MICROSOFT®

OFFICE 20

BASICS

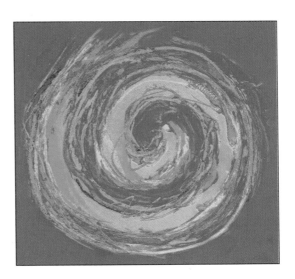

by Pasewark and Pasewark

THOMSON

COURSE TECHNOLOGY

Australia • Canada • Mexico • Singapore • Spain • United Kingdom • United States

THOMSON
COURSE TECHNOLOGY

Microsoft® Office 2003 BASICS
by Pasewark and Pasewark*

Authors

William R. Pasewark, Sr., Ph.D.
Professor Emeritus,
Texas Tech University

**William R. Pasewark, Jr.,
Ph.D., CPA**
Professor of Accounting,
Texas Tech University

Carolyn Pasewark Denny, M.Ed.
National Computer Consultant,
Reading and Math Certified
Elementary Teacher, Certified
Counselor, K-12

Scott G. Pasewark, B.S.
Occupational Education,
Computer Technologist

Jan Pasewark Stogner, MBA
Financial Planner

Beth Pasewark Wadsworth, B.A.
Graphic Designer

Publishers

Cheryl Costantini
Executive Director

Kim Ryttel
Senior Marketing Manager

Alexandra Arnold
Senior Editor

David Rivera
Product Manager

Trevor Kallop
Senior Manufacturing
Coordinator

Meagan Putney
School Market Specialist

Justine Brennan
Editorial Assistant

Rose Marie Kuebbing, CEP, Inc.
Managing Developmental Editor

Jean Findley, CEP, Inc.
Production Editor

GEX Publishing Services
Compositor

Banta Menasha
Printer

COPYRIGHT © 2005 Course Technology, a division of Thomson Learning, Inc. Thomson Learning™ is a trademark used herein under license.

*Pasewark and Pasewark is a trademark of the Pasewark LTD.

The Keyboarding Touch System Improvement Appendix is an excerpt from Keyboarding Skill Builder for Computers, Copyright 1996 by William R. Pasewark, Sr.

Printed in the United States of America

3 4 5 6 7 8 9 BM 07 06 05

For more information, contact Course Technology, 25 Thomson Place, Boston, Massachusetts, 02210.

Or find us on the World Wide Web at: www.course.com

For permission to use material from this text or product, contact us by
Tel (800) 730-2214
Fax (800) 730-2215
www.thomsonrights.com

Disclaimer
Course Technology reserves the right to revise this publication and make changes from time to time in its content without notice.

Microsoft and the Office logo are either registered trademarks or trademarks of the Microsoft Corporation in the United States and/or other countries. Course Technology/Thomson Learning is an independent entity from Microsoft Corporation and not affiliated with Microsoft Corporation in any manner. This text may be used in assisting students to prepare for a Microsoft Office Specialist exam (MOS). Neither Microsoft Corporation, its designated review company, nor Course Technology/ Thomson Learning warrants that use of this publication will ensure passing the relevant MOS exam.

ISBN 0-619-18335-7

Experience Office Now and in the Future...
With these exciting new products!

TABLE OF CONTENTS

UNIT 1   INTRODUCTION

UNIT 2   MICROSOFT WORD

UNIT 3   MICROSOFT POWERPOINT

UNIT 4 MICROSOFT® EXCEL

UNIT 5 MICROSOFT ACCESS

UNIT 6 MICROSOFT PUBLISHER

Overview of This Book

What makes a good computer instructional text? Answer: Sound pedagogy and the most current, complete materials. That is what you will find in *Microsoft® Office 2003 BASICS*. Not only will you find an inviting layout, but also many features to enhance learning.

Objectives—Objectives are listed at the beginning of each lesson, along with a suggested time for completion of the lesson. This allows you to look ahead to what you will be learning and to pace your work.

Learning Boxes—These boxes expand and enrich learning with additional information or activities: Hot Tips, Did You Know?, Computer Concepts, Internet, Extra Challenge, and Teamwork.

Cross-Curricular Activities—Icons are interspersed throughout each lesson for language arts, math, science, and social studies exercises.

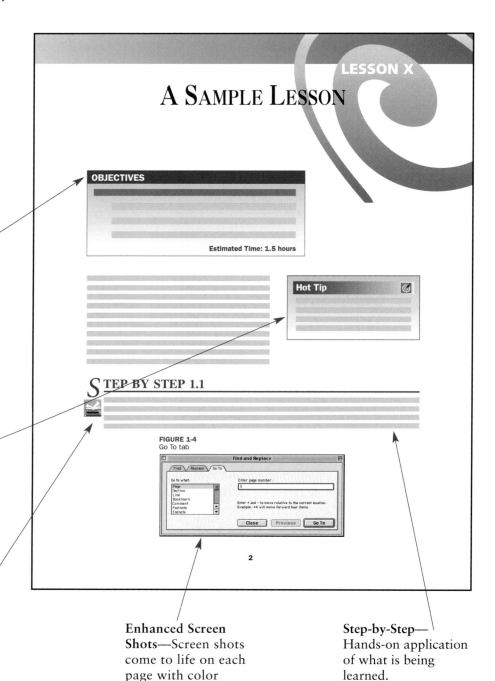

LESSON X

A SAMPLE LESSON

OBJECTIVES

Estimated Time: 1.5 hours

Hot Tip

STEP BY STEP 1.1

FIGURE 1-4
Go To tab

2

Enhanced Screen Shots—Screen shots come to life on each page with color and depth.

Step-by-Step—Hands-on application of what is being learned.

Overview of This Book

Summaries— Summaries at the end of each lesson prepare you to complete the end-of-lesson activities.

Vocabulary/Review Questions—Review material at the end of each lesson and each unit prepares you to assess the content presented.

Lesson Projects— End-of-lesson hands-on application of what has been learned in the lesson allows you to actually apply the techniques covered. Also includes web and teamwork projects.

Critical Thinking Activities—Each lesson gives you an opportunity to apply creative analysis and use the Help system to solve problems.

Command Summary—At the end of each unit is a Command Summary for quick reference.

End-of-Unit Projects—End-of-unit hands-on application of concepts learned in the unit. Provides opportunity for a comprehensive review.

Lesson X Unit Sample   Intro Excel   **3**

SUMMARY

VOCABULARY *Review*

REVIEW *Questions*

PROJECTS

CRITICAL *Thinking*

COMMAND SUMMARY

REVIEW *Questions*

PROJECTS

PORTFOLIO *Checklist*

Capstone Simulation—There is a comprehensive simulation at the end of the text when you apply all of the skills you have learned.

Portfolio Checklist— At the end of each unit is a list of files that can be added to your portfolio.

Appendices— Appendices cover Windows Basics, Computer Concepts, Concepts for Microsoft Office Programs, and Keyboarding Touch System Improvement.

GUIDE FOR USING THIS BOOK

Please read this Guide before starting work. The time you spend now will save you much more time later and will make your learning faster, easier, and more pleasant.

Terminology

This text uses the term *keying* to mean entering text into a computer using the keyboard. *Keying* is the same as "keyboarding" or "typing."

Text means words, numbers, and symbols that are printed.

You will "tap" keys rather than "strike" or "press" them. Tapping keys lightly improves your keyboarding skill and helps prevent carpel tunnel syndrome.

Type Style and What You Will Do

The different type styles used in this book have special meanings. They will save you time because you will soon automatically recognize from the type style the nature of the text you are reading and what you will do.

WHAT YOU WILL DO	TYPE STYLE	EXAMPLE
Text you will key	**Bold**	Key **Don't litter** rapidly.
Individual keys you will tap	**Bold**	Tap **Enter** to insert a blank line.
WHAT YOU WILL SEE	**TYPE STYLE**	**EXAMPLE**
Filenames in book	**Bold upper and lowercase**	Open **Step2-1** from the data files.
Vocabulary terms in book	***Bold and italics***	The ***menu bar*** contains menu titles.
Words on screen	*Italics*	Highlight the word *pencil* on the screen.
Menus and commands	**Bold**	Open the **File** menu and choose **Open**.
Options/features with long names	*Italics*	Select **Normal** from the *Style for following paragraph* text box.
Names of sections/boxes	*Italics*	Click **Monthly Style** in the *Print Style* box.

Cross-Curricular Icons

Throughout the text you will periodically see cross-curricular icons. These icons are placed with step-by-step exercises and with end-of-lesson projects and activities to indicate places where the material covers one of the four core subject areas: Language Arts, Math, Social Studies, or Science. The exercises with these icons are ones which will give you an opportunity to expand upon knowledge you have gained in one of these areas.

 Language Arts   Social Studies

 Math   Science

Learning Boxes

Learning Boxes expand and enrich learning for all students and provide extra activities for fast learners:

 Computer Concepts—technology principles that apply to all computers

 Did You Know?—interesting facts about the task students are completing

 Extra Challenges—additional activities similar to or extending the scope of the task

 Hot Tips—reminders and other important information to help students complete tasks

Review Pack CD

All data files necessary for the Step-by-Step exercises, end-of-lesson Projects, end-of-unit Projects, and Capstone Simulation exercises in this book are located on the Review Pack CD. Data files for the *Activities Workbook* are also stored on the Review Pack CD.

Data files are named according to the lesson number and the first exercise in which they are used. A data file for the first Step-by-Step exercise in Lesson 1 would have the filename **Step1-1**. Other data files have the following formats:

- End-of-lesson projects: **Project1-1**
- End-of-unit projects: **Project2**

AN IDEAL BOOK FOR EVERYONE

Microsoft Office 2003 BASICS is an ideal book:

1. For courses with learners who have varying abilities and previous computer experiences that includes novice, competent and skilled students. It includes a wide range of learning experiences from activities with only several commands to simulations and projects that can challenge and sharpen problem-solving skills for fast learners.

2. For many educational settings such as middle schools, charter schools, technical schools, career schools, adult education courses, in-service teacher courses, in-service company programs, military programs, correctional facility courses, government funded programs such as Workforce, and all who want to self learn Office 2003.

3. For a wide variety of class time schedules because the book is both comprehensive and flexible.

4. For all students who want a quick start and a fast finish learning Office 2003 because the instructions are clear, concise, and direct.

New Features

This book includes the following *new* features:

1. Applications such as optical illusions, zoos, how airplanes fly, and spelling improvement through mnemonics that will appeal to all learners

2. Approximately 20% less words than traditional computer books

3. Appropriate reading level for middle school and high school learners.

4. Cross-curricular activities that are interspersed throughout the lessons for Language Arts, Math, Science and Social Studies

5. Spanish Glossary on the Instructor Resources CD

6. A PowerPoint unit that includes interactive, animated, and live projects

7. A field-tested Keyboard Touch System Improvement appendix

8. New keyboarding terminology so students "tap" instead of "strike" or "press" keys.

Office 2003 BASICS includes all of the features in the authors' two predecessor best-selling books on Office 2000 and Office XP that have won "Texty Awards" as the best computer books in two consecutive years. See page xvii for these features.

Features

Each <u>Lesson</u> contains the following features designed to promote learning

- Objectives that specify goals students should achieve by the end of each lesson
- Screen captures that illustrate the concept
- Step-by-Step exercises for students to practice each concept
- Cross-Curricular activities interspersed throughout each lesson
- Review Questions that test students
- Projects so students can apply what they learn
- Critical Thinking Activities to help students to solve problems
- Web and Teamwork Projects
- Learning Boxes to enrich learning

Each <u>Unit</u> contains a Unit Review with the following features:

- Cross-curricular related projects
- A Command Summary that reviews menu commands and toolbar shortcuts
- Review Questions that check what students have learned
- Projects by which students apply skills learned
- Portfolio Checklist of students' files
- A simulation about real-world tasks

Summary

Microsoft Office 2003 BASICS is adoptable for all grade levels in all types of schools for students with a wide variety of abilities. It makes learning easy and enjoyable.

Because computers are such an important subject for all learners, teachers need a well-designed educationally sound textbook that is supported by strong ancillary instructional materials. *Microsoft Office 2003 BASICS* is just such a book.

TEACHING AND LEARNING RESOURCES FOR THIS BOOK

Instructor Resources CD

The *Instructor Resources CD* contains a wealth of instructional material you can use for teaching Office 2003. The CD contains:

- Student data files and the teacher's solution files
- ExamView® tests for each lesson
- *Instructor's Manual* that includes:
    - Lecture notes and teaching tips for each lesson
    - Computer or lab set-up requirements
    - Quick quizzes and discussion questions
- Copies of figures in the student text, that you can use to prepare transparencies
- Answers to the lesson and unit review questions
- Suggested schedules for teaching the lessons
- Answers to the *Activities Workbook* exercises
- PowerPoint presentations for enhancing and supporting the material in the text
- Spanish Glossary

Activities Workbook

An *Activities Workbook* is available that contains more than 2,000 questions and hands-on computer applications for each unit of this book.

ASSESSMENT INSTRUMENTS

SAM 2003 Assessment and Training

SAM 2003 helps you energize your class exams and training assignments by allowing students to learn and test important computer skills in an active, hands-on environment.

With SAM 2003 Assessment, you create powerful interactive exams on critical applications such as Word, Outlook, PowerPoint, Windows, the Internet, and much more. The exams simulate the application environment, allowing your students to demonstrate their knowledge and think through the skill by performing real-world tasks.

- Build hands-on exams that allow the student to work in the simulated application environment.

- Add more muscle to your lesson plan with SAM 2003 Training. Using highly interactive text, graphics, and sound, SAM 2003 Training gives your students the flexibility to learn computer applications by choosing the training method that fits them the best.

- Create customized training units that employ various approaches to teach computer skills.

- Designed to be used with the Microsoft Office 2003 series, SAM 2003 Assessment & Training includes built-in page references so students can create study guides that match the Microsoft Office 2003 textbooks you use in class. Powerful administrative options allow you to schedule exams and assignments, secure your tests, and run reports with almost limitless flexibility.

- Deliver exams and training units that best fit the way you teach.

- Choose from more than one dozen reports to track testing and learning progress.

Exam View

ExamView is a powerful, objective-based test generator that enables you to create paper, LAN, or Web-based tests from test banks designed specifically for your Course Technology text. Utilize the ultra-efficient QuickTest Wizard to create tests in less than five minutes by taking advantage of Course Technology's question banks, or customize your own exams from scratch.

MESSAGE FROM THE AUTHORS

Our Mission Statement

The Pasewark authors have more than 90 years of combined experience authoring award-winning textbooks. During that time, they developed their mission statement:

> **To help our students live better lives.**

When students learn how computers can help them in their personal, career, school, and family activities, they can live better lives — now and in the future.

Our Commitment

In writing *Microsoft Office 2003 BASICS*, we have dedicated ourselves to creating a comprehensive and appealing instructional package to make teaching and learning an interesting, challenging, and rewarding experience.

With these instructional materials, instructors can create realistic learning experience so learners can successfully master concepts, knowledge, and skills that will help them live better lives—now and in the future.

Award Winning Books by the Pasewarks

The predecessors to this book, *Microsoft® Office 2000: Introductory* and *Microsoft Office XP: Introductory*, won the Text and Academic Authors Association *Texty Award* for the best el-hi computer book for the years 2000 and 2002.

In 1994, the Pasewarks also won a *Texty* for their Microsoft Works computer book. Their book, *The Office: Procedures and Technology*, won the first William McGuffey Award for Textbook Excellence and Longevity. *Microsoft® Works 2000 BASICS* won the Texty Award for the best computer book for the year 2001.

ABOUT THE AUTHORS

Pasewark LTD is a family-owned business. We use Microsoft® Office in our business, career, personal, and family lives. Writing this book, therefore, was a natural project for six members of our family who are identified on the title page of this book.

The authors have written more than 100 books about computers, accounting, and office technology.

Pasewark LTD authors are members of several professional associations that help authors write better books.

They have been recognized with numerous awards for classroom teaching. Effective classroom teaching is a major ingredient for writing effective textbooks.

Back row: Beth Pasewark Wadsworth, Carolyn Pasewark Denny, Scott Pasewark
Front row: Bill Pasewark, Jr., Bill Pasewark, Sr., Jan Pasewark Stogner

Acknowledgments

The authors gratefully thank Rhonda Davis for her valuable work coordinating manuscript and for using her business experiences to write several segments of Office 2003. The authors also acknowledge the work of these computer teachers: Billie Conley for her advice and writing contributions and Brenda Bass for her assistance. Our co-op school/work student, LaChell Lemond, assumed more and more responsibilities to help produce this book. Tom Tyner, Course Technology, Regional Sales Manager has provided valuable insights for this and other Pasewark books.

All of our books are a coordinated effort by the authors and scores of professionals working with the publisher. The authors appreciate the dedicated work of all these publishing personnel and particularly those with whom we have had direct contact:

- Course Technology: Cheryl Costantini, Alexandra Arnold, Kim Ryttel, Meagan Putney, Justine Brennan, and David Rivera

- Custom Editorial Productions (CEP), Inc.: Jean Findley and Rose Marie Kuebbing

- Many professional Course Technology sales representatives make educationally sound presentations to instructors about our books. We appreciate their valuable work as "bridges" between the authors and instructors.

START-UP CHECKLIST

MINIMUM CONFIGURATION

- ✓ PC with Pentium 233 MHz or higher processor, Pentium III recommended.
- ✓ RAM requirements
    - ✓ Windows XP – 128 MB of RAM
    - ✓ Windows 2000 Professional – 128 MB of RAM
- ✓ Hard disk with 400 MB free for typical installation

- ✓ CD-ROM drive
- ✓ Super VGA monitor with video adapter, (800 × 600) or higher-resolution
- ✓ Microsoft Mouse, IntelliMouse, or compatible pointing device
- ✓ For e-mail, Microsoft Mail, Internet SMTP/POP3, or other MAPI-compliant messaging software
- ✓ Printer

INTRODUCTION

Unit 1

Lesson 1   1.5 hrs
Microsoft® Office 2003 Basics and the Internet

Estimated Time for Unit: 1.5 hours

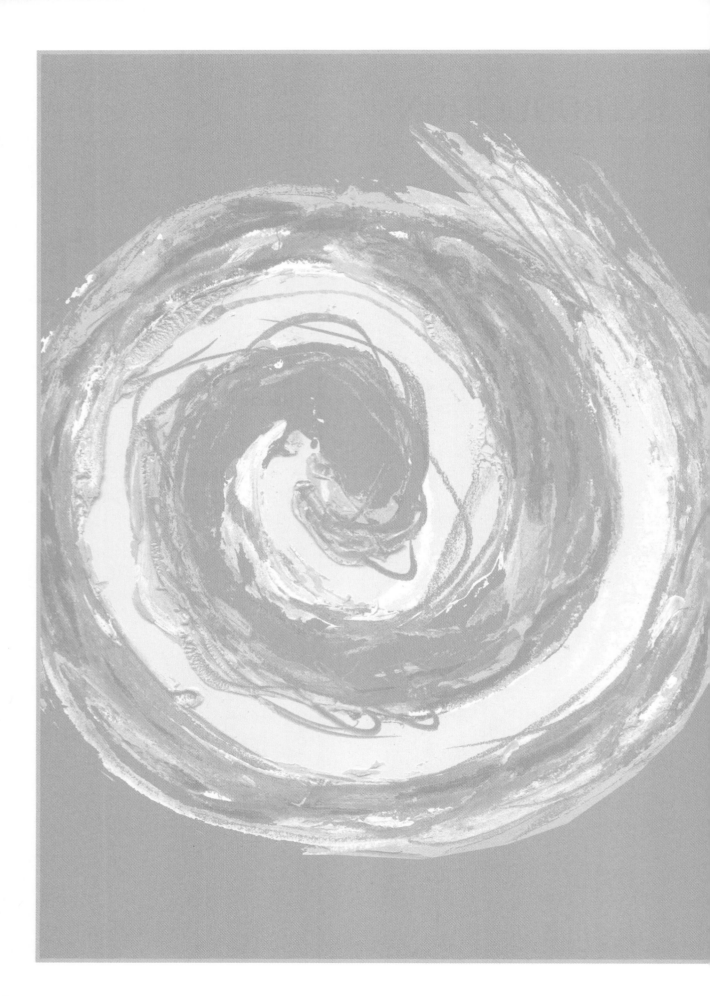

MICROSOFT® OFFICE 2003 BASICS AND THE INTERNET

OBJECTIVES

In this lesson, you will:

■ Start an Office program.

■ Explain an Office program's opening screen and how to use the menus and toolbars.

■ Open an existing Office document.

■ Save and close an Office document.

■ Know the shortcuts for opening recently used documents.

■ Use the Office Help system, including the Office Assistant.

■ Quit an Office application.

■ Access the Internet and use a Web browser.

Estimated Time: 1.5 hours

Introduction to Microsoft Office 2003

Microsoft Office 2003 is a group of computer programs. Office 2003 includes a word-processing program (Word), a presentation program (PowerPoint), a spreadsheet program (Excel), a database program (Access), and a desktop publishing program (Publisher). Table 1-1 describes each of these programs.

Internet

For more information on Microsoft Word and other Microsoft products, visit Microsoft's Web site at *http://www.microsoft.com*.

Computer Concepts

You can open a new file from within an application by opening the **File** menu and choosing **New**. You can also click the **New** button in the standard toolbar to create a new file. In the Word program, the button is titled **New Blank Document**.

TABLE 1-1
Applications in the Office 2003 program

ITEM	FUNCTION
Word	The word-processing program helps you to create documents such as letters and reports.
PowerPoint	The presentation program is used to create slides, outlines, speaker's notes, and audience handouts.
Excel	The spreadsheet program lets you work with numbers to create items such as budgets and loan payments.
Access	The database program helps you to create lists of information, such as addresses.
Publisher	The desktop publishing program helps you to design professional-looking documents.

Before starting Step-by-Step 1.1, please go to pages viii, ix, x, xi and read the Overview of This Book and the Guide for Using This Book. The time you spend reading this information will save you much more time later. It will also make your learning faster, easier, and more pleasant.

STEP-BY-STEP 1.1

1. Click the **Start** button to open the Start menu.

2. Point to **All Programs** (in Windows 2000, point to **Programs**) and then **Microsoft Office**. Click **Microsoft Office PowerPoint 2003.** PowerPoint starts and a blank presentation appears, as shown in Figure 1-1.

FIGURE 1-1
A blank presentation in the PowerPoint program

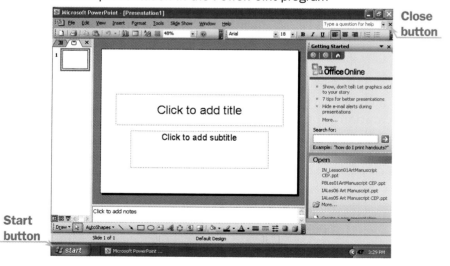

3. Click the **Close** button on the right side of the menu bar to close the blank presentation. The PowerPoint program will remain open.

STEP-BY-STEP 1.1 Continued

4. Click the **Start** button again.

5. Point to **All Programs**, point to **Microsoft Office**, and then click **Microsoft Office Word 2003.** Word starts and a blank document appears, as shown in Figure 1-2. Leave Word and PowerPoint open for use in the following Step-by-Steps.

FIGURE 1-2
Word opening screen

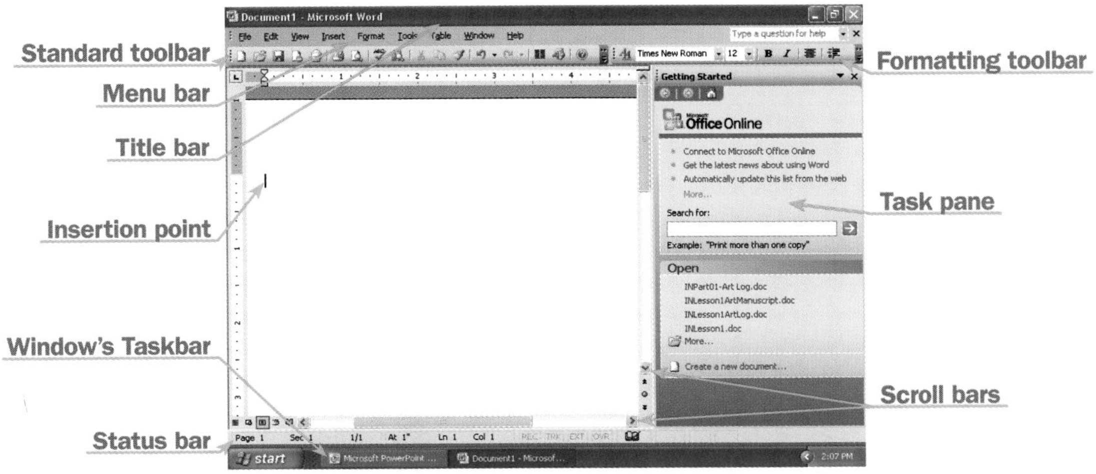

Understanding the Opening Screen

Most of the options you will use in an Office program can be found on the opening screen of each program. Look carefully at the parts of the opening screen for the Word program labeled in Figure 1-2. These basic parts of the screen are similar in all of the Office programs and are discussed below in Table 1-2.

TABLE 1-2
Understanding the opening screen

ITEM	FUNCTION
Title bar	Displays the name of the Office program and the current file.
Menu bar	Contains the menu titles from which you can choose a command. All options in a program can be accessed from within the menus.
Standard toolbar	Contains buttons you can use for common tasks.
Formatting toolbar	Contains buttons you can use for changing formatting, such as type styles.
Insertion point	Shows where text will appear when you begin keying.
Scroll bars	Allow you to move quickly to other areas of an Office application.
Status bar	Tells you the status of what is shown on the screen.
Taskbar	Shows the Start button, the Quick Launch toolbar, and all open programs.
Task pane	Opens automatically when you start an Office application. Contains commonly used commands for that program.

The *task pane* is a separate window on the right-hand side of the opening screen, as shown in Figures 1-1 and Figure 1-2. It opens automatically when you start an Office application. The task pane contains commonly used commands that can help you work faster. To close the task pane, simply click the Close button in the upper right corner of the task pane. To view the task pane, open the View menu and choose Task Pane.

Using Menus and Toolbars

A *menu* in an Office application is like a menu in a restaurant. You look at the menus to see what the program has to offer. Each title in the menu bar represents a separate *drop-down menu*. When you choose a command from a drop-down menu, you tell the program what you want to do. To see an expanded menu with all the commands, click the arrows at the bottom of the menu. Figure 1-3 compares the short and expanded versions of the Edit menu.

FIGURE 1-3
Short menu vs. expanded menu

Arrows

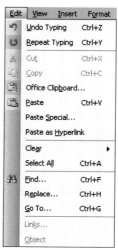

Toolbars provide another quick way to choose commands. The toolbars use *icons*, or small pictures, to remind you of each button's function. Toolbars can also contain drop-down menus.

As with the menus, toolbars initially display buttons only for basic commands. To see additional buttons, click Toolbar Options (the button at the far right on each toolbar) on the toolbar and choose from the list that appears, as shown in Figure 1-4.

Computer Concepts

If you do not know the function of a toolbar button, move the mouse pointer to the button, but do not click. The name of the function will appear below the button.

Did You Know?

Only the Standard and Formatting toolbars are displayed, but many more toolbars are available. To see a list of the toolbars you can use, right-click anywhere on a toolbar, or you can open the View menu and select Toolbars.

FIGURE 1-4
Toolbar Options list

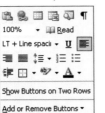

Opening, Saving, and Closing Office Documents

In all Office programs, you *open*, *save*, and *close* files in the same way. Opening a file means loading a file from a disk onto your screen. Saving a file stores it on a disk. Closing a file removes it from the screen.

Opening an Existing Document

In all Office programs, when you open an existing document, the Open dialog box appears (see Figure 1-5).

FIGURE 1-5
Open dialog box

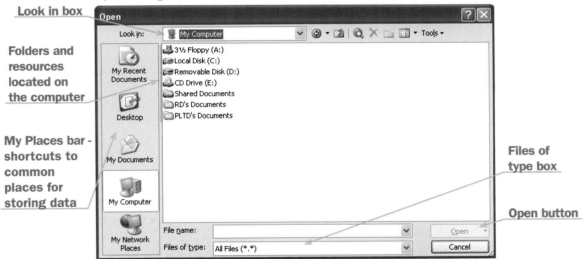

Look in box

Folders and
resources
located on
the computer

My Places bar -
shortcuts to
common
places for
storing data

Files of
type box

Open button

The Open dialog box allows you to open a file from any available disk or folder. A *folder* is a location where files and other folders are stored on a disk. The *Look in* box, near the top of the dialog box, is where you locate the disk drive that contains the file you want to open. Below that is a list that shows you the folders or resources that are on the disk.

Hot Tip

The My Places bar on the left side of the dialog box provides a shortcut for accessing some of the common places to store documents.

STEP-BY-STEP 1.2

1. With Word on the screen, click **More...** in the *Open* section of the Getting Started task pane. The Open dialog box appears, as shown in Figure 1-5. If the **More...** option is not displayed, choose **Open...** instead. (If the task pane is not displayed, open the **View** menu and choose **Task Pane**.)

2. Click the down arrow to the right of the *Look in* box to display the available disk drives.

3. Click the drive that contains your data files and locate the **Booster Club** folder, as shown in Figure 1-6.

FIGURE 1-6
Booster Club folder

4. Double-click the **Booster Club** folder. The folders within the Booster Club folder appear, as shown in Figure 1-7.

FIGURE 1-7
Contents of the Booster Club folder

5. Double-click the **Perez** folder. The names of all the files in the Perez folder display. (If necessary, click the down arrow at the right of the *Files of type* box and select **All Files** to display all the files.)

6. Click **Schedule Memo** to select it and then click **Open** to open the file. Leave the file open for the next Step-by-Step.

You can see how folders help organize and identify documents. The Perez folder also contains a spreadsheet with the schedule for working the booth at the County Fair. In the next Step-by-Step, you will start Excel, the Office spreadsheet application, and open the spreadsheet that goes with the memo.

STEP-BY-STEP 1.3

1. Open another Office document by clicking the **Start** button.

2. Point to **All Programs** (in Windows 2000, point to **Programs**) and then **Microsoft Office**. Click **Microsoft Office Excel 2003.** Excel starts and a blank spreadsheet appears.

3. Open the **File** menu and choose **Open**. The Open dialog box appears.

4. Click the down arrow at the right of the *Look in* box. If necessary, click the drive that contains your data files and locate the Booster Club folder.

5. Double-click the **Booster Club** folder, then double-click the **Perez** folder.

6. Double-click **Fair Schedule** to open the file. The Fair Schedule spreadsheet appears on the screen, as shown in Figure 1-8. Leave the file open for the next Step-by-Step.

FIGURE 1-8
Fair Schedule file

Microsoft Excel - Fair Schedule.xls

Schedule for Booth time at the County Fair - July 8th to 22nd

		Sa 8	Su 9	M 10	Tu 11	W 12	Th 13	F 14	Sa 15	Su 16	M 17	Tu 18	W 19	Th 20	Fr 21	Sa 22	Total hrs:
6	Acker, Jude		8				6			8					6	8	36
7	Aldridge, Hunter	8		4		4	6				4		4		6		36
8	Bledsoe, Samantha	4	4		4		4		4	4	4		4			4	36
9	Carrizales, Cody	8			4		4	8			4		4			8	40
10	Daniel, Alexa	4	4	4		4		6			4		4		6		36
11	Davis, Hillary		8						8	8						8	32
12	Glass, Katie		8	4		4		6		8	4	4					38
13	Hamilton, Eric	8			4		4		8		4			4	6		38
14	Jones, Logan		8					6		8					6	8	36
15	Lewis, Scott	8	4		4			6			4		4		6		36
16	Miller, Josh	4	4		4		4		4	4		4		4		4	36
17	Perez, Mike	8			4		4	8			4		4			8	40
18	Rafael, Kristin			4		4		6	4	4	4		4		6		36
19	Stone, Heather		8						8	8						8	32
20	Weinhold, Ashley		8	4		4		6		8	4	4					38
21	Wong, Keri	8			4		4	8			4			4	6		38

Ready — NUM

Saving a File

Saving is done two ways. The Save command saves a file on a disk using the current name. The Save As command saves a file on a disk using a new name. The Save As command can also be used to save a file to a new location.

FILENAMES

A filename may contain up to 255 characters and may include spaces. However, you will probably never need this many characters to name a file. Name a file with a name that will remind you of what the file contains, such as Research Paper or Art Club Flyer. The filename can include most of the characters found on the keyboard. Table 1-3 lists the characters that cannot be used in a filename.

TABLE 1-3
Characters that cannot be used in filenames

CHARACTER	NAME	CHARACTER	NAME
*	asterisk	<	less than sign
\	backslash	;	semicolon
[ ]	brackets	/	slash
:	colon	"	quotation mark
=	equal sign	?	question mark
>	greater than sign	I	vertical bar

STEP-BY-STEP 1.4

1. *Fair Schedule* should be on the screen from the last Step-by-Step. Open the **File** menu and choose **Save As**. The Save As dialog box appears, as shown in Figure 1-9.

FIGURE 1-9
Save As dialog box

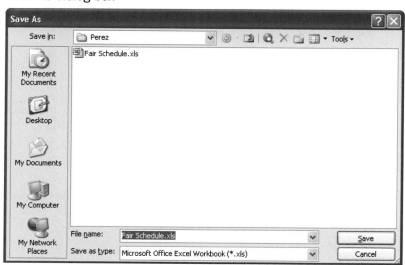

STEP-BY-STEP 1.4 Continued

2. In the *File name* box, key **Fair Work Schedule**, followed by your initials.

3. Click the down arrow to the right of the *Save in* box and choose the **Booster Club** folder.

4. Double-click the **Lewis** folder.

5. Click **Save** to save the file with the new name in the Lewis folder. Leave the document open for the next Step-by-Step.

Closing an Office Document

You can close an Office document either by choosing Close on the File menu or by clicking the Close button on the right side of the menu bar. If you close a file, the program will still be open and ready for you to open or create another file.

> **Did You Know?**
>
> All of the programs in Office 2003 allow you to open new documents while you are working in other documents. You can even work in documents created in another Office program, such as Excel, while working in Word. To move back and forth between documents, just click the taskbar button for the document you want to display.

STEP-BY-STEP 1.5

1. Open the **File** menu and choose **Close**. *Fair Work Schedule* closes.

2. Click the **Microsoft Word** button on the taskbar to make it active. *Schedule Memo* should be displayed.

3. Click the **Close** button in the right corner of the menu bar to close *Schedule Memo*.

4. Leave Word open for the next Step-by-Step.

Shortcuts for Loading Recently Used Files

Office offers you two shortcuts for opening recently used files. The first shortcut is to choose My Recent Documents from the Start menu. A menu will open listing the fifteen most recently used documents, as shown in Figure 1-10. To open one of the recently used files, click the file you wish to open.

FIGURE 1-10
Most recently used files

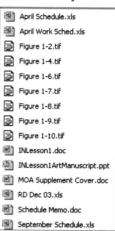

The second and third shortcuts can be found on each Office application's File menu and task pane. The bottom part of the File menu and the Open section of the task pane show the filenames of the four most recently opened documents. The most recently opened document is listed first, as shown in Figure 1-11. When a new file is opened, each filename moves down to make room for the new most recently opened file. To open one of the files, you simply choose it as if it were a menu selection. If the document you are looking for is not on the File menu, use Open to locate and select the file.

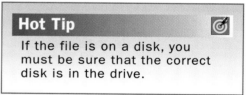

Hot Tip

If the file is on a disk, you must be sure that the correct disk is in the drive.

FIGURE 1-11
Most recently used files on the File menu and task pane

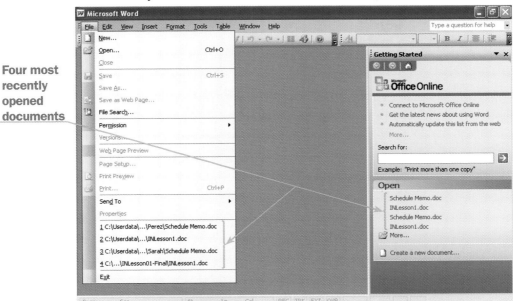

Office Help

This lesson has covered only a few of the many options in the Office programs. For more information, use Office Help when you have a question about an option. You can access Office Help from the Help menu. Or, key a question in the *Type a question for help* box on the menu bar. Then, from the Help task pane shown in Figure 1-12, you can display a Table of Contents or search the Help system for information.

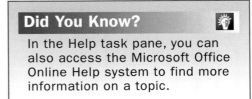

Did You Know?

In the Help task pane, you can also access the Microsoft Office Online Help system to find more information on a topic.

FIGURE 1-12
Word Help task pane

Many topics in the Help program are linked. A *link* is displayed with colored, underlined text. By clicking a link, you can "jump" to more information about that topic.

STEP-BY-STEP 1.6

1. Display the Word Help task pane, shown in Figure 1-12, by opening the **Help** menu and choosing **Microsoft Office Word Help**.

2. Click the **Table of Contents** link to display a list of topics. If you have Internet access, this information is downloaded from the Microsoft Online Help system. If you do not have Internet access, the information is accessed from the Offline Table of Contents.

3. Click the topic **Working with Text**, click **Copy and Paste**, and then click **Move or copy text and graphics**. A list of topics displays in a separate window.

4. Click the **Move or copy a single item** topic in the Microsoft Office Word Help window.

5. Read the contents of the Help window and leave it open for the next Step-by-Step.

When you want to search for help on a topic, you can key a word into the *Search for* box. The list of topics is searched to find a match. You can then click a topic to see it explained in the Help window, as shown in Figure 1-13.

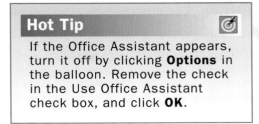

Hot Tip

If the Office Assistant appears, turn it off by clicking **Options** in the balloon. Remove the check in the Use Office Assistant check box, and click **OK**.

FIGURE 1-13
Help topic explained in the Help window

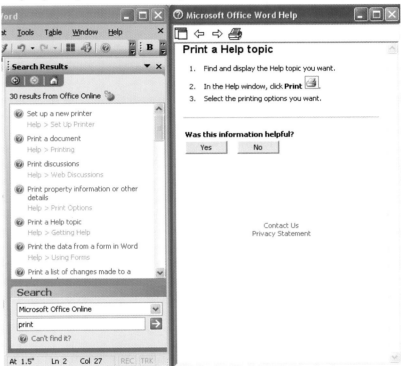

STEP-BY-STEP 1.7

1. Double-click the green back arrow at the top of the Word Help task pane to display the *Search for* box. (*Note:* You may need to drag the Microsoft Office Word Help window out of the way to see the task pane.)

2. Click in the *Search for* box to place the insertion point within it, key **print**, and click the green *Start searching* arrow.

3. Search through the list of results until you find **Print a Help topic**. Click it to display information in the Microsoft Office Word Help window, as shown in Figure 1-13.

4. Read the information, then print the information by following the instructions you read.

5. Close the Help program by clicking the **Close** button in the Help window as well as in the task pane.

Office Assistant

The Office Assistant is a feature found in all the Office programs and is another way to get help. The Assistant, shown in Figure 1-14, is an animated character that offers tips, solutions, instructions, and examples to help you work faster. The default Office Assistant character is a paper clip, named Clippit. A *default* setting is the one used unless another option is chosen.

Hot Tip

You can change the way the Office Assistant provides help. Click on the Office Assistant, click **Options**, choose the **Options** tab, and make your selections.

FIGURE 1-14
Default Office Assistant

The Office Assistant keeps track of the work you are doing and notices when you might need help. It appears on the screen with tips on how to save time or use the program more effectively. For example, if you start writing a letter in Word, the Assistant pops up to ask if you want help, as shown in Figure 1-15.

FIGURE 1-15
Office Assistant asking if you need help

If you have a specific question, you can use the Office Assistant to search for help. To display the Office Assistant if it is not on the screen, choose Show the Office Assistant from the Help menu. Key your question and click Search. The Assistant searches for a match and then displays a list of help topics.

S TEP-BY-STEP 1.8

1. If necessary, open the **Help** menu and choose **Show the Office Assistant**. The Office Assistant appears, as shown in Figure 1-14. Click the **Office Assistant** to display the text box.

2. Key **How do I use the Office Assistant?** in the text box.

3. Click **Search**. A list of Help topics is displayed in the Search Results task pane.

<u>**STEP-BY-STEP 1.8 Continued**</u>

4. Choose one of the topics listed and click it to display information in the Microsoft Office Help window.

5. Read and print the information.

6. Click the **Close** boxes in the Help window and the task pane to remove the Help window from the screen.

7. Click the **Office Assistant** to display the text box again. Click **Options**. In the *Show tips about* section, click to place a check mark in the *Using features more effectively* box. Click **OK**.

8. Click the **New Blank Document** button in the standard toolbar to open a new Word document.

9. Key **Dear Zack,** and tap **Enter**. A message from the Office Assistant appears asking if you want help writing your letter, as shown in Figure 1-15. (*Note:* If the message does not appear, you may not have keyed the comma after Zack. Add the comma and tap Enter again. The message should display.)

10. Click **Just type the letter without help**.

11. Close the Word document without saving. Leave Word open for the next Step-by-Step.

Quitting an Office Application

To quit Word or any other Office program, open the File menu and choose Exit. You can also click the Close button on the right side of the title bar. Exiting an Office program takes you to another open program or back to the Windows desktop.

*S*TEP-BY-STEP 1.9

1. Open the **File** menu. Notice the files listed toward the bottom of the menu. These are the four most recently used files mentioned previously in this lesson.

2. Choose **Exit**. Word closes and Excel is displayed on the screen.

3. Click the **Close** button in the right corner of the title bar. Excel closes and the desktop appears on the screen. The taskbar shows that an application is still open.

4. Click the **PowerPoint** button on the taskbar to display it on the screen. Exit PowerPoint. The desktop appears on the screen again.

Accessing the Internet

The *Internet* is a vast network of computers linked to one another. The Internet allows people around the world to share information and ideas through Web pages, newsgroups, mailing lists, chat rooms, e-mail, and electronic files.

Connecting to the Internet requires special hardware and software and an Internet Service Provider. Before you can use the Internet, your computer needs to be connected, and you should know how to access the Internet.

The *World Wide Web* allows you to use links on "pages" to share information. The Internet is its carrier. To identify the links, the Web uses addresses called *Uniform Resource Locators (URLs)*. Here are some examples of URLs:

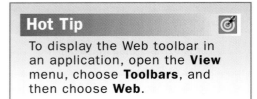

Hot Tip

To display the Web toolbar in an application, open the **View** menu, choose **Toolbars**, and then choose **Web**.

http://www.senate.gov

http://www.microsoft.com

The Web toolbar, shown in Figure 1-16, is available in all Office programs. It contains buttons for opening and searching documents. You can use the Web toolbar to access documents on the Internet, on an *intranet* (a company's private Web), or on your computer. Table 1-4 describes the function of each button on the Web toolbar.

FIGURE 1-16
Web toolbar

TABLE 1-4
Web toolbar

BUTTON	FUNCTION
Back	Takes you to the previous page.
Forward	Takes you to the next page.
Stop	Stops loading the current page.
Refresh	Reloads the current page.
Start Page	Loads your **home page**, the first page that appears when you start your browser.
Search the Web	Opens a page where you can key a word to search the Web.
Favorites	Shows a list of your favorite Web sites.
Go	Takes you to a different site.
Show Only Web Toolbar	Hides all the toolbars except the Web toolbar.
Address box	Takes you to the address that you have keyed in the box.

To view documents on the Web, you need special software. A *Web browser* is software used to display Web pages on your computer monitor. Microsoft's *Internet Explorer* is a browser for navigating the Web that is included with the Office programs. Figure 1-17 shows a Web page using Internet Explorer as a browser.

FIGURE 1-17
Web browser

Did You Know?

Toolbars display buttons for basic commands only. To see additional buttons, click **Toolbar Options** on the toolbar and choose from the list that appears. When you use a button from the list, it is added to the toolbar. If you haven't used a button recently, it is added to the Toolbar Options list.

Computer Concepts

There are two basic types of Internet connections, dial-up and direct. Dial-up access uses a modem and a telephone line to communicate between your computer and the Internet. Most individual users have dial-up access. Direct access uses a special high-speed connection, such as a DSL cable, between your computer and the Internet. This access is faster but more expensive than dial-up access. Most businesses and institutions, and some individuals, have direct access.

S TEP-BY-STEP 1.10

1. Connect to your Internet Service Provider if you are not connected already.

2. Open **Word**. Open the **View** menu, choose **Toolbars**, and then choose **Web** from the submenu if the Web toolbar isn't displayed already.

3. Click the **Start Page** button on the Web toolbar. The Start Page begins loading, as shown in Figure 1-17. Wait a few moments for the page to load. (Since this page is updated every day, your start page may not look exactly like the one shown.)

4. Close Internet Explorer by clicking its **Close** button, and return to Microsoft Word.

5. Click the **Search the Web** button. The Internet Explorer program opens and displays the MSN Search screen.

6. Key **pets** in the *Search* box.

7. Click **Search** and a list of pet-related Web sites appears.

8. Click on one of the Web sites to display more information on pets.

9. Click the **Back** button to return to the previous page. Click another Web site to display.

10. Click the **Home** button to return to the Start Page for Internet Explorer.

11. Close Internet Explorer. Close Word. If a message appears asking you if you want to save changes, click **No**.

12. If necessary, disconnect from your Internet Service Provider.

Hot Tip

You can display the Web toolbar in any Office application and use it to access the World Wide Web.

Hot Tip

To start your Web browser, you can click the **Start Page** button, click the **Search the Web** button, or key an **URL** in the *Address* box of the Web toolbar. Depending on your type of Internet connection, you may have to connect to your Internet Service Provider first.

SUMMARY

In this lesson, you learned:

■ Microsoft Office 2003 is a group of computer programs. Office 2003 includes a word-processing program (Word), a presentation program (PowerPoint), a spreadsheet program (Excel), a database program (Access), and a desktop-publishing program (Publisher).

■ The basic parts of the opening screen are similar in all of the Office programs. The task pane is a separate window on the right-hand side of the opening screen. The task pane contains commonly used commands that can help you work faster.

■ Each title in the menu bar represents a separate drop-down menu. When you choose a command from a drop-down menu, you tell the program what you want to do. To see an expanded menu with all of the commands, click the arrows at the bottom of a menu.

■ Toolbars provide another quick way to choose commands. The toolbars use icons, or small pictures, to remind you of each button's function. Toolbars can also contain drop-down menus.

■ In all Office programs, when you open an existing document, the Open dialog box appears. The Open dialog box allows you to open a file from any available disk or folder.

■ No matter which Office application you are using, files are opened, saved, and closed the same way. Filenames may contain up to 255 characters and may include spaces.

■ Recently used files can be opened quickly by choosing the filename from the bottom of the File menu or from the task pane. You can also click the Start button and select My Recent Documents to list the fifteen most recently used files. To exit an Office application, choose Exit from the File menu or click the Close button on the title bar.

■ Use Office Help when you have a question about an option. You can access Office Help from the Help menu. Or, key a question in the *Type a question for help* box on the menu bar. From the Help task pane, you can then display a Table of Contents or search the Help system for information.

■ The Office Assistant is a feature found in all Office programs and is another way to get help. It offers tips, advice, and hints on how to work more effectively. You can also use it to search for help on any given topic.

■ The Internet is a vast network of computers linked to one another. The Internet allows people around the world to share information and ideas through Web pages, newsgroups, mailing lists, chat rooms, e-mail, and electronic files.

■ The World Wide Web allows you to use links on "pages" to share information. The Internet is its carrier. To identify the links, the Web uses addresses called Uniform Resource Locators (URLs).

■ The Web toolbar is available in all Office programs. It contains buttons for opening and searching documents. You can use the Web toolbar to access documents on the Internet, on an intranet (a company's private Web), or on your computer.

VOCABULARY *Review*

Define the following terms:

Close	Internet Explorer	Task pane
Default	Intranet	Toolbar
Drop-down menu	Link	Uniform Resource Locators
Home page	Menu	(URLs)
Icon	Open	World Wide Web
Internet	Save	Web browser

REVIEW *Questions*

WRITTEN QUESTIONS

Write a brief answer to the following questions.

1. List four of the applications that are included in Office 2003.

2. How do you start an Office application?

3. What is the difference between the Save and Save As commands?

4. If the Web toolbar is not on the screen, how do you display it?

5. What is the location and the function of the title bar, menu bar, status bar, and taskbar?

TRUE/FALSE

Circle T if the statement is true or F if the statement is false.

T   F   1. In all Office applications, you open, save, and close files in the same way.

T   F   2. A filename may include up to 356 characters and may include spaces.

T   F   3. The Office Assistant is available in all Office programs.

T   F   4. The Web uses addresses called URLs to identify the links on Web pages.

T   F   5. As you work in Office, the menus are adjusted to display the commands used most frequently.

PROJECTS

PROJECT 1-1

As President of the Booster Club, you need to save a copy of Fair Work Schedule into each of the Booster Club members' folders.

1. Open Word and a blank document appears.

2. Open Excel. Use the **File** menu to locate the **Booster Club** folder in the data files. Open the **Fair Schedule** file from the **Perez** folder.

3. Use the **Save As** command to save the file as **Fair Work Schedule,** followed by your initials, in the **Acker** folder.

4. Repeat the process to save the file in the **Bledsoe, Glass, Jones, Miller,** and **Stone** folders.

5. Close **Fair Work Schedule** and exit Excel. The blank Word document should be displayed.

6. Use the task pane to open the **Schedule Memo** Word file from the **Perez** folder.

7. Save the file with the same name in the **Lewis** folder.

8. Close **Schedule Memo.** Close the Word document without saving and exit Word.

PROJECT 1-2

1. Open Word and access the Help system.

2. Search on the word **tip.**

3. Choose from the list of topics to find out how to show the tip of the day when Word starts.

4. Print the information displayed in the Microsoft Office Help window.

5. Search on the question **What should I do if the Office Assistant is distracting?**

6. Choose from the list of topics to find out how to troubleshoot Help.

7. In the Microsoft Office Help window, choose the option to find out what to do if the Office Assistant is distracting.

8. Print the information displayed in the Microsoft Office Help window.

9. Close the Help system and exit Word.

PROJECT 1-3

1. If necessary, connect to your Internet Service Provider.

2. Open your Web browser.

3. Search for information on the Internet about computers.

4. Search for information about another topic in which you are interested.

5. Return to your home page.

6. Close your Web browser and disconnect from the Internet, if necessary.

WEB *Project*

PROJECT 1-4

If necessary, connect to your Internet Service Provider. Open your Web browser. Search for information on a vacation site in which you are interested. Print one page of the information. Close your Web browser and disconnect from the Internet, if necessary.

TEAMWORK *Project*

PROJECT 1-5

In a small group, discuss how you would use each of the Office programs in your personal life. Write down each program and the possible uses for each one. Pick one of the applications and describe, in writing, how you would use it.

CRITICAL *Thinking*

ACTIVITY 1-1

Use the Office Help system to find out how to change the Office Assistant from a paper clip to another animated character. Write down the steps and then change your Office Assistant to another character.

MICROSOFT WORD

Unit 2

Estimated Time for Unit: 9 hours

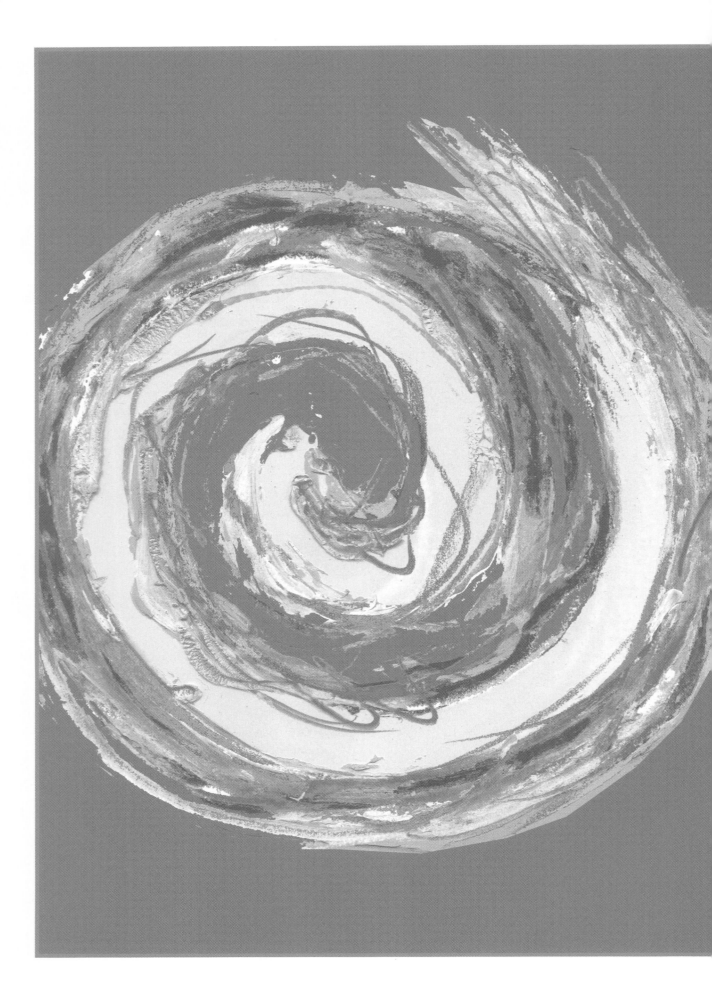

WORD BASICS

What Is Word?

Word is the word processing application in the Microsoft Office 2003 suite of programs. Word is used to enter and edit text. You can easily create and edit documents such as letters and reports. You can also create documents that are more complex such as newsletters and Web pages.

STEP-BY-STEP 1.1

1. With Windows running, click **Start** on the taskbar.

start

2. Point to **All Programs** (in Windows 2000, point to **Programs**), and then point to **Microsoft Office**. Click **Microsoft Office Word 2003** on the submenu. A blank page appears, as shown in Figure 1-1.

FIGURE 1-1
Document in Normal view

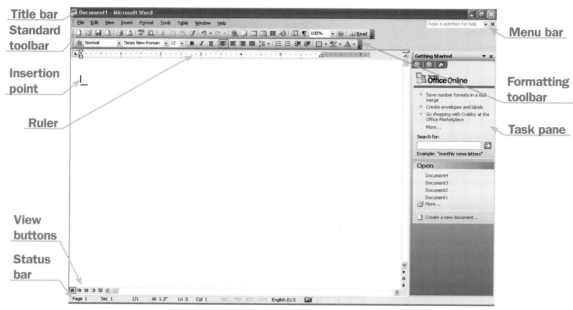

3. Leave the blank Word document open for the next Step-by-Step.

Parts of the Opening Screen

Look at the parts of the opening screen labeled in Figure 1-1. Now find the parts on your computer screen. Some of the features of the opening screen are described in Table 1-1.

TABLE 1-1
Understanding the opening screen

PARTS OF SCREEN	FUNCTION
Standard toolbar	Contains buttons for common tasks, such as printing and opening documents.
Formatting toolbar	Contains buttons for changing the format of characters and paragraphs.
Ruler	Changes indents, tabs, and margins.
Insertion point	Shows where text will appear when you begin keying.
View buttons	Changes views.
Status bar	Shows the portion of the document on the screen and the location of the insertion point. Also shows status of Word features.
Task pane	Window on the right side of the document window. Contains most-used commands for functions such as styles, clip art, and research.

The mouse pointer looks like an I-beam in the text area of the window. When moving out of the text area toward the toolbars, it turns into an arrow. You can then point and click easily on toolbar buttons and menu names.

Text Entry and Word Wrap

To enter text in a new document, begin keying at the insertion point. The insertion point moves to the right as you key. If the text you key goes beyond the right margin, it automatically moves to the next line. This is called *word wrap* because words are "wrapped around" to the next line.

Tap Enter once to start a new paragraph or to end a line at a specific place. To insert a blank line, tap Enter twice.

STEP-BY-STEP 1.2

1. If the task pane is visible, close it by clicking the **Close** button on the task pane.

2. Key the text from Figure 1-2. Watch how the words at the end of lines wrap to the next line as they are keyed.

FIGURE 1-2

Learning to type quickly and accurately is a skill that will help you the rest of your life. To type fast by touch, curve your fingers and make sharp quick strokes. Try to keep your eyes on the copy and not on your hands or the screen. Sit with your feet flat on the floor and your back erect. You should also arrange your work area so that you are comfortable with the position of the keyboard and the document.

3. If you make a mistake, continue to key. You will learn how to correct errors in the next lesson. Leave the document open for the next Step-by-Step.

Document Views

The five ways to view a document on the screen are Normal view, Web Layout view, Print Layout view, Outline view, and Reading Layout view. The table below describes each view.

TABLE 1-2
Document screen views

VIEW	FUNCTION
Normal ≣	Shows a simplified layout of the page so you can key, edit, and format text.
Web Layout ⬚	Shows how a document looks when it is viewed as a Web page.
Print Layout ⊟	Shows how a document looks when it is printed.
Outline ⊯	Shows the headings and text in outline form. You can then see the structure of the document and reorganize it easily.
Reading Layout 📖 📖 Read	Shows text on the screen in a form that is easy to read.

STEP-BY-STEP 1.3

1. Open the **View** menu and choose **Web Layout** to change the document to Web Layout view.

2. Open the **View** menu and choose **Print Layout** to change the document to Print Layout view.

3. Open the **View** menu and choose **Outline** to change the document to Outline view.

4. Open the **View** menu and choose **Reading Layout** to change the document to Reading Layout view. Click the **Close** button on the Reading Layout toolbar.

5. Open the **View** menu and choose **Normal** to change to Normal view.

6. Leave the document open for the next Step-by-Step.

> **Hot Tip**
>
> You can also change views by clicking the view buttons at the bottom left of the document windows.

Moving the Insertion Point

To move the insertion point in a short document, it is faster to use the mouse. Place the I-beam where you want the insertion point and then click the left mouse button. The blinking insertion point appears.

In a long document, it is faster to use the keyboard to move the insertion point. Table 1-3 shows the keys you can tap to move the insertion point.

TABLE 1-3
Keyboard shortcuts for moving the insertion point

PRESS	TO MOVE THE INSERTION POINT
Right arrow	Right one character
Left arrow	Left one character
Down arrow	To the next line
Up arrow	To the previous line
End	To the end of a line
Home	To the beginning of a line
Page Down	To the next page
Page Up	To the previous page
Ctrl+right arrow	To the next word
Ctrl+left arrow	To the previous word
Ctrl+End	To the end of the document
Ctrl+Home	To the beginning of the document

STEP-BY-STEP 1.4

1. Tap **Ctrl+Home** to move to the beginning of the document.

2. Tap **Ctrl+right arrow** three times to move to the fourth word (*quickly*) in the first line.

3. Tap **End** to move to the end of the first line.

4. Tap the **down arrow** to move to the next line.

5. Tap **Ctrl+End** to move to the end of the document.

6. Click **Ctrl+Home** to move to the beginning of the document. Leave the document open for the next Step-by-Step.

Saving a Document

When you save a file for the first time, you will need to choose Save As on the File menu. The Save As dialog box appears as shown in Figure 1-3. This is where you name the file and choose where to save it.

FIGURE 1-3
Save As dialog box

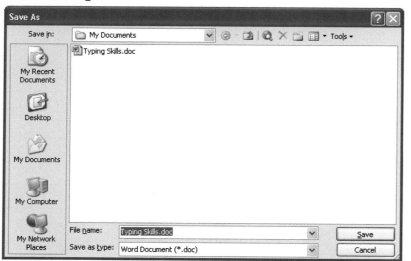

The next time you want to save changes to the document, you only need to choose Save on the File menu. Word saves the document by overwriting the previous version. After you have already saved a file, you can use Save As to save it again using a different name or to save it to a new location.

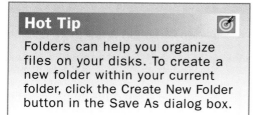

Hot Tip

Folders can help you organize files on your disks. To create a new folder within your current folder, click the Create New Folder button in the Save As dialog box.

STEP-BY-STEP 1.5

1. Open the **File** menu and choose **Save As**. The Save As dialog box appears.

2. Click the down arrow at the right of the *Save in* box to display the disk drives.

3. Choose the drive where you want to save the file.

4. In the *File name* box, select the name of the file if necessary. Key **Typing Skills** followed by your initials.

5. Click **Save**.

6. Word returns you to the Normal view screen. Open the **File** menu and choose **Close** to close the document.

Opening a Document

With Word on the screen, you can open a file from any disk or folder using the Open dialog box, as shown in Figure 1-4. You can also open documents using the task pane.

FIGURE 1-4
Open dialog box

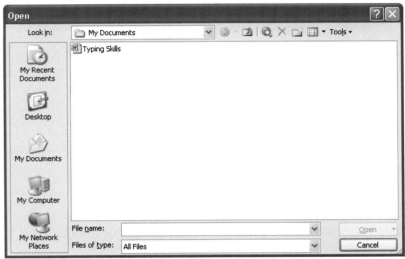

STEP-BY-STEP 1.6

1. Open the **File** menu and choose **Open**. The Open dialog box appears.

2. Click the down arrow to the right of the *Look in* box to display the available disk drives.

3. Select the drive where you saved the file **Typing Skills**.

4. Click to select the file. Click **Open**. The *Typing Skills* document appears on the screen. Leave the document open for the next Step-by-Step.

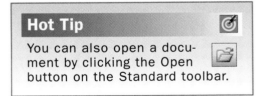

Hot Tip

You can also open a document by clicking the Open button on the Standard toolbar.

Zoom View

The **Zoom view** allows you to magnify and reduce your document on the screen. When changing the magnification of a document, the higher the magnification, the larger the document and the lower the magnification, the smaller the document.

Full Screen View

Many times, it is difficult to see the entire document on your screen. **Full Screen View** removes the toolbars, rulers, and scrollbars from the screen. It leaves only the document and the Close Full Screen button on the screen.

STEP-BY-STEP 1.7

1. Open the **View** menu and choose **Zoom**. The Zoom dialog box appears.

2. In the *Zoom to* section, click to select **200%**. Click **OK**. The document is magnified to 200%.

3. Open the **View** menu and choose **Zoom**. In the *Zoom to* section, click to select **100%**. Click **OK**. The document is reduced to 100%.

4. Open the **View** menu and choose **Full Screen**. The document changes to Full Screen view.

5. Click the **Close Full Screen** button. The document returns to Normal view.

6. Save and leave the document open for the next Step-by-Step.

> **Hot Tip**
>
> You can also click the arrow on the Zoom box on the Standard toolbar to change the magnification.

Previewing a Document

The **Print Preview** command shows you how a document will look when it is printed. The print preview window will look similar to Figure 1-5. The Print Preview toolbar contains options for viewing the document, as shown in Figure 1-6.

> **Hot Tip**
>
> It is always good to preview a document before you print it. Correcting errors before you print the document will save time and paper.

FIGURE 1-5
Print Preview

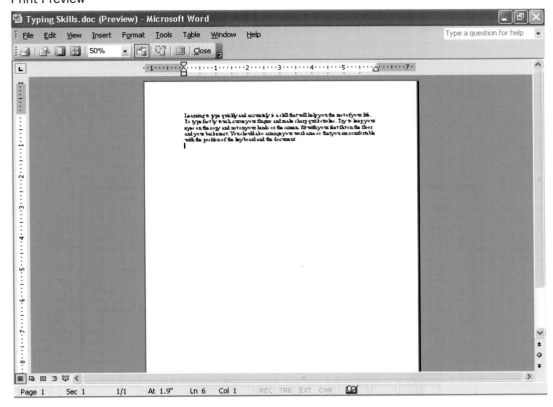

FIGURE 1-6
Print Preview toolbar

Print

Magnifier

One Page

Multiple
Pages

Zoom

View Ruler

Shrink to Fit

Close
Preview

Full Screen

Selecting a Page Orientation

There are two ways to print text on a page in Word. Documents printed in *portrait orientation* are longer than they are wide, as shown in Figure 1-7. Documents printed in *landscape orientation* are wider than they are long, as shown in Figure 1-8. By default, Word is set to print pages in portrait orientation. You can change the page orientation in the Page Setup dialog box, as shown in Figure 1-9.

FIGURE 1-7
Portrait orientation

FIGURE 1-8
Landscape orientation

FIGURE 1-9
Page Setup dialog box

STEP-BY-STEP 1.8

1. Open the **File** menu and choose **Print Preview**. Notice that the page orientation of the document is portrait.

2. Click the **Close** button on the Print Preview toolbar to return to the Normal view screen.

3. Open the **File** menu and choose **Page Setup**. The Page Setup dialog box appears.

4. Click the **Margins** tab if it is not already selected.

5. In the *Orientation* section, choose the **Landscape** option. Click **OK**.

6. Open the **File** menu and choose **Print Preview**. The document is now in landscape orientation. Click the **Close** button.

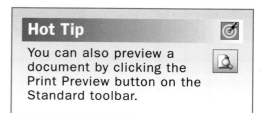

Hot Tip

You can also preview a document by clicking the Print Preview button on the Standard toolbar.

7. Save the document and leave it open for the next Step-by-Step.

Printing Your Document

You can print a full document, a single page, or multiple pages from a document on the screen. The Print dialog box, as shown in Figure 1-10, contains other options for printing a document.

FIGURE 1-10
Print dialog box

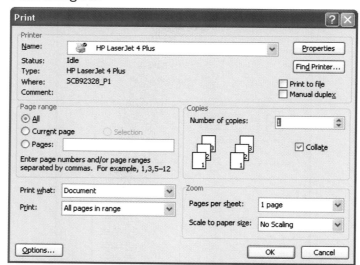

STEP-BY-STEP 1.9

1. Open the **File** menu and choose **Print.** The Print dialog box appears.

2. Print the document using the default settings by clicking **OK**.

3. Open the **File** menu and choose **Close** to close the document. (Click **Yes** to save any changes if you are prompted.)

> **Hot Tip**
>
> You can also print a document by clicking the Print button on the Standard toolbar or on the Print Preview toolbar. Word will not open the Print dialog box, but will begin printing immediately using the default settings.

SUMMARY

In this lesson, you learned:

- Word is a word processing program that can be used to create documents such as letters, memos, forms, and even Web pages.

- The key elements of the Normal view screen are the Standard and Formatting toolbars, ruler, insertion point, view buttons, status bar, and task pane.

- You can view the document screen in Normal view, Web Layout view, Print Layout view, Outline view, and Reading Layout view.

- When text is entered, the word wrap feature automatically wraps words around to the next line if they will not fit on the current line.

- When corrections or additions need to be made, the insertion point can be placed anywhere within a document using the keyboard or mouse.

- When you save a document for the first time, the Save As dialog box appears. This is where you name a file and choose where to save it.

- You can locate and open an existing document through the Open dialog box.

- Zoom view allows you to magnify or reduce your document on the screen.

- Full Screen view makes it easier to view a document on the screen by removing the toolbars, rulers, and scroll bars.

- Use the Print Preview command to see a document as it will appear when printed.

- Use the Page Setup dialog box to change the page orientation to portrait orientation or landscape orientation.

- Print a document by choosing the Print command from the File menu or by clicking the Print button on the Standard toolbar.

VOCABULARY *Review*

Define the following terms:

Full Screen view	Print Preview	Word wrap
Landscape orientation	Word	Zoom view
Portrait orientation		

REVIEW *Questions*

MULTIPLE CHOICE

Select the best response for the following statements.

1. The Normal view screen contains all except the following:
   A. title bar
   B. view buttons
   C. Save in box
   D. insertion point

2. What dialog box do you use to save a file for the first time?
   A. Save
   B. Locate File
   C. Save As
   D. Save File

3. Clicking the Print button on the toolbar causes Word to
   A. begin printing immediately using default settings.
   B. display the Print dialog box.
   C. switch to the Print Preview screen.
   D. show the document on the screen as it will appear when printed.

4. To move the insertion point to the end of the document, tap
   A. the down arrow.
   B. End.
   C. Page Down.
   D. Ctrl+End.

5. Which of the following is *not* a method for opening an existing document?
   A. Click the Print Preview button on the Standard toolbar.
   B. Choose Open on the File menu.
   C. Click the Open button on the Standard toolbar.
   D. Use the task pane.

FILL IN THE BLANK

Complete the following sentences by writing the correct word or words in the blanks provided.

1. _____ view allows you to enter and format text quickly.

2. To insert a blank line in a document, tap the _____ key twice.

3. Documents printed in _____ orientation are wider than they are long.

4. The blinking _____ shows where text will appear when you begin keying.

5. _____ can help you organize files on your disks.

PROJECTS

PROJECT 1-1

Create a flyer announcing an upcoming Car Wash to help support the band.

1. Open **Project1-1** from the data files. Save the document as **Car Wash** followed by your initials.

2. Change the view to **Full Screen.**

3. Place the insertion point at the end of the first sentence. Key the following text: **All proceeds will help purchase new band uniforms.**

4. Click **Ctrl+End** to move the insertion point to the end of the last line.

5. Insert a blank line and key: **Thank you for your support!**

6. Close Full Screen view.

7. Change the orientation of the document to landscape.

8. Preview the document

9. Save, print, and close the document.

PROJECT 1-2

Write a letter thanking the principal for his generous donation at the band car wash.

1. Open the **File** menu and choose **New**. Click **Blank Document** on the task pane to create a new Word document.

2. Key the following text:

Dear Mr. Jones,

Thank you for participating in the Thomas Jefferson Junior High Car Wash. We appreciate your generous donation. It helped us achieve our goal of purchasing new uniforms for our band members. The car wash was a huge success because of people like you. Thank you for supporting our fund-raiser.

Sincerely,

3. Insert four blank lines after *Sincerely*, and key your name.

4. Change the document to **Normal** view.

5. Change the document to **Print Layout** view.

6. Change the document to **Reading Layout** view.

7. Change the document back to **Normal** view.

8. Save the document as **Thank You** followed by your initials.

9. Print and close the document.

PROJECT 1-3

1. Open **Project1-3** from the data files. Save the document as **Eagle** followed by your initials.

2. Click **Ctrl + End** to move the insertion point to the end of the last line. Tap **Enter** twice to insert a blank line.

3. Key the following facts about the bald eagle. Insert a blank line after each fact.

It is a species unique to North America.

They are 29-42 inches long, weigh 7-15 pounds, and have a wingspan of 6-8 feet making them one of the largest birds in North America.

Bald Eagles are located in every U.S. state except for Hawaii.

They eat mainly fish but also eat small animals such as ducks, turtles, and rabbits.

Bald Eagles can fly approximately 100 miles per hour in a level flight.

4. Preview the document.

5. Save, print, and close the document.

PROJECT 1-4

1. Open **Project1-4** from the data files. Save the document as **Constitution** followed by your initials.

2. Change the Zoom to **100%**.

3. Change to **Full Screen** view.

4. Read the document to become familiar with it. Click **Ctrl+Home** to place the insertion point at the beginning of the document if necessary.

5. Click **Ctrl+right arrow** four times to move the insertion point to the fifth word. Key **United** followed by a space.

6. Click **Ctrl+End** to place the insertion point at the end of the document. Key the text:

   It reflects fundamental principles that are timeless.

7. Insert a blank line and key:

   At the time the Constitution was written, it was considered a radical plan of government. Some of the new and untried principles were limited government, separation of powers, and individual rights. It is the responsibility of each of us to preserve and protect this document.

8. Close the Full Screen view. Preview the document.

9. Save, print, and close the document.

WEB*Project*

PROJECT 1-5

In 1787, seventy-two delegates from the thirteen colonies gathered in Philadelphia to write the Constitution. Some well-known Americans such as George Washington and Benjamin Franklin attended this convention. Other delegates were James Madison, Alexander Hamilton, Gouverneur Morris, Roger Sherman, William Paterson, and Luther Martin.

1. Open a new Word document.

2. Use the Internet to research one of the delegates listed above.

3. Write a paragraph about the delegate you selected. Use at least five facts including which colony the delegate represented.

4. Save the document as **Delegate** followed by your initials.

5. Print and close the document.

TEAMWORK*Project*

PROJECT 1-6

In small groups, think of reasons why the band needs new uniforms.

1. Open a new Word document.

2. Key the reasons the band needs new uniforms. Tap **Enter** after each reason.

3. Save the document as **Uniforms** with the initials of the group. Print and close the document.

4. Share your group's ideas with the rest of the class.

CRITICAL*Thinking*

 ## ACTIVITY 1-1

The band is raising money to purchase new band uniforms. Type a persuasive paragraph stating the reasons why the band needs new uniforms. Be sure to include reasons from the Teamwork Project. Save it as **Persuasive Paragraph**. Preview and print the document.

BASIC EDITING

Selecting Text

Selecting is highlighting a block of text. Blocks can be as small as one character or as large as an entire document. After selecting a block of text, you can edit the entire block at once. You can select text using the mouse or using the keyboard. Table 2-1 summarizes ways to select text. To remove the highlight, click the mouse button.

TABLE 2-1
Selecting blocks of text

TO SELECT THIS	DO THIS
Word	Double-click the word.
Line	Click one time in the left margin beside the line.
Line (or lines)	Click one time in the left margin beside the line, and then drag the mouse downward to select the following lines. Or Position the insertion point at the beginning of a line, tap and hold down Shift, and tap down arrow once to select one line or several times to select more lines.
Sentence	Hold down Ctrl, and click in the sentence.
Paragraph	Triple-click anywhere in the paragraph. Or Double-click in the left margin of the paragraph.
Multiple paragraphs	Double-click in the left margin beside the paragraph; then drag to select following paragraphs.
Entire document	Triple-click in the left margin. Or Hold down Ctrl, and click one time in the left margin. Or Choose Select All from the Edit menu.

S TEP-BY-STEP 2.1

1. With Word open, open the **File** menu and click **Open**. The Open dialog box appears.

2. Open **Step2-1** from the data files. Save the document as **Typing Skills2** followed by your initials.

3. Click one time in the margin to the left of the word *Learning* to select the first line.

> **Hot Tip**
>
> You can also select text items that are not next to each other. Select the first item you want, and hold down the **Ctrl** button; then select the other items.

4. Click one time anywhere in the document to remove the highlight.

5. Double-click the word **Learning** to select it.

6. Click anywhere in the document to remove the highlight.

7. Triple-click anywhere in the first paragraph to select the entire paragraph. Remove the highlight.

STEP-BY-STEP 2.1 Continued

8. Position the insertion point before the *T* in the word *To* in the second sentence of the paragraph. Click and drag the pointer to select the entire sentence. Remove the highlight.

9. Open the **Edit** menu and choose **Select All** to select the entire document. Remove the highlight.

10. Leave the document open for the next Step-by-Step.

Using the Backspace and Delete Keys

You might find that you need to delete characters or words. You can delete characters by using the Backspace key or the Delete key. Tapping Backspace deletes the character to the left of the insertion point. Tapping Delete deletes the character to the right of the insertion point. You can also easily remove a number of characters or words by first selecting them and then tapping either Backspace or Delete.

> **Hot Tip**
>
> Many times, it is easier to select and edit sentences and paragraphs if you can view the sentence and paragraph markers. To view the formatting markers, click the Show/Hide button on the Standard toolbar. Being able to see these hidden characters can help you edit your text.

Using Overtype

In *Overtype mode,* the text you key replaces, or types over, existing text. Overtype mode is especially useful for correcting misspelled words or for replacing one word with another word of the same length. You can turn Overtype on or off by double-clicking OVR on the status bar. You can also tap the Insert key. After replacing text, turn off the Overtype mode by double-clicking OVR or tapping the Insert key.

STEP-BY-STEP 2.2

1. Place the insertion point after the word *flat* in the fourth sentence of the document.

2. Tap **Backspace** until the words *flat* and the extra blank space disappear.

3. Place the insertion point before the word *also* in the fifth sentence.

4. Tap **Delete** until the word *also* and the blank space after it disappear.

5. In the first sentence, select the words *the rest of your.* Tap **Delete**. The words disappear.

6. Double-click **OVR** on the status bar. OVR appears in black, as shown in Figure 2-1.

FIGURE 2-1
Overtype mode

STEP-BY-STEP 2.2 Continued

7. Move the insertion point to the left of the *l* in the word *location* in the last sentence. Key **position**.

8. Double-click **OVR** on the status bar to turn Overtype off.

9. Save and leave the document open for the next Step-by-Step.

Using Undo and Redo

When working on a document, you will sometimes delete text accidentally or change your mind about the changes you have made. To undo or reverse recent actions, use the Undo command. Click the down arrow next to the Undo button on the toolbar to see a drop-down list of your recent actions. The most recent action appears at the top of the list, as shown in Figure 2-2. Choose the action you want to undo. Word will undo that action and all the actions listed above it.

Hot Tip

If the **Redo** button is not visible, you can display it by clicking the **Toolbar Options** button on the Standard toolbar; then choose it from the list of buttons.

FIGURE 2-2
Undo list

Similar to the Undo command is the Redo command. The Redo command reverses an Undo action. As with the Undo command, when you click the down arrow next to the Redo button, a list of recent actions appears.

STEP-BY-STEP 2.3

1. Click the arrow on the **Undo** button on the toolbar. A drop-down list appears, as shown in Figure 2-2.

2. Scroll down the list—all choices will be highlighted as you scroll—and click **Typing p**. (The description should read *Undo 8 Actions*.) The word *position* changes back to *location*.

3. Click the down arrow on the **Redo** button on the toolbar. A drop-down list appears.

4. Scroll down the list and click **Typing n**. (The description should read *Redo 8 Actions*.) The word *location* changes back to *position*.

STEP-BY-STEP 2.3 Continued

5. Double-click the word **keyboard** in the same sentence to select it. Tap **Delete**.

6. Click the **Undo** button. The word *keyboard* reappears.

7. Save and leave the document open for the next Step-by-Step.

Cutting and Copying Text

At some point when you are editing a document, you will probably want to move or copy text to a different location. The feature that makes these moving and copying operations easy is the Office Clipboard. The *Clipboard* is a temporary storage place in the computer's memory. The Clipboard is displayed in the task pane as shown in Figure 2-3.

FIGURE 2-3
Office Clipboard in the task pane

Cutting Text

Use the Cut and Paste commands to move text from one location to another. The *Cut* command removes the selected text from the document and places it on the Clipboard. When you *paste* the text, it is copied from the Clipboard to the location of the insertion point. Moving text in this manner is often referred to as cutting and pasting.

STEP-BY-STEP 2.4

1. Open the **Edit** menu and choose **Office Clipboard** to display the Clipboard.

2. Click the **Clear All** button to clear any items that are on the Clipboard if necessary.

3. Hold down **Ctrl** and click the last sentence of the document to select it. Open the **Edit** menu and choose **Cut.** The sentence you selected disappears from the screen. It has been placed on the Clipboard.

4. Position the insertion point at the end of the second sentence.

5. Hover the pointer over the sentence on the Clipboard. Click the arrow to the right of the sentence. Click **Paste**. The sentence appears at the insertion point.

6. Save the document, and leave it open for the next Step-by-Step.

Hot Tip

To cut text, you can also click the Cut button on the Standard toolbar. To paste text, you can also click the Paste button on the Standard toolbar.

Copying Text

The Copy command is similar to the Cut command. However, when you choose the *Copy* command, a copy of the selected text is placed on the Clipboard. The original text remains in the document. You also retrieve the copied text from the Clipboard.

STEP-BY-STEP 2.5

1. Hold down **Ctrl** and click the second sentence, which begins *To type.* Open the **Edit** menu and click **Copy**. A copy of the sentence is placed on the Clipboard.

2. Position the insertion point at the end of the paragraph. Open the **Edit** menu and click **Paste.** A copy of the sentence appears at the insertion point.

3. Hold down **Ctrl** and click the second sentence. Open the **Edit** menu and click **Cut** to remove the sentence.

4. Click the **Close** button on the Office Clipboard to close it.

5. Save and leave the document open for the next Step-by-Step.

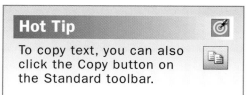

Hot Tip

To copy text, you can also click the Copy button on the Standard toolbar.

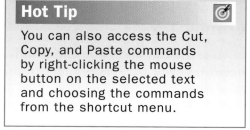

Hot Tip

You can also access the Cut, Copy, and Paste commands by right-clicking the mouse button on the selected text and choosing the commands from the shortcut menu.

Using Drag and Drop

When copying or moving text a short distance, you can use a quick method called *drag and drop*. Place the mouse pointer on the selected text and hold down the mouse button until a small box appears below the insertion point. While still holding down the mouse button, drag the text to the desired location.

> **Hot Tip**
>
> You can also use the drag and drop method to copy text by holding down Ctrl while dragging the text.

STEP-BY-STEP 2.6

1. Select the third sentence of the document, which begins *Try to.*

2. Position the pointer over the selected text.

3. Click and hold. A dotted insertion point will appear at the pointer and a box will appear below the pointer.

4. Drag the pointer to the end of the paragraph. Position the pointer after the period ending the paragraph and release the mouse button. The sentence is moved.

5. Adjust spacing between sentences if necessary.

6. Save and leave the document open for the next Step-by-Step.

Automatic Spell Checking

Automatic spell checking identifies misspellings and words that are not in Word's dictionary by underlining them with a wavy red line after you key them. To correct a misspelled word that is underlined, position the pointer on the word and click with the right mouse button. A shortcut menu appears with a list of correctly spelled words. Click with the left mouse button on the suggestion that you want, and it replaces the misspelled word.

> **Did You Know?**
>
> The automatic spell checker sometimes incorrectly identifies words as being misspelled, such as proper names. This is because the spell checker could not find the word in its dictionary.

Automatic Grammar Checking

Similar to the automatic spell checker feature, *automatic grammar checking* checks the document for grammatical errors. When it finds a possible error, Word underlines the word, phrase, or sentence with a wavy green line. To see the suggested corrections, right-click on the word or phrase. Choose a suggestion from the shortcut menu, or choose Grammar to learn more about the particular grammar error that has been identified.

Computer Concepts

Although the grammar checker is a helpful tool, you still need to have a good working knowledge of English grammar. The grammar checker can identify a possible problem, but you must decide if the change should be made depending on the context of the sentence.

STEP-BY-STEP 2.7

1. Place the insertion point at the end of the paragraph.

2. Key the following sentences with the misspelled word **typping.**
   Are you making more than two errors per minute. Then you are typping too fast.

3. The automatic grammar checker underlined the grammar error in green. The automatic spell checker underlined the misspelled word in red.

4. Position the I-beam on the underlined misspelled word *typping*, and click the *right* mouse button. A shortcut menu appears, as shown in Figure 2-4.

FIGURE 2-4
Automatic spell checker shortcut menu

5. With the left mouse button, click the correct spelling of *typing*. The misspelled word is replaced with the correctly spelled word, and the wavy red underline disappears.

6. Position the I-beam on the green underlined word *minute*, and click the *right* mouse button. A shortcut menu appears, as shown in Figure 2-5.

STEP-BY-STEP 2.7 Continued

FIGURE 2-5
Automatic grammar checker shortcut menu

7. Click the suggested change **minute?** at the top of the shortcut menu. The sentence is corrected.

8. Save, print, and close the document.

Using the Spelling and Grammar Checker

In addition to checking your spelling and grammar as you type, you can also check the document after you finish keying by using the *Spelling and Grammar Checker.* When a spelling error is detected, the Spelling and Grammar dialog box appears, as shown in Figure 2-6. Figure 2-7 shows the Spelling and Grammar dialog box as it appears when a grammar error is identified. Table 2-2 explains the options for correcting spelling errors. Table 2-3 explains the options for correcting grammar errors. The options in the Spelling and Grammar dialog box change depending on the nature of the error.

Hot Tip

You can use the Spelling and Grammar checker to check an entire document or portions of a document.

FIGURE 2-6
Spelling and Grammar dialog box (Spelling)

FIGURE 2-7
Spelling and Grammar dialog box (Grammar)

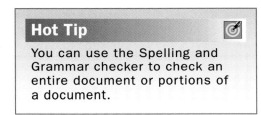

TABLE 2-2
Spelling and Grammar dialog box options for Spelling

OPERATION	ACTION
Ignore Once	Ignores only the word displayed in red. The button changes to Resume if you click in the document.
Ignore All	Ignores all instances of the same word.
Add to Dictionary	Adds the selected word to the custom dictionary.
Change	Corrects only the selected word.
Change All	Corrects all instances of the same misspelling.
AutoCorrect	Adds the word and its correction to your AutoCorrect list.
Suggestions	Displays a list of proposed spelling changes.
Options	Allows you to change default spelling and grammar check settings.
Undo/Undo Edit	Reverses your last spelling change.
Cancel/Close	Before you make a spelling change, Cancel stops the spelling check. At the end of a spell check, Close stops the spelling check and saves all the changes you have made. After your first spelling change, the button name Cancel changes to Close.

TABLE 2-3
Spelling and Grammar dialog box options for Grammar

OPERATION	ACTION
Ignore Once	Ignores only the grammar error displayed in green. The button changes to Resume if you click in the document.
Ignore Rule	Ignores all instances of the same occurrence of the rule.
Next Sentence	Accepts the manual changes you made to a document and continues with the spelling and grammar check.
Change	Corrects only the displayed grammar error.
Explain	Provides an explanation of the grammar or style rule being applied.
Suggestions	Displays a list of proposed spellings or grammar changes.
Options	Allows you to change default spelling and grammar check settings.
Undo	Reverses your last grammar change.
Cancel/Close	Before you make a grammar change, Cancel stops the grammar check. At the end of a grammar check, Close stops the grammar check and saves all the changes you have made. After your first grammar change, the button name Cancel changes to Close.

STEP-BY-STEP 2.8

1. Open **Step2-8** from the data files.

2. Save the document as **Trip Letter** followed by your initials.

3. Tap **Ctrl+Home** to move the insertion point to the beginning of the document, if necessary.

4. Click the **Spelling and Grammar** button on the toolbar.

5. The word *deposet* is displayed in red type in the Spelling and Grammar dialog box. Note that suggested words are listed in the *Suggestions* box. Click the word **deposit**, if not already selected.

6. Click **Change**. Word replaces the misspelled word and continues checking.

7. The word *has* is displayed in green. The word *have* is in the *Suggestions* box. Click **Change**.

8. The word *vald* is displayed in red. The word *valid* is in the *Suggestions* box. Click **Change.**

9. The word *departur* is displayed in red. The word *departure* is displayed in the *Suggestions* box. Click **Change All**. Word replaces the error each time it occurs in the document and continues checking.

10. The word *a* is displayed in green. Click **Change** to change it to *an.*

11. The message *The spelling and grammar check is complete* appears. Click **OK**.

12. Save the document, and leave it open for the next Step-by-Step.

Using Find and Replace

Find and Replace are useful editing commands that let you find specific words in a document quickly. If you want, you can replace them instantly with new words. Both commands are chosen from the Edit menu. The Find and Replace dialog box appears as shown in Figure 2-8. (Click More to see the expanded dialog box.)

FIGURE 2-8
Find tab in the Find and Replace dialog box

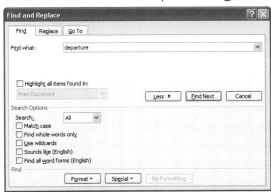

The Find Command

The Find command allows you to quickly search for the occurrence of a specific word or phrase you key in the *Find what* box. The Find command moves the insertion point to each occurrence of the word or phrase.

Find can locate whole or partial words. You can display options for searching for words by clicking the More button. The options in the Find and Replace dialog box are explained in Table 2-4.

TABLE 2-4
Find dialog box options

OPERATION	ACTION
Search	Lets you search from the location of the insertion point up, from the location of the insertion point down, or all (the entire document).
Match case	Searches for words with the same case as that keyed in the Find what box.
Find whole words only	Finds only the word *all*—not words with *all* in them such as *allow* and *rally*.
Use wildcards	Makes it possible to search for words using special characters such as a question mark or asterisk, along with a word or characters in the Find dialog box.
Sounds like	Locates words that sound alike but are spelled differently. For example, if you key the word *so*, Word would also find the word *sew*.
Find all word forms	Lets you find different forms of words. For example, if you search for the word *run*, Word would also find *ran, runs,* and *running*.
Find Next	Goes to the next occurrence of the word.
Cancel	Stops the search and closes the dialog box.
More/Less	Displays the Find and Replace options/Hides the options.
Format	Lets you search for formatting, such as bold, instead of searching for a specific word. It also allows you to search for words with specific formatting, such as the word *computer* in bold.
Special	Lets you search for special characters that may be hidden, such as a paragraph mark, or special characters that are not hidden, such as an em dash (—).

The Replace Command

The Replace command is an extended version of the Find command. Replace has all the features of Find. The Replace command, shown in Figure 2-9, also allows you to replace a word or phrase in the *Find what* box with another word or phrase you key in the *Replace with* box.

FIGURE 2-9
Replace tab in the Find and Replace dialog box

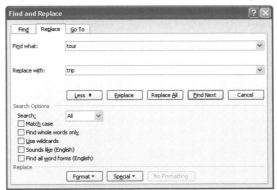

S TEP-BY-STEP 2.9

1. Open the **Edit** menu and choose **Find**. The Find and Replace dialog box appears.

2. In the *Find what* box, key **departure**.

3. In the *Search Options* section, check the **Find all word forms** option. Click the **More** button to expand the dialog box if necessary.

4. Click **Find Next**. Word selects and stops on *departure*. (If the Find and Replace dialog box is covering the word, click on the title bar and drag the box down until the word is displayed.)

5. Continue to click **Find Next** until the dialog box appears stating that Word has finished searching the document. *Departure* appears three times in the document.

6. Click **OK**. Click **Close** on the Find and Replace dialog box.

7. Tap **Ctrl+Home** to move the insertion point to the beginning of the document if necessary. Carefully read the document and note where the word *tour* appears.

8. Open the **Edit** menu and choose **Replace**. Key **tour** in the *Find what* box.

9. Key **trip** in the *Replace with* box. Uncheck the *Find all word forms* option.

10. Click **Replace All**. The following message appears: *Word has completed its search of the document and has made 3 replacements*. Click **OK**.

11. Click **Close** on the Find and Replace dialog box. Read the document again. Notice the word *tour* has been replaced with the word *trip*.

12. Save and leave the document open for the next Step-by-Step.

> **Hot Tip**
>
> One of the quickest ways to move through a long document is to use the Go To command. Go To allows you to skip to a specific part of a document. To use the Go To command, open the **Edit** menu and choose **Go To**. In the *Go to what:* box, you can select where you want to move in the document.

Using the Thesaurus

The *Thesaurus* is a useful feature for finding a synonym (a word with a similar meaning) for a word in the document. For some words, the Thesaurus also lists antonyms, or words with opposite meanings. Use the Thesaurus to find the exact word to express your message or to avoid using the same word repeatedly in a document. You can select an appropriate synonym in the Research task pane, as shown in Figure 2-10.

FIGURE 2-10
Research task pane (Thesaurus)

STEP-BY-STEP 2.10

1. Select the word **outstanding** in the first paragraph.

2. Open the **Tools** menu and point to **Language.** Click **Thesaurus** on the submenu. The Research task pane opens with a list of synonyms.

3. Scroll down to view the synonyms. Under the *exceptional (adj.)* meaning, click the arrow next to the word *wonderful*. Click **Insert** from the submenu. Don't forget to change the preceding *an* to *a.*

4. Select the word **advise** in the last sentence of the second paragraph.

5. Key **advise** in the *Search for* box on the Research task pane. Click the **Start searching** arrow next to the *Search for* box.

6. Using the *counsel (v.)* meaning, replace *advise* with the synonym *recommend.*

> **Computer Concepts**
>
> Even synonyms can have different shades of meaning. Be sure a synonym makes sense in context before replacing a word with it.

STEP-BY-STEP 2.10 Continued

7. Click **Close** on the Research task pane.

8. Save and leave the document open for the next Step-by-Step.

Inserting the Date and Time

You can easily insert the current date and time into a word processing document. In the Date and Time dialog box, shown in Figure 2-11, you will need to select one of the formats available.

FIGURE 2-11
Date and Time dialog box

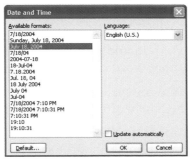

STEP-BY-STEP 2.11

1. Place the insertion point on the first blank line of the document.

2. Open the **Insert** menu and choose **Date and Time**.

3. Click on the format similar to *September 22, 2006*. There should *not* be a check in the *Update automatically* box.

4. Click **OK**. The current date is inserted in the letter.

5. Save, print, and close the document.

SUMMARY

In this lesson, you learned:

- You can speed up operations by selecting blocks of text.

- You can delete text using Backspace and Delete. Overtype mode allows you to replace existing text with the new text that is keyed. Overtype is especially useful for correcting misspelled words.

- You can undo recent actions by using the Undo command. When you click the down arrow next to the Undo button, a drop-down list of your recent actions appears. You can redo an action using the Redo button.

- You can send text to the Clipboard by using either the Cut or Copy command from the Edit menu or toolbar. Then you can retrieve that text or graphic by using the Paste command.

- The Find command moves the insertion point from its present position to the next occurrence of the word or phrase for which you are searching.

- Replace has all the features of Find. In addition, Replace allows you to replace a word or phrase in the Find box with another word or phrase you key in the Replace box.

- Automatic spell checking identifies misspellings and words that are not in Word's dictionary by underlining them in red immediately after you key them.

- Automatic grammar checking automatically checks your document for grammatical errors. When Word finds an error, it underlines the word, phrase, or sentence with a wavy green line.

- The Spelling and Grammar dialog box contains options that allow you to check the spelling and grammar of words, ignore words, make changes, and add words to your own custom dictionary.

- The Thesaurus is a useful feature for finding a synonym (a word with a similar meaning) for a word in your document. For some words, the Thesaurus also lists antonyms.

- The Date and Time command is especially useful when including the date in a letter or memo.

VOCABULARY *Review*

Define the following terms:

Automatic grammar checking	Cut	Selecting
Automatic spell checking	Drag and Drop	Spelling and Grammar
Clipboard	Overtype mode	Checker
Copy	Paste	Thesaurus

REVIEW *Questions*

TRUE/FALSE

Circle T if the statement is true or F if the statement is false.

T F 1. You can edit an entire block of text by selecting it.

T F 2. A green wavy line indicates a grammar error.

T F 3. Use Overtype mode to reverse a recent action.

T F 4. The Replace command is an extended version of the Find command.

T F 5. The Clipboard provides long-term storage, just as saving a file does.

WRITTEN QUESTIONS

Write a brief answer to the following questions.

1. How do the Cut and Copy commands differ?

2. How do you access the Thesaurus?

3. What are the three ways to select an entire document?

4. When is the Undo command useful?

5. What are the two ways to delete characters?

PROJECTS

PROJECT 2-1

Create a list of commonly misspelled words.

1. Open a new Word document. Key the list of commonly misspelled words shown below. Be sure to tap **Enter** after each word.

   Calendar

   Immediate

   Equipment

   Schedule

   Receipt

   Privilege

   Column

   Occurrence

   Exceed

   Apparent

2. Key the word **Installation** below *Immediate*.

3. Click the **Undo** button. The word *Installation* disappears.

4. Click the **Redo** button. The word *Installation* appears again.

5. Use Overtype to replace the word *Exceed* with the word **Precede**. Turn off Overtype.

6. Use drag and drop to alphabetize the spelling list.

7. Save the document as **Spelling List** followed by your initials. Print and close the document.

PROJECT 2-2

In your communications class you are learning about verbal and nonverbal communication. The class assignment is to create a handout with examples of how to use body language.

1. Open **Project2-2** from the data files. Save the document as **Body Language** followed by your initials.

2. Print the document.

3. Many times the spell checker will not identify incorrect words in a document because they are spelled correctly. Find ten words that are incorrect in the document and circle them.

4. Save and close the document.

PROJECT 2-3

Ms. Jones, the government teacher, is sponsoring an end-of-the-year trip to Washington, D.C. Update the itinerary to send to eighth grade students participating on the trip.

1. Open **Project2-3** from the data files. Save the document as **Itinerary** followed by your initials.

2. Correct the spelling and grammar errors in the document.

3. Insert the current date after *Date:*.

4. Use Cut and Paste to switch Day 3 and Day 4. Be sure each day has the correct heading.

5. Place the insertion point below Day 5 and key the following text:

   Breakfast at hotel

   Tour the Ford's Theatre

   Leave for the airport at 1:30 p.m.

   Arrive home at 7:00 p.m.

6. Delete the *Day 6* heading.

7. Highlight the word *Itinerary* in the title and use the Thesaurus to find a synonym.

8. Preview the document. Print from the Print Preview window.

9. Save, print, and close the document.

PROJECT 2-4

Your teacher has asked you to prepare a flyer about the history of Washington, D.C. This flyer will be included in an information packet for each student going on the trip.

1. Open **Project2-4** from the data files. Save the document as **History** followed by your initials.

2. Tap **Ctrl+Home** to move the insertion point to the beginning of the document. Use the Spelling and Grammar checker to correct the errors.

3. Delete the last sentence in the document.

4. Use the Thesaurus to replace the following words with synonyms: *select, designed, attractive,* and *portion*.

5. Copy the clip art and the text, and paste it at the bottom of the page. Leave four blank lines between blocks of text.

6. Preview the document.

7. Save, print, and close the file.

WEB *Project*

PROJECT 2-5

The teacher thought it would be fun to go on an Internet hunt to find clues about the White House.

1. Open **Project2-5** from the data files. Save the document as **White House** followed by your initials.

2. Search Web sites about the White House and answer the questions on the document.

3. Save, print, and close the document.

Extra Challenge

After researching the Web sites, create new questions about the White House for the hunt. Trade questions with a classmate. Answer the new questions.

TEAMWORK *Project*

PROJECT 2-6

Your teacher has asked the students to help promote excitement about the Washington, D.C., trip by preparing a document about one of the places you will visit. Use the Washington, D.C., itinerary in Project 2-3 to choose a place to research.

1. With a partner, use the Internet to find information about one of the places you will visit in Washington, D.C.

2. Write a paragraph about the place you are researching. Share the information with your classmates.

3. Save the document as **Washington D.C.** followed by three letters to identify it. Print and close the document.

Extra Challenge

Find other places you would like to visit in Washington, D.C. Add additional days to the itinerary that include these locations.

CRITICAL *Thinking*

ACTIVITY 2-1

In Project 2-1, you typed a list of commonly misspelled words. One way to remember how to spell difficult words is to use mnemonics. Mnemonics uses association techniques as an aid to help remember things such as frequently misspelled words. Some examples are:

Compliment – praise	"I" is the favorite pronoun
Complement – go together	The two letter e's go together
Accommodate	Double date of c's and m's

With a partner, choose a word from the list of frequently misspelled words in Project 2-1 or you can choose a word from the lists of misspelled words on the Internet. On a Word document, create a mnemonic to help you remember how to spell the word. Save the document as **Mnemonics** followed by three letters to identify it. Share the information with the class.

FORMATTING TEXT

OBJECTIVES

In this lesson, you will:

■ Apply different fonts and font styles to the text.

■ Change the size and color of the text.

■ Use different underline styles and font effects.

■ Highlight text.

■ Copy formats using the Format Painter.

■ Apply and clear styles.

■ Change character spacing.

Estimated Time: 2 hours

Formatting Text

Once you have keyed text into the document, Word provides many useful tools to change the appearance of the text. Arranging the shape, size, type, and general makeup of a document is called *formatting*. To format text, you can use the Font dialog box, as shown in Figure 3-1. You can also use the buttons on the formatting toolbar, as shown in Figure 3-2.

FIGURE 3-1
Font dialog box

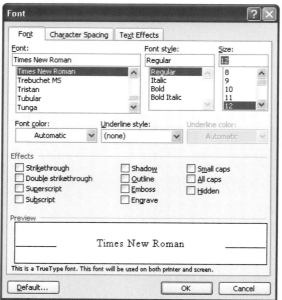

FIGURE 3-2
Formatting toolbar

Changing the Font, Style, Size, and Color

Designs of type are called *fonts*. Just as clothing comes in different designs, fonts have different designs. Like clothing, fonts can be dressy or casual. When you are creating a document, you should consider what kind of impression you want the text to make. Do you want the document to look formal or informal? Using the fonts shown in Figure 3-3 would result in very different looking documents.

Hot Tip ◎

If the Formatting toolbar on the screen does not show all of the buttons shown in Figure 3-2, click the **Toolbar Options** button and then choose the **Add or Remove Buttons** option. Select **Formatting**. A drop-down list of available buttons appears. Click the buttons you would like to appear on the toolbar.

FIGURE 3-3
Different fonts

This font is called Times New Roman.

This font is called Arial.

This font is called Broadway.

𝔗𝔥𝔦𝔰 𝔣𝔬𝔫𝔱 𝔦𝔰 𝔠𝔞𝔩𝔩𝔢𝔡 𝔒𝔩𝔡 𝔈𝔫𝔤𝔩𝔦𝔰𝔥 𝔗𝔢𝔵𝔱 𝔐𝔗.

𝓣𝓱𝓲𝓼 𝓯𝓸𝓷𝓽 𝓲𝓼 𝓬𝓪𝓵𝓵𝓮𝓭 𝓢𝓬𝓻𝓲𝓹𝓽 𝓜𝓣 𝓑𝓸𝓵𝓭.

THIS FONT IS CALLED CASTELLER.

Changing the Font

You can apply a new font by selecting one in the Font dialog box, as shown in Figure 3-1. You can also use the Font box on the Formatting toolbar, as shown in Figure 3-4. You can change the font of text already keyed by selecting it first and then choosing a new font. To change the font of text not yet keyed, first choose the font and then key the text.

FIGURE 3-4
Font box

STEP-BY-STEP 3.1

1. Open **Step3-1** from the data files.

2. Save the document as **Proofreading** followed by your initials.

3. Open the **Edit** menu and choose **Select All** to select all the text.

4. Open the **Format** menu and choose **Font.** The Font dialog box appears, as shown in Figure 3-1. Click the **Font** tab if necessary.

5. In the *Font* box, scroll down and click **Times New Roman**. Notice the *Preview* box shows text in the new font.

STEP-BY-STEP 3.1 Continued

6. Choose **OK**. The text in the document changes to Times New Roman. Click anywhere in the document to remove the highlight.

7. Select the title of the document, *Proofreading Guidelines*.

8. Click the arrow at the right of the *Font* box on the Formatting toolbar. A list of fonts appears.

   | Times New Roman ▾ |

9. Choose **Arial** from the list of fonts. The title appears in the selected font. Click the mouse button to remove the highlight.

10. Save the document, and leave it open for the next Step-by-Step.

Changing Font Style

Font style is a set of formatting features you can apply to text to change its appearance. Common font styles are bold, italic, and underline. These styles can be applied to any font. Figure 3-5 illustrates some of the styles applied to the Times New Roman font.

FIGURE 3-5
Different font styles

This is Times New Roman bold.

This is Times New Roman italic.

This is Times New Roman underline.

This is Times new Roman bold, italic, and underline.

The easiest way to change font style is to select the text and click the Bold, Italic, or Underline buttons on the Formatting toolbar. To remove a style from the selected text, click the corresponding style button on the toolbar. Clicking a toolbar button to turn a feature on or off is called *toggling*. Styles can also be applied from the Font style list box in the Font dialog box.

| **B** | *I* | <u>U</u> |

Hot Tip

A faster way to access the **Font** dialog box is by right-clicking in the document and choosing **Font** from the shortcut menu or by tapping **Ctrl+D**.

STEP-BY-STEP 3.2

1. Select the title. Open the **Format** menu and choose **Font.** In the *Font style* box, click **Bold**.

2. Click **OK**. The title changes to bold style.

3. Triple-click in the first paragraph to select it.

4. Click the **Italic** button on the Formatting toolbar. The text changes to italic. Click the mouse button to remove the highlight.

STEP-BY-STEP 3.2 Continued

5. Tap **Ctrl** and click on the second sentence in the first paragraph to select it.

6. Click the **Underline** button on the Formatting toolbar. The sentence is underlined.

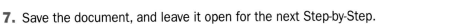

7. Save the document, and leave it open for the next Step-by-Step.

Changing Font Size

Font size is determined by measuring the height of characters in units called *points*. There are 72 points in an inch. A standard font size for text is 12 points. The higher the point size, the larger the characters. Figure 3-6 illustrates the Arial font in 10, 14, and 18 point. You can change font size by using the Font Size box on the Formatting toolbar or the Font dialog box.

Hot Tip

If you want to use a font size that is not on the drop-down menu of the Font size box, key the point size in the Font Size box and tap Enter.

FIGURE 3-6
Different font sizes

This is Arial 10 point.

This is Arial 14 point.

This is Arial 18 point.

Changing the Color of Text

You can change the color of text to emphasize words or data. Select the text and click the arrow on the Font Color button on the Formatting toolbar. Choose the color you want to apply from the palette, as shown in Figure 3-7. You can also use the Font dialog box to change the color of text on the screen.

Hot Tip

If you are not sure of the color on the Font Color palette, hover the pointer over the color box and the name of the color will appear.

FIGURE 3-7
Font Color palette

STEP-BY-STEP 3.3

1. Select the entire document. Open the **Format** menu and choose **Font**. In the *Size* box, scroll down and click **14**.

2. Click **OK**. Remove the highlight.

3. Select the title. Click the arrow to the right of the *Font Size* box on the Formatting toolbar. A list of font sizes appears.

4. Choose **20**. The title appears in 20-point size.

5. With the title still selected, open the *Format* menu and choose **Font.** The Font dialog box appears.

6. Click the arrow next to the *Font color* box. A palette of colors appears. Click **Red**. Notice the text in the *Preview* box changes to red.

7. Click **OK**. Remove the highlight. The title appears in red.

8. Select the first heading *Check Accuracy*. Click the arrow next to the *Font Size* box on the Formatting toolbar. Click **16**. The heading changes to 16-point size.

9. Click the arrow next to the *Font Color* box on the Formatting toolbar. Click **Blue**. Remove the highlight.

10. Save the document, and leave it open for the next Step-by-Step.

Changing Underline Style and Color

In the Font dialog box, you can choose an underline color or an underline style. See Table 3-1 for some examples of underlining style options.

TABLE 3-1
Underline styles

UNDERLINE STYLES	
Single Line	Dotted Line
Double Line	Wavy Line
Thick Line	Dot/Dash Line

Changing Font Effects

Word offers font effects to help you enhance the text. These font effects are shown in Table 3-2. To select a font effect, choose one of the options in the Effects section of the Font dialog box.

TABLE 3-2
Font effects

FONT EFFECT	RESULT
Strikethrough	~~No turning back~~
Double strikethrough	~~Caution: Hot~~
Superscript	The mountain is ^high^.
Subscript	The pool is ~deep~.
Shadow	By invitation only
Outline	Thursday
Emboss	December 18
Engrave	Jack and Claire
Small caps	CALYPSO STREET
All caps	GLENMERLE
Hidden	Part of the text is hidden

STEP-BY-STEP 3.4

1. Select the title. Open the **Format** menu and choose **Font.**

2. In the *Effects* section, choose **Shadow**.

3. Click **OK**. The words now have a shadow effect. Remove the highlight.

4. Select the heading *Check Accuracy*. Right-click on the heading, and choose **Font** from the shortcut menu to display the Font dialog box.

5. Click the arrow next to the *Underline style* box. Choose the double-line style from the list.

6. Click the arrow next to the *Underline color* box. Choose blue from the palette.

7. Click **OK**. The heading is now double-underlined in blue.

8. Save the document, and leave it open for the next Step-by-Step.

Extra Challenge

Open a new document. Key the words *happy, sad, angry, afraid, confident, excited,* and *bored*. Select each word, and change the font, size, style, color, and effect to reflect the meaning of the word.

Highlighting

To emphasize an important part of a document, you can *highlight* it in color. To highlight text, click the arrow next to the Highlight button on the Formatting toolbar. Choose the color you want from the palette, as shown in Figure 3-8.

FIGURE 3-8
Highlight color palette

STEP-BY-STEP 3.5

1. Select the last sentence of the last paragraph.

2. Click the arrow next to the **Highlight** button on the toolbar.

3. Click **Yellow** on the color palette. The selected text is highlighted with a yellow background on the screen.

4. Save the document, and leave it open for the next Step-by Step.

Copying Format and Style

Often you will spend time formatting an area of text and then find that you need the same format in another part of the document. The Format Painter button on the Standard toolbar allows you to copy the format of text rather than the text itself. You can use the command to quickly apply a complicated format and style to text.

STEP-BY-STEP 3.6

1. Select the heading *Check Accuracy*.

2. With the heading still selected, click the **Format Painter** button on the toolbar. The pointer changes to a paintbrush and I-beam.

3. Scroll down and select the heading *Be Consistent*. The font size, underline style, and underline color formatting that were copied are applied.

STEP-BY-STEP 3.6 Continued

4. Click the **Format Painter** button again. Select the heading *Check Facts*. The new format is applied.

5. Save, print, and close the document.

Applying Styles

In Word, a *style* is a predefined set of formatting options that have been named and saved. Applying styles to text can save time and add uniformity to a document. To apply a style, use the Style box on the Formatting toolbar or the Styles and Formatting task pane, as shown in Figure 3-9.

FIGURE 3-9
Styles and Formatting task pane

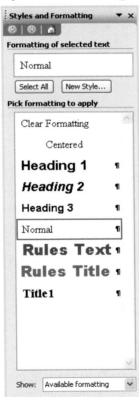

To clear a style from text, select the text to be cleared. Use the Clear Formatting button on the Style box on the Formatting toolbar or in the Styles and Formatting task pane.

Character Spacing

Character spacing controls the amount of space between each letter. You can change character spacing on the character spacing tab in the Font dialog box as shown in Figure 3-10.

FIGURE 3-10
Character Spacing tab

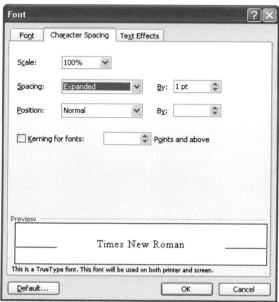

STEP-BY-STEP 3.7

1. Open **Step3-7** from the data files. Save the document as **Rules** followed by your initials.

2. Select the title. Open the **Format** menu and choose **Styles and Formatting.** The Styles and Formatting task pane appears.

3. In the *Formatting of selected text* box, notice the name of the style for the selected text is *Title1*. Hover the mouse pointer over *Title1* and read the description. The format of the Title1 style is Normal with 14 point font and it is bolded.

4. With the title still selected, click **Clear Formatting** in the *Pick formatting to apply* section. The *Title* formatting is now cleared from the text. In the *Formatting of selected text* box, the name of the style changes to *Normal*.

5. With the title still selected, click **Rules Title** in the *Pick formatting to apply* section. The Rules Title style is applied to the title. Close the Styles and Formatting task pane.

6. Select the first rule.

7. Click the arrow next to the *Style* box on the Formatting toolbar. Click **Rules Text**. The rule is changed to the Rules Text style.

   Normal ▾

STEP-BY-STEP 3.7 Continued

8. Apply the Rules Text style to the other rules.

9. Select the title. Open the **Format** menu and choose **Font**. Click the Character Spacing tab.

10. In the *Spacing* box, click **Expanded**. In the *By* box increase the points to **1.5**. Click **OK**. The space between the characters in the title is increased to 1.5.

11. Save, print, and close the document.

SUMMARY

In this lesson, you learned:

■ Fonts are designs of type that can be used to change the appearance of a document.

■ Common font styles are bold, italic, and underline. These styles can be applied to any font.

■ Font size is measured in points. The higher the point size, the larger the characters.

■ You can change the color of text, style of underline, color of underline, and font effects from the Font dialog box.

■ Highlights can be used to emphasize important text.

■ You can easily copy the format and style of blocks of text using the Format Painter.

■ Styles are predefined sets of formatting options that save time and add consistency to a document.

■ You can adjust the spacing between characters.

VOCABULARY*Review*

Define the following terms:

Font size	Formatting	Styles
Font style	Highlight	Toggling
Fonts	Points	

REVIEW *Questions*

TRUE/FALSE

Circle T if the statement is true or F if the statement is false.

T   F   1. The Format Painter command will copy text but not the format of the text.

T   F   2. The standard font size is 10 point.

T   F   3. In the Font dialog box, the *Font* box shows the current font.

T   F   4. Common font styles are strikethrough, shadow, and engrave.

T   F   5. You can change space between characters by expanding or condensing the space.

WRITTEN QUESTIONS

Write a brief answer to each of the following questions.

1. What are two ways to clear a style from text?

2. What are two quick ways to open the Font dialog box?

3. What are five ways to change the appearance of text using the Font dialog box?

4. What are two ways to emphasize text?

5. What are three common font styles?

PROJECTS

PROJECT 3-1

You have been asked to prepare a certificate for the student of the month at your school.

1. Open **Project3-1** from the data files. Save the document as **Certificate** followed by your initials.

2. Change all text to Old Century, 20 point, Light Blue. If the font is not available, choose another appropriate font.

3. Change the font effect of all text to Emboss.

4. Change the first *Student of the Month* to 36 point, bold, and the font effect to Small caps.

5. Change *Todd James* to Arial, 28 point, and the font effect to All caps.

6. Change *October 2006* to 28 point, bold, italic.

7. Change page orientation to Landscape.

8. Preview the document. Save, print, and close.

PROJECT 3-2

Create a flyer for a Stargazing Party sponsored by the Oakland Astronomy Club.

1. Open **Project 3-2** from the data files. Save the document as **Stargazing** followed by your initials.

2. Change all text to Andy, 20 point, Red. If the font is not available, choose another appropriate font.

3. Change the title to Signboard, 36 point, Emboss. If the font is not available, choose another appropriate font.

4. Change the word *Where:* to Signboard, 24 point, Italic, Emboss.

5. Use the Format Painter to copy the format of *Where:* to *Date:* and *Time:*.

6. Change the last sentence to Signboard, 22 point.

7. Highlight the last sentence in yellow.

8. Preview the document. Save, print, and close.

PROJECT 3-3

As a member of the Oakland Astronomy Club, you need to format a paper about the Big Dipper.

1. Open **Project 3-3** from the data files. Save the document as **Big Dipper** followed by your initials.

2. Read the document about the Big Dipper.

3. Change all text to Arial, 12 point.

4. Apply **Heading 1** style to the title *The Big Dipper*.

5. Apply **Heading 2** style to the three headings in the document.

6. Change the character spacing of the title to 2.0.

7. Highlight the last two sentences with Gray-25% from the color palette.

8. Preview the document. Save, print, and close.

PROJECT 3-4

1. Open **Project 3-4** from the data files. Save the document as **Civil War** followed by your initials.

2. Change all the text to Old Century, plum. If the font is not available, choose another appropriate font.

3. Change the title to 26 point, italic, dark blue. Underline the title with a dark blue, wavy underline.

4. Use the **Format Painter** to copy the format of *Civil War* to *Underground Railroad*.

5. Preview the document. Save, print, and close the document.

WEB*Project*

PROJECT 3-5

There are many Web sites with photos of Earth taken from space. Find a Web site where you can zoom in and view your school from space. Copy the photo to a Word document. Save the document as **Satellite Photos** followed by your initials.

TEAMWORK*Project*

 **PROJECT 3-6**

With a partner, choose a constellation and research it. Write a paragraph about the constellation and present the information to the class. Be sure to include in what season the constellation can be viewed from the Northern Hemisphere. Save the document as **Constellation** followed by three letters to identify it.

CRITICAL*Thinking*

 **ACTIVITY 3-1**

After hearing the reports on constellations, create a new constellation with your partner. Write a paragraph about the constellation that includes its name and a description of the constellation. It should also include a story about why the constellation appears in the sky. Save the document as **New Constellation** followed by three letters to identify it.

ACTIVITY 3-2

An effective way to capture a reader's attention is to animate text. Use the Help system to learn how to animate text. Open the **Stargazing** document you created in Project 3-2. Animate the title with the text animation of your choice. Save the document as **Stargazing Animation** followed by your initials.

FORMATTING PARAGRAPHS AND DOCUMENTS

OBJECTIVES

In this lesson, you will:

- Set the margins of a document.
- Align text.
- Adjust indents and line spacing.
- Insert page breaks.
- Change vertical alignment.
- Set and modify tabs.
- Insert and format tables.
- Apply bullet and numbering formats.
- Create an outline numbered list.

Estimated Time: 2 hours

Formatting Documents

Just as you apply formatting to text, you can also use Word features to format a document. Formatting presents a consistent and attractive style throughout a document, allowing your readers to understand your message more easily.

Setting Margins

Margins are the blank areas around the top, bottom, and sides of a page. Word sets predefined, or default, margin settings, which you may keep or change. To change margin settings, use the Page Setup dialog box, as shown in Figure 4-1.

FIGURE 4-1
Page Setup dialog box

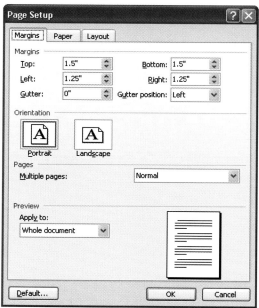

STEP-BY-STEP 4.1

1. Open the **Step4-1** document from the data files. Save the document as **Money** followed by your initials.

2. Preview the document to see the existing margins. Close Print Preview.

3. Open the **File** menu and choose **Page Setup**. Click the **Margins** tab if necessary.

4. In the *Margins* section, click the up arrow next to the *Top* box to **1.2"**.

5. Tap **Tab** to go to the bottom margin setting. Notice that the margins of the sample document change as you tap Tab.

6. Click the down arrow to **.8"**.

7. Key **1** as the left and right margin settings.

8. Click **OK**.

9. Preview the document to see the new margins. Close Print Preview.

10. Save and leave the document open for the next Step-by-Step.

Aligning Text

*A**lignment*** refers to the position of text between the margins. As Figure 4-2 shows, you can choose left-aligned, centered, right-aligned, or justified for the text alignment.

Left-aligned and justified are the two most commonly used text alignments in documents. For invitations, titles, and headings, select Centered as the alignment for the text. Right alignment occurs frequently for page numbers and dates.

FIGURE 4-2
Text alignment

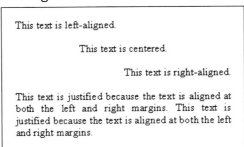

To align text, use the Paragraph dialog box, shown in Figure 4-3. You can also change alignment by clicking the alignment buttons on the Formatting toolbar, shown in Figure 4-4.

FIGURE 4-3
Paragraph dialog box

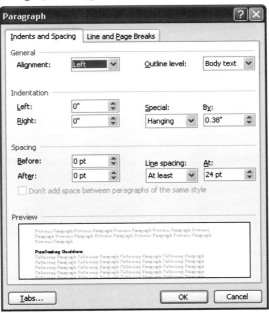

FIGURE 4-4
Alignment buttons

S TEP-BY-STEP 4.2

1. Select the title. Open the **Format** menu and choose **Paragraph.**

2. In the *General* section, click the arrow next to the *Alignment* box and click **Centered**. Click **OK**. The title is centered.

3. Select the date above the title.

4. Click the **Align Right** button on the toolbar. (If the button is not displayed, choose it from the **Toolbar Options** menu.) The date is right-aligned.

5. Select the first paragraph. Click the **Justify** button on the toolbar. The paragraph is justified.

6. Save and leave the document open for the next Step-by-Step.

Changing Indents

An ***indent*** is the space you insert between text and a document's margin. You can indent text either from the left margin, from the right margin, or from both the left and right margins. You indent text by using the indent markers on the horizontal ruler, shown in Figure 4-5. To indent text, drag the indent markers to the desired point on the ruler.

FIGURE 4-5
Indent markers

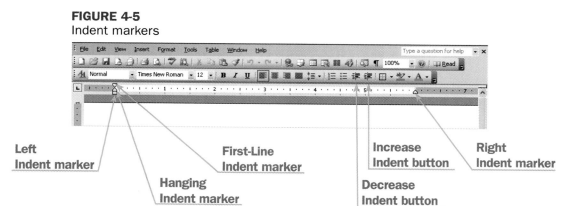

Left
Indent marker

First-Line
Indent marker

Hanging
Indent marker

Increase
Indent button

Decrease
Indent button

Right
Indent marker

Setting a First-Line Indent

The paragraph format where the first line indents more than the following lines is a first-line indent. Using the first-line indent marker, you can indent paragraphs as shown in Figure 4-6. After you set a first-line indent in one paragraph, all subsequent paragraphs you key will have the same first-line indent.

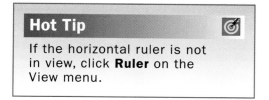

Hot Tip

If the horizontal ruler is not in view, click **Ruler** on the View menu.

FIGURE 4-6
First-line indent

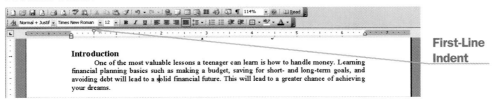

Setting a Hanging Indent

You can also create hanging indents in which the first full line of text is not indented but the following lines are, as shown in Figure 4-7. To set a hanging indent, drag the hanging indent marker to the right of the first-line indent marker. Hanging indents appear commonly in lists and documents such as glossaries.

FIGURE 4-7
Hanging indent

Indenting from Both Margins

Indenting from both margins, as shown in Figure 4-8, sets off paragraphs from the main body of text. You might use this type of indent for long quotations.

FIGURE 4-8
Indent from both margins

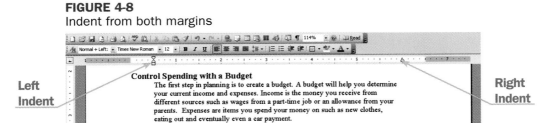

S TEP-BY-STEP 4.3

1. With the **Money** document open, position the insertion point anywhere in the first paragraph.

2. Click on the First-line indent marker, and drag it to the **.5**-inch mark, as shown in Figure 4-6. You have created a first-line indent.

3. Select the second paragraph.

4. Click the Left Indent marker and drag to the **.5**-inch mark. You have created a left indent.

5. With the paragraph still selected, click the **Right Indent** marker and drag to the **5.5**-inch mark. You have created a right indent. The second paragraph is now indented from both margins.

6. Save and leave the document open for the next Step-by-Step.

Adjusting Line Spacing

Line spacing refers to the amount of space between lines of text. By default, Word single-spaces text. Single-spacing has no extra space between each line. To make text more readable, you can add space between lines of text. The 1.5 lines option adds half a line of space between lines. Double-spaced text has a full blank line between each line of text. (Figure 4-9 illustrates different spacing options.) To change line spacing, use the Paragraph dialog box. You can also use the Line Spacing button on the Formatting toolbar.

FIGURE 4-9
Line spacing options

The line spacing of this paragraph is single.
The paragraph is single-spaced.

The line spacing of this paragraph is 1.5 lines.
This paragraph is 1.5-spaced.

The line spacing of this paragraph is double.

This paragraph is double-spaced.

Inserting Page Breaks

In a multipage document, Word must select a place to end one page and begin the next. The place where one page ends and another begins is called a *page break*. Word automatically inserts page breaks where they are necessary. You also can insert a page break manually. For example, you might want to do this to prevent an

Hot Tip

Another way to increase the readability of a page is to add spaces between paragraphs. You can add space before or after a paragraph by opening the Format menu and choosing Paragraph. In the Spacing section, change the values in the Before or After boxes.

automatic page break from separating a heading from the text that follows. To insert a page break manually, open the Break dialog box from the Insert menu, as shown in Figure 4-10.

FIGURE 4-10
Break dialog box

In Normal view, an automatic page break is shown as a dotted line across the page. A manual page break is also shown as a dotted line across the page, but it has the words *Page Break* in the middle, as shown in Figure 4-11. To delete manual page breaks, select the page break line and tap Backspace or Delete.

FIGURE 4-11
Manual page break

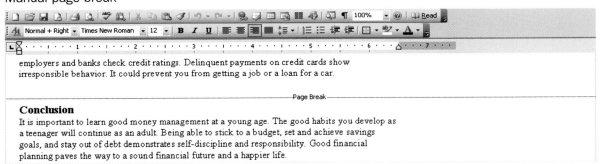

S TEP-BY-STEP 4.4

1. Select the first paragraph of the document. Open the **Format** menu and choose **Paragraph**.

2. In the *Spacing* section, click the arrow next to the **Line spacing** box.

3. Click **Double**. Notice the text under *Preview* changes to double-spaced.

4. Click **OK**. The paragraph is double-spaced.

5. Switch to Normal view if necessary.

6. Place the insertion point to the left of the subheading *Conclusion*.

STEP-BY-STEP 4.4 Continued

7. Open the **Insert** menu and choose **Break**. The Break dialog box appears.

8. In the *Break types* area, *Page break* should be selected. Choose **OK**. The dotted line with the words *Page Break* in the middle indicates that a manual page break has been inserted.

9. Save, print, and close the document.

> **Hot Tip**
>
> You can access the Paragraph dialog box quickly by right-clicking and choosing **Paragraph** from the shortcut menu.

Changing Vertical Alignment

V*ertical alignment* refers to positioning text between the top and bottom margins of a document. You can align text with the top of the page, center the text, distribute the text equally between the top and bottom margins, or align the text with the bottom of the page. To vertically align text, use the Page Setup box, as shown in Figure 4-12.

FIGURE 4-12
Layout tab in the Page Setup dialog box

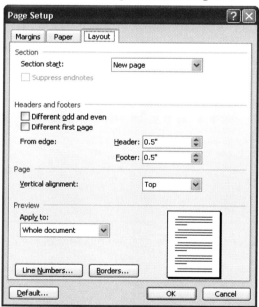

S TEP-BY-STEP 4.5

1. Create a new Word document.

2. Key the following text:

   Your name
   Accounting 101
   Get a Grip on Your Money

3. Select the text. Click the **Center** button on the Formatting toolbar to center the text.

4. Change the font to Arial and the font size to 18.

5. Open the **File** menu and choose **Page Setup.** Click the **Layout** tab to select it.

6. Click the arrow on the **Vertical alignment** box. Choose **Center**. Click **OK**.

7. Preview the document to see that the text aligns vertically. Close Print Preview.

8. Save the document as **Money Title** followed by your initials.

9. Print and close the document.

Setting Tab Stops

Tab stops, or *tabs*, mark the place where the insertion point will stop when you tap the Tab key. Tab stops are useful for creating tables or aligning numbered items. Text alignment can be set with decimal, left, right, or center tab stops, as shown in Figure 4-13. See Table 4-1 for a description of common tab stops.

FIGURE 4-13
Types of tabs

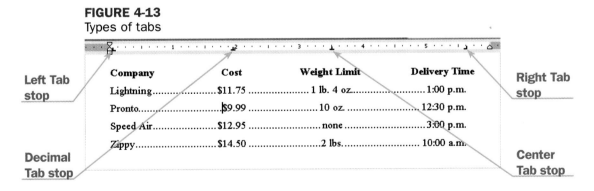

Left Tab stop

Right Tab stop

Decimal Tab stop

Center Tab stop

Company	Cost	Weight Limit	Delivery Time
Lightning	$11.75	1 lb. 4 oz.	1:00 p.m.
Pronto	$9.99	10 oz.	12:30 p.m.
Speed Air	$12.95	none	3:00 p.m.
Zippy	$14.50	2 lbs.	10:00 a.m.

TABLE 4-1
Common tab stops

TAB	TAB NAME	FUNCTION
⊾	Left Tab stop	Left-aligns selected text at the point indicated on the horizontal ruler. This is the default tab.
⅃	Right Tab stop	Right-aligns selected text at the point indicated on the horizontal ruler. This is useful for aligning page numbers in a table of contents.
⊥	Center Tab stop	Centers selected text at the point indicated on the horizontal ruler. This is used with titles and announcements.
⊥	Decimal Tab stop	Aligns selected text on the decimal point at the point indicated on the horizontal ruler. This is helpful when preparing price lists, invoices, and menus.

To set tabs, use the Tabs dialog box as shown in Figure 4-14. Another way to set a tab stop is by clicking the tab box at the far left of the ruler. To remove a tab, drag it off the ruler. You can also add *leaders*, which are solid, dotted, or dashed lines that fill the blank space before a tab setting.

Hot Tip

Hover the pointer over the tab box on the ruler to see the type of tab selected.

FIGURE 4-14
Tabs dialog box

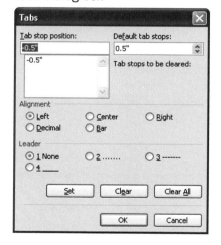

STEP-BY-STEP 4.6

1. Open **Step4-6** from the data files. Save the document as **Computer** followed by your initials.

2. Select all data except the title.

3. Open the **Format** menu and choose **Tabs**. The Tabs dialog box appears, as shown in Figure 4-14. Click **Clear** to clear the –0.5 tab.

4. Key **1.5** in the *Tab stop position* box.

STEP-BY-STEP 4.6 Continued

5. In the *Alignment* section, click **Left** if necessary. Click **Set**.

6. Select **1.5** in the *Tab stop position* box and key **5.75** in the *Tab stop position* box.

7. In the *Alignment* section, click **Decimal** and in the *Leader* section, click **2 ....** . Click **Set**.

8. Click **OK**. The dialog box closes, and text in the second column lines up at the tab you set with leaders.

9. Save, print, and close the document.

Inserting and Formatting Tables

A *table* is an arrangement of text or numbers in rows and columns, similar to a spreadsheet. Tables are sometimes easier to use than trying to align text with tabs.

To create a table, use the Insert Table dialog box, shown in Figure 4-15. To enter text in a table, position the insertion point in the cell where you want to begin. A cell is where a row and column intersect. Key the text, and then use the Tab or an arrow key to move to the next cell where you want to insert data. Tap the Enter key only if you want to insert a second line in a cell. You can also insert a table by clicking the Insert Table button on the Standard toolbar.

> **Hot Tip**
>
> You can covert text you have already typed into a table by opening the **Table** menu and clicking **Convert**.

FIGURE 4-15
Insert Table dialog box

S TEP-BY-STEP 4.7

1. Open **Step4-7** from the data files. Save the document as **Training** followed by your initials.

2. Position the insertion point on the second blank line below the second paragraph.

3. Open the **Table** menu and choose **Insert** and **Table** on the submenu. The Insert Table dialog box appears.

4. In the *Number of columns* box, key **3**.

5. In the *Number of rows* box, key **6**.

6. Click **OK**. The table is inserted.

7. Key the data in the table as shown in Figure 4-16.

FIGURE 4-16
Data in a table

Date	Session	Time
9/15	CPR	1:00 – 4:00 p.m.
9/28	CPR	7:00 – 10:00 p.m.
9/15	First Aid	7:00 – 9:00 p.m.
9/28	First Aid	1:00 – 3:00 p.m.
9/12	General Information	7:00 – 8:30 p.m.

8. Save your changes, and leave the document open for the next Step-by-Step.

Formatting and Revising a Table

After you have created a table, you can revise it by inserting and deleting rows and columns and changing formats within cells. To change the format of a cell, click in a specific table cell. You can also select the entire row or column and then change the format. To insert a row or a column, use Insert on the Table menu. You can also delete a column or row by choosing Delete on the Table menu. To select the entire table, click the table resize handle. You can change column width or row height manually by clicking on the border of the column or row and dragging the border to expand or decrease the width or height.

Many of the commands on the Table menu are available on the Tables and Borders toolbar, shown in Figure 4-17. To display the toolbar, open the View menu, choose Toolbars, and then click Tables and Borders.

FIGURE 4-17
Tables and Borders toolbar

S TEP-BY-STEP 4.8

1. Click to the left of *Date* (outside the table) to select the first row.

2. Click the **Center** button on the Formatting toolbar. All three of the headings are centered.

3. With the first row still selected, change the font size to 14-point, bold. Remove highlight.

4. Position the pointer at the top of the *Date* column. When the pointer changes to a downward-pointing arrow, click to select the entire column.

5. Choose the **Center** button on the Formatting toolbar. The text in the entire column is centered.

6. Drag the right border of the *Date* column to the left to reduce the column width. The column should be only slightly wider than the column heading.

7. Click to the left of the *9/12* row to select it.

8. Open the **Table** menu and choose **Insert.** Choose **Rows Below** on the submenu. A new row is inserted below the one you selected.

9. In the new row, key the following data:

   9/25   General Information   1:00 – 2:30 P.M.

10. Hover the mouse pointer over the table move handle until it changes to a four-headed arrow. Click to select the entire table. Click the **Center** button on the Formatting toolbar.

11. Save your changes, and leave the document open for the next Step-by-Step.

Merging Table Cells

You can make other modifications to the structure of a table using tools on the Tables and Borders toolbar. You can split cells to transform one column or row into two or more. You can merge cells to create one large cell out of several small cells. Use the Table menu to split or merge cells.

S TEP-BY-STEP 4.9

1. Select the first row. Open the **Table** menu and choose **Insert.** Choose **Rows Above** on the submenu.

2. In the new first row, key **Training Sessions.**

3. Select the new first row. Open the **Table** menu and click **Merge Cells.** Center the text if necessary.

4. Save your changes, and leave the document open for the next Step-by-Step.

Borders and Shading

You can change the borders and shading of one cell, one column or row, or the entire table. Select the area to be formatted. To add borders and shading to a table, use the Table Properties dialog box. Click the Borders and Shading button and make your changes in the Borders and Shading dialog box.

Hot Tip

Word has many different predesigned formats that you can apply to a table. Open the Table menu and choose Table AutoFormat.

STEP-BY-STEP 4.10

1. Select the table. Open the **Table** menu and choose **Table Properties**.

2. Click the **Borders and Shading** button.

3. Click the Borders tab if necessary. Click the **All** button in the *Setting* section if necessary.

4. Click the arrow next to the *Color* box and choose **Orange**. Click the arrow next to the *Width* box and choose **2¼ pt**.

5. Click the Shading tab. In the *Fill* section, choose **Turquoise** from the palette of colors. Click **OK**. Click **OK** again to close the Table Properties dialog box.

6. Click outside the table to deselect it.

7. Preview the document.

8. Save, print, and close the document.

Bulleted and Numbered Lists

Sometimes you may want to create a bulleted or numbered list in a document. A numbered list is useful when items appear sequentially, such as instructions. A bulleted list often is used when the order of items does not matter. A **bullet** is any small character that appears before an item. Pictures, symbols, and icons may all serve as bullets.

To create a bulleted or numbered list, use the Bullets and Numbering dialog box, as shown in Figure 4-18. You can also click the Bullets and Numbering buttons on the Formatting toolbar. To finish a bulleted or numbered list, tap Enter twice. Alternatively, to convert existing text into a bulleted or numbered list, select the text and click the Bullets or Numbering button on the toolbar or use the Bullets and Numbering dialog box.

FIGURE 4-18
Bulleted tab in the Bullets and Numbering dialog box

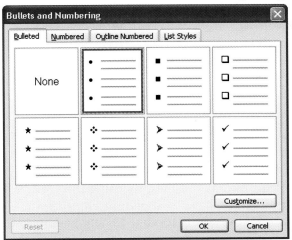

S TEP-BY-STEP 4.11

1. Open **Step4-11** from the data files. Save the document as **Metric** followed by your initials.

2. Place the insertion point at the end of the first paragraph. Tap **Enter** twice to insert a blank line.

3. Open the **Format** menu and choose **Bullets and Numbering**. Select the Bulleted tab if necessary.

> **Hot Tip**
>
> You can customize the bullets and the numbers in a list, by clicking the Customize button in the Bullets and Numbering dialog box.

4. Click on a bullet option. Click **OK**. A bullet appears with a tabbed space so you can begin keying a bulleted list.

5. Key **Kilo = thousand**. Tap **Enter**. Notice how Word automatically continues formatting a bulleted list.

6. Key the remaining prefixes as shown below.

    Hector = hundred

    Deka = ten

    Deci = tenth

    Centi = hundredth

    Milli = thousandth

7. After you key the fifth item, tap **Enter** twice to stop the bulleted list formatting.

8. Select the four units of measure under the second paragraph.

9. Click the **Bullets** button on the Formatting toolbar. The guidelines list is now bulleted.

STEP-BY-STEP 4.11 Continued

10. Select the three guidelines under the third paragraph.

11. Click the **Numbering** button on the Formatting toolbar. The guidelines are now numbered.

12. Save, print, and close the document.

Outline Numbered List

An *outline numbered list* is a list with two or more levels of bullets or numbering. You can create multilevel lists, such as outlines, by using the Outline Numbered tab in the Bullets and Numbering dialog box, as shown in Figure 4-19. Use the Increase Indent and Decrease Indent buttons on the Formatting toolbar to help you build the hierarchy of your multi-level list.

FIGURE 4-19
Outline Numbered tab

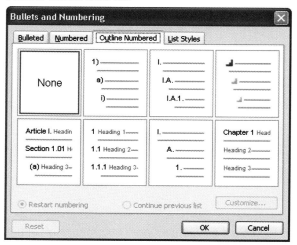

STEP-BY-STEP 4.12

1. Open **Step4-12** from the data files. Save the document as **Constitution2** followed by your initials.

2. Place the insertion point at the end of the first paragraph. Tap **Enter** twice to insert a blank line.

3. Open the **Format** menu and choose **Bullets and Numbering.** The Bullets and Numbering dialog box appears.

4. Click the **Outline Numbered** tab. Click the second format on the top row. Click **OK**. The number *1)* and an indent appear.

> **Hot Tip**
>
> You can also tap the **Tab** button to indent an item or tap **Shift+Tab** to decrease the indent on an item.

STEP-BY-STEP 4.12 Continued

5. Key **Evolution of Democratic Government** and tap **Enter.**

6. Click the **Increase Indent** button. The indent is increased, and the letter *a.* appears.

7. Key **Historical Influences** and tap **Enter**.

8. Click the **Increase Indent** button. The indent is increased, and the number *i.* appears.

9. Key **The Magna Carta** and tap **Enter**.

10. Key **The Declaration of Independence** and tap **Enter**.

11. Key **The Federalist Papers** and tap **Enter**.

12. Click the **Decrease Indent** button. The indent decreases, and the letter *b.* appears.

13. Key the remaining items in the multilevel list below.

    b) Early attempts at representative government

        i)   The Virginia House of Burgesses

        ii)   The Articles of Confederation

        iii) The federalist/anti-federalist debate

  2) Role of the Constitution in Our Democracy

    a) Principles reflected in the Constitution

        i)   Limited government

        ii)   Separation of powers

        iii) Individual Rights

    b) Constitution as a living document

        i)   Historical conflicts, states' rights

        ii)   Role of Supreme Court, current debates

        iii) Bill of Rights, amending the Constitution

14. Save, print, and close the document.

SUMMARY

In this lesson, you learned:

■ Margins are the blank areas around the top, bottom, and sides of a page. You can change the margin settings by choosing Page Setup on the File menu.

■ You can align text by choosing Paragraph on the Format menu or by clicking the buttons on the Formatting toolbar. You can also change the vertical alignment in the Page Setup dialog box.

■ You can indent text either from the left margin, from the right margin, or from both the left and right margins.

■ Single-spacing has no extra space between each line. Double-spacing has one full line space between each line of text.

■ Word automatically inserts page breaks where they are necessary. You also can insert a page break manually by choosing Break on the Insert menu and choosing Page break.

■ Text alignment can be set with decimal, left, right, or centered tabs. Leaders can be used with any kind of tab.

■ Tables are used to show data in columns and rows. They are usually easier to use than trying to align text with tabs. You can change the format of tables to best display your data.

■ You can use the Bullets or Numbering buttons on the toolbar to create bulleted or numbered lists. To change the appearance of a list, choose Bullets and Numbering on the Format menu to access the Bullets and Numbering dialog box.

■ Outlines are useful for creating a document with a hierarchical structure. Use the Bullets and Numbering dialog box to create an outlined numbered list.

VOCABULARY *Review*

Define the following terms:

Alignment	Line spacing	Table
Bullet	Margin	Tabs
Indent	Outline numbered list	Vertical alignment
Leader	Page break	

REVIEW *Questions*

TRUE/FALSE

Circle T if the statement is true or F if the statement is false.

T F 1. You can change the vertical alignment of text on a page in the Page Setup dialog box.

T F 2. Tabs are useful for adding space between lines.

T F 3. Documents are normally aligned left or justified.

T F 4. A hanging indent indents the lines that follow the first full line of text.

T F 5. Your document will have no margins unless you specify them.

MULTIPLE CHOICE

Select the best response for the following statements.

1. What type of text has a full blank line between each line of text?
   A. single-spaced
   B. indented
   C. double-spaced
   D. aligned

2. Which tab in the Bullets and Numbering dialog box contains predefined formats for multilevel lists?
   A. Numbered
   B. Bulleted
   C. Outline Numbered
   D. all of the above

3. The upper triangle at the left edge of the ruler indicates the
   A. first-line indent marker.
   B. decrease indent marker.
   C. hanging indent marker.
   D. left indent marker.

4. Text can be aligned using all of the following types of tab stops except
   A. justified.
   B. decimal.
   C. right.
   D. center.

5. In an outline numbered list, which button moves a heading to a higher level?
   A. Plus
   B. Increase Indent
   C. Decease Indent
   D. Tab

PROJECTS

PROJECT 4-1

You have been asked to update the *Proofreading Guidelines* document.

1. Open **Project4-1** from the data files. Save the document as **Proofreading2** followed by your initials.

2. Change top and bottom margins to 1".

3. Center the title.

4. Create a first line indent at .5" to each paragraph.

5. Select all text except the title. Change the line spacing to **1.5** lines.

6. Insert a manual page break before the *Check Spelling* heading.

7. Add bullets to the *Spelling* list.

8. Preview the document. Save, print, and close the document.

PROJECT 4-2

1. Open **Project4-2** from the data files. Save the document as **Verb Tense** followed by your initials.

2. Display the ruler if it is not already showing.

3. Center and bold the title. Increase the font size to **18**.

4. Select all text but the title. Set the left indent tab to the 1-inch mark on the ruler.

5. Set a decimal tab with dash style leaders at **5** inches.

6. Center and bold the headings. Increase the font size to **16**.

7. Preview the document. Save, print, and close the document.

PROJECT 4-3

Your science class has been studying erosion. You have been asked to format a document about erosion.

1. Open **Project4-3** from the data files. Save the document as **Erosion** followed by your initials.

2. Set the top and bottom margins at **1.5** inches.

3. Change the left and right margins to **1** inch.

4. Double-space the text.

5. Select the list of causes. Change the left indent to .5 inch. Change the right indent to **5** inches.

6. Bullet the list.

7. Select the types of weathering. Change the left indent to .5 inch. Change the right indent to 5 inches.

8. Number the list.

9. Vertically align the text in the center of the document.

10. Preview the document. Save, print, and close the document.

 PROJECT 4-4

A good example of erosion is the Grand Canyon. Create an outline with facts about the history of the Grand Canyon.

1. Open a new Word document.

2. Create an outlined numbered list using the information in Figure 4-20.

FIGURE 4-20
Outline of Grand Canyon

Grand Canyon

I. Creation of Grand Canyon
    A. Colorado river erodes the Colorado Plateau
    B. The erosion took 4-6 million years
    C. The canyon is 250 miles long and 20 miles wide
II. History
    A. Native Americans
        1. Paleohunters – roamed the area more than 11,000 years ago
        2. Anasazi – agricultural tribe lived in the canyon from 500 to 1200 AD
        3. Navajo – largest American tribe in United States, lived in area from 1400 to present day
    B. The Spanish
        1. Francisco Vasquez de Coronado first European to explore the area
        2. Garcia Lopez de Cardenas first European to see the Grand Canyon
    C. Expansion of the West
        1. United States gains most of the Southwest in 1848, after the war with Mexico
        2. Lt. Joseph Ives surveyed the Grand Canyon in 1857
        3. Major John Wesley Powell was the first man to travel through the Grand Canyon on the Colorado River
        4. President Theodore Roosevelt names the Grand Canyon a national monument

3. The title should be 16 point, bold, and centered.

4. Preview the document.

5. Save the document as **Grand Canyon** followed by your initials. Print and close the document.

WEB*Project*

 PROJECT 4-5

Some important rivers in the world are the Yangtze, the Nile, the Amazon, the Mississippi, and the Rhine. On the Internet, find the length of each river and the continent where it is located.

1. Open a new Word document.

2. Create a table with three columns and six rows.

3. Key *River, Continent,* and *Length* as headings for each column.

4. Key the information about the rivers in the table.

5. Insert a new row at the top of the table. Key **Important Rivers of the World** in the first cell. Merge the cells.

6. Center the title. Change the font to 16 point, bold.

7. Change the borders to 2 1/4 point, blue. Change the shading to pale blue.

8. Save the document as **Rivers** followed by your initials.

9. Print and close the document.

TEAMWORK*Project*

 PROJECT 4-6

With a partner, choose a topic from the Grand Canyon outline. Research and find five facts about the topic. Key the facts in a new Word document. Add a title about the topic. Use what you have learned in Lesson 4 to double-space, bullet, and vertically align the text. Save the document as **Facts** followed by three letters to identify it. Share the information with your classmates.

CRITICAL*Thinking*

ACTIVITY 4-1

Use Help to find out how to Sort text. Sort the rivers in the table you created in Project 4-5 alphabetically. Save the document as **River Sort** followed by your initials.

LESSON 5

WORKING WITH GRAPHICS

OBJECTIVES

In this lesson, you will:

- Format text into columns.
- Add borders and shading to paragraphs.
- Insert and scale clip art.
- Wrap text around graphics.
- Add borders to pages.
- Draw objects.
- Select, resize, cut, copy, and paste objects.
- Add text to drawings.

Estimated Time: 2 hours

Working with Graphics

Word allows you to enhance documents by adding graphics. ***Graphics*** are pictures that help illustrate text and make the page more attractive. Word has predefined shapes, as well as pictures. Word also includes drawing tools that enable you to create your own graphics and add them to your documents. To access Word's graphics and drawing tools, you can use the Drawing toolbar, as shown in Figure 5-1. To work with graphics, you must be in Print Layout view.

FIGURE 5-1
Drawing toolbar

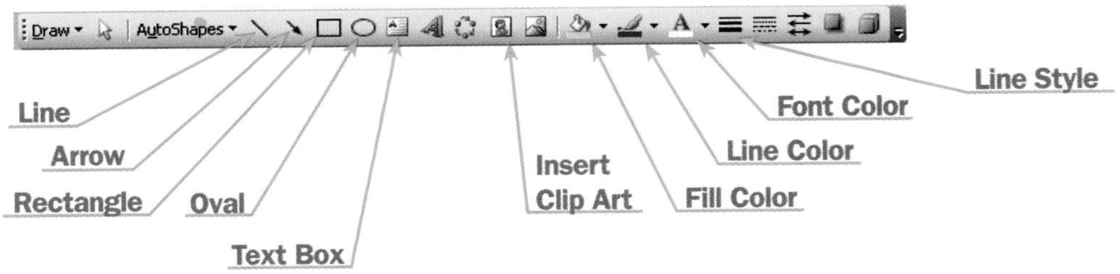
Draw
AutoShapes
Line
Arrow
Rectangle
Oval
Text Box
Insert
Clip Art
Fill Color
Line Color
Font Color
Line Style

Creating Columns

Sometimes a document can be more effective if the text is formatted in multiple columns. A newsletter is an example of a document that often has two or more columns. Columns are easy to create using the Columns dialog box, as shown in Figure 5-2. You can indicate whether you want a line separating the columns. You can also create columns in a document using the Columns button on the Standard toolbar.

FIGURE 5-2
Columns dialog box

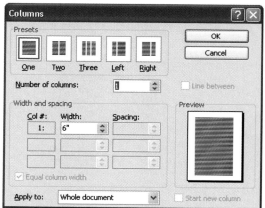

STEP-BY-STEP 5.1

1. Open **Step5-1** from the data files. Save the document as **Library** followed by your initials.

2. Open the **Format** menu and choose **Columns.**

3. In the *Presets* box, choose **Two**.

4. In the *Width and spacing* box under *Spacing,* click the up arrow until it reads **0.6"**.

5. Click the **Line between** box to insert a check mark. Click **OK**.

6. Click **Print Preview** to view the columns. Close Print Preview.

7. Save and leave the document open for the next Step-by-Step.

Adding Borders and Shading to Paragraphs

Borders and shading add interest and emphasis to text. *Borders* are single, double, thick, or dotted lines that appear around text. You can also add *shading*—grays or colors—to paragraphs or lines to emphasize text. To add borders and shading, use the Borders and Shading dialog box, as shown in Figure 5-3 and Figure 5-4.

FIGURE 5-3
Borders tab in Borders and Shading dialog box

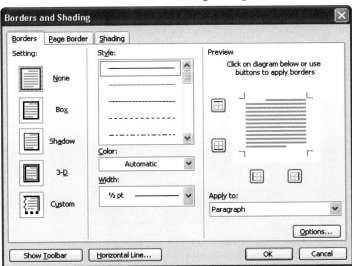

FIGURE 5-4
Shading tab in Borders and Shading dialog box

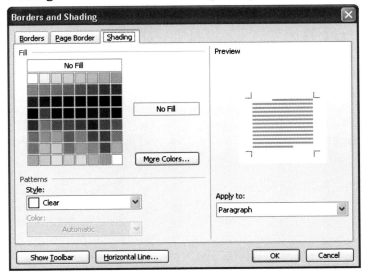

S TEP-BY-STEP 5.2

1. Select the heading *To volunteer, please call 435-555-8024.*

2. Open the **Format** menu and choose **Borders and Shading**.

3. Click the **Borders** tab if necessary.

4. In the *Setting* section, click the **Box** button.

5. In the *Width* box, click the arrow and choose the **2¼ pt** width from the menu.

6. In the *Color* box, choose **Blue**.

7. Click the **Shading** tab. In the *Fill* section, choose **Light Yellow**.

8. Click **OK**. In addition to the blue border, the text now contains light yellow shading, as shown in Figure 5-5.

FIGURE 5-5
Text with border and shading

> **To volunteer, please call 435-555-8024**

Friends of the Library
The Friends of the Library Association

9. Save and leave the document open for the next Step-by-Step.

Inserting Clip Art

Graphics that are already drawn and available for use in documents are called *clip art*. Clip art libraries offer artwork of common objects that may improve the quality of your work. To insert clip art, use the Clip Art task pane, as shown in Figure 5-6.

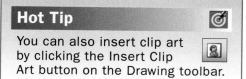

Hot Tip

You can also insert clip art by clicking the Insert Clip Art button on the Drawing toolbar.

Computer Concepts

The Media Gallery includes other media types besides clip art, such as photographs, movies, and sounds. You can also connect to the Web to access more images.

FIGURE 5-6
Clip Art task pane

S TEP-BY-STEP 5.3

1. In the first column, place the insertion point on the blank line above the *Teen Summer Reading Program* heading.

2. Open the **Insert** menu and choose **Picture**. Click **Clip Art** on the submenu. The Clip Art task pane appears.

3. In the *Search for* box, key **books**. Click **Go**.

4. Click the arrow next to the books image of your choice. Click **Insert** on the submenu. The clip art is inserted in the text.

5. Place the insertion point to the left of the heading *Movie and Popcorn Night*.

6. In the *Search for* box, key **movie**. Click **Go**.

7. Click the arrow next to the movie image of your choice. Click **Insert** on the submenu. The clip art is inserted in the text.

8. Close the Clip Art task pane.

9. Save and leave the document open for the next Step-by-Step.

Selecting Clip Art

Although clip art is already created, you can alter the way it appears on a page. To edit clip art, you must first select it. To select clip art, position the insertion point over the clip art and click. A box with eight small squares appears around the clip art, as shown in Figure 5-7. The box is called the *selection rectangle*. The squares are called *sizing handles*. You can use the Picture toolbar, as shown in Figure 5-8, or the Format Picture dialog box, as shown in Figure 5-9, to edit clip art.

FIGURE 5-7
Selection rectangle with sizing handles

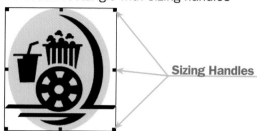

FIGURE 5-8
Picture toolbar

FIGURE 5-9
Format Picture dialog box

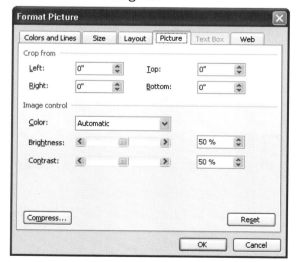

Resizing Clip Art

Once the clip art has been inserted, it can be resized to fit better in the text. To resize the clip art, first select it, and then click on a sizing handle. The insertion point becomes a crosshair. Drag the handle inward or outward to make the object smaller or larger. After adjusting the clip art to the desired size, click anywhere in the window to deselect it.

> **Hot Tip**
>
> You can quickly access the Format Picture dialog box by selecting the object and then right-clicking the mouse button. Choose **Format Picture** on the shortcut menu.

To change the size, or *scale*, of a graphic so its proportions are precise, use the Format Picture dialog box, as shown in Figure 5-10. You can also resize clip art while maintaining its proportions by holding down the shift key and dragging the sizing handle or by dragging the corner handles inward or outward.

FIGURE 5-10
Size tab in Format Picture dialog box

STEP-BY-STEP 5.4

1. Click the picture of the books to select it.

2. Use the handles to resize it to approximately 1½ inches tall by 2 inches wide.

3. Click the **Center** button on the Formatting toolbar. The book clip art is centered in column 1. Deselect the clip art.

4. Click the picture of the movie to select it.

5. Open the **Format** menu and choose **Picture.**

STEP-BY-STEP 5.4 Continued

6. Click the **Size** tab. In the *Scale* section, click the *Height* down arrow until *35%* appears in the box. Notice that the *Width percentage* and the *Size measurements* in inches also change.

7. Click **OK**. The clip art is smaller.

8. Save and leave the document open for the next Step-by-Step.

Wrapping Text around Clip Art

To save space and make a document look more professional, you may want to wrap text around the clip art. To wrap text, use the Layout tab in the Format Picture dialog box, as shown in Figure 5-11. The *Wrapping style* samples show how the text will flow around the graphic.

FIGURE 5-11
Layout tab in Format Picture dialog box

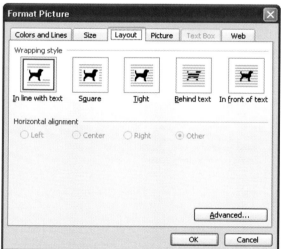

STEP-BY-STEP 5.5

1. Select the movie clip art if it is not already selected.

2. Open the **Format** menu and choose **Picture**. Click the Layout tab if necessary.

3. In the *Wrapping Style* section, click **Square**. Click **OK**. Click anywhere in the window to deselect the movie clip art. The document should appear similar to the one in Figure 5-12.

FIGURE 5-12
Text wrapping with clip art

Movie and Popcorn Night
Join us for the Summer Movie Series every Tuesday night at 7:00 p.m. Pick up a schedule at the check out desk, or view

STEP-BY-STEP 5.5 Continued

4. Preview the document. If the newsletter is more than one page, adjust spacing of the text or the size of the clip art.

5. Save, print, and close the document.

Adding Borders to Pages

The same way you add borders to paragraphs, you can add borders to entire pages. Use the Page Border tab in the Borders and Shading dialog box to choose the setting, line style, width, and color of border you want. See Figure 5-13. In the *Art* box, you can choose predefined art borders. To specify the amount of space between the border and the text or edge of the page, click the Options button and make the changes in the Border and Shading Options dialog box.

FIGURE 5-13
Page Border tab in Borders and Shading dialog box

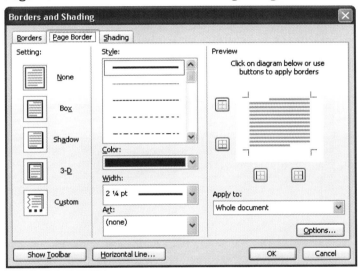

STEP-BY-STEP 5.6

1. Open **Step5-6** from the data files. Save the file as **Invitation** followed by your initials.

2. Open the **Format** menu and choose **Borders and Shading**.

3. Click the **Page Border** tab. In the *Setting* section, click the **Box** button.

STEP-BY-STEP 5.6 Continued

4. Click the arrow on the *Art* box, and choose a predefined art border appropriate for a birthday invitation. You can see a preview of how the document will look in the *Preview* section.

5. Click the **Options** button. The Border and Shading Options dialog box appears.

6. Click the arrow on the *Measure from* box and select **Text**. Click **OK** twice to close the dialog boxes.

7. Change the color of the text to match the border.

8. Click the **Print Preview** button to see how your document will appear. Close **Print Preview**.

9. Save, print, and close the document.

Drawing Graphics

Word provides tools for you to create graphic images. The Drawing toolbar contains buttons for drawing and manipulating objects, such as lines, arcs, rectangles, circles, and free-form shapes. Table 5-1 summarizes the basic drawing tools that appear in the Drawing toolbar.

TABLE 5-1
Drawing tools

BUTTON	NAME	FUNCTION
▢	Rectangle	Draws rectangles and squares. To use, click and hold the mouse button; then drag to draw. To create a perfect square, hold down the Shift key as you drag.
◣	Line	Draws straight lines. To use, position the pointer where you want the line to begin; then click and hold the mouse button, and drag to where you want the line to end.
◯	Oval	Draws ovals and circles. To use, click and hold the mouse button; then drag to draw the oval or circle. To create a perfect circle, hold down the Shift key as you drag.
�	Select Objects	Lets you select and manipulate objects. To use, click on the arrow. The insertion point assumes the pointer shape.

S TEP-BY-STEP 5.7

1. You want to create a map to the birthday party. Open a new Word document. Study the map in Figure 5-14. You will be drawing a map similar to this one.

FIGURE 5-14
Park map

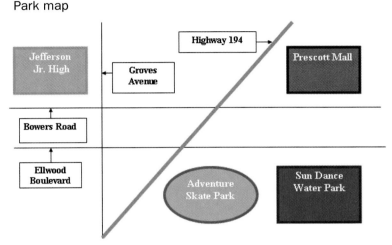

2. Change the orientation to landscape.

3. If necessary, click the **Drawing** button on the Standard toolbar to display the Drawing toolbar.

4. Click the **Line** button. The drawing canvas appears on the document and the mouse pointer changes to a crosshair. You may want to use Zoom to decrease the size of the document to view it better.

5. Draw a line positioned similar to *Groves Avenue* shown in Figure 5-14. Position the pointer in the upper portion of the document about a third from the left side of the document. Drag to draw a line from the upper portion to the lower portion. Release the mouse button when your line is in position.

6. Use the **Line** button to create the other roads on the map. Be sure to click the Line button each time you draw a line. You will learn how to change the color and the width of the lines later in the lesson.

7. Draw an oval similar to *Adventure Skate Park*. Click the **Oval** button. The mouse pointer changes to a crosshair.

8. Press and hold the mouse button. Drag to draw an oval about **1½** inches tall by **3** inches wide. Release the mouse button when your oval is approximately the same size and in the same position as the skate park shown in Figure 5-14. You will learn how to add color to a shape later in the lesson.

9. Preview your document and make any necessary adjustments.

10. Save the document as **Water Park Map** followed by your initials. Leave the document open for the next Step-by-Step.

Editing Drawings

As with clip art, you can change the way your drawings appear in a document. To edit a drawing object, you must first select it. Position the insertion point over the object and click. Handles appear around the object, and a four-sided arrow appears with the arrow pointer. Drag one of the handles inward or outward to make the object smaller or larger. Click anywhere in the window to deselect the object. Select and press Delete or Backspace to delete an object.

You can cut, copy, and paste objects the same way you do text. The Cut and Copy commands place a copy of the selected image on the Clipboard. Pasting an object from the Clipboard places the object in your drawing. To move an object, select it; then press and hold the mouse button while you drag the object to its new location.

STEP-BY-STEP 5.8

1. Click the **Rectangle** button.

2. Position the pointer in the upper-left corner of your document.

3. Drag to draw a rectangle similar to *Jefferson Jr. High* on the map. When you release the mouse button, the rectangle is still selected.

4. Click the **Copy** button on the toolbar.

5. Click the **Paste** button. A copy of the rectangle appears.

6. Click the **Paste** button again. Another copy of the rectangle appears.

7. The last rectangle you pasted is still selected. Place the pointer in the middle of the rectangle, and hold down the mouse button. Drag the rectangle to the right side of the document so it is in the same position as *Prescott Mall* on the map.

8. Select the next rectangle, and drag it to the same position as *Sun Dance Water Park* on the map. Use the handles to create a square **1½** inches by **1½** inches. Deselect the square.

9. Save and leave the document open for the next Step-by-Step.

Adding Color and Style to Objects

Color adds life to your drawings. Word allows you to fill objects with color and change the color of lines. To change the color, use the Fill Color button or the Line Color button on the Drawing toolbar, as shown in Figures 5-15 and 5-16. To choose a color from the color box, simply click the color you want.

FIGURE 5-15
Fill Color button with color box

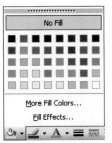

FIGURE 5-16
Line Color button with color box

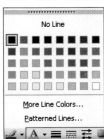

Another way to change the appearance of drawings is to change the line style. You can change the style of the line or lines that make up an object, such as a rectangle. Word gives you many choices for line styles, including thick and thin lines, dotted lines, and arrows. To change the line style, use the Line Style button on the Drawing toolbar, as shown in Figure 5-17.

FIGURE 5-17
Line Style menu

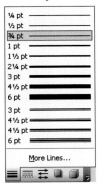

S TEP-BY-STEP 5.9

1. Select the oval on the map.

2. Click the arrow on the **Fill Color** button on the Drawing toolbar. Click **Lime** on the color palette. The oval is filled with the color lime green.

3. Select the *Sun Dance Water Park* rectangle on the drawing.

4. Click the arrow on the **Fill Color** button, and click the color **Light Blue**. The square is filled with the color light blue.

5. Fill the *Prescott Mall* rectangle with **Gray 40%.** Fill the *Jefferson Jr. High* rectangle with **Light Orange**.

STEP-BY-STEP 5.9 Continued

6. Select the line labeled *Highway 194* on the map in Figure 5-14.

7. Click the arrow on the **Line Color** button on the Drawing toolbar. Click **Red** on the color palette.

8. With the line still selected, click the **Line Style** button. A menu of line styles appears.

9. Click the **4½ pt** solid line. The line on the drawing thickens.

10. Select the oval, and click the **Line Color** button. Click the color **Green**. The line around the oval is now green.

11. With the oval still selected, click the **Line Style** button. Click the **6 pt** solid line. The line around the oval thickens. Deselect the oval.

12. Select the light blue rectangle, and click the **Line Color** button. Click the color **Dark Blue**. The line around the rectangle is now dark blue.

13. With the rectangle still selected, click the **Line Style** button. Click the **6 pt** solid line. The line around the rectangle thickens. Deselect the rectangle.

14. Change the line color of the gray rectangle to **Gray 80%** and a **6 pt** solid line.

15. Change the line color of the orange rectangle to **Orange** and a **6 pt** solid line.

16. Save and leave the document open for the next Step-by-Step.

Adding Text to Your Drawings

Often the drawings will require labels. Word provides several ways to add text to a document. The easiest way is to right-click in the object and choose Add Text on the shortcut menu.

Another way to add text to your drawing is to insert text boxes. To add a text box, click the Text Box button on the Drawing toolbar or open the Insert menu and choose Text Box. A crosshair pointer appears. Position the pointer where you want the text box to appear; then click and drag to create a text box. An insertion point appears inside the text box so you can key the text you want. Text within a text box can be formatted like regular text.

Once a text box is inserted into a document, it can be treated similarly to a graphic. You can format, resize, or change the position of a text box using the same commands as you would with a drawing object. To move a text box, click and drag it to the location you want.

S TEP-BY-STEP 5.10

1. Select the skate park. Right-click and choose **Add text** on the submenu to insert text.

2. Key **Adventure Skate Park**. Format text as Times New Roman, 18 point, centered, white, bold.

3. Key **Sun Dance Water Park**, **Prescott Mall**, and **Jefferson Jr. High** in the three rectangles. Center the text and format it as Times New Roman, 18 point, centered, white, bold.

4. Click the **Text Box** button on the Drawing toolbar.

5. To create a label for *Highway 194,* place the crosshair above and to the left of the red diagonal line, as shown on the map in Figure 5-14. Click and drag the mouse to draw a text box approximately ½ inch tall and 2 inches wide. Release the mouse button.

6. With the insertion point in the text box, key **Highway 194**. Format as Times New Roman, 16 point, centered, bold.

7. Repeat steps 5 and 6 to insert the text boxes for *Groves Avenue, Bowers Road*, and *Ellwood Boulevard* as shown on the map.

8. Click the **Arrow** button on the Drawing toolbar. Draw an arrow from the text box labeled *Highway 194* to the red diagonal line. Draw arrows for the text boxes labeled *Groves Avenue, Bowers Road*, and *Ellwood Boulevard* as shown in Figure 5-14.

9. Preview the document. Make adjustments as needed.

10. Save, print, and close the document.

SUMMARY

In this lesson, you learned:

- You can create documents with multiple columns. You can specify the number of columns and whether you want a line separating them.

- Borders and shading add interest and emphasis to text.

- You can insert clip art and scale it to fit your document.

- To wrap text around an object, select the object and choose Picture on the Format menu.

- You can add borders to an entire page similar to the way you add borders to paragraphs.

- You can also draw graphics to add to word processing documents. The Drawing toolbar allows you to draw shapes such as lines, rectangles, and ovals.

- Drawing objects can be resized, copied, and moved.

- Text boxes can be created to contain special text. They can be formatted, resized, or moved just like drawing objects.

VOCABULARY *Review*

Define the following terms:

Borders	Scale	Shading
Clip art	Selection rectangle	Sizing handles
Graphics		

REVIEW *Questions*

FILL IN THE BLANK

Complete the following sentences by writing the correct word or words in the blanks provided.

1. Choose the _____ tab in the Borders and Shading dialog box to add a border to an entire page.

2. Word will insert clip art at the _____ in the document.

3. The _____ toolbar contains tools you can use to draw and manipulate objects.

4. To add text to an object, right-click in the object and choose _____ on the shortcut menu.

5. To resize an object, drag the _____ inward or outward.

MATCHING

Match the correct term in Column 2 to its description in Column 1.

Column 1

___ 1. Add a preset design to a diagram.

___ 2. Format a document into columns.

___ 3. Insert a border on four sides of a paragraph.

___ 4. Format clip art.

___ 5. Add color to an object.

Column 2

A. Format Picture button

B. Fill Color button

C. Columns button

D. AutoShapes button

E. AutoFormat button

F. Format Painter button

G. Box button

PROJECTS

PROJECT 5-1

You have been asked to help with a newsletter for your school. The counselor has given you some information and asked you to format it into a one-page newsletter.

1. Open **Project5-1** from the data files. Save the document as **School Newsletter** followed by your initials.

2. Center the title and date.

3. Change the font of *Jefferson Jr. High* to 26 point, dark red, bold. Change *PTA Newsletter* to 18 point, dark red, bold. Change the font of the date to 14 point, gold, bold.

4. Place the insertion point in front of the sentence *From Our Principal*. Format the document with two columns, with a line, and with 0.4-inch spacing between each column. Select the *This point forward* option from the *Apply to* drop-down list.

5. Format the headings *From Our Principal, From the PTA President, Fall Festival-October 25th, New Faculty, Jefferson T-shirts for Sale*, and *Tennis Team Tryouts* as 14 point, dark red, bold. Center the headings in the columns.

6. Apply bullets to the the names of the new faculty.

7. Place a 3-point dark red border around the list of dates and shade it gold. Be sure to include the title.

8. Place the insertion point above the title *Fall Festival*. Insert appropriate clip art. Key **fall** in the *Search for* box. Center and resize the clip art to fit the newsletter.

9. Place the insertion point above the title *Tennis Team Tryouts*. Insert appropriate clip art. Key **tennis** in the *Search for* box. Center and resize the clip art to fit the newsletter.

10. Preview the document. Adjust the spacing within the document if necessary.

11. Save, print, and close the document.

PROJECT 5-2

Reformat the *Eagle* document.

1. Open **Project5-2** from the data files. Save the document as **Eagle2** followed by your initials.

2. Change the list of facts to 18 point. Bullet the list.

3. Change the bulleted list of facts into two columns.

4. Place the insertion point above the title. Insert appropriate clip art. Key **eagle** in the *Search for* box. Center and resize the clip art to fit the document.

5. Place an appropriate page border on the document. Be sure the border is measured from the text.

6. Preview the document. Save, print, and close the document.

PROJECT 5-3

You need to create a timeline about events that led to the Revolutionary War.

1. Open a new Word document. You will create a timeline similar to Figure 5-18.

FIGURE 5-18
Timeline

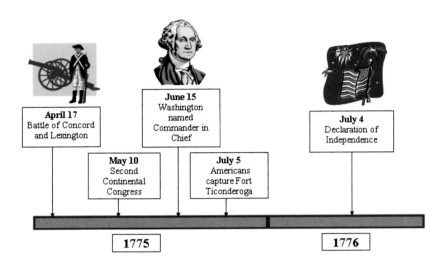

2. Change the page orientation to landscape.

3. Draw a long, slender rectangle in the lower portion of the document similar to the red rectangle in Figure 5-18. Fill the rectangle with the color red. Add a 3-point, blue border.

4. Draw a vertical line in the rectangle as a division between the years similar to Figure 5-18. Change the line to 6 point, blue.

5. Add a text box under the first portion of the timeline. Key **1775** in the text box. Change the font to 20 point, bold and centered.

6. Add a text box under the second portion of the timeline. Key **1776** in the text box. Change the font to 20 point, bold and centered.

7. Add a text box above the first portion of the year 1775. Key **April 17 Battle of Concord and Lexington**. Change the font to 14 point. Bold the date.

8. Create similar text boxes for the other dates on the timeline. Change the font of the text in each box to 14 point. Bold each date.

9. Use arrows to connect each text box to the appropriate place on the timeline.

10. Insert appropriate clip art for the date April 17. Key **Soldier** in the *Search for* box. Select the clip art and click **Insert**. Resize the clip art and move it above the April 17 text box.

11. Insert appropriate clip art for June 15 and July 4. Key **George Washington** in the *Search for* box for the date June 15. Key **flag** in the *Search for* box for the date July 4. Resize and move the clip art so it is similar to Figure 5-18.

12. Preview the document. Make adjustments as needed.

13. Save the document as **Timeline** followed by your initials. Print and close the document.

PROJECT 5-4

You have been asked to add graphics to the Big Dipper document.

1. Open **Project5-4** from the data files. Save the document as **Big Dipper2** followed by your initials.

2. Select the first paragraph including the heading. Add a 3 pt, yellow border with Sky Blue shading.

3. Place the insertion point above the title. Insert appropriate clip art. Key **Big Dipper** in the *Search for* box. Center and resize the clip art to fit the document if necessary.

4. Place the insertion point to the left of the first line in the second paragraph. Insert appropriate clip art. Key **Ursa Major** or **bear** in the *Search for* box. Resize the clip art to fit the document. Wrap the text around the clip art.

5. Place the insertion point to the left of the first line in the third paragraph. Insert clip art that looks like the North Star. Key **star** in the *Search for* box. Resize the clip art to fit the document. Wrap the text around the clip art.

6. Preview the document. Save, print, and close the document.

WEB*Project*

PROJECT 5-5

The AutoShapes submenu contains a selection of flowchart symbols. You have been asked to create a table describing the function of some of the symbols.

1. Open a new Word document. Create a table similar to the one in Figure 5-19.

FIGURE 5-19
Flowchart Symbols table

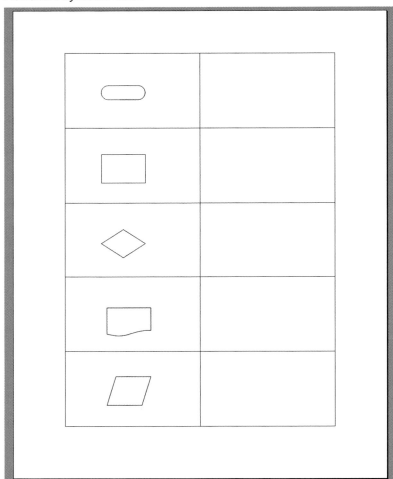

2. Use the Internet to research the function of each symbol. Key a description of the symbol in the second column.

3. Save the document as **Flowchart Symbols** followed by your initials. Print and close the document.

TEAMWORK *Project*

PROJECT 5-6

You have been assigned to write a research paper for your language arts class. With a partner, create a flowchart to show the steps of writing a research paper. Use the symbols from the chart you created in Project 5-5. Save the document as **Research Paper** followed by your initials.

CRITICAL *Thinking*

ACTIVITY 5-1

Use the drawing tools to create a map that would guide a person from your school to your home. Save the map as **Neighborhood** followed by your initials.

MICROSOFT WORD

COMMAND SUMMARY

FEATURE	MENU COMMAND	TOOLBAR BUTTON	LESSON
Align Text	Format, Paragraph, Alignment		4
Bold	Format, Font, Bold		3
Borders	Format, Borders and Shading		5
Bullets	Format, Bullets and Numbering		4
Clip Art	Insert, Picture, Clip Art		5
Close	File, Close		1
Columns	Format, Columns		5
Copy	Edit, Copy		2
Create a New Document	File, New, Blank document		1
Cut	Edit, Cut		2
Date and Time Insert	Insert, Date and Time		2
Delete Character	Backspace or Delete		2
Delete Page Break Line	Select page break line, Delete or Backspace		4
Drawing Graphics	View, Toolbars, Drawing		5
Find	Edit, Find		2
Font	Format, Font	Times New Roman	3
Font Color	Format, Font		3
Font Effects	Format, Font		3
Font Size	Format, Font	12	3
Grammar Check	Tools, Spelling and Grammar		2
Highlight	Highlight		3
Indentation	Format, Paragraph		4
Italic	Format, Font		3
Line Spacing	Format, Paragraph		4
Margins	File, Page Setup, Margins		4
Normal View	View, Normal		1

FEATURE	MENU COMMAND	TOOLBAR BUTTON	LESSON
Numbering	Format, Bullets and Numbering		4
Open Existing Document	File, Open		1
Outline Numbered	Format, Bullets and Numbering		4
Overtype			2
Page Breaks	Insert, Break		4
Paste	Edit, Paste		2
Preview Document	File, Print Preview		1
Print Document	File, Print		1
Print Layout View	View, Print Layout		1
Redo	Edit, Redo		2
Replace	Edit, Replace		2
Save	File, Save or Save As		1
Select Entire Document	Edit, Select All		2
Shading	Format, Borders and Shading		5
Sort	Table, Sort		
Spell Check	Tools, Spelling and Grammar		2
Style	Format, Styles and Formatting	Normal	3
Table Insert	Table, Insert, Table		4
Tabs	Format, Tabs		4
Text Box	Insert, Text Box		5
Thesaurus	Tools, Language, Thesaurus		2
Underline	Format, Font		3
Undo	Edit, Undo		2
Vertical Alignment	File, Page Setup		4
Web Layout View	View, Web Layout		1

REVIEW *Questions*

MATCHING

Match the correct term in Column 2 to its description in Column 1.

Column 1

___ 1. List of options from which to choose

___ 2. Designs of type

___ 3. Predefined set of formatting options

___ 4. Setting used unless another option is chosen

___ 5. File that contains formatting with text you can customize

Column 2

A. fonts

B. default

C. taskbar

D. menu

E. font effects

F. style

G. template

WRITTEN QUESTIONS

Write a brief answer to the following questions.

1. What are two ways to check the spelling in a document?

2. How do you align text? What are the four text alignment positions?

3. How do you resize an object?

4. What are the two ways to set tabs?

5. What is the Clipboard?

PROJECTS

PROJECT 1

1. Open **Project1** from the data files.

2. Save the document as **Camp** followed by your initials.

3. Check the document for spelling and grammar errors. Make changes as needed.

4. Change the Zoom to **75%**.

5. Select the entire document and change the font to Arial.

6. Find the word *program*, and replace it with **activity** each time it occurs in the document. Be sure to check *Find all word forms*.

7. Move the heading *Registration Information* and the paragraph that follows to the end of the document.

8. Replace the word *spectacular* in the first paragraph with a synonym that makes sense in context.

9. Change the line spacing of the document to **1.5**.

10. Change the orientation to landscape.

11. Add an appropriate page border.

12. Center align the text vertically on the page.

13. Change the title *Camp Piney Ridge* to 28 point, centered. Change the font of the title to one of your choice. Change the color to one that matches the page border.

14. Change each of the headings to the **Heading 3** style. Change the color to match the page border.

15. Center the last heading. Indent the last paragraph 1 inch on each side.

16. Create a 3-point border around the last heading and paragraph. Change the color of the border and shade it with colors that match the page border.

17. Preview the document. Save, print, and close the document.

PROJECT 2

1. Open **Project2** from the data files.

2. Save the document as **Honors** followed by your initials.

3. Change the left and right margins to **1.75"**.

4. Center the letterhead. Change the first line of the letterhead to 14 point, bold.

5. Insert the date on the fourth blank line below the letterhead.

6. Place the insertion point above the letterhead. Insert clip art. Key **diploma** in the *Search for* box. Adjust the size to **30%** height and **30%** width.

7. Use the thesaurus to find a synonym for the word *aim* in the third sentence.

8. Insert a table with three columns and six rows after the first paragraph.

9. Key the data in the table as shown in Figure UR-1.

FIGURE UR-1
Tutoring schedule

Subject	Member	Day
Algebra	Carrie Jones	Tuesday
Chemistry	John Wilson	Tuesday
Language Arts	Belinda White	Thursday
Spanish	Trina Garcia	Thursday
History	Yolanda Hernandez	Thursday

10. Center the three headings, and change the font size to 14 point, bold.

11. Add a new row after the *History* row, and key the following data:

   Computer   **Adam Richards**   **Thursday**

12. Add a new row above the first row, and key **Tutoring Schedule**; merge the cells.

13. Center the heading if necessary and change to 16 point, bold.

14. Change the borders to 3 point, dark red and shading to Sky Blue.

15. Save, print, and close the file.

PROJECT 3

1. Open **Project3** from the data files.

2. Save the document as **Pizza** followed by your initials.

3. Change all the text to 14 point, Arial, green.

4. Change the left and right margins to 1 inch.

5. Center the title *Luigi's Pizza*. Change it to all caps, Arial Black, 24 point, red with shadow effect.

6. Center the subtitle *"The Best Pizza in Town"*. Change it to 16 point, bold, italic.

7. Indent the first line of the first paragraph .5 inches.

8. Change the *Specialty Pizzas* heading to red, 18 point, bold, small caps, with a red double underline.

9. Copy the format of the *Specialty Pizzas* heading to the *Pasta Dishes* and *Build Your Own Pizza* headings.

10. Number the items in the *Specialty Pizzas* and *Pasta Dishes* lists.

11. Change the line spacing of the first paragraph to **1.5** and the list of toppings to double-spacing.

12. Format the list of pizza toppings into three columns with **.4** inches between them.

13. Center and change *Come again!* to red, 18 point, bold, italic.

14. Preview the document. Print from the Preview screen.

15. Save and close the document.

PROJECT 4

Your school is having an open house. You have been asked to create a flyer to inform the students and parents.

1. Open a new Word document.

2. Create the poster in Figure UR-2 using what you have learned in this unit. Follow the instructions shown on the poster.

FIGURE UR-2
Open House poster

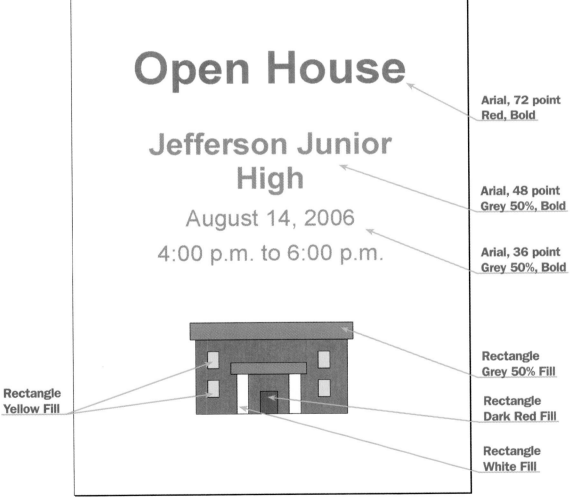

3. Save the document as **Open House** followed by your initials.

4. Print and close the document.

 PROJECT 5

1. Open **Project5** from the data files.

2. Save the document as **Roman Numerals** followed by your initials.

3. Use Find and Replace to replace the word *numberal* with *numeral*.

4. Change the title to 24 point, Plum, centered with Emboss effect.

5. Change the character spacing of the title to 2 points.

6. Place the insertion point above the title. Insert clip art. Key **Roman numeral** in the *Search for* box. Resize the clip art so it is appropriate for the document.

7. Insert a table with two columns and eight rows after the first paragraph.

8. Key the data in the table as shown in Figure UR-3.

FIGURE UR-3
Roman numeral table

Numeral	Value
I	1
V	5
X	10
L	50
C	100
D	500
M	1000

9. Change the headings of the first table to 14 point, bold.

10. Center the text in the columns of the first table. Resize the columns so that they are only slightly wider than the headings.

11. Center the first table.

12. Change the borders of both tables to 2 ¼ point, Plum.

13. Number the rules in the second paragraph.

14. Calculate the Arabic numeral for the Roman numeral in the second table. Key the correct Arabic numeral in the second column.

15. Preview the document. Save, print, and close the document.

PORTFOLIO *Checklist*

Include the following files from this unit in your student portfolio:

Lesson 1
- ___ Typing Skills
- ___ Car Wash
- ___ Thank You
- ___ Eagle
- ___ Constitution
- ___ Delegate
- ___ Uniforms
- ___ Persuasive Paragraph

Lesson 2
- ___ Body Language
- ___ History
- ___ Itinerary
- ___ Spelling List
- ___ Trip Letter
- ___ Typing Skills2
- ___ Washington D.C.
- ___ White House
- ___ Mnemonics

Lesson 3
- ___ Big Dipper
- ___ Certificate
- ___ Proofreading
- ___ Rules
- ___ Stargazing
- ___ Civil War
- ___ Satellite Photos
- ___ Constellation
- ___ New Constellation
- ___ Stargazing Animation

Lesson 4
- ___ Computer
- ___ Constitution2
- ___ Erosion
- ___ Metric
- ___ Money
- ___ Money Title
- ___ Proofreading2
- ___ Rivers
- ___ Training
- ___ Verb Tense
- ___ Grand Canyon
- ___ Facts
- ___ River Sort

Lesson 5
— Big Dipper2
— Eagle2
— Flowchart Symbols
— Invitation
— Library
— Neighborhood
— Research Paper
— School Newsletter
— Timeline
— Water Park Map

Unit Review
— Camp
— Honors
— Open House
— Pizza
— Roman Numerals

MICROSOFT POWERPOINT

Unit 3

Estimated Time for Unit: 7 hours

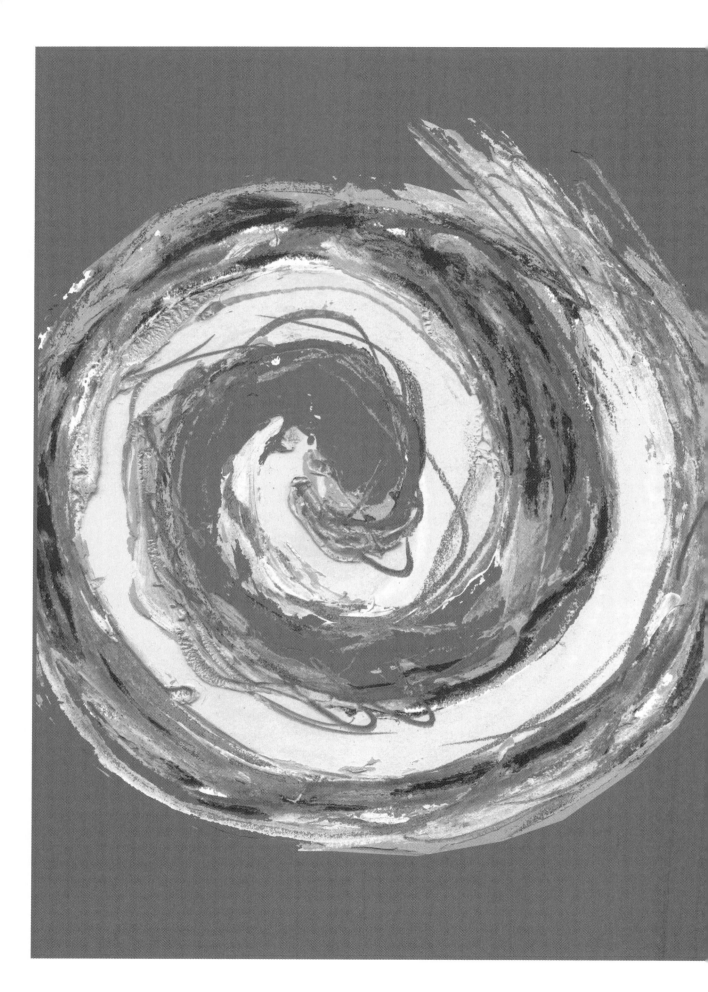

POWERPOINT BASICS

What Is PowerPoint?

PowerPoint is the presentation application of the Microsoft Office 2003 suite of programs. *Presentations* help you show your ideas using slides, outlines, speaker's notes, and audience handouts. A presentation can include text, clip art, graphs, tables, and charts. Presentations can also include multimedia features such as Flash files, animated GIFs, and sound or video clips.

PowerPoint presentations are usually viewed using a projector on a screen, but you can also use a television monitor, your computer screen, or an additional monitor connected to your computer. PowerPoint presentations can also be broadcast or published on the Internet. *Broadcasting* a presentation allows you to deliver a live presentation over the Internet. *Publishing* a presentation allows others to see your work at any time by using the Internet.

Hot Tip

The PowerPoint screen contains Standard, Formatting, and Drawing toolbars, similar to those found in Word. The screen also contains the task pane, located on the right side of the screen.

PowerPoint provides features such as design templates and wizards that make creating a presentation easier. This lesson introduces you to some of the features available in PowerPoint 2003.

Computer Concepts

The task pane has features that are related to the task on which you are currently working. If the task pane is not displayed, right-click the Standard toolbar and click Task Pane to display it.

Starting PowerPoint

Like other Office applications, you start PowerPoint by clicking the Start button, selecting All Programs (or Programs in Windows 2000), Microsoft Office, and clicking Microsoft Office PowerPoint 2003. The PowerPoint program opens, as shown in Figure 1-1.

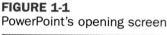

FIGURE 1-1
PowerPoint's opening screen

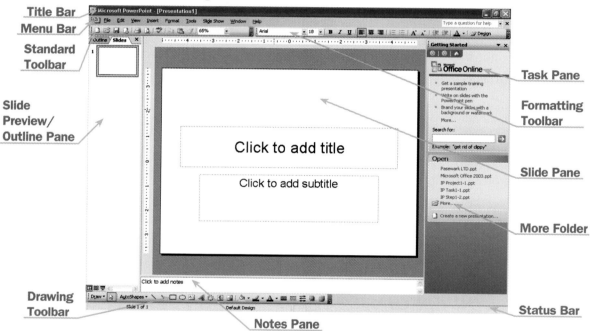

S TEP-BY-STEP 1.1

1. Click the **Start** button to open the Start menu.

2. Point to **All Programs** (or **Programs** in Windows 2000), point to **Microsoft Office**, and then select Microsoft Office PowerPoint 2003.

3. The PowerPoint opening window appears (Figure 1-1). Leave the program on the screen for the next Step-by-Step.

Opening and Viewing an Existing Presentation

To open an existing presentation, choose the presentation from the list in the PowerPoint task pane under the heading *Open*. This list shows recently opened presentations. Click the presentation you want to open.

If the presentation you want to open is not in the list, click the *More* folder (see Figure 1-1). The More folder is not available if presentations are not listed in the task pane. If the *More* folder is not displayed, choose Open instead. This choice displays the Open dialog box, as shown in Figure 1-2. Locate the presentation you want to open, click the file name, and click the Open button. The presentation you selected appears on the screen, as shown in Figure 1-3.

FIGURE 1-2
Open dialog box

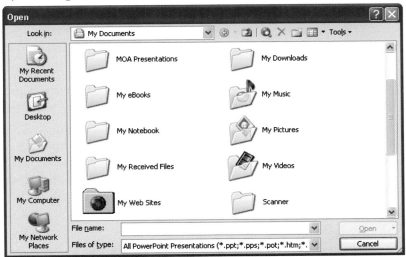

FIGURE 1-3
Opening a presentation

The View Show option on the Slide Show menu allows you to view a presentation as you would when you present it. During a presentation, click your mouse to view the next slide.

Text or pictures that have motion are called *animation*. When you give a presentation, you speak to the audience. You tell them more details about the topic on each slide. PowerPoint allows you to delay the animation until you trigger it by clicking the mouse. As you view the presentation in Step-by-Step 1.2, messages appear at the bottom of each slide indicating when you should advance to the next animation or slide. (See Figure 1-4.)

FIGURE 1-4
Presentation message

Click your mouse or tap the right arrow key to continue.

STEP-BY-STEP 1.2

1. In the task pane, click the **More** link. If the More option is not available, click **Open** from the **File** menu. The Open dialog box is displayed.

2. In the Open dialog box, display the disk drive and/or folder containing the data files for this course, click **Step1-2,** and then click **Open.** The file appears as shown in Figure 1-3.

3. Click **View Show** from the **Slide Show** menu.

4. Tap the right arrow key or click the mouse to trigger the animation on the first slide. A picture of an airplane appears, and moves across the screen. If you have a sound card and speakers, you should also hear the sound of an airplane engine. A message at the bottom of the screen tells you to click the mouse or tap the right arrow key.

5. Click the mouse to display the title of the presentation on the screen. A message appears again telling you to click the mouse or tap the right arrow key.

6. Click the mouse again. A second plane moves across the screen.

7. Click your mouse again. Another plane flies across the screen.

8. Click your mouse to advance to the next slide. Notice that the animation on the slide advances automatically.

9. Click your mouse again to advance to the next slide. The text of this slide appears automatically. A small green box with a picture of a speaker also appears next to the text.

10. Click the green box to hear the pronunciation of the word *aerodynamics*.

11. Click your mouse again to trigger the next text line. Continue to click to advance the slides. The instructions on the slides guide you through the presentation. As the presentation continues, notice the different examples of animation. Leave the presentation open for the next Step-by-Step.

> ### Hot Tip
>
> You can tap the **Esc** key anytime during a presentation to return to the view displayed prior to running the show.

Saving a Presentation

When you create a presentation, you will want to save it. To save a new presentation, choose Save As from the File menu or click the Save button on the toolbar to display the *Save As* dialog box, as shown in Figure 1-5. Click the down arrow to the right of the *Save in* box and click the drive where you will save your presentation. Select the contents of the *File name* box, key a file name, and choose Save.

FIGURE 1-5
Save As dialog box

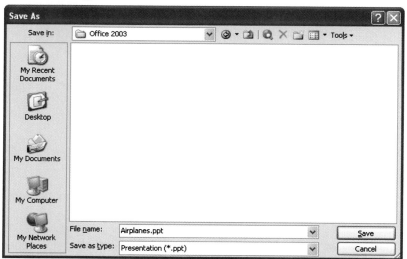

The next time you want to save changes to your presentation, click the Save button on the toolbar or choose Save from the File menu. These commands update the file and do not open the dialog box.

S TEP-BY-STEP 1.3

1. Choose **Save As** on the **File** menu. The Save As dialog box appears, as shown in Figure 1-5.

2. Click the down arrow to the right of the *Save in* box and choose the drive and folder in which you want to save the presentation.

3. In the *File name* box, key **Airplanes,** followed by your initials.

4. Click **Save.** Leave the program on the screen for the next Step-by-Step.

Changing Views

Yௌou can view a presentation four different ways using options on the View menu: Normal, Slide Sorter, Slide Show, and Notes Page. (See Figure 1-6.) You can also change the view quickly by clicking one of the buttons on the bottom-left of the screen, shown in Figure 1-7.

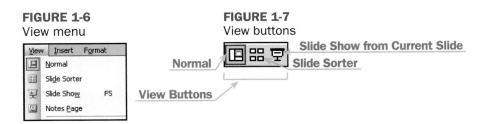

FIGURE 1-6
View menu

FIGURE 1-7
View buttons

Normal View

You have been working in *Normal view*. This view has four panes, the slide preview and outline pane, the task pane, the slide pane, and the notes pane.

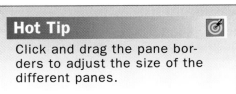

Hot Tip

Click and drag the pane borders to adjust the size of the different panes.

Using the Slide Preview and Outline Pane

PowerPoint displays all your slides in the outline pane on the left side of your screen. This pane has two tabs at the top, the Outline tab and the Slides tab. The *Outline tab* displays all the text on your slides in outline form. The *Slides tab* displays your slides as small pictures or thumbnails. To switch between the modes, click the Slides tab or the Outline tab.

To move between the slides, click the thumbnail in the Slides mode or click on the text in the Outline mode. The Outline mode allows you to edit text in the outline. You can also view the slides in your presentation by scrolling up and down. To close the pane, click the Close button in the top-right corner of the pane. Choose Normal on the View menu to display this pane if it is closed.

Hot Tip

You can also tap the **Page Down** key to view the next slide or tap **Page Up** to view the previous slide.

STEP-BY-STEP 1.4

1. If it is not already selected, click the **Outline** tab on the left side of the window.

2. Use the scroll bar to scroll down to slide **16**.

3. Highlight the word *Roman*. Key the word **Greek**.

4. Scroll to slide **17**.

5. Highlight the word *Roman* and key the word **Greek**.

6. Click the **Slides** tab. Leave the presentation on the screen for the next Step-by-Step.

Using the Task Pane

The *task pane* on the right side of the screen contains common tasks that you use frequently when creating a presentation. The task pane defaults to open when you start PowerPoint. You can change this option by selecting Options from the Tools menu, and clicking the View tab. Below Show you can choose to turn this option on or off by checking or un-checking Startup Task Pane.

STEP-BY-STEP 1.5

1. Click the **Design** button on the Formatting toolbar. (This opens the task pane if it is not already open.) The *Slide Design* task pane opens.

2. Scroll to view the different design templates.

3. Click **Color Schemes** and **Animation Schemes** to view the color schemes and animations available for your use. Click **Design Templates** to return to the *Design Templates* task pane. Leave the program on the screen for the next Step-by-Step. See Figure 1-8.

FIGURE 1-8
Design Templates, Color Schemes, Animation Schemes

Using the Slide Pane

The *slide pane* is the workbench for PowerPoint presentations. It displays one slide at a time in an area large enough to work in easily.

S TEP-BY-STEP 1.6

1. Use the scroll bar to scroll down to slide **16** if it is not already displayed in the slide pane.

2. Select the text that is formatted white. A text edit box appears around the text.

3. Use the Formatting toolbar to change the text size to **32**. Highlight the word *aerios*. Make it **bold** and **italics**, as shown in Figure 1-9.

FIGURE 1-9
Text edit box

4. Use the scroll bar to scroll to slide **17**. Select the text that is formatted white and change the text size to **32**. Highlight the word *dynamis*. Make it **bold** and **italics**. Leave the program on the screen for the next Step-by-Step.

Notes Page View

The *Notes Page view* displays your slides on the top portion of the page, with the speaker notes for each slide in the notes pane on the bottom of the page. To add speaker notes, click in the notes pane and begin keying, or you can open the View menu and choose Notes Page. You can use these notes to help you as you make a presentation, or give them to the audience as a handout to guide them through your presentation. You will learn more about using the notes pane in Lesson 2.

Slide Sorter View

Slide Sorter view, as shown in Figure 1-10, displays miniature versions of the slides on the screen so that you can move and arrange slides easily. The Slide Sorter toolbar helps you set the length of time a slide is displayed and select any special effects used to display the new slide. To switch to the Slide Sorter view, open the View menu and choose Slide Sorter.

FIGURE 1-10
Slide Sorter view

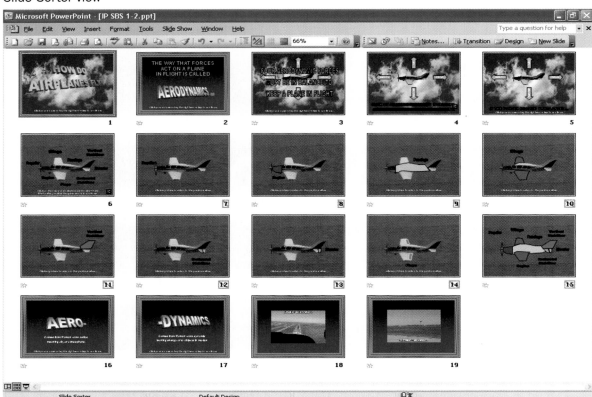

STEP-BY-STEP 1.7

1. Click the **Slide Sorter View** button. The screen appears, as shown in Figure 1-10.

2. Click slide **16** so that it is outlined in bold.

3. Drag slide **16** to the space between slide 2 and slide 3. A line appears between the two slides. Release the mouse button. Slide 16 moves to become slide 3. All other slides move down and they are renumbered.

4. Drag slide **17** and drop it between slide 3 and slide 4. Slide 17 becomes slide 4. All other slides move down and they are renumbered.

5. Click slide **1**.

STEP-BY-STEP 1.7 Continued

6. Click the **Slide Show** button on the bottom-left corner of the screen. Slide 1 appears on the screen.

7. Click the mouse to advance through all the slides. Once you have advanced through all the slides, a black screen displays.

8. Click to exit the presentation and return to the PowerPoint Slide Sorter screen.

9. Save the presentation and leave it open for the next Step-by-Step.

Slide Show View

In the *Slide Show view*, you can run your presentation on the computer as if it were a slide projector to preview how it will look. To access this view, choose Slide Show from the View menu or tap the F5 key.

Using Menus and Toolbars

When you first use PowerPoint, the short menu displays only the basic commands. To see an expanded menu with all the commands, click the arrows at the bottom of the menu. As you work, PowerPoint adjusts the menus to display the commands you use most frequently. When you use a command, it is added to the short menu. If you haven't used a command recently, it is dropped from the short menu. It can still be selected from the full menu.

In Normal view, the three toolbars displayed on the screen by default are the Standard, Formatting, and Drawing toolbars. They are shown in Figures 1-11, 1-12, and 1-13. The Standard and Formatting toolbars generally share the same row. To see additional buttons, click the Toolbar Options button on the toolbar and choose from the list that appears. When you use a button from the list, it is added to the toolbar.

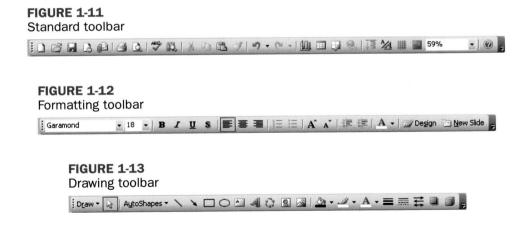

FIGURE 1-11
Standard toolbar

FIGURE 1-12
Formatting toolbar

FIGURE 1-13
Drawing toolbar

The status bar, shown in Figure 1-14, appears at the bottom of your screen. The area on the left side of the status bar shows which slide is displayed. The second area indicates the design currently in use. You can double-click the name of the design to bring up the *Slide Design Template* task pane. The third area displays a spell-check icon or the currently loaded language dictionary.

> **Hot Tip**
>
> To hide or display a toolbar, right-click any toolbar on the screen and choose a toolbar from the shortcut menu.

FIGURE 1-14
Status bar

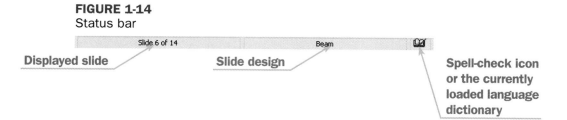

Displayed slide   Slide design   Spell-check icon or the currently loaded language dictionary

Deleting Slides

A presentation you create using the AutoContent Wizard includes a predetermined number of slides based on the type of presentation you choose. If you decide that a slide does not fit your presentation, you can easily delete it. With that slide displayed, choose Delete Slide from the Edit menu. If you accidentally delete the wrong slide, immediately choose Undo Delete Slide from the Edit menu to restore the slide or click the Undo button on the toolbar.

> **Hot Tip**
>
> If you make a mistake while using an Office program, you can tap **Ctrl+Z** to undo the last entry. By default, you can undo up to 20 entries in PowerPoint. You can change the number of actions you can undo by selecting **Options** from the **Tools** menu and clicking the **Edit** tab.

STEP-BY-STEP 1.8

1. If necessary, click the **Slide Sorter View** button.

2. Hold down the Control (Ctrl) key on your keyboard, and click on slides **18** and **19** so that they are outlined with a bold line. Right-click on either slide to display a shortcut menu.

3. Click **Delete Slide** from the shortcut menu.

4. Click slide **1**.

5. Click the **Slide Show** button and the presentation appears on the screen.

6. Click the mouse button to advance through all the slides. Notice that the original slides 18 and 19 have been deleted from the presentation.

7. Save and leave the presentation open for the next Step-by-Step.

Printing a Presentation

PowerPoint offers several print options that can enhance your presentation to an audience. If you don't print your presentation in color, you can choose either the *Grayscale* or *Pure Black and White* option in the Print dialog box (see Figure 1-15). To make sure the slides print on the page correctly, there is a *Scale to fit paper* option. With the *Frame slides* option, you can choose to print a border around each slide.

FIGURE 1-15
Print dialog box

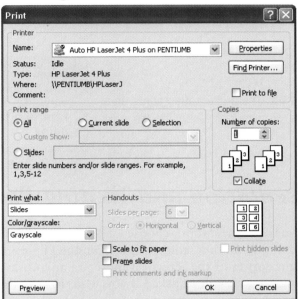

STEP-BY-STEP 1.9

1. Open the **File** menu and choose **Print**. The Print dialog box appears (Figure 1-15).

2. In the *Print range* section, click **Current slide**.

3. Click the arrow on the *Print what* box, and click **Slides** if necessary.

4. Click the **Preview** button. The slide appears as it would if you printed it.

5. Click the **Print** button and then click **OK** to print the slide.

6. Open the Print dialog box again.

7. Click the arrow on the *Print what* box, and click **Outline View.**

8. Click the **Scale to fit paper** option.

> **Computer Concepts**
>
> You can preview what your presentation will look like when printed in black and white by choosing **Color/Grayscale, Pure Black and White** from the **View** menu.

STEP-BY-STEP 1.9 Continued

9. Click the **Preview** button. The slide appears as it would if you printed it.

10. Click **Print** and click **OK**. The presentation prints as an outline on one page.

11. Open the Print dialog box again.

12. In the *Print what* box, choose **Handouts.**

13. In the Handouts section, click the down arrow next to the *Slides per page* box and choose **9.**

14. Choose **Horizontal** as the order, if it is not already chosen.

15. Click the **Preview** button. The slide appears as it would if you printed it.

16. Click **Print** and click **OK**. The presentation prints as a handout. Leave the presentation open for the next Step-by-Step.

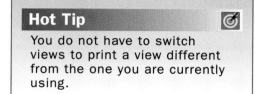

Hot Tip

You do not have to switch views to print a view different from the one you are currently using.

Closing a Presentation and Exiting PowerPoint

When you want to close a presentation, choose Close from the File menu or click the presentation's Close button. To exit PowerPoint, choose Exit from the File menu or click the PowerPoint Close box in the upper-right corner of the screen. If there are any unsaved changes to a presentation you have been working on, you will be asked if you want to save them before exiting.

STEP-BY-STEP 1.10

1. Open the File menu and choose **Close** to close the presentation. Click **Yes** if prompted to save your changes.

2. Click the **Close** box in the upper-right corner of the screen to exit PowerPoint.

SUMMARY

In this lesson, you learned:

■ PowerPoint is an Office application that can help you create a professional presentation. When you start PowerPoint, you have the choice of opening an existing presentation or creating a new one.

■ You can view your presentation four different ways: Normal view, Slide Sorter view, Slide Show view, and Notes Page view. Each view has its own advantages.

- Using the Print dialog box, you can print your presentation as slides using the Slides option, with notes using the Notes Pages option, or as an outline using the Outline View option. You can also choose to print handouts with two, three, four, six, or nine slides per page.

- To exit PowerPoint, choose Exit from the File menu.

VOCABULARY *Review*

Define the following terms:

Animation	Outline tab	Slide Show view
Broadcast	Presentation	Slide Sorter view
Normal view	Publish	Slides tab
Notes Page view	Slide pane	Task pane

REVIEW *Questions*

MULTIPLE CHOICE

Select the best response for the following statements.

1. When an existing file you want to open is not shown in the PowerPoint dialog box, choose
   A. Open Another File
   B. Search
   C. More
   D. Browse

2. Which toolbar is not displayed by default in Normal view?
   A. Outlining
   B. Standard
   C. Formatting
   D. Drawing

3. Which of the following is not one of the presentation views?
   A. Outline
   B. Notes Page
   C. Slide Show
   D. Slide Sorter

4. How do you display the task pane if it is not displayed?
   A. Click Display Task Pane in the Help menu
   B. Click Task Pane on the View menu
   C. Click the Task Pane button in Normal view
   D. None of the above. The task pane is always displayed.

5. Which option in the Print dialog box lets you choose to print a border around each slide?
   A. Grayscale
   B. Print border
   C. Scale to fit
   D. Frame slides

FILL IN THE BLANK

Complete the following sentences by writing the correct word or words in the blanks provided.

1. The list under the heading _____ shows recently opened presentations.

2. Tap the _____ key to advance and the _____ key to review slides in a presentation.

3. The _____ tab displays all of the text on your slides in outline form.

4. _____ view displays miniature versions of the slides on screen so that you can move and arrange slides easily by dragging.

5. You can print _____ that contain small pictures or thumbnails of your slides.

PROJECTS

PROJECT 1-1

1. Open **Project1-1** from the data files.

2. Save the presentation as **Vacation Hot Spots** followed by your initials.

3. Run the presentation as a slide show.

4. Leave the presentation open for the next project.

PROJECT 1-2

1. Select and delete slide **6** (titled Arizona) and slide **8** (titled The End).

2. Print the presentation as audience handouts with six slides per page.

3. Run the presentation as a slide show.

4. Save and close the presentation.

WEB *Project*

PROJECT 1-3

1. Search the Internet for a PowerPoint project about a subject that interests you.

2. Save the presentation as **Project 1-3** followed by your initials.

3. Run the presentation as a slide show.

4. Print the presentation as audience handouts with four slides per page.

5. Save and close the presentation.

TEAMWORK *Project*

PROJECT 1-4

1. Present the PowerPoint project you found in Project 1-3 to your class.

2. Give the handouts that you made in step 4 of Project 1-3 to your audience.

CRITICAL *Thinking*

ACTIVITY 1-1

You can change the way that PowerPoint displays when you initially open the program. Use PowerPoint Help to find out how to change the default view.

ACTIVITY 1-2

It is helpful to plan a presentation before you actually create it on the computer. Sketch out ideas on paper for a presentation on one of the topics below or make up your own. The presentation should have at least four slides. Include a title slide and indicate where you would put clip art.

- Help start a community campaign to keep your city clean.

- Encourage people to donate blood in the blood drive campaign next week.

- Explain the procedure for some safety technique (performing CPR, fire prevention, how to baby-proof a house, or performing first aid).

- Offer the audience the opportunity to become involved in a community project or volunteer organization.

- Explain the advantages of adopting an animal from the local shelter.

- Provide information about a new class that will be available in the fall.

CREATING POWERPOINT PRESENTATIONS

Creating a Presentation

When you start PowerPoint, you can choose to create a new presentation or open an existing presentation. A short list of recently opened presentations is displayed in the task pane (see Figure 2-1). Simply click the name of a presentation to open it.

FIGURE 2-1
Getting Started task pane

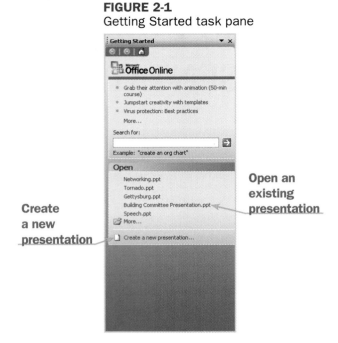

Create
a new
presentation

Open an
existing
presentation

If you click *Create a new presentation,* the task pane shown in Figure 2-2 displays four choices for creating a presentation: *Blank presentation, From design template, From AutoContent wizard,* and *From existing presentation.* The New Presentation task pane also contains a Templates section. If PowerPoint has already been used on your computer, the list of recently used templates contains the last four opened template files.

FIGURE 2-2
New Presentation task pane

Select an option to
create a new
presentation
that doesn't use a
template listed below

Select an option
to use one of the
listed templates
when creating
a new presentation

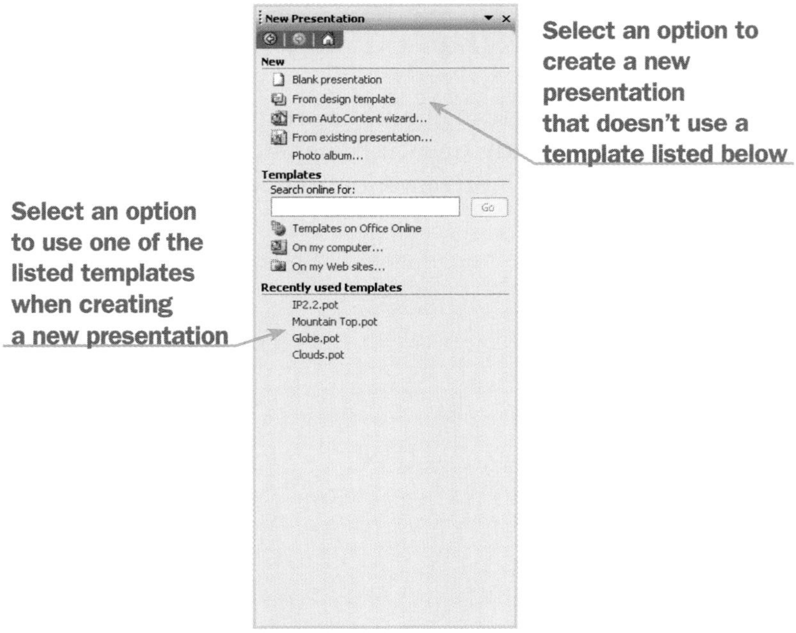

The *Blank presentation* feature lets you create a presentation from scratch, using a new combination of layout, format, colors, and styles. If you decide to create a presentation using the *From design template* option, you can choose a design template that is right for the presentation you have planned. The design templates that come with PowerPoint are already formatted with certain colors, fonts, and layouts. Click the task pane drop-down menu shown in Figure 2-2 or select a template from the list of recently used templates to access the design templates. The *AutoContent Wizard* guides you through a series of questions about the type of presentation, output options, presentation style, and presentation options. The Wizard offers ideas and an organization for a new presentation based on your answers.

> **Computer Concepts**
>
> Unless you have a particular reason for creating a presentation from a blank document, it is easier to use the wizard or a design template. You can always modify the presentation as you go along.

STEP-BY-STEP 2.1

1. Start PowerPoint. In the Getting Started task pane, choose **Create a new presentation**. Remember, if the task pane is not displayed, you can show it by right-clicking the Standard toolbar and clicking **Task Pane.** The New Presentation task pane appears, as shown in Figure 2-2.

2. In the New Presentation task pane, choose **From AutoContent wizard**. The AutoContent Wizard dialog box appears, as shown in Figure 2-3.

FIGURE 2-3
AutoContent Wizard dialog box

3. Read the screen and click **Next**.

4. This screen displays the types of presentations in categories that the AutoContent Wizard can help create. The wizard defaults to the General category. Click the **All** button and view all of the categories.

5. If necessary, select **Generic** as the type of presentation you are going to create. Click **Next**.

6. If necessary, choose **On-screen presentation** as the output. Click **Next**.

7. In the Presentation title box, key **Virtual Zoo**.

8. In the Footer box, key **Visit our website – www.cityzoo.org**.

9. Click the **Date last updated** box to remove the check mark. Click **Next**.

<u>**STEP-BY-STEP 2.1 Continued**</u>

10. Click **Finish**. Your presentation appears on the screen, similar to Figure 2-4.

FIGURE 2-4
AutoContent presentation

11. Save the presentation as **Virtual Zoo** followed by your initials and leave it open for the next Step-by-Step.

Applying a Design Template

You can use a design template to change the appearance of your slides without changing the content. *Design templates* are predesigned graphic styles that you can apply to your slides. You can change the color scheme, font, formatting, and layout of your slides in a design template to create a different look.

To view the available design template options, click Slide Design in the drop-down menu on the task pane. The Slide Design task pane displays all the available design templates. When you hover over (place your mouse pointer over an object without clicking) a design template, the name of the template appears and an

> **Hot Tip**
>
> When using the AutoContent Wizard to create a presentation, PowerPoint automatically inserts the registered User Information on the opening slide. You can change this information by selecting the **Tools** menu, choosing **Options**, and clicking the **General** tab.

arrow for a drop-down menu (Figure 2-5) appears on the right side of the design template. The menu options apply the template to all of the slides in your presentation or to only select slides. There is also an option to view the templates in the large or small format. Choose Apply to All Slides from the drop-down menu to change all your slides to the new design.

FIGURE 2-5
Design template drop-down menu

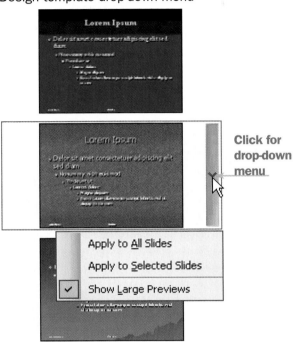

If you cannot find any templates that you like, you can choose one from another location, download one from the Internet, or create one of your own. To choose another template from Microsoft's Web site, scroll to the bottom of the Slide Design task pane and click the slide that says "Design Templates on Microsoft Office Online" if it is available. You must have an Internet connection to do this. To choose a template from another location, click the Browse button at the bottom of the Slide Design task pane and select the template from the correct file location.

STEP-BY-STEP 2.2

1. If necessary, click the **Design** button to display the task pane. Select **Slide Design** from the task pane drop-down menu if it is not already selected.

2. At the bottom of the Slide Design task pane, click on the **Browse** button. The Apply Design Template dialog box appears. Locate the template named **Step2-2.pot** in the student data files. (Depending on the version of Windows and the settings on your computer, the .file name extensions might not be displayed.) Click on the file name and click the **Apply** button. PowerPoint applies the template to all of the slides in the presentation, and adds the template to the Slide Design task pane. The current presentation is displayed on your screen with a new design. Your screen should look like Figure 2-6.

FIGURE 2-6
Opening slide with new design template applied

3. Save and leave the presentation open for the next Step-by-Step.

Changing Color Scheme

To apply a different color scheme to your presentation, while still in the Slide Design task pane, click Color Schemes in the task pane, hover over the color scheme you want to apply, and click the drop-down arrow. To apply the scheme to all of your slides, click Apply to All Slides. This feature is also available from the task pane drop-down menu by clicking Slide Design – Color Schemes.

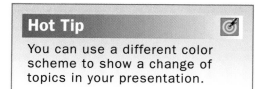

Hot Tip

You can use a different color scheme to show a change of topics in your presentation.

You can apply the color scheme to only specific slides by selecting the slides from the Slide Preview pane or using the Slide Sorter view. You can select more than one slide by holding down the Ctrl button while clicking the slides. To apply color schemes to only the selected slides, click Apply to Selected Slides from the drop-down menu.

Adding or Changing Slide Animation

When you *animate* an object, text, or slide, you add a sound or visual effect. Animation enhances your presentation and increases audience interest. To add or change slide animation, while still in the Slide Design task pane, click Animation Schemes in the task pane. This feature is also available from the task pane drop-down menu by clicking Slide Design – Animation Schemes.

You can apply an animation to the current (displayed) slide or to all slides. This feature applies animation to all text items on the slide. You can also individually animate text boxes, pictures, and transitions into the slide. You will learn how to do this in a following lesson. The two buttons at the bottom of the task pane allow you to preview the animation. Click Play to activate the animation in the current screen. The Slide Show button shows the slide in full screen, as it would appear in a slide show.

STEP-BY-STEP 2.3

1. Select the Slide Design task pane, if necessary, and click **Slide Design - Animation Schemes** in the task pane.

2. In the task pane, scroll down and click **Pinwheel**, as shown in Figure 2-7.

FIGURE 2-7
Animation schemes

STEP-BY-STEP 2.3 Continued

3. Click **Apply to All Slides**.

4. Click **Play** (if necessary) to view the slide animation.

5. Save and leave the presentation open for the next Step-by-Step.

Formatting a Single Slide

You can use a design template to change the appearance of a single slide without changing the rest of the slides in the presentation. Click the Design button to display the Slide Design task pane. Previously, you learned how to apply these features to an entire presentation. In this Step-by-Step you apply these features to a single slide.

STEP-BY-STEP 2.4

1. Select slide **9**. Click the **Design** button on the Formatting toolbar to display the Slide Design task pane (if it is not already selected).

2. Click **Design Templates** to display the templates in the task pane.

3. Scroll down and hover over the design template named **Clipboard.pot**. When the list arrow appears, click **Apply to Selected Slides**. The current slide is displayed on your screen with a new design.

Hot Tip

If Clipboard.pot is not displayed with your design templates, you can locate it in the student data files.

4. Click **Color Schemes** in the task pane. Select the first color scheme in the list.

5. Click **Animation Schemes** in the task pane.

6. Select **Unfold** from the **Animation Schemes** menu. Do *not* click the Apply to Master button or the Apply to All Slides buttons, because you are applying the animation only to this slide.

7. View the presentation to see your additions. Save the presentation and leave it open for the next Step-by-Step.

Using the Slide Master

The *slide master* controls the formatting for all the slides in the presentation. You can use the slide master to change such items as the font, size, color, style, alignment, spacing, and background. Changing the slide master affects the appearance of all of the slides in a presentation associated with that master slide, and gives them a consistent look. You can add headers and footers to slides and place an object, such as a logo or graphic, on every slide by placing the object on the slide master. To access the master title slide, shown in Figure 2-8, choose Master from the View menu, and then select Slide Master from the submenu.

FIGURE 2-8
Slide master

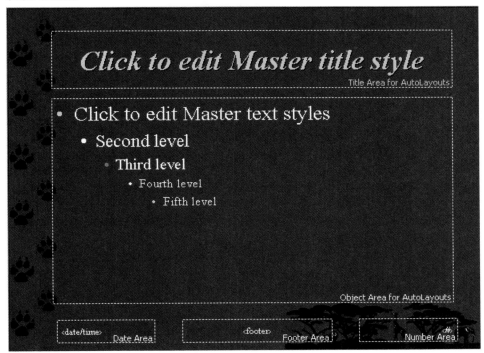

When you are in the Slide Master view, the Slide/Outline pane displays the title master and the slide master. Presentations can contain more than one design. The Slide Master view will display a master slide for each design that has been applied to the presentation. See Figure 2-9. As you hover over a slide or title master in the Slide/Outline pane, the name of the template and the slide numbers where it is applied appear.

FIGURE 2-9
Slide and title masters in Slide/Outline pane

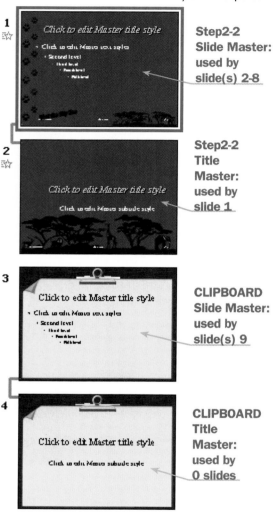

To make changes to a slide or title master, click on the correct master to display it in the slide workspace. When you have finished making changes to the slide master, click Close on the Slide Master View toolbar shown in Figure 2-10.

FIGURE 2-10
Slide Master View toolbar

PowerPoint has other masters that work like the slide master. The *handout master* lets you add items that you want to appear on all the handouts for a presentation. Masters frequently include a logo, the date, the time, and page numbers. On the *notes master*, include any text or formatting that you want to appear on all your speaker notes. Click View, choose Master from the menu, and choose the specific master from the submenu.

> **Computer Concepts**
>
> You can override the formats applied to the presentation by the slide master. Simply make changes directly to individual slides.

S TEP-BY-STEP 2.5

1. Click slide 1. Click **View** and choose **Master** on the menu and **Slide Master** on the submenu. Select the master slide called *Step2-2 Slide Master*.

2. Click the **Insert WordArt** button from the drawing toolbar at the bottom of the PowerPoint screen. The WordArt Gallery dialog box appears, as shown in Figure 2-11.

FIGURE 2-11
WordArt Gallery dialog box

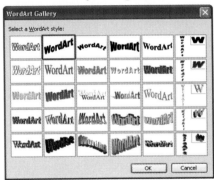

3. Click the WordArt example that is located at the top of the second column and click **OK**. The Edit WordArt Text dialog box appears.

4. In the *Text* box, key **Visit the City Zoo**, and click **OK**. The words you keyed appear on the slide template.

STEP-BY-STEP 2.5 Continued

5. Resize the WordArt by "grabbing" the top-right handle. Drag the handle down and to the left. Click the WordArt and drag it to the bottom of the slide. Drop it to the right of the animal track picture. See Figure 2-12 for proper size and placement.

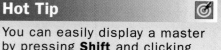

Hot Tip

You can easily display a master by pressing **Shift** and clicking the **Normal View**, **Slide Sorter View**, or the **Slide Show** buttons in the bottom-left corner of your screen.

FIGURE 2-12
Positioning and resizing the picture on the slide master

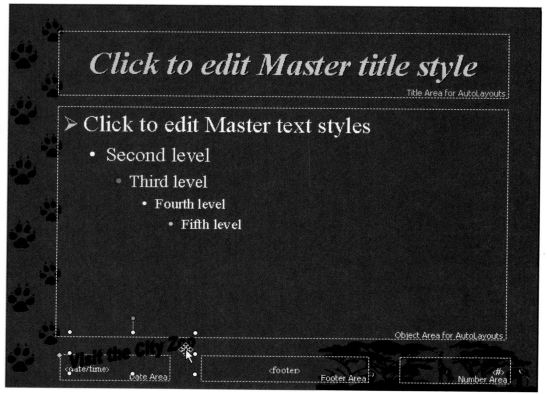

6. Click **Close Master View** on the Slide Master View toolbar. Scroll through the presentation to see that the WordArt appears on all slides except for the first and last slides.

7. Save the presentation, and leave it open for the next Step-by-Step.

Working with Text

Adding Text to Slides

When the AutoContent Wizard helps you create a presentation, it creates placeholders on each slide that tell you what kind of information can go there. A *placeholder* reserves a space in the presentation for the type of information you want to insert. To replace a text placeholder, click the text. A box with a hashed-line border appears around the text. You can then select the existing text and key whatever you like.

If you cannot see the text clearly, it is helpful to use the Zoom feature. Click the arrow next to the Zoom box on the Standard toolbar. The menu contains preset percentages so you can enlarge or reduce the size of the presentation on screen or you can choose Fit to allow PowerPoint to use all the space available to display the slide.

You can also replace text on a slide by keying the text in the Outline view of the Slide/Outline pane. Select the text that you want to replace, and key the new text.

> **Computer Concepts**
>
> To find and replace text, open the **Edit** menu and choose **Replace**. In the first box, key the text you want to find. In the second box, key the new replacement text. Click **Find Next** to find the next occurrence, **Replace** to replace the next occurrence, or **Replace All** to replace all occurrences.

79%

S TEP-BY-STEP 2.6

1. Display slide **2**. Highlight the words *State the purpose of the discussion* and *Identify yourself*. A box appears around all of the text. Key the following:

   These are some of the animals you will find at the City Zoo.

2. Click slide **3**. Highlight the words *Topics of Discussion*, and key **Gorilla**.

3. Highlight the rest of the words on the slide that read *State the main ideas you'll be talking about*. A box appears around all of the text. Key the following:

   - **Lives in Africa**
   - **Found in tropical rain forests, and lowland forests**
   - **Eats plants, ants, and termites**
   - **Lives 25 - 30 years in the wild**
   - **Lives in small families of 6 - 8**
   - **Adult eats about 50 lbs of food a day**
   - **Endangered**

> **Hot Tip**
>
> You can add text to the top or bottom of a slide by inserting a header or footer. You can also add the slide number, date, or time in a header or footer. Open the **View** menu and choose **Header and Footer**. Select the options and key the text you want.

STEP-BY-STEP 2.6 Continued

Bold the text you just keyed. See Figure 2-13.

FIGURE 2-13
Slide 3 with new text

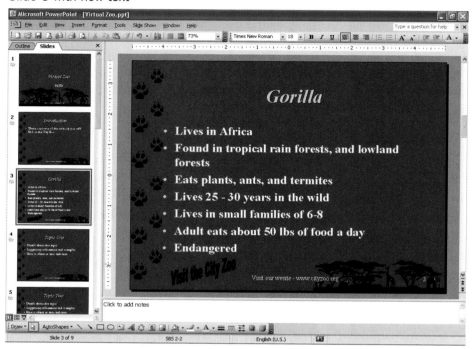

4. You have learned how to change the text by editing it directly on the slide. You will edit the rest of the presentation using the Outline mode. Click the **Outline** tab in the Slide Preview pane. Highlight the text next to the icon for slide **4** that reads *Topic One*. Key the word **Zebra**. Highlight the rest of the text and replace it with the following:

- **Lives in Africa**
- **Found on savannas (grassy plains)**
- **Herbivore (only eats plants and grasses)**
- **Lives 25 - 30 years in the wild**
- **Very social, lives in large herds**
- **Needs to drink water often**
- **Can run up to 40 mph**

STEP-BY-STEP 2.6 Continued

Bold the text you just keyed. See Figure 2-14.

FIGURE 2-14
Slide 4 with new text

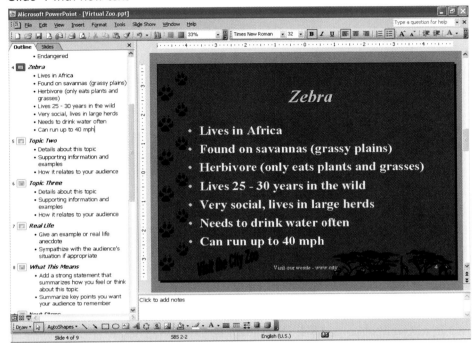

5. On slide **5**, replace the words *Topic Two* with **Orangutan**. Highlight all the text below the title and key the following:

- **Name means "man of the forest"**
- **Lives in Southeast Asia**
- **Found in tropical rain forests**
- **Omnivore (eats plants and animals such as leaves and insects)**
- **Lives 30 - 45 years in the wild**
- **Endangered**

Bold the text you just keyed.

6. Replace *Topic Three* on slide **6** with **African Elephant**. Replace the rest of the text with:

- **Lives in Africa**
- **Found on grasslands**
- **Eats roots, grasses, leaves, fruit, and bark**
- **Lives 60 - 70 years in the wild**
- **Lives in family groups**
- **Largest land mammals**
- **Endangered**

Bold the text you just keyed.

STEP-BY-STEP 2.6 Continued

7. Replace *Real Life* on slide **7** with **Tiger**. As you key the following text, notice that PowerPoint automatically adjusts the font size to fit the slide.

   - **Lives in Asia**
   - **Found in forests**
   - **Carnivore (eats other animals)**
   - **Lives 10 - 15 years**
   - **Mostly solitary**
   - **Very good nighttime vision**
   - **Retractable claws**
   - **Needs an area of 10 - 30 square miles to provide enough prey to survive**
   - **Good swimmers**
   - **Endangered**

   Bold the text you just keyed.

8. Replace *What This Means* on slide **8** with **Lion**. Replace the rest of the text with the following:

   - **Lives in Africa**
   - **Found in savannas, open woodlands, and brush**
   - **Carnivore**
   - **Lives 10 - 15 years in the wild**
   - **Lives in a pride that contains 4 - 20 members**
   - **Runs up to 35 mph and can jump 30 feet**

   Bold the text you just keyed.

9. On slide **9** replace *Next Steps* with **Zoo Information**. Replace the rest of the text with the following:

   - **Location: 26 Nantucket Road**
   - **Hours: 9 am – 7 pm**
   - **Cost: Adults $10.00 Children under 5 free**

   Bold the text you just keyed.

10. Click **Slide Show**, and choose **View Show** from the menu. Click the mouse to advance through the presentation.

11. Save the presentation and leave it open for the next Step-by-Step.

> ### Computer Concepts
> If you want to add text to a slide that does not have a text placeholder, click the **Text Box** button on the **Drawing** toolbar or open the **Insert** menu and choose **Text Box**.

> ### Hot Tip
> To move a text box, click to select the box, drag it, and drop it in the new location. To resize, click a handle and drag it.

Adding Notes to a Slide

To add speaker notes, click in the notes pane below the slide or switch to the Notes Page view by opening the View menu and choosing Notes Page. If the text is too small to read in the Notes Page view, you can increase the size by using the Zoom feature on the Standard toolbar. A good PowerPoint presentation generally contains brief, main points about the subject. Use the speaker notes to remind yourself of any additional information you need to include in your speech.

Change Alignment, Spacing, Case, and Tabs

To change text alignment, select the text and click one of the alignment buttons on the toolbar. Text can be left-aligned, centered, right-aligned, or justified.

Line spacing identifies the size of the area between the lines of text or the area before or after each paragraph. To change spacing, select the text, open the Format menu, click Line Spacing, and make changes in the Line Spacing dialog box.

Case identifies the capitalization used in displayed text. To change the case of text, select the text, open the Format menu, and click Change Case. Choose one of the five options in the Change Case dialog box.

A tab is used to align text inside the document's left and right margins. To set or clear tabs, display the ruler by choosing Ruler from the View menu. Set a tab by selecting the text, clicking the tab button at the left end of the horizontal ruler to select the type of tab, and clicking the location on the ruler where the tab will be placed. Clear a tab by dragging the tab marker off the ruler.

S TEP-BY-STEP 2.7

1. Return to the Normal view if necessary, and select the text on slide **9** below the slide title *Zoo Information*.

2. Click the **Center** button on the toolbar.

3. Open the **Format** menu and click **Line Spacing**. The Line Spacing dialog box appears as shown in Figure 2-15. In the Line Spacing section, click the up arrow until it reads **2**. Click **OK**.

FIGURE 2-15
Line Spacing dialog box

STEP-BY-STEP 2.7 Continued

4. Highlight the words *Location: 26 Nantucket Road* in the first sentence. Open the **Format** menu and click **Change Case**. The Change Case dialog box appears as shown in Figure 2-16. Choose **UPPERCASE** and click **OK**.

FIGURE 2-16
Change Case dialog box

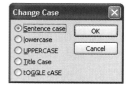

5. Repeat Step 4 for the words *Hours: 9 am – 7 pm* in the second sentence and *Cost: Adults $10.00 Children under 5 free* in the third sentence.

6. Select all of the text on the slide and click the Bullets icon on the Formatting toolbar to remove the bullets from the slide.

7. Place your cursor between the words *$10.00* and *Children* and tap the **Enter** key.

8. Save the presentation and leave it open for the next Step-by-Step.

Working with Bullets

If you want bullets on a slide, you can add them by selecting the text or placeholder and clicking the Bullets button on the toolbar. You can customize a bulleted list after it has been created. You can change the appearance of the bullets—such as their shape, size, or color—and you can also adjust the distance between the bullets and the text. To change the appearance of the bullets throughout the presentation, make the changes on the slide master. You cannot select a bullet to make changes; you must select the associated text.

To change all the bullets in a bulleted list, select the entire list. When you click Format and click Bullets and Numbering, the Bullets and Numbering dialog box appears, as shown in Figure 2-17. On the Bulleted tab, you can select a preset bullet or add a graphical bullet by clicking the Picture button. You can also change the color or the bullet size in relation to the text.

> **Computer Concepts**
>
> If your list is numbered rather than bulleted, choose the **Numbered** tab in the Bullets and Numbering dialog box to customize the list.

FIGURE 2-17
Bullets and Numbering dialog box

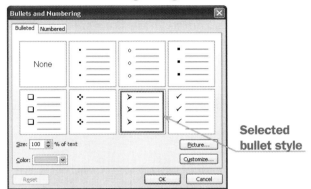

Selected bullet style

STEP-BY-STEP 2.8

1. Display the slide master by opening the **View** menu, selecting **Master,** and selecting **Slide Master** from the submenu.

2. Choose the **Step2-2 Slide Master** if it is not already displayed.

3. Highlight **Click to edit Master text styles**. Be sure to choose "text," not "title."

4. Open the **Format** menu and choose **Bullets and Numbering**.

5. Choose the **Bulleted** tab (if it is not already selected), as shown in Figure 2-17.

6. Select the bullet style shown in Figure 2-17 with the box around it. (Your bullet choices may not match the figure exactly.) If that bullet is not available, click another appropriate one. Click the down arrow in the Size box until it reads **90**. Click **OK**.

7. Close the Slide Master and advance through the presentation to view the changes.

8. Save the presentation and leave it open for the next Step-by-Step.

Extra Challenge

Change the bullets in your presentation to arrows, dots, stars, check marks, or some other character by choosing **Bullets and Numbering** from the **Format** menu.

Hot Tip

Tap the **Tab** key to demote a bullet one level.

Changing Text Appearance

If you use a design template, the format of the text on your slides is predetermined so that the layout, color scheme, font, size, and style are consistent throughout the presentation. You can alter the format of individual slides by making changes directly to the slides. You change the font, font style, size, effects, and color in the Font dialog box, shown in Figure 2-18, which you access by choosing Font from the Format menu.

FIGURE 2-18
Font dialog box

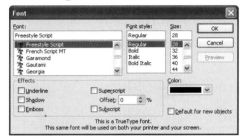

You can also use the Formatting toolbar as a shortcut to changing the font, font size, font style, and font color, as shown in Figure 2-19. The Increase Font Size and Decrease Font Size buttons allow you to change the font size quickly in preset increments.

FIGURE 2-19
Formatting toolbar

S TEP-BY-STEP 2.9

1. Display slide **9** and highlight the text below the title.

2. Open the **Format** menu and choose **Font**.

3. In the Font box of the Font dialog box, choose **Freestyle Script** or another font that appears similar to the font in Figure 2-20. In the Size box, choose **28** if necessary. Click **OK**.

4. Save the presentation and leave it open for the next Step-by-Step.

STEP-BY-STEP 2.9 Continued

FIGURE 2-20
Slide 9 with Freestyle Script font

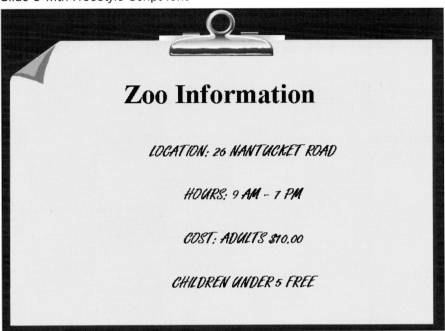

Check Spelling, Style, and Usage

Automatic spell-checking identifies misspellings and words that are not in its dictionary by underlining them with a wavy red line immediately after you key them. To correct a misspelled word, position the pointer on the underlined word and click with the right mouse button. A shortcut menu appears with a list of correctly spelled words. Click the suggestion that you want with the left mouse button and PowerPoint replaces the misspelled word. You can turn the automatic spell checker on, off, or change the way that it checks your document. Open the Tools menu, select Options, and click the Spelling and Style tab.

You can also check the spelling in a presentation after it is complete by clicking the Spelling button on the Standard toolbar. The Spelling dialog box contains options for ignoring words, making changes, or adding words to your own custom dictionary.

Another useful PowerPoint tool is the Thesaurus. To use the Thesaurus, select the word you want to check, open the Tools menu, and click Thesaurus. The Research task pane appears and offers a selection of alternative words with the same or similar meanings.

STEP-BY-STEP 2.10

1. Click slide **1** so that it is displayed. Open the **Tools** menu and click **Spelling**.

2. Correct any errors found by the spell checker.

3. Save the presentation and leave it open for the next Step-by-Step.

An effective presentation should be consistent, error-free, and visually appealing. PowerPoint helps you determine if your presentation conforms to the standards of good style. For instance, title text size should be at least 36 points. A light bulb appears (see Figure 2-21), to alert you to problems with visual clarity such as appropriate font usage and legibility, inconsistent capitalization, and end punctuation. To make changes, click the light bulb and choose an option from the menu.

FIGURE 2-21
Light bulb

If it is installed, an Office Assistant also appears to offer help using PowerPoint. You can control how the Office Assistant and light bulb work. Click the Office Assistant and click the Options button. The Office Assistant dialog box appears. This dialog box enables you to choose the way tips are displayed.

In the Style Options dialog box, you can customize what PowerPoint considers style errors or inconsistencies. Open the Tools menu, choose Options, and click the Spelling and Style tab. Click the Style Options button to access the Style Options dialog box as shown in Figure 2-22. Make any changes you want or click the Defaults button to restore the original settings.

FIGURE 2-22
Style Options dialog box

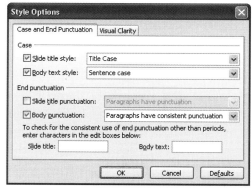

Adding Slides

Adding New Slides

You can add a slide to a presentation by clicking the New Slide button on the toolbar or by choosing New Slide from the Insert menu. In the Normal view, PowerPoint places the new slide after the currently displayed slide. Choosing New Slide displays the Slide Layout dialog box in the task pane, which allows you to choose a layout for the new slide. The Slide Layout task pane has 29 layouts. Choose a layout and apply it to the slide as you did earlier.

> **Hot Tip**
>
> If you have problems while creating a presentation, you can use the Office Assistant. If the Office Assistant is not visible, choose **Show the Office Assistant** from the **Help** menu.

STEP-BY-STEP 2.11

1. Display slide **3** titled *Gorilla*. The area on the left of the status bar should read *Slide 3 of 9*.

2. Click the **New Slide** button on the toolbar. The Slide Layout task pane is displayed.

3. Click the layout in the task pane named *Content*, if it is not already chosen.

4. Click the icon that reads *Insert Picture*, as shown in Figure 2-23. The Insert Picture dialog box appears.

FIGURE 2-23
Insert Picture

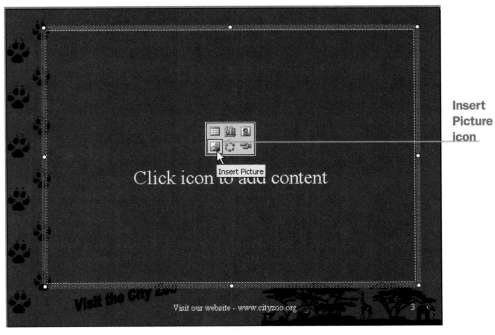

STEP-BY-STEP 2.11 Continued

5. Locate the picture named Gorilla.jpg and select it. Click the Insert button to insert the picture on the slide. Adjust the size of the picture and place it on the slide so that it looks similar to Figure 2-24.

FIGURE 2-24
Proper placement of the picture

6. Display slide **6** titled *Orangutan*. The area on the left of the status bar should read *Slide 6 of 10*.

7. Click the **New Slide** button on the toolbar. The Slide Layout task pane is displayed.

8. Click the layout in the task pane named *Blank*, if it is not already chosen.

9. Open the **Insert** menu and choose **Movies and Sounds** from the menu, and select **Movie from File** from the submenu. The Insert Movie dialog box appears, as shown in Figure 2-25.

FIGURE 2-25
Insert Movie dialog box

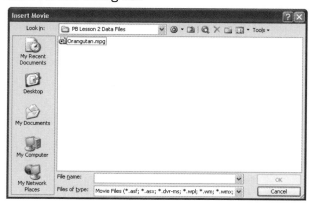

STEP-BY-STEP 2.11 Continued

10. Locate the movie named **Orangutan.mpg** and select it. Click the **OK** button to insert the movie on the slide. A dialog box appears asking if you want the movie to start automatically or when clicked. Click **Automatically**. See Figure 2-26. Adjust the size of the movie and center it on the slide.

FIGURE 2-26
Movie dialog box

11. Save and close the presentation.

Adding New Slides from Other Presentations

Another way to add a slide is to copy it from another presentation. Open the Insert menu and choose Slides from Files. Locate and open the presentation from which you want to copy a slide. Click Display if necessary. Select the slides you want to copy and click Insert. PowerPoint inserts the slide after the one displayed on the screen. You can choose to keep the same format of the slides that you are copying into the presentation by placing a check next to *Keep source formatting* on the Slide Finder dialog box.

STEP-BY-STEP 2.12

1. Locate and open the presentation called **Step2-12.ppt** in the data files. View the presentation and close it when you are finished.

2. Locate and open your presentation (*Virtual Zoo*). Display slide **5** titled *Zebra*. The area on the left of the status bar should read *Slide 5 of 11*.

3. Open the **Insert** menu and choose **Slides from Files**. The Slide Finder dialog box appears.

4. Click the **Browse** button. The Browse dialog box appears. Locate the **Step2-12.ppt** file again, and click the **Open** button. The Slide Finder dialog box appears again (see Figure 2-27), but this time it contains the slides from the *IP2.14* presentation.

FIGURE 2-27
Slide Finder dialog box

STEP-BY-STEP 2.12 Continued

5. Click the **Insert All** button, and then click the **Close** button.

6. View the presentation and notice that all of the slides are inserted into your presentation. The formatting from the *Virtual Zoo* presentation is applied to the new slides.

7. Make any necessary formatting changes to display the text and graphics correctly.

8. Save the presentation and leave it open for the next Step-by-Step.

Arranging Slides

You can easily move slides around in a presentation by using the Slide Sorter feature on the View menu. You can drag the slides to any position in a presentation.

STEP-BY-STEP 2.13

1. Switch to the Slide Sorter view by clicking **View** and choosing **Slide Sorter** from the menu.

2. Drag slide **7** (the picture of the hippopotamus) so that it is between slide **11** (the slide about the hippopotamus) and slide **12** (the slide about the giraffe). See Figure 2-28 to see how your screen should look.

FIGURE 2-28
Slide Sorter View

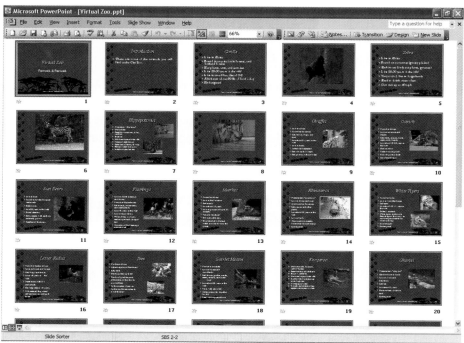

STEP-BY-STEP 2.13 Continued

3. Drag the current slide **7** (the picture of the elephant) so that it is between slide **29** (the slide about the elephant) and slide **30** (the slide about the tiger).

4. Continue to arrange the slides by moving the slides that have the pictures of the tiger and lion follow the slide that tells about the animal.

5. Switch back to the Normal view and view the presentation.

6. Save the presentation and leave it open for the next Step-by-Step.

Use Slide Transitions

When you run a presentation, *slide transitions* determine how one slide is removed from the screen and how the next one appears. You can set the transitions between slides by opening the Slide Show menu, clicking Slide Transition, and making choices in the Slide Transition task pane shown in Figure 2-29.

FIGURE 2-29
Slide Transition task pane

The *Apply to selected slides* portion of the dialog box displays a list of effects. You can select the speed at which a slide displays and add a sound under *Modify transition*. In the *Advance slide* section, you determine whether to advance the slides manually by clicking the mouse or set the timing to advance slides automatically. To set slides to advance automatically, click *Automatically after* and enter the number of seconds you want the slide to be displayed

Computer Concepts

If you choose Random Transition in the list box, PowerPoint randomly chooses a transition effect for each slide when you run the presentation.

on the screen. In the *Sound* section you can choose a sound effect that will play while the slide transition occurs. If you click *Apply to All Slides,* the selections you made affect all slides in the presentation. You can apply a transition to several slides by holding the Control (Ctrl) key down, and clicking on the slides in the Outline/Slide pane.

STEP-BY-STEP 2.14

1. Select slide **1**. Open the **Slide Show** menu and choose **Slide Transition**. The Slide Transition task pane is displayed, as shown in Figure 2-29.

2. Choose **Cover Right-Down** in the list box. Choose **Medium** as the speed. In the *Advance slide* section, **On mouse click** should be chosen and no sound should be selected in the *Sound* section.

3. Select slide **32**. Choose **Wipe Up** in the list box. Choose **Slow** as the speed.

4. Select slides **2–31** by holding down the **Shift** key and clicking on the slides **2** and **31**. Choose **Newsflash** from the list box. Choose **Medium** as the speed.

5. Save and close the presentation.

SUMMARY

In this lesson, you learned:

- You can use PowerPoint to create a new presentation and apply design templates, color schemes, slide animations, and text formatting.
- You can use the slide master to make changes.
- You can change the appearance of text and bullets in PowerPoint.
- You can add a slide to a PowerPoint presentation.
- You can add slides from an existing presentation.
- You can use the Slide Sorter view to arrange slides.
- You can check spelling and style.
- You can use slide transitions.

VOCABULARY *Review*

Define the following terms:

Animate	Design template	Placeholder
AutoContent Wizard	Handout master	Slide master
Blank Presentation	Notes master	Slide transitions

REVIEW *Questions*

MATCHING

Write the letter of the term in the right column that best matches the description in the left column.

Column 1	**Column 2**
___ 1. Controls formatting for all slides in a presentation	**A.** AutoContent Wizard
___ 2. Guides you through a series of questions about the type of presentation, output options, presentation style, and presentation options to offer ideas and an organization for a new presentation based on your answers	**B.** slide transition
	C. slide master
	D. design template
	E. Outline view
___ 3. Adding sound effects or special visuals	**F.** animate
___ 4. Determines how one slide is removed from the screen and the next one appears	**G.** slide layout
___ 5. Predesigned graphic styles that can be applied to your slides	

WRITTEN QUESTIONS

Write a brief answer to the following questions.

1. What option would you use to create a presentation from scratch using the layout, format, colors, and style you prefer?

2. What option guides you through a series of questions about the type of presentation, output options, presentation style, and presentation options?

3. What three ways can you trigger an object to be animated?

4. How do you display the Outlining toolbar?

5. What determines how one slide is removed from the screen and how the next one appears?

PROJECTS

 PROJECT 2-1

1. Start PowerPoint.

2. Open the presentation **Project2-1.ppt** from the data files.

3. Save the presentation as **Seven Wonders** followed by your initials.

4. Switch to **Slide Sorter** view. Move slide **4** so that it appears between slides 2 and 3.

5. Set the slide transition for all slides so the effect is **Box Out** and the speed is **Slow**.

6. Switch to **Slide Show** view and run the presentation on your computer.

7. Save the presentation and print it as handouts with four slides on a page. Leave the presentation open for the next project.

PROJECT 2-2

1. Adjust the text (not the titles) on each slide so that it is centered within the textbox.

2. Change the font size to **22**.

PROJECT 2-3

1. Add a transition of your choice to each slide.

2. Save and print the entire presentation as handouts with six slides on a page.

3. Close the presentation and exit PowerPoint.

WEB*Project*

PROJECT 2-4

1. With your instructor's permission, search the Internet for sites that have PowerPoint design templates. Use the sites to get ideas for creating your own design template.

2. Research the Microsoft Web site at www.microsoft.com to learn how to create your own design templates.

3. Create your own design template. Save it as **Design Template** followed by your initials. Print the template.

TEAMWORK*Project*

PROJECT 2-5

1. In a small group, use the AutoContent Wizard to create a presentation that sells a product or service of your choice.

2. Print handouts of your presentation using six slides per page.

3. Take turns giving the presentation to your group. Save the file as **AutoContent Wizard** followed by your initials.

CRITICAL*Thinking*

ACTIVITY 2-1

Use the AutoContent Wizard and the skills you learned in this lesson to create a presentation for an organization to which you belong. Be sure to check your presentation for correct spelling, punctuation, and grammar usage. Save and print the entire presentation as handouts with six slides on a page. Save the file as **Organization** followed by your initials.

ACTIVITY 2-2

Create a presentation using the ideas you organized in Critical Thinking Activity 1-2 in Lesson 1. Choose a design template and clip art. Include slide transitions and animation. Run the presentation for your class. Save the file as **Organization2** followed by your initials.

ENHANCING POWERPOINT PRESENTATIONS

OBJECTIVES

In this lesson, you will:

- Build and modify an organization chart.
- Create and modify tables.
- Add a header or footer.
- Draw an object.
- Add shapes and apply formatting.
- Fill an object.
- Scale and size an object.
- Create a text box.

Estimated Time: 1.5 hours

Working with Organization Charts

Organization charts are useful for showing relationships within an organization. To add an organization chart to a slide, you can use the Diagram or Organization Chart slide layout. This layout contains a placeholder for an organization chart. Double-click the placeholder to open the Diagram Gallery dialog box, which displays different diagram options, as shown in Figure 3-1. Click the Organization Chart icon and then click OK.

FIGURE 3-1
Diagram Gallery dialog box

To fill in the chart, click in a box and key text. Use the box tools on the icon bar to add more boxes to the organization chart. Click the tool on the icon bar for the box you want to create and then click the box in the chart to which you want to attach it. Add a chart title by replacing the text placeholder. When you are ready to return to the presentation, click the Close box and choose to update the object when a message box appears.

STEP-BY-STEP 3.1

1. Open **Step3-1** from the data files.

2. Save the presentation as **US Government** followed by your initials.

3. Click the **New Slide** button on the Formatting toolbar to add another slide to the presentation.

4. Click on the first slide to select it.

5. Click on the slide and click the **Design** button on the Formatting toolbar to open the Slide Design task pane.

6. Choose **Slide Layout** from the drop-down menu in the Slide Design task pane. The Slide Layout dialog box appears in the task pane.

7. Under *Text Layouts*, select the layout named **Title Slide** and click it to apply it to the slide. Click in the box that says *Click to add title*, and key **THE GOVERNMENT OF THE UNITED STATES** in all capital letters. Click in the box that says *Click to add subtitle*, and key **An Organizational Chart**.

8. Select the second slide. Under *Other Layouts,* select the layout named **Title and Diagram or Organization Chart** and click it to apply it to the slide. The slide displays with a placeholder for a diagram or an organization chart. Double-click the placeholder.

9. The Diagram Gallery appears, as shown in Figure 3-1. Click the **Organization Chart** icon if necessary and click **OK**. The chart template appears on the slide and the Organization Chart toolbar appears, as shown in Figure 3-2.

FIGURE 3-2
Chart template and Organization Chart toolbar

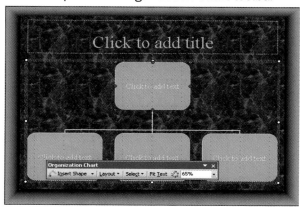

STEP-BY-STEP 3.1 Continued

10. Click in the top box, key **The Constitution**, and **bold** the text.

11. Click in the first text box on the second level, key **Legislative Branch**, and **bold** the text.

12. Click in the middle text box on the second level, key **Executive Branch,** and **bold** the text.

13. Click in the third text box on the second level, key **Judicial Branch**, and **bold** the text.

14. Click the text box that contains **Legislative Branch**, click the arrow on the **Insert Shape** button on the Organization Chart toolbar, and then click **Subordinate**. Notice that a new level is added to the chart.

15. In the box you just added, key **The Congress** and **bold** the text.

16. Click the text box that contains **Executive Branch,** click the arrow on the **Insert Shape** button on the Organization Chart toolbar, and then click **Subordinate**.

17. In the box you just added, key **President** and **bold** the text.

18. Click the **Judicial Branch** box, click the **Insert Shape** list arrow, and then click **Subordinate** to add a new box on the next level.

> **Hot Tip**
>
> If you make a mistake, you can tap **Ctrl+Z** to undo your previous actions.

19. In the box you just added, key **The Supreme Court of the United States**, and **bold** the text.

20. Notice that the text you keyed will not fit in the shape. **Right-click** on the shape and a menu appears. Click **Format AutoShape**, as shown in Figure 3-3. The Format AutoShape dialog box appears.

FIGURE 3-3
Menu

STEP-BY-STEP 3.1 Continued

21. Click the **Text Box** tab if necessary, and click the box next to **Word wrap text in AutoShape** so a check appears showing the feature is selected, as shown in Figure 3-4. Click **OK** to close the dialog box. Notice that the text fits within the AutoShape.

FIGURE 3-4
Select word wrap

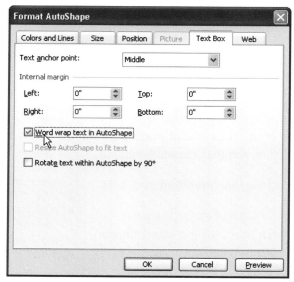

22. Click the **The Congress** box again. Click the **Insert Shape** list arrow, and then click **Assistant** to add a new box on this level.

23. Click the **The Congress** box again. Click the **Insert Shape** list arrow, and then click **Assistant** to add another new box on this level. Two boxes are now added below the current box.

24. In the first box you just added, key **Senate**. In the second box, key **House**.

25. Click the box that says **The Supreme Court of the United States**. Click the **Insert Shape** list arrow, and then click **Assistant** to add a new box on the next level.

26. In the new box under President, key **Vice President**. Your screen should look like Figure 3-5.

STEP-BY-STEP 3.1 Continued

FIGURE 3-5
Organization chart

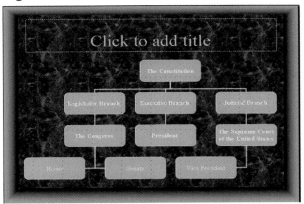

27. Save the presentation and leave it open for the next Step-by-Step.

Modifying an Organization Chart

To modify an organization chart, click the chart to activate it. To reorganize the arrangement of boxes in the chart, select a box and drag it over another box to attach it to the second box. You can change text or box formatting, including font, font style, font size, alignment, color, shadows, and borders, by double-clicking the outer edge of a box and choosing a command from the Format AutoShape dialog box. To change the background color of the chart, double-click the background and choose a command from the Format Organization Chart. Note that you cannot change colors or shadows on charts that have been created using the Autoformat feature.

S TEP-BY-STEP 3.2

1. Click the second slide to select it if it is not already selected. Select the box around the title place-holder, as shown in Figure 3-6. Tap the **Delete** key to delete the placeholder.

FIGURE 3-6
Title placeholder

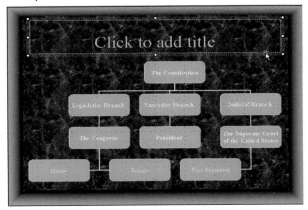

STEP-BY-STEP 3.2 Continued

2. Click the Organizational chart to select it. Click the **Autoformat** button on the Organization Chart toolbar. The Organization Chart Style Gallery dialog box appears, as shown in Figure 3-7.

FIGURE 3-7
Organization Chart Style Gallery dialog box

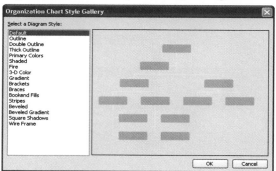

3. Click **Bookend Fills** and click **OK**. The diagram style is applied to the organization chart.

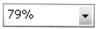

Hot Tip

You can resize the slide to make the text easier to read by increasing the number in the Zoom box on the toolbar. This does not change anything on the slide.

4. Select the words **The Constitution** in the top box of the chart. On the Formatting toolbar, change the font to **Tahoma**.

5. Click the **Vice President** box and drag it on top of the President box. A dotted outline appears around the box. Release the mouse button. The box is now a subordinate below the President box.

6. Resize and move the organizational chart so that it appears correctly aligned on the slide.

Hot Tip

Close the task pane to make your working area larger. You can open it again by clicking **View** and selecting **Task Pane** from the menu.

7. Select the entire chart and add the **Faded Zoom** animation to be triggered as **Start With Previous**.

8. Save the presentation and leave it open for the next Step-by-Step.

Working with Tables

Tables are useful when you need to include large amounts of data. The data can be displayed in rows and columns so that it is easier to read.

Hot Tip

To make formatting changes to more than one box, click and drag to place a selection box around all the boxes you want to change.

Creating Tables

To include a table on a slide, you can use the slide layout that has a placeholder for a table. When you double-click the placeholder, the Insert Table dialog box appears. Choose the number of columns and rows you want and a table is inserted on your slide. Key text in the table. Tap the Tab key to move between cells.

> **Computer Concepts**
>
> If you want to create a more complex table, use the Draw Table feature on the Tables and Borders toolbar.

S TEP-BY-STEP 3.3

1. Select the second slide if necessary. Click the **New Slide** button to access the Slide Layout task pane. Change the slide layout to the one named **Title and Content**.

2. Click the Insert Table icon in the placeholder. The Insert Table dialog box opens, as shown in Figure 3-8.

FIGURE 3-8
Insert Table dialog box

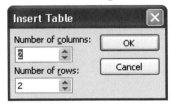

3. In the *Number of columns* box, key **3**.

4. In the *Number of rows* box, key **10**. Click **OK**. PowerPoint inserts a table with three columns and ten rows on the slide.

5. Select the Title placeholder and tap the **Delete** key. Reposition the table on the slide if necessary.

6. Click in the first cell and key the data as shown in Figure 3-9.

FIGURE 3-9
Table slide

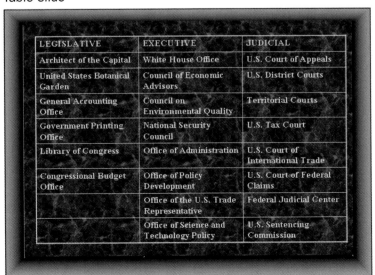

LEGISLATIVE	EXECUTIVE	JUDICIAL
Architect of the Capital	White House Office	U.S. Court of Appeals
United States Botanical Garden	Council of Economic Advisors	U.S. District Courts
General Accounting Office	Council on Environmental Quality	Territorial Courts
Government Printing Office	National Security Council	U.S. Tax Court
Library of Congress	Office of Administration	U.S. Court of International Trade
Congressional Budget Office	Office of Policy Development	U.S. Court of Federal Claims
	Office of the U.S. Trade Representative	Federal Judicial Center
	Office of Science and Technology Policy	U.S. Sentencing Commission

STEP-BY-STEP 3.3 Continued

7. Select all of the cells in the table by clicking in the top-left corner of the slide and dragging your cursor to the bottom-right corner of the slide.

8. Change the font to **Tahoma**, and the font size to **18**.

9. Save the presentation and leave it open for the next Step-by-Step.

Modifying Tables

To modify a table's borders, fill, or text boxes, select the table and choose Table from the Format menu. (A table must be selected to make this option available.) The Format Table dialog box appears, as shown in Figure 3-10.

FIGURE 3-10
Format Table dialog box

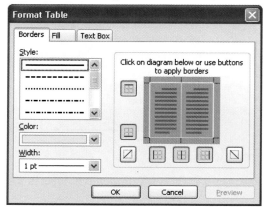

When you are modifying a table, it is helpful to display the Tables and Borders toolbar, shown in Figure 3-11. If it is not displayed, you can display it by right-clicking the Standard toolbar and choosing the toolbar you want from the menu. Using the Tables and Borders toolbar, you can insert columns and rows, merge or split cells, change the alignment and fill color, and format the borders.

FIGURE 3-11
Tables and Borders toolbar

To change the width of a column or row, click and drag a border. To insert or delete a column or row, click the Table button on the Tables and Borders toolbar and choose the appropriate command.

S TEP-BY-STEP 3.4

1. Select all of the text in the table, click the **Center** button on the Formatting toolbar, and the **Center Vertically** button on the Tables and Borders toolbar.

2. Select all of the text in the first row and display the **Format Table** dialog box, shown in Figure 3-10.

3. Click the **Fill** tab, and click the box next to Fill color so that a check appears in the box. Click the down arrow and select **Automatic** from the color palette that is displayed. Click **Semitransparent** so that a check appears in the box and click **OK**. Your slide should appear similar to Figure 3-12.

FIGURE 3-12
Completed slide

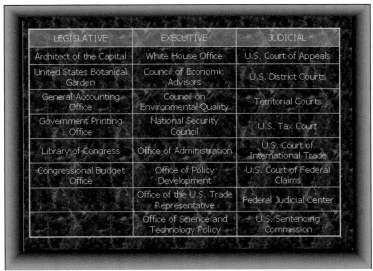

4. Save and leave the presentation open for the next Step-by-Step.

Adding a Header or Footer

Y ou can add a header or footer on the Slide Master or by selecting Header and Footer from the View menu. The AutoContent Wizard automatically creates a footer during the setup process.

When you select Header and Footer, the Header and Footer dialog box appears on the screen as shown in Figure 3-13. You can add the date and time, slide number, and any text you want to the footer of the slide. When you click the Notes and Handouts tab you also have the option of creating a header. Some items that you might include in a header or footer are the presenter's name, e-mail address, Web site address, or phone number.

FIGURE 3-13
Header and Footer dialog box

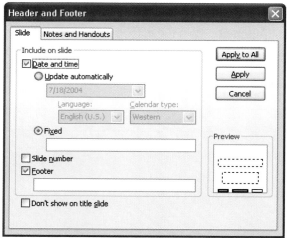

S TEP-BY-STEP 3.5

1. Select **Header and Footer** from the **View** menu. The Header and Footer dialog box appears on the screen.

2. Click in the Footer text box and key **Source: THE UNITED STATES GOVERNMENT MANUAL**. Click **Don't show on title slide** so that a check appears in the box.

3. Click the **Notes and Handouts** tab.

4. Click the **Date and time** option if it is not already selected.

5. Click **Update automatically**.

6. In the Header text box, key your name.

7. Click **Apply to All**.

8. View the presentation and the Notes Page view to see your changes.

9. Save the presentation. Print and close it.

Creating and Changing Shapes and Objects

You can add shapes and other drawing objects to your presentation by using the AutoShapes and drawing tools on the Drawing toolbar. AutoShapes are premade shapes such as circles, cones, and stars that you can include in your presentation to add interest to a slide.

Drawing an Object

The Drawing toolbar, shown in Figure 3-14, displays by default when you start PowerPoint. It contains buttons for drawing objects such as lines, circles, arrows, and squares. Click the corresponding button to activate the tool. The Rectangle tool draws rectangles and squares. The Oval tool draws ovals and circles. To use a tool, click and hold the mouse button, and then drag to draw. To create a perfect circle or square, hold down the Shift key as you drag.

FIGURE 3-14
Drawing toolbar

Adding a Shape

Add a variety of other shapes by clicking the AutoShapes tool on the Drawing toolbar. A menu appears that has lines, connectors, arrows, and other kinds of objects to help draw the shape you want. Click the slide to insert the shape with a predefined size.

Selecting an Object

When you click an inserted object to select it, little squares appear at the edges of the graphic. As you learned in Lesson 2, these small squares are called handles. They indicate that the object is selected and they allow you to manipulate the object. When you choose another tool, the selection handles around an object disappear.

Scaling and Sizing an Object

Handles do more than indicate that an object is selected. They make it easy to resize an object that is too large or too small. Select the object to make the handles appear and then drag one of the handles inward or outward to make the object smaller or larger. Changing the size of an object this way may distort the image.

To *scale* an object, hold down Shift and drag a corner handle. This maintains an object's proportions so the result is not distorted. You scale and size clip art graphics just as you do objects. Many AutoShapes have a yellow diamond adjustment handle that you can drag to change the appearance of the object.

Computer Concepts

You can size an object more precisely by clicking **Format** and choosing **AutoShape** from the menu. Click the **Size** tab and specify a height and width.

Extra Challenge

Create a new slide in the current presentation. Add an object such as clip art, WordArt, or AutoShapes to the slide. Practice resizing the object by using the scaling feature, and then resize it without using the scaling feature. When you have finished, delete the slide.

Copying or Moving an Object

To move an object, select it and then drag it into place. You can cut, copy, and paste objects the same way you do text. The Cut and Copy commands place a copy of the selected image on the Office Clipboard. Pasting an object from the Office Clipboard places the object in your drawing. You can then move it into position.

S TEP-BY-STEP 3.6

1. Open **Step3-6** from the data files.

2. Save the presentation as **Optical Illusions** followed by your initials.

3. **View** the presentation.

4. Switch to the **Normal** view if necessary, and click between slides 3 and 4. Click the **New Slide** button and access the Slide Layout task pane. Change the slide layout to the one named **Blank**.

5. Click on the new slide to select it if necessary.

6. Click the **AutoShapes** button on the Drawing toolbar. Choose **Basic Shapes** from the menu and click the **Smiley Face** icon on the submenu as shown in Figure 3-15.

FIGURE 3-15
Smiley Face on Basic Shapes menu

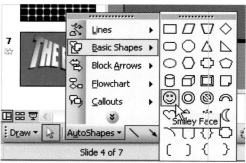

7. Click in the upper-left corner of the slide and drag to draw a box about the size of a nickel. When you release the mouse button, the smiley face appears with handles. Refer to Figure 3-16 for approximate placement and size. The initial fill color of your images may differ from the color shown in the figures.

STEP-BY-STEP 3.6 Continued

FIGURE 3-16
Slide with AutoShapes

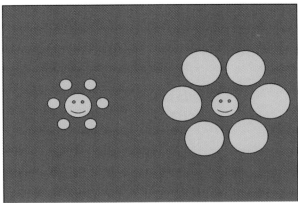

8. Right-click on the smiley face and select **Copy** from the menu.

9. Right-click on the smiley face again, and select **Paste** from the menu. Refer to Figure 3-16 for approximate placement.

10. Click the **Oval** button on the Drawing toolbar. Click above and to the left of the first smiley face you created, and draw a circle similar to Figure 3-16. The initial fill color of your images may differ from the color shown in the figures.

11. Right-click on the circle you just created, and select **Copy** from the menu. Choose **Clipboard** from the task pane menu. Click the circle you just copied five times to place five copies of the object on the slide. Arrange the circles around the first circle as shown in Figure 3-16.

12. Click the **Oval** button on the Drawing toolbar again. Click above and to the left of the second smiley face you created, and draw a circle about the size of a quarter similar to Figure 3-16.

13. Right-click on the circle you just created, and select **Copy** from the menu. Choose **Clipboard** from the task pane menu if necessary. Click the circle you just copied five times to place five copies of the object on the slide. Arrange the circles around the second circle as shown in Figure 3-16.

14. Save the presentation and leave it open for the next Step-by-Step.

Working with Objects

Once you have created an object, you can rotate, fill, scale, or size an object, as well as change its color and position. To work with an object, you must select it. When working with more than one object, you can group the items so that you can apply any changes to all of the objects at the same time.

Applying Formatting

The Drawing toolbar contains various ways to apply formatting to visual elements in a presentation. You can change the fill, line, or font color. You can also change the line, dash, or arrow style, add shadows, and make an object 3D.

Filling an Object

Select the object you want to fill and click the Fill Color button on the Drawing toolbar. When you click the down arrow, a box appears, as shown in Figure 3-17.

FIGURE 3-17
Color Fill dialog box

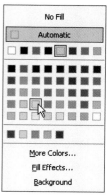

To change an object back to the default fill color, click Automatic. To choose a color in the color scheme, click one of the eight choices below Automatic. Your selected object is filled with the color you click. To fill an object with a color not in the presentation's color scheme, click More Fill Colors. To fill an object with a gradient, texture, pattern, picture, or add a shading style, click Fill Effects. The Fill Effects dialog box appears, as shown in Figure 3-18.

FIGURE 3-18
Fill Effects dialog box

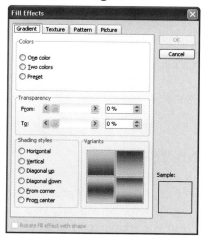

Changing Line Color

Another way to apply formatting to a drawing object is to change the line color. Click the arrow next to the Line Color button on the Drawing toolbar and click an option in the Line Color box that appears. The Line Color box is very similar to the Fill Color box.

STEP-BY-STEP 3.7

1. Double-click the first smiley face. The Format AutoShape dialog box appears. Click the arrow next to **Fill Color**. A box appears, as shown in Figure 3-17. Click the color **Yellow**.

2. In the Line section, change the weight of the line to **2.5 pt**. Click **OK** to apply the changes to the smiley face.

3. Double-click the second smiley face. Click the arrow next to **Color** in the Fill section, and click the color **Yellow**.

4. In the Line section, change the weight of the line to **2.5 pt**. Click **OK**. Your slide should look similar to Figure 3-19.

FIGURE 3-19
Colors and lines applied to AutoShapes

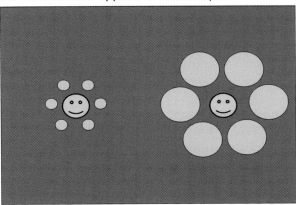

5. Save the presentation and leave it open for the next Step-by-Step.

Selecting an Object

As you learned earlier in the lesson, when you select an object, square handles surround it. To select an object, be sure the Select Objects tool is chosen on the toolbar, position the insertion point over the object, and click. The selection handles appear around the object and you can move the object. A four-sided arrow appears with the arrow pointer. To deselect an object, click another object or any blank area in the window.

Selecting More Than One Object

Sometimes you will want to select more than one object. PowerPoint gives you two ways to select more than one object. The first method is *Shift-clicking*. In the second method, you draw a selection box around a group of objects.

Shift-Clicking

To Shift-click, hold down the Shift key and click each of the objects you want to select. Use this method when you need to select objects that are not close to each other or when the objects you need to select are near other objects you do not want to select. If you select an object by accident, click it again to deselect it—still holding down the Shift key.

Drawing a Selection Box

Using the Select Objects tool, you can drag a selection box around a group of objects. Use a selection box when all of the objects you want to select are near each other and can be surrounded with a box. Be sure your selection box is large enough to enclose all the selection handles of the various objects. If you miss a handle, the corresponding item will not be selected.

Combining Methods

You can also combine these two methods. First, use the selection box and then Shift-click to include objects that the selection box might have missed.

Grouping Objects

As your drawing becomes more complex, you might find it necessary to "glue" objects together into groups. *Grouping* allows you to work with several items as if they were one object. To group objects, select the objects you want to group, click Draw on the Drawing toolbar, and choose Group from the menu. To ungroup objects, select the group on the slide and use the Ungroup command.

S TEP-BY-STEP 3.8

1. Click to select any one of the circles surrounding the first smiley face that you created. Hold down the Shift key, and click on the rest of the circles surrounding the first smiley face only.

2. Right-click on one of the circles that you selected, select **Grouping** from the menu, and select **Group** from the submenu, as shown in Figure 3-20. After you group the objects, your slide should appear similar to Figure 3-21. The initial fill color of your images may differ from the color shown in the figures.

STEP-BY-STEP 3.8 Continued

FIGURE 3-20
Grouping circles

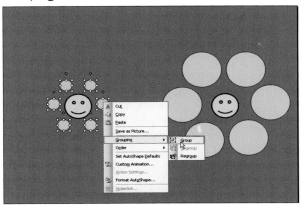

FIGURE 3-21
Grouped circles

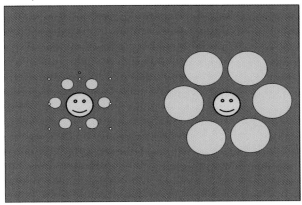

3. Using the same technique as above, select the circles surrounding the second smiley face that you created. Right-click on one of the circles that you selected, click **Grouping** on the menu, and click **Group** on the submenu.

4. Double-click any of the circles around the first smiley face. The Format AutoShape dialog box appears. Click the arrow next to **Color** in the Fill section. Click the color **Indigo**.

5. In the Line section, change the weight of the line to **2 pt** if necessary. Click **OK** to apply it to the circle. Notice that because you grouped the circles, the formatting is applied to all of the circles.

6. Double-click any of the circles around the second smiley face. Click the arrow next to **Color** in the Fill section. Click the color **Indigo**.

STEP-BY-STEP 3.8 Continued

7. In the Line section, change the weight of the line to **2 pt** if necessary. Click **OK**. Your slide should look similar to Figure 3-22.

FIGURE 3-22
Formatted circles

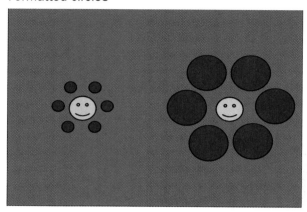

8. Click on the first group of circles to select it. Hold down the Shift key and click on the second group of circles to select it. Open the task pane, if necessary, and select **Custom Animation** from the task pane menu. The Custom Animation task pane appears.

9. Click the **Add Effect** button. Choose **Entrance** from the menu and **Grow & Turn** from the submenu. Note that if Grow & Turn is not available, click **More Effects** to open the Add Entrance Effect menu, as shown in Figure 3-23. The Grow & Turn animation has been applied to both groups of circles.

FIGURE 3-23
Add Entrance Effect dialog box

STEP-BY-STEP 3.8 Continued

10. In the task pane, click the animation that represents the first group of circles. Hold down the Shift key, and select the second animation, which represents the second group of circles. Click the down arrow next to the second animation, and click **Start With Previous** from the menu. (You can also click the down arrow next to *Start* above the animations to select the animation settings.) See Figure 3-24. Because you selected the animations together, the timing for both animations will be the same. Note that the numbers behind each group in Figure 3-24 may differ from your numbers, depending on which circle you chose in Steps 1 and 3.

FIGURE 3-24
Custom Animation task pane

11. Click the first smiley face, hold down the Shift key, and click the second smiley face to select it.

12. Click the **Add Effect** button. Choose **Entrance** from the menu and **Zoom** from the submenu. Remember that if Zoom is not available on this menu, click **More Effects** to open the Add Entrance Effect menu.

13. In the task pane, click the animation that represents the first smiley face. Click the down arrow next to the second animation, and click **Start After Previous** from the menu.

14. In the task pane, click the animation that represents the second smiley face. Click the down arrow next to the second animation, and click **Start With Previous** from the menu.

STEP-BY-STEP 3.8 Continued

15. Click the first smiley face to select it. Click the **Add Effect** button. Choose **Motion Paths** from the menu and **Right** from the submenu. Trigger this animation to **Start After Previous**.

16. Click the second smiley face to select it. Click the **Add Effect** button. Choose **Motion Paths** from the menu and **Left** from the submenu. Trigger this animation to **Start With Previous**. Your screen should look like Figure 3-25.

FIGURE 3-25
Slide with animation

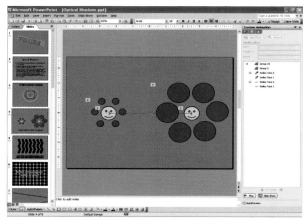

17. Save the presentation and leave it open for the next Step-by-Step.

Create a Text Box

If you want to add text on a slide that does not have a placeholder for it, you can create a text box. Click the Text Box tool on the Drawing toolbar. Click the mouse button and drag to create a text box the size you want, as shown in Figure 3-26. To move the box, drag it to a new location. To resize the box, drag one of the handles. To insert text, click inside the text box and begin keying.

FIGURE 3-26
Text box

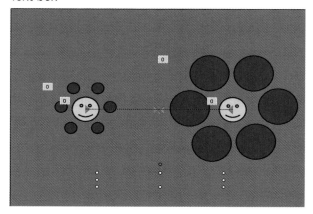

S TEP-BY-STEP 3.9

1. With slide **4** still selected, click the **Text Box** tool on the Drawing toolbar.

2. Click below the first group of circles, and drag your pointer to the right and down slightly. Release the mouse button. A text box appears on the screen, as shown in Figure 3-26.

3. Key **Which smiley face is larger?** in the text box.

4. Select the text you just keyed in the text box. **Center** and **bold** it. Change the font size to **40**. The text wraps to a second line. Drag the left and right handles so that the text box is centered on the slide as shown in Figure 3-27.

FIGURE 3-27
Text box on side

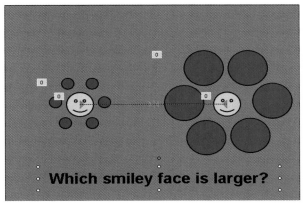

5. Click the **Add Effect** button. Choose **Entrance** from the menu and **Rise Up** from the submenu. Trigger this animation to **Start After Previous**.

6. Click the **Add Effect** button. Choose **Exit** from the menu and **Sink Down** from the submenu. Trigger this animation to **Start On Click**.

7. In the task pane, click the animation that represents the entrance of the text box, and click the **Re-Order up arrow** so that the animation is below the entrance of the second smiley face.

STEP-BY-STEP 3.9 Continued

8. Click the animation that represents the exit of the text box, and click the **Re-Order up arrow** so that the animation is below the entrance of the text box, as shown in Figure 3-28.

FIGURE 3-28
Slide animation

9. View the presentation. Save and close the presentation.

SUMMARY

In this lesson, you learned:

- You can create and modify organization charts in a presentation.

- You can insert a table on a slide using the Insert Table dialog box and then modify it using the Tables and Borders toolbar.

- You can add shapes and objects to your presentation using the AutoShapes and drawing tools on the Drawing toolbar. You can rotate, fill, scale, or size an object as well as change its fill or line color.

- You can add text on a slide or inside a shape by creating a text box. You can wrap text inside a text box.

VOCABULARY *Review*

Define the following terms:

Grouping	Scale	Shift-clicking
Organization charts		

REVIEW *Questions*

TRUE/FALSE

Circle T if the statement is true or F if the statement is false.

T   F   1. The background color of an organization chart must be the same as the color of the slide.

T   F   2. When you double-click a table placeholder on a slide, the Insert Table dialog box appears.

T   F   3. Using the Select Objects tool, you can drag a selection box around a group of objects.

T   F   4. To change an object back to the default fill color, click Default in the Fill Color box.

T   F   5. To place text inside a shape, choose Insert Text from the Draw menu.

MULTIPLE CHOICE

Select the best response for the following statements.

1. When working with tables, _____ can be displayed in rows and columns so that it is easier to read.
   A. pictures
   B. clip art
   C. data
   D. none of the above

2. The small squares surrounding a selected graphic are called _____.
   A. buttons
   B. tabs
   C. handles
   D. boxes

3. _____ allows you to work with several items as if they were one object.
   A. Gathering
   B. Grouping
   C. Selecting
   D. Aligning

4. You can fill an object with _____.
   A. gradients
   B. texture
   C. patterns
   D. all of the above

5. Which key do you hold down to maintain an object's proportions when resizing?
   A. Ctrl
   B. Shift
   C. Alt
   D. Tab

PROJECTS

PROJECT 3-1

Open the **Optical Illusions** presentation you created in this lesson. Save it as **Optical Illusion1** followed by your initials.

1. Select slide **4**, and click on the first group of indigo circles to select it. Hold down the **Shift** key, and click on the second group of circles to select it.

2. Click the **Add Effect** button. Choose **Exit** from the menu and select **Pinwheel** from the submenu.

3. In the task pane, click the animation that represents the exit animation of the first group of circles. Click the down arrow next to the second animation, and click **Start After Previous** from the menu.

4. In the task pane, click the animation that represents the exit animation of the first group of circles. Click the down arrow next to the second animation, and click **Start With Previous** from the menu.

5. In the task pane, click the animation that represents the exit animation of the first group of circles. Hold down the **Shift** key, and click the animation that represents the exit animation of the second group of circles.

6. Use **Re-Order up-arrow** to move the animation triggers so that they follow the exit animation trigger for the text.

7. View the presentation.

8. Save the presentation and leave it open for the next project.

PROJECT 3-2

With the **Optical Illusion1** presentation open, do the following:

1. Display slide **4** if necessary.

2. Click the first smiley face to select it. Hold down the **Shift** key, and click on the second smiley face to select it.

3. Right-click on either smiley face to display the menu.

4. Select **Order** from the menu, and select **Bring to Front** from the submenu.

5. Save the presentation and close it.

WEB*Project*

PROJECT 3-3

1. With your instructor's permission, search the Internet for Web sites that have more information about optical illusions.

2. Use the Web sites to get ideas for creating a new slide for your presentation.

3. Add a new slide containing your illusion before the slide at the end of the presentation.

4. Save the presentation as **Optical Illusion2** and close it.

TEAMWORK*Project*

PROJECT 3-4

1. In a small group, use the Internet to research a company.

2. Use the information you find to create a presentation about the company that includes an organization chart, a table, and drawing objects. Save the presentation as **Organization Chart**.

3. Print handouts of your presentation using six slides per page.

4. Take turns giving the presentation to your group.

CRITICAL*Thinking*

ACTIVITY 3-1

Create a presentation on a topic of your choice that includes at least four slides. Each slide should contain at least three AutoShapes. Save the presentation as **Activity 3-1**.

ACTIVITY 3-2

You want to make some changes to some text boxes. Use the Help system to find out how to do the following:

1. Change the shape of a text box to an AutoShape.

2. Display text vertically instead of horizontally in a text box.

3. Change the margins around the text in a text box.

ACTIVITY 3-3

Use the Help system to find out how to rotate objects on a slide.

EXPANDING ON POWERPOINT BASICS

OBJECTIVES

In this lesson, you will:

- Integrate PowerPoint with other Office programs.
- Replace text fonts in an entire presentation.
- Use the Format Painter.
- Deliver a presentation.
- Change the output format.

Estimated Time: 2 hours

Integrating PowerPoint with Other Office Programs

You can import data from other Office programs to create new presentations. A Word outline is the easiest kind of document to import because it is formatted with heading levels that will convert to the same levels in PowerPoint. For example, the text in the Heading 1 level of Word is converted to slide titles. The next level is converted to bulleted text on the PowerPoint slide.

STEP-BY-STEP 4.1

1. Start Word and then open **Step4-1.doc** from the data files. Notice how the document is formatted as an outline.

2. Close the file and exit Word.

3. Open PowerPoint. Click **File** and choose **Open** on the menu. The Open dialog box appears.

4. From the *Files of type* drop-down list box, choose **All Outlines**.

5. Locate **Step4-1.doc** in the data files and choose **Open**. PowerPoint imports the Word document text into a presentation and formats it as slides.

6. Save the presentation as **Solar System** followed by your initials.

7. Change the design template to **Orbit**.

8. Display slide **1**, if necessary. Key the following at the end of the second item (delete the period following the word *second*):

   —faster than any other planet.

9. Save and leave the presentation open for the next Step-by-Step.

Embedding Data

In the previous Step-by-Step you edited a document that was created in Microsoft Word. When you move data from Microsoft Word by cutting or copying the text and pasting it into PowerPoint, the text is changed to the format used by PowerPoint.

When it is easier to edit the information using the original application, you can *embed* the information as an object by using the Insert Object dialog box, shown in Figure 4-1. The embedded information becomes part of the new file, but it is a separate object that can be edited using the application that created it. For example, if you insert a table from a Word document into a PowerPoint presentation, PowerPoint uses Word to edit the document instead of PowerPoint.

FIGURE 4-1
Insert Object dialog box

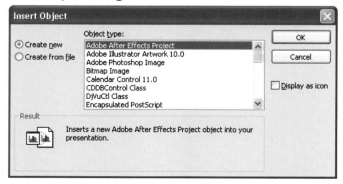

S TEP-BY-STEP 4.2

1. Minimize the PowerPoint file.

2. Start Word and open the file named **Step4-2.doc** (Word file) from the data files.

3. Select all of the text in the document. Click **Edit** and choose **Copy** from the menu to copy the text to the Clipboard. Close the Word document.

4. Maximize the PowerPoint file that you minimized in Step 1.

5. Switch to **Slide Sorter** view, if that is not the current view. You may want to close the task pane if necessary to see more of the slides on your screen.

6. Click in front of slide 1, as shown in Figure 4-2.

FIGURE 4-2
Insert new slide

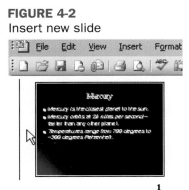

7. Insert a new slide with a blank layout.

8. Double-click the new **slide 1** to display it.

9. Click **Insert** and choose **Object** from the menu and click **Microsoft Word Document** in the *Object type* section of the Insert Object dialog box (see Figure 4-1). Click **OK**.

STEP-BY-STEP 4.2 Continued

10. Click inside the Word document placeholder. Click **Edit** and choose **Paste** from the menu. Click outside the document. Center the text box on the slide. Your slide should look similar to Figure 4-3.

FIGURE 4-3
Embed a Word Document

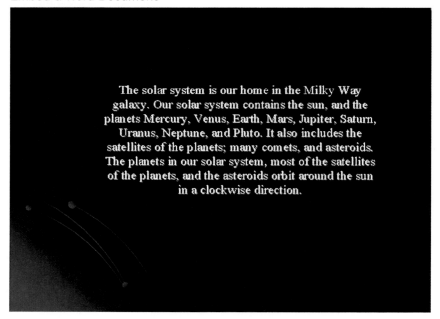

The solar system is our home in the Milky Way galaxy. Our solar system contains the sun, and the planets Mercury, Venus, Earth, Mars, Jupiter, Saturn, Uranus, Neptune, and Pluto. It also includes the satellites of the planets; many comets, and asteroids. The planets in our solar system, most of the satellites of the planets, and the asteroids orbit around the sun in a clockwise direction.

11. Save and leave the presentation open for the next Step-by-Step.

Editing Embedded Data

To make changes to the Word file embedded in the PowerPoint presentation, double-click the text you want to edit. Word, the application in which the text was created, opens so that you can edit the text. When you finish and return to PowerPoint, the presentation includes the changes you made to the text.

STEP-BY-STEP 4.3

1. Display slide **1** if it is not already displayed.

2. Double-click on the text to enable the Word edit feature. Click in front of the word *clockwise*, and key **counter-**, so the sentence reads: *The planets in our solar system, most of the satellites of the planets, and the asteroids orbit around the sun in a counter-clockwise direction.*

3. Click outside the placeholder again to exit Word. Notice the changes you made are now part of the presentation.

4. Save and leave the presentation open for the next Step-by-Step.

Import Excel Charts into a Presentation

In Lesson 3, you learned how to build and modify a chart on a slide. You can also create a chart by importing data from an existing Excel worksheet.

STEP-BY-STEP 4.4

1. Switch to **Slide Sorter** view, if that is not the current view. Click between slide 1 and slide 2. Insert a new slide with a blank layout.

2. Double-click the new slide **2** to display it.

3. Click **Insert,** choose **Object** from the menu, and click **Microsoft Excel Chart**. Click **OK**. Your screen should look similar to Figure 4-4.

FIGURE 4-4
Embedded Excel chart

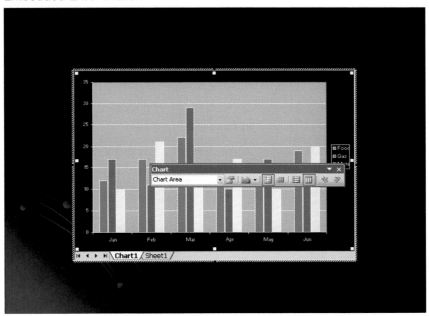

4. Click the tab at the bottom of the chart named **Sheet 1**. Click cell **A1** and drag to cell **E8**. Notice that cells A1:D7 are filled with sample text, but the text might not be visible because the slide background is black. Press the **Delete** key to delete the sample text.

5. Minimize the Solar System file.

6. Open **Step4-4.xls** (Excel file) from the data files.

7. Select all of the text in the worksheet. Click **Edit** and choose **Copy** from the menu to copy the text to the Clipboard. Close the Excel workbook.

8. Maximize the PowerPoint file that you minimized in Step 5. Double-click the chart object if necessary.

STEP-BY-STEP 4.4 Continued

9. Click in cell **A1** again. Click **Edit** and choose **Paste** from the menu. If the cells from the sample data are still highlighted, a message will be displayed warning you that the selected area is a different size than the data you are pasting. Click **OK** to paste the new data. Adjust the columns so you can read all of the text.

10. Click the **Chart 1** tab to display the chart.

11. Right-click in the chart area to display the Chart menu, as shown in Figure 4-5.

FIGURE 4-5
Chart menu

12. Click **Source Data**. The Source Data dialog box appears (Figure 4-6).

FIGURE 4-6
Source Data dialog box

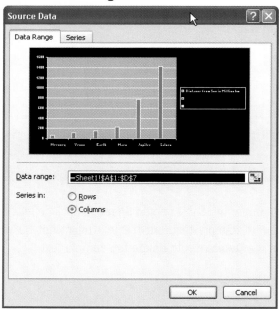

13. If necessary, click the **Series** tab. Delete the two items in the series column named **blank series** by highlighting them and clicking the **Remove** button.

STEP-BY-STEP 4.4 Continued

14. Click the **Collapse Dialog** button to the right of the *Name* series. Highlight cell **B1**. Click the **Expand Dialog** button to display the Source Data dialog box again.

15. Click the **Collapse Dialog** button to the right of the *Values* series. Highlight cells **B2:B10**. Click the **Expand Dialog** button to display the Source Data dialog box again.

16. Click the **Collapse Dialog** button to the right of the *Category (X) axis labels* box. Highlight cells **A2:A10**. Click the **Expand Dialog** button to display the Source Data dialog box again. Click **OK**.

17. Right-click in the chart area to display the Chart menu, as shown in Figure 4-5. Click **Chart Options**. The Chart Options dialog box appears. Click the **Legend** tab and remove the check mark next to *Show legend*. Click **OK**.

18. Click outside the chart boundaries. Center the chart box on the slide. Your slide should look similar to Figure 4-7.

FIGURE 4-7
Embedded Excel chart

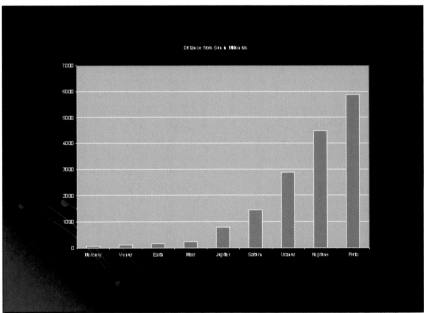

19. Save and leave the presentation open for the next Step-by-Step.

Insert Word Tables on Slides

Earlier in this lesson you learned how to embed a Word file on a slide. You can also insert tables from Word.

S TEP-BY-STEP 4.5

1. Switch to Slide Sorter view if that is not the current view. Insert a new slide with a Blank layout between slides 2 and 3.

2. Double-click the new slide **3** to display it.

3. Click **Insert**, choose **Object** from the menu, and click **Microsoft Word Document**. Click **OK**.

4. Click inside the Word document placeholder, and then click the **Tables and Borders** button on the toolbar. The Table and Borders dialog box appears. Click the **Insert Table** button. The Insert Table dialog box appears. In the *Table size* area, change the number of columns to **2** and the number of rows to **10**. Click **OK**. Enter the data into the new table as it appears below.

PLANET	TIME TO ROTATE AROUND SUN
Mercury	88 Earth days
Venus	224.7 Earth days
Earth	365.3 days
Mars	687 Earth days
Jupiter	12 Earth years
Saturn	29.5 Earth years
Uranus	84 Earth years
Neptune	165 Earth years
Pluto	248 Earth years

5. Change the text size to **24** and **bold** it. Change the text color to **Gray-25%** and **center** it.

6. Click outside the table boundaries. Center the text box on the slide. Your screen should look similar to Figure 4-8.

STEP-BY-STEP 4.5 Continued

FIGURE 4-8
Embed a Word document

7. Print the presentation with six slides per page. Save and close the presentation.

Send a Presentation to Word

You can send a presentation to Word to use as a handout or to create other documents using the text and slides from the presentation.

To send the presentation to Word, choose Send To from the File menu, and select Microsoft Word from the submenu. The Send To Microsoft Office Word dialog box appears, as shown in Figure 4-9. The options in the dialog box enable you to send your presentation to Word in several different formats.

FIGURE 4-9
Send To Microsoft Office Word dialog box

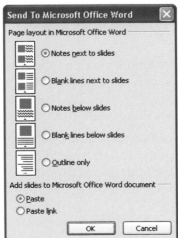

STEP-BY-STEP 4.6

1. Open the data file **Step4-6**.

2. Click **File**, choose **Send To** from the menu, and select **Microsoft Office Word** on the submenu. The Send To Microsoft Office Word dialog box appears.

3. Click **Blank lines next to slides** in the dialog box, if necessary.

4. Click **OK**. The presentation is exported into Word and formatted as a document, as shown in Figure 4-10.

FIGURE 4-10
FrontPage as a Word document

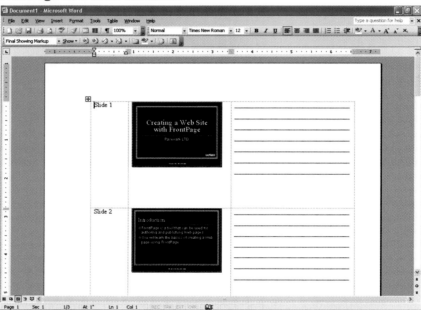

5. Save the document as **FrontPage** followed by your initials. Print the document and close it. Close the PowerPoint presentation.

Working with Multiple Masters

PowerPoint will allow you to apply more than one slide master to a presentation. This is useful if your presentation will contain slides with more than one layout, slide design, or any other features that are controlled by the slide master. This will save time as you are creating the presentation, because you can choose which slides will use each slide master.

There are several ways that you can create a new master. Display the Slide Masters by clicking View, choosing Master from the menu, and selecting Slide Master from the submenu. Click the Insert New Slide Master button on the Slide Master toolbar. See Figure 4-11.

FIGURE 4-11
Slide Master toolbar

Another way to create slide masters is to display the Slide Designs menu in the task pane, click on the design you want to apply to the presentation, choose the drop-down arrow next to the slide, and click Add Design on the submenu. This will add two new masters, a Slide Master and a Title Master. See Figure 4-12.

FIGURE 4-12
New Slide Masters

S TEP-BY-STEP 4.7

1. Open the file named **Solar System** that you last saved in Step-by-Step 4.5. Switch to **Slide Sorter** view if that is not the current view.

2. Click to the right of slide **12**. You will insert slides from the file named *Step 4-7*, as you learned to do in Step-by-Step 2.12.

3. Choose **Slides from Files** on the **Insert** menu. The Slide Finder dialog box appears.

4. Click **Browse,** locate the file named **Step4-7**, and click **Open**.

5. Click the box labeled **Keep source formatting**.

STEP-BY-STEP 4.7 Continued

6. Click **Insert All**. The slides are inserted after slide 12 in the presentation. Click the **Close** button to close the dialog box.

7. Drag slide **13** so that it is in front of slide **1**.

8. Drag the current slide **14** (titled *Sun*) to place it between slides **4** and **5**.

9. Drag the current slide **15** (picture of the sun) to place it between slides **5** and **6**.

10. Continue to place the slides with the pictures of each planet after the slide that describes it. The last slide in the presentation should be a picture of the moon.

11. Switch to the Slide Master view by clicking **View**, choosing **Master** from the menu, and selecting **Slide Master** from the submenu. Two new slide masters (1_Orbit Slide Master and 1_Orbit Title Master) appear in the Slide Master task pane, as shown in Figure 4-12.

12. In the Slide Master task pane, right-click the slide named **1_Orbit Title Master** and click **Delete Master** from the menu.

13. Click the other new slide master named **1_Orbit Slide Master** to display it.

14. Hover over the picture on the slide so that your pointer changes and click to select it as shown in Figure 4-13. Click the Delete button to delete it from the slide master.

FIGURE 4-13
Delete figure from slide master

15. Click **View** and choose **Normal** from the menu to return to the Normal view.

STEP-BY-STEP 4.7 Continued

16. Click on slide **6** to display it and open the Slide Design task pane. Scroll through the slide designs and click on the new slide design named **1_Orbit**. Click the down arrow next to the slide design and click **Apply to Selected Slides**.

17. Switch to the Slide Sorter view, and select all of the slides with pictures on them. Use the **Ctrl** key to select multiple slides. Apply the **1_Orbit** slide design to these slides if necessary.

18. View the presentation.

19. Save the presentation and leave it open for the next Step-by-Step.

Formatting Text and Objects

In earlier lessons you learned the basics of formatting text and objects. PowerPoint has several helpful features to make formatting easier.

Replace Text Fonts

You can change a font throughout your presentation by clicking Format and choosing Replace Fonts on the menu. The Replace Font dialog box appears, as shown in Figure 4-14. In the *Replace* box, choose the font you want to replace. In the *With* box, choose the font you want to use as a replacement, and then click Replace.

FIGURE 4-14
Replace Font dialog box

Use the Format Painter

If you format an object with certain attributes, such as fill color and line color, and you want to format another object the same way, use the *Format Painter* feature. Select the object that has the attributes you want to copy, click the Format Painter button, and then click the object you want to format. You can use the same process to copy text attributes, such as font, size, color, or style to other text. To copy attributes to more than one object or section of text, double-click the Format Painter button, click each object or text you want to format, and click the Format Painter button when you are finished.

> **Computer Concepts**
>
> To apply one slide's color scheme to another slide, switch to **Slide Sorter** view, select the slide with the color scheme you want to copy, click **Format Painter**, and then click the slide to which you want to apply the color scheme.

STEP-BY-STEP 4.8

1. Switch back to the **Normal** view if necessary. Click **Format** and choose **Replace Fonts** from the menu. The Replace Font dialog box appears.

2. The labels on the pictures of the planets are in the Times New Roman font. In the *Replace* box, choose **Times New Roman** if necessary.

3. In the *With* box, choose **Arial**, if necessary, as shown in Figure 4-14. Click **Replace**. All the text in Times New Roman font throughout the presentation is replaced with the Arial font. Notice that the font in the table on slide 4 is not changed because the data for the table was created in Microsoft Word.

4. Click **Close** to close the Replace Fonts dialog box.

5. Display slide **6**. Select the word **Sun**.

6. Change the font color to **orange**, **60-point**, **bold**.

7. With *Sun* still selected, click the **Format Painter** button. The pointer changes to an I-beam with a paintbrush next to it.

8. Display slide **8** (Mercury). Click and drag the pointer over the word *Mercury*. The format changes so it is the same as *Sun*. Use the same process to format the rest of the slides with pictures. Remember, you can double-click the Format Painter button to apply the same format more than once.

9. View the presentation.

10. Save the presentation and leave it open for the next Step-by-Step.

Aligning Text and Pictures

A good presentation uses short phrases, pictures, and graphs to convey its point. Presentations that contain text or pictures that are out of alignment can distract from the point of the presentation. To align a text box or picture, you can add grid lines and picture guides to the slide as you are creating it. Click View and choose Grid and Guides from the menu. The Grid and Guides dialog box appears, as shown in Figure 4-15. The grid lines and picture guides are displayed only in the Normal and Notes Pages views. They are not visible when you run the slide presentation.

FIGURE 4-15
Grid and Guides dialog box

The *Snap to* area of the dialog box moves an object to the closest gridline on a slide. The *Grid settings* section sets the spacing between the intersections of the gridlines. You can also choose to display the grid from this area, as shown in Figure 4-16.

FIGURE 4-16
Grid displayed on screen

The *Guide settings* area displays a set of crosshairs on the screen to help you align an object in the center, left, right, top, or bottom of the slide, as shown in Figure 4-17. This helps you place the object exactly where you want it.

FIGURE 4-17
Guides displayed on screen

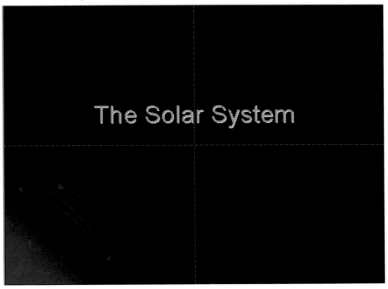

S TEP-BY-STEP 4.9

1. Display slide **6** (picture of the sun).

2. Click **View** and choose **Grid and Guides** from the menu. The Grid and Guides dialog box appears.

3. If necessary, click the boxes next to **Display grid on screen** and **Display drawing guides on screen** to select the options. Click **OK**.

4. Select **Sun** so that the text box is highlighted.

5. Drag the text box so that the top handles rest on the second horizontal gridline from the bottom of the slide.

6. Now drag the text box so that the center handles rest on the center vertical gridline of the slide.

7. Use the same process to format the rest of the slides with pictures. When you have finished aligning the text on the slides, click **View** and choose **Grid and Guides** from the menu to turn off the grid and drawing guides.

8. View the presentation to make sure the changes look correct.

9. Save the presentation and leave it open for the next Step-by-Step.

Delivering a Presentation

To start a presentation, click the Slide Show view button. You can start the slide show on any slide by displaying or selecting the slide you want to begin with before clicking the Slide Show view button. If you want a particular slide to be hidden when you run your presentation, select the slide in Slide Sorter view, click Slide Show, and choose Hide Slide from the menu.

On-screen navigation tools control a presentation while presenting it. When you run the presentation, a navigational toolbar appears in the bottom left of the screen. Click the rectangle button to display a menu, as shown in Figure 4-18.

FIGURE 4-18
On-screen navigation tools

When you click the mouse, the slides advance in order. You can choose the Previous or Next buttons to display the slide before or after the current one. To go to another slide, choose Go to Slide from the displayed menu and select Slide Navigator from the submenu. The Slide Navigator menu appears, as shown in Figure 4-19. Click the slide you want to display. To exit the slide show, choose End Show from the menu.

FIGURE 4-19
Slide Navigator menu

Another on-screen tool is the Action button. Action buttons allow you to jump from slide to slide. Action buttons are assigned hyperlinks to direct the actions (the presentation in the first lesson had several Action buttons). To insert an Action button, click Slide Show, choose Action Buttons from the menu, and choose the button you want from the submenu as shown in Figure 4-20.

FIGURE 4-20
Action Button menu

When you move your mouse, an arrow appears so that you can point out parts of the slide. When you click the Pointer Options button and choose Arrow Options, three choices appear: Automatic, Visible, and Hidden. Automatic will display the arrow as you move it around a slide, but will hide it if you do not move the mouse for a short period of time. Visible will display the arrow all of the time during a presentation, and Hidden hides the arrow during a presentation. The Ball Point Pen, Felt Tip Pen, and Highlighter are tools that allow writing or highlighting features on the screen. You can choose the colors from the Ink Colors menu. The Eraser tool erases any ink it touches. Erase All Ink on Slide deletes all ink marks.

S TEP-BY-STEP 4.10

1. Click slide **3** to display it. Choose **Slide Show**, point to **Action Buttons**, and click the **Forward or Next** button as shown in Figure 4-20. The pointer changes to a cross shape. Click in the bottom right corner of the slide, and drag the pointer down and right to draw a button as shown in Figure 4-21. The Action Settings dialog box appears.

FIGURE 4-21
Action button on slide

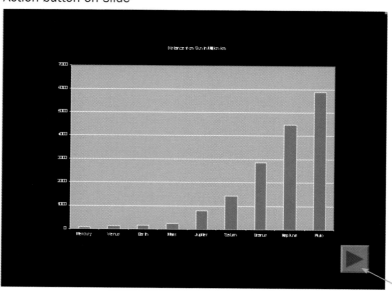

Action button

2. Click **Hyperlink to** if necessary, and click the down arrow next to the selection box to display the selection menu. Scroll down and click **Slide**. The Hyperlink to Slide dialog box appears. Click **Slide 6**, click **OK**, and click **OK** again. The Action button is hyperlinked to slide 6.

3. Click slide **6** to display it. Choose **Slide Show**, point to **Action Buttons**, and click the **Return** button. Create a return button in the bottom right corner of the slide that hyperlinks back to slide 3.

4. View the show. When you get to slide 3, click the Action button to jump to slide 6. Click the Action button on slide 6 to return to slide 3. Continue viewing the presentation.

5. Switch to **Slide Sorter** view and select slide **25**.

6. Click **Slide Show** and choose **Hide Slide** from the menu. Repeat this process for slide **26**.

7. Select slide **5** and click the **Slide Show** view button. The presentation begins on slide 5.

8. Click the menu button on the bottom left of the screen.

9. Choose **Go to Slide** from the menu and click **1 The Solar System**. Slide 1 is displayed.

10. Click to advance to slide **5**.

11. Right-click your mouse, choose **Pointer Options** from the on-screen navigation tools menu, and select **Felt Tip Pen** from the submenu. Right-click your mouse again, and click **Pointer Options**, **Ink Color**, and **Red** from the submenu.

STEP-BY-STEP 4.10 Continued

12. Underline the phrases *75% hydrogen* and *25% helium.*

13. Choose **Pointer Options** from the on-screen navigation tools menu and **Arrow** from the submenu. The pen changes to a pointer.

14. Choose **End Show** from the menu to exit the slide show. You will be prompted by a dialog box asking if you want to keep or discard your ink annotations. Click **Discard**. Leave the presentation on the screen for the next Step-by-Step.

Set Up a Slide Show

PowerPoint has many features to help make a presentation interesting and effective. Choose from several options for delivering a presentation. A presentation can be set up as a self-running presentation that can be viewed, for example, at a trade show booth. An individual can view a presentation over a company Intranet or on the Web. However, the most common method is to run a presentation with a speaker who directs the show.

To set up the slide show, choose Set Up Show from the Slide Show menu. The Set Up Show dialog box appears (Figure 4-22), which has six sections:

■ *Show type* determines how the show will be viewed.

■ *Show slides* allows you to choose which slides you are showing.

■ *Show options* allows you to choose features that you want to include when making your presentation.

■ *Advance slides* determines whether you advance the slides manually or automatically.

■ *Multiple monitors* sets up your computer when you are using a secondary monitor or projector.

■ *Performance* adjusts your computer's settings to give the best picture at the fastest speed.

FIGURE 4-22
Set Up Show dialog box

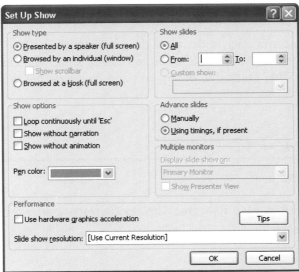

STEP-BY-STEP 4.11

1. Switch back to the **Normal** view if necessary. Click **Slide Show** and choose **Set Up Show** from the menu. The Set Up Show dialog box appears, as shown in Figure 4-22.

2. In the *Show type* section, click **Presented by a speaker** if it is not already selected.

3. In the *Show slides* section, click **From**. The first box should be **1**. Change the second box to **24**.

4. In the *Advance slides* section, click **Using timings, if present**, if it is not already selected.

5. Click **OK**.

6. View the presentation to see the changes. Leave the presentation on the screen for the next Step-by-Step.

Rehearse Timing

PowerPoint can automatically advance the slides in your presentation at preset time intervals. This is helpful in the case of an unattended presentation at a kiosk or sales booth or if you must make a presentation within a specific time limit.

To rehearse timing for a presentation, choose Rehearse Timings from the Slide Show menu. The slide show automatically starts. The Rehearsal toolbar with a timer for the slide and a timer for the presentation appears on the screen, as shown in Figure 4-23. When you finish a slide, click on the Next button. The presentation advances to the next slide and the slide timer starts over. You can pause the timer by clicking on the Pause button. The Repeat button resets the slide timer back to zero and the presentation timer back to the time that had elapsed through the previous slide. When you get to the end of the show, a dialog box appears asking if you want to keep the slide timings for the presentation.

FIGURE 4-23
Rehearsal toolbar

To view rehearsal times for each slide, view the presentation in the Slide Sorter view. The time allotted to each slide is listed in the lower-left corner of each slide. You can further edit the timing of each slide by opening the Slide Transition dialog box and changing the time below the *Advance slide area* of the dialog box.

STEP-BY-STEP 4.12

1. Switch to **Slide Sorter** view.

2. Click **Slide Show** and choose **Rehearse Timings** from the menu. The slide show starts and the timers for the slide and the slide show begin.

STEP-BY-STEP 4.12 Continued

3. Click the **Next** button every four to five seconds. Don't worry if you make a mistake. If you need to pause the presentation, click the **Pause** button.

4. When you reach the end of the slide show, a dialog box appears asking if you want to keep the timings. Click **Yes**. The presentation returns to the Slide Sorter view.

5. Click the **Transition** button on the toolbar. The Slide Transition task pane appears. Correct the timing of any slides if needed by adjusting the time below *Advance slide*.

6. Click **Slide Show** and choose **View Show** from the menu. The slides will automatically advance at the rate you set for each slide. Leave the presentation on the screen for the next Step-by-Step.

Embedding Fonts

Not all computers have every font style installed on them. If you are giving your presentation on a computer other than your own, your presentation text might not look exactly as it did when you created it. PowerPoint can embed fonts into your presentation so that your text appears exactly as you originally created it. You do not have to embed common fonts, such as Times New Roman, Arial, or Courier New, that are installed with Windows.

To embed fonts in your presentation click File, and choose Save As from the menu. Click Tools on the toolbar. The Tools menu appears, as shown in Figure 4-24.

FIGURE 4-24
Tools menu

Click Save Options, and the Save Options dialog box appears. Click on *Embed True Type Fonts,* and then click on *Embed characters in use only*.

STEP-BY-STEP 4.13

1. Click **File** and choose **Save As** from the menu.

2. Click **Tools** on the toolbar. The Tools menu appears, as shown in Figure 4-24.

STEP-BY-STEP 4.13 Continued

3. Click **Save Options**. The Save Options dialog box appears, as shown in Figure 4-25.

FIGURE 4-25
Save Options dialog box

4. Click the check box **Embed TrueType fonts**.

5. Choose **Embed characters in use only**.

6. Click **OK**.

7. Click **Save** to finish saving the file. Leave the presentation on the screen for the next Step-by-Step. If a dialog box appears asking if you want to replace a file that already exists, click Yes.

Use Package for CD and Copying Presentations to Folders

If you are giving your presentation on another computer, you can use Package for CD to compact all your presentation files into a single, compressed file that fits on a CD. You can then unpack the files when you reach your destination computer.

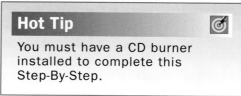

Hot Tip

You must have a CD burner installed to complete this Step-By-Step.

To use this feature, click File, and choose Package for CD from the menu. The Package for CD dialog box appears, as shown in Figure 4-26. The dialog box gives several options for preparing your presentation. The Add Files button selects the presentation you want to package. The Copy to Folder button allows you to choose the destination of your files. The Options button opens another dialog box where you can choose the linked files and fonts you want to package. If the computer on which you are giving your presentation does not have PowerPoint installed, the wizard can download a PowerPoint Viewer. This dialog box also allows you to include a password on your PowerPoint file.

FIGURE 4-26
Package for CD dialog box

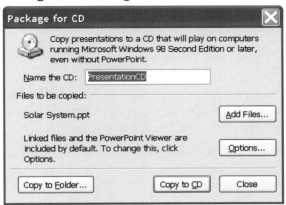

STEP-BY-STEP 4.14

1. Minimize the presentation to display your desktop. Create a new folder on your desktop by right-clicking on the desktop. Choose **New** from the menu and select **Folder** from the submenu. Name this new folder **Solar System** followed by your initials.

2. Maximize the presentation, click **File**, and choose **Package for CD** from the menu. The **Package for CD** dialog box appears, as shown in Figure 4-26. The open presentation is already listed. If you want to include additional presentations, click the Add Files button to select the additional presentations.

3. Click the **Copy to Folder** button. The Copy to Folder dialog box appears.

4. Click the **Browse** button and locate the folder you just created. Highlight the folder and click the Select button. The folder location appears in the *Location* section of the Copy to Folder dialog box. Click **OK**, and the files are copied to the folder.

5. Click the **Options** button. The Options dialog box appears. It opens another dialog box where you can choose the linked files and fonts you want to package.

6. Since this presentation does not include any linked files and you embedded the fonts in the previous Step-by-Step, deselect both the linked files and embedded fonts boxes.

7. Include the Viewer, if it is not already selected. Click **OK**.

8. Click **Copy to CD** (you must have a writable CD in the drive), and the files are copied to the destination disk.

9. Minimize the presentation and delete the Solar System folder by right-clicking it and selecting **Delete** from the menu. Click **Yes**.

10. Maximize the presentation and close it.

SUMMARY

In this lesson, you learned:

- You can create a new presentation from existing slides and you can copy a slide from one presentation into another.

- To replace fonts throughout an entire presentation, choose Replace Fonts from the Format menu. You can copy the formatting of an object or text by clicking the Format Painter button. Click a second object to apply the format to the object.

- When delivering a presentation, you can start the slide show on any slide. To navigate through a presentation while it is running, click the triangle in the corner of the screen and choose from the menu.

- You can use your pointer as a pen to draw or write on a slide while running a presentation. To change the color of the pen, choose Pen Color from the Pointer Options menu and choose a color.

- You can import text from Word to create a new presentation or add slides. It is easiest for PowerPoint to convert the text to slides when the Word document is in outline form.

- Embedding is another way to integrate data between applications. Information is embedded as an object so that it can be edited using the original application.

- To make changes to an embedded object, double-click on it to open the application that created it. Changes made when editing are reflected in the destination file.

VOCABULARY *Review*

Define the following terms:

Embed	Grid settings	Snap to
Format Painter	Guide settings	

REVIEW *Questions*

FILL IN THE BLANK

Complete the following sentences by writing the correct word or words in the blanks provided.

1. When running a presentation, click the _____ in the bottom-left corner of the screen to display a menu of navigation tools.

2. If you format an object with certain attributes, such as fill color and line colors, and then want to format another object the same way, use the _____ feature.

3. When importing text from Word, a(n) _____ is the easiest document for PowerPoint to convert.

4. PowerPoint can _____ fonts into your presentation so that your text appears exactly as you originally created it.

5. To display your speaker notes on the screen, choose _____.

MATCHING

Write the letter of the term in the right column that best matches the description in the left column.

1. Dialog box you use to copy a slide from another presentation   A. Format Painter

2. View button you click to start a presentation   B. Insert Hyperlink

3. Dialog box where you alter the output format of a presentation   C. Page Setup

4. Used to copy attributes of text or objects   D. Slide Finder

5. Dialog box you access to embed information   E. Insert Object

    F. Slide Navigator

    G. Slide Show

PROJECTS

PROJECT 4-1

1. Start PowerPoint and open the **Solar System** file you worked on earlier in this lesson. Save the presentation as **Solar System 2** followed by your initials.

2. Change the output format so that handouts print in landscape orientation.

3. Replace the Arial font throughout the presentation with **Tahoma**. (If that font is not available, choose another appropriate one.)

4. Select the title *The Solar System* on slide **1**.

5. Change the font to **Impact, 48**-point.

6. Use the **Format Painter** to apply that title format to the rest of the titles in the presentation.

7. Publish the presentation as a Web page and preview it in a browser.

8. Save, print the presentation as handouts with four slides per page, and close.

PROJECT 4-2

1. Open the **Solar System** presentation.

2. Save the presentation as **Solar System 3**.

3. Insert a new slide with a blank layout between slides 24 and 25.

4. Insert a Word table that contains the following information:

PLANET	NUMBER OF MOONS
Mercury	0
Venus	0
Earth	1
Mars	2
Jupiter	16
Saturn	18
Uranus	15
Neptune	8
Pluto	1

5. Change the text size to **24** and bold it. Change the text color to **blue** and center it.

6. Center the text box on the slide.

7. View the presentation.

8. Save, print, and close the presentation.

WEB*Project*

PROJECT 4-3

1. Search the Internet for Web sites that offer suggestions about making good PowerPoint presentations.

2. Print the suggestions and save them as **Project 4-3**.

TEAMWORK*Project*

PROJECT 4-4

1. Form small groups and discuss the suggestions that you found in the project above.

2. Open the **Solar System** presentation and create handouts with six slides per page. Give the handouts to your audience.

3. Take turns running the slide presentation for the other members of your group using the suggestions you found on the Internet.

CRITICAL*Thinking*

ACTIVITY 4-1

Your supervisor wants you to insert a movie file into the presentation you are editing for him. Use the Help system to find out how to insert a Windows Media Player movie file onto a slide in the presentation.

ACTIVITY 4-2

Create an outline in Word using heading styles. Enter at least three items using the Heading 1 style so your presentation has at least three slides. Import the text into PowerPoint to create a new presentation. Convert the presentation into a Web page and view it with your browser.

MICROSOFT POWERPOINT

COMMAND SUMMARY

FEATURE	MENU COMMAND	TOOLBAR BUTTON	LESSON
Align Left	Format, Alignment, Align Left	▤	2
Align Right	Format, Alignment, Align Right	▥	2
AutoShapes	Insert, Picture, AutoShapes	AutoShapes ▾	3
Bold	Format, Font	**B**	2
Bulleted List	Format, Bullets and Numbering, Bulleted	▤	2
Center	Format, Alignment, Center	▤	2
Clip Art	Insert, Picture, Clip Art	🖼	1
Close	File, Close		1
Copy	Edit, Copy	📋	3
Collapse Dialog Box		🖳	3
Create a New Presentation	File, New	📄	2
Cut	Edit, Cut	✂	3
Design		📝	1
Delete a Slide	Edit, Delete Slide		2
Find	Edit, Find		2
Font	Format, Font	Arial ▾	2
Font Color	Format, Font	A	2
Font Size	Format, Font	18 ▾	2
Format Painter		🖌	4
Free Rotate			3
Header and Footer	View, Header and Footer		2
Hyperlink	Insert, Hyperlink	🔗	4
Insert Table	Insert, Table	▦	3
Line Color		🖊 ▾	3
Move Up		⬆	2
New Slide	Insert, New Slide	📋	1
Next		▱	1

FEATURE	MENU COMMAND	TOOLBAR BUTTON	LESSON
Numbered List	Format, Bullets and Numbering, Numbered		2
Office Assistant	Help, Show the Office Assistant		1
Open	File, Open		1
Paste	Edit, Paste		3
Print	File, Print		1
Replace	Edit, Replace		2
Replace Fonts	Format, Replace Fonts		4
Save	File, Save		1
Select Objects			3
Slide Show			1
Spell Check	Tools, Spelling		2
Text Box	Insert, Text Box		3
Underline	Format, Font		2
Undo	Edit, Undo		2
Views	View, desired view		1

REVIEW *Questions*

TRUE/FALSE

Circle T if the statement is true or F if the statement is false.

T F   1. If the presentation you want to open is not in the task pane, click the *More presentations* folder for more options.

T F   2. A slide transition allows you to make an adjustment to an effect.

T F   3. It is not possible to cut and copy objects the way you do text.

T F   4. Changing the slide master will affect the appearance of all the slides.

T F   5. To navigate through a running presentation, click the triangle in the screen corner and choose from the menu.

MULTIPLE CHOICE

Select the best response for the following statements.

1. Which of the following features does *not* allow you to create a new presentation?
    A. Blank Presentation
    B. More Presentations
    C. From Design Template
    D. From AutoContent Wizard

2. What reserves space in the presentation for the type of information you want to insert?
    A. master
    B. object box
    C. template
    D. placeholder

3. Slide design allows you to change all of the following parts of a slide except:
    A. design templates
    B. color schemes
    C. animation schemes
    D. effects

4. What should you use to show hierarchical structure and relationships in a company?
    A. table
    B. graph
    C. text box
    D. organization chart

5. You can apply changes to the entire presentation using all of the following, except:
    A. Slide Master
    B. Handout Master
    C. Design Template Master
    D. Notes Master

PROJECTS

PROJECT 1

1. Open **PB UR-1** from the student data files.

2. Save the presentation as **Words** followed by your initials.

3. Insert a new slide.

4. Display Slide **2** and click the **Design** button on the toolbar.

5. Choose **Slide Layout** from the Other Task Panes drop-down menu. The Slide Layout task pane appears.

6. Under *Text Layouts*, select the layout named *Title Slide* and click it to apply it to the slide.

7. The slide is displayed with a placeholder for a Title and Subtitle. Click the **Title** placeholder and key **Fun with the English Language**.

8. Click the **Subtitle** placeholder and key *your name*.

9. Move slide **2** so that it is in front of slide **1**.

10. Add two more new slides with a *Title and Text* format between slides 1 and 2.

11. Save and leave the presentation open for the next project.

PROJECT 2

1. Click between slides 3 and 4.

2. Choose **Slides from Files** from the **Insert** menu. The Slide Finder dialog box appears.

3. Locate the file named **PB UR-2**, and insert all of the slides into your presentation.

4. Save and leave the presentation open for the next project.

PROJECT 3

1. Click slide **2** to select it. In the title section, key **Synonyms**.

2. In the text area, key the following sentence:

   A word with the same meaning as another word.

3. Click slide **3** to select it. In the title section, key **Homonyms**.

4. In the text area, key the following sentence:

   A word that is spelled or pronounced in the same way as one or more other words but has a different meaning.

5. Save and leave the presentation open for the next project.

PROJECT 4

1. Click slide **2** to select it. Open the **WordArt Gallery,** and add a WordArt object that says **Intelligent,** and uses the format selected in Figure UR-1.

FIGURE UR-1
Insert first WordArt object

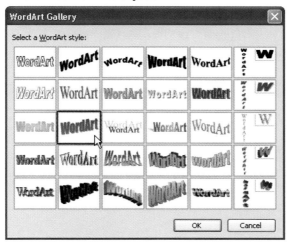

2. Add another WordArt object that says **Smart.** Place the objects on the slide as shown in Figure UR-2.

FIGURE UR-2
Placement of WordArt objects

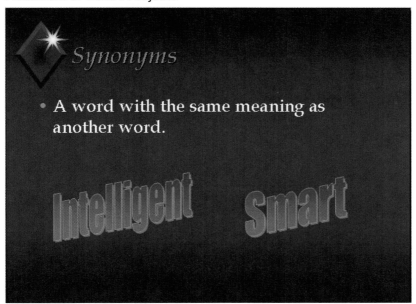

3. Click slide **3** to select it. Add a WordArt object that says **TWO**, and uses the format shown in Figure UR-3.

FIGURE UR-3
Add a WordArt object

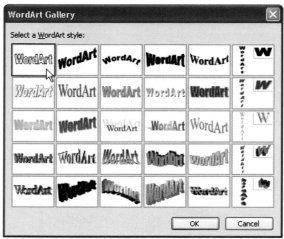

4. Format the WordArt object by right-clicking and selecting **Format WordArt** from the menu. The Format WordArt dialog box appears. Format the WordArt by making changes to the Format WordArt dialog box as shown in Figure UR-4.

FIGURE UR-4
Format WordArt object

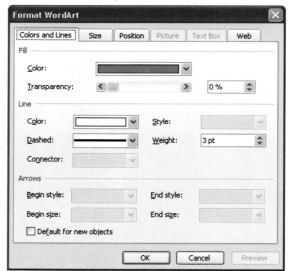

5. Add two more WordArt objects that say **TO** and **TOO**. Format and place the objects on the slide as shown in Figure UR-5.

FIGURE UR-5
WordArt objects inserted

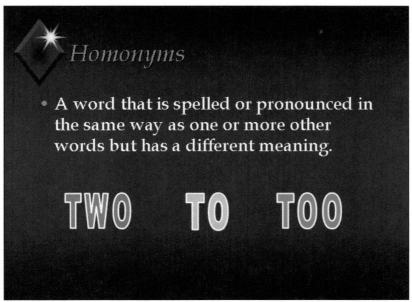

6. Save and leave the presentation open for the next project.

PROJECT 5

1. Click slide **2** to select it. Click the word **Intelligent** to select it.

2. Add a **Blast** animation from the **Emphasis** menu to the WordArt object. If necessary, select **More Effects** to see the Blast option. Trigger the object to **Start With Previous.** See Figure UR-6. The colors in your task pane may not match the colors in the figure.

FIGURE UR-6
Add animation to WordArt object

3. Click the word **Smart** to select it.

4. Add a **Blast** animation from the **Emphasis** menu to the WordArt object. Trigger the object to **Start After Previous.**

5. Click slide **3** to select it. Click the word **TWO** to select it.

6. Add a **Faded Zoom** animation from the **Entrance** menu to the WordArt object. If necessary, select **More Effects** to see the Faded Zoom option. Trigger the object to **Start With Previous.**

7. Click the word **TO** to select it.

8. Add a **Faded Zoom** animation from the **Entrance** menu to the WordArt object. Trigger the object to **Start With Previous.**

9. Click the word **TOO** to select it.

10. Add a **Faded Zoom** animation from the **Entrance** menu to the WordArt object. Trigger the object to **Start With Previous**.

11. View the presentation. Print handouts with four slides per page.

12. Save and close the presentation.

Extra Challenge

Add animation and slide transitions. Run the presentation.

PORTFOLIO *Checklist*

Include the following files from this unit in your student portfolio:

Lesson 1
___ Airplanes
___ Vacation Hot Spots
___ Project 1-3
___ Activity 1-1
___ Activity 1-2

Lesson 2
___ Virtual Zoo
___ Seven Wonders
___ Project 2-4
___ AutoContent Wizard
___ Organization
___ Organization2

Lesson 3
___ US Government
___ Optical Illusions
___ Optical Illusions1
___ Optical Illusions2
___ Organization Chart
___ Activity 3-1
___ Activity 3-2
___ Activity 3-3

Lesson 4
___ Solar System
___ Solar System2
___ Solar System3
___ Project 4-3
___ Activity 4-1
___ Activity 4-2

Unit Review
___ Words

MICROSOFT EXCEL

Unit 4

Estimated Time for Unit: 9.5 hours

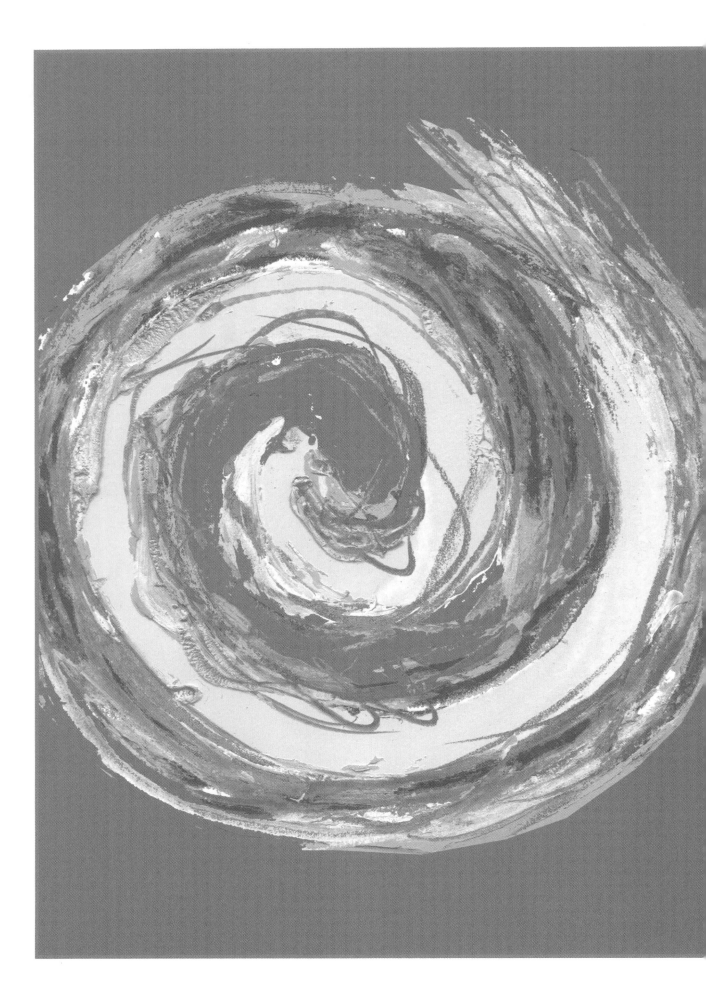

EXCEL BASICS

What Is Excel?

Excel is the spreadsheet application in the Microsoft Office 2003 suite of programs. A *spreadsheet* is a grid of rows and columns that holds numbers, words, and formulas. A spreadsheet is used to solve problems that involve numbers. A *worksheet* is a computerized spreadsheet in Excel. A collection of related worksheets is referred to as a *workbook*.

FIGURE 1-1
Excel worksheet

Standard toolbar

Getting Started task pane

Highlight

Formula bar

Column letters

Formatting toolbar

Sheet tabs

Scroll bars

STEP-BY-STEP 1.1

1. With Windows running, click the **Start** button, point to **All Programs** (in Windows 2000, point to **Programs**), point to Microsoft Office, and then click **Microsoft Office Excel 2003**.

2. Excel starts and a blank workbook titled *Book1* appears, as shown in Figure 1-1. The first page of the workbook is the worksheet titled *Sheet1*. Leave the blank worksheet on the screen for use in the next Step-by-Step.

Parts of the Worksheet

Columns are identified by letters at the top of the worksheet. *Rows* are identified by numbers on the left side of the worksheet. A *cell* is the meeting point of a row and column, and is identified by the column letter and row number (for example, A1, B2, C4). The mouse pointer is a thick plus sign when it's in the worksheet. The cell that is ready for data entry has a dark border around it. This is sometimes referred to as a *highlight*.

The cell that contains the highlight is the *active cell*. The *formula bar* is below the toolbar in the worksheet. The formula bar shows the data that is being entered in the active cell. On the far left side of the formula bar is the *name box*, which shows the active cell.

> **Did You Know?**
>
> Excel comes with several template files that you may use to build commonly used spreadsheets, such as invoices, expense statements, and purchase orders. To open these files, open the **File** menu and choose **New**. In the *Templates* section of the New Workbook task pane, click **On my computer**. In the Templates dialog box, click the **Spreadsheet Solutions** tab, and double-click the template file you want to open.

Opening a Workbook

As you learned, when you start Excel, the program displays a new workbook titled *Book1*. This workbook is eliminated if you open another file.

S TEP-BY-STEP 1.2

1. Click **More . . .** in the *Open* section of the Getting Started task pane. The Open dialog box appears. If the **More . . .** option is not displayed, choose **Open . . .** instead.

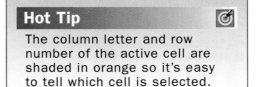

Hot Tip

The column letter and row number of the active cell are shaded in orange so it's easy to tell which cell is selected.

2. Click the arrow at the end of the *Look in* box, and go to the folder that contains the data files for this lesson. The files appear in the display window.

3. Double-click the filename **Step1-2**. The worksheet appears on the screen, similar to that shown in Figure 1-2. Leave the workbook open for the next Step-by-Step.

FIGURE 1-2
Opening a workbook

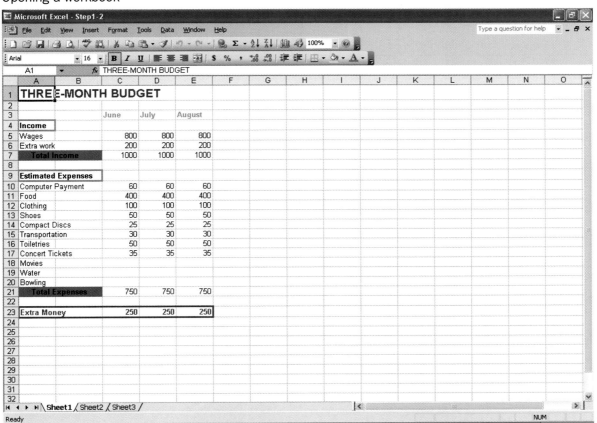

Moving in the Worksheet

To move the highlight to a cell, move the mouse pointer to the cell and click. You can also move the highlight to different parts of the worksheet using the keyboard or the Go To command on the Edit menu.

Using Keys to Move the Highlight

You can move the highlight by tapping certain keys or key combinations, as listed in Table 1-1. Many of these key combinations might be familiar to you if you use Microsoft Word. As in Word, when you hold down an arrow key, the highlight will move repeatedly and quickly.

TABLE 1-1
Keyboard options for moving the highlight in a worksheet

TO MOVE	TAP
Left one column	Left arrow
Right one column	Right arrow
Up one row	Up arrow
Down one row	Down arrow
To the first cell of a row	Home
To cell A1	Ctrl+Home
To the last cell containing data	Ctrl+End
Up one window	Page Up
Down one window	Page Down

STEP-BY-STEP 1.3

1. The highlight should be in cell **A1**. Move to the last cell in the worksheet that contains data by tapping **Ctrl+End**. The highlight moves to cell **E23**.

2. Move to the first cell of row 23 by tapping **Home**. The highlight appears in cell A23, which contains the words *Extra Money*.

3. Move up three rows by tapping the up arrow key three times. The highlight moves to cell A20, which contains the word *Bowling*.

4. Open the **Edit** menu and choose **Go To**. The Go To dialog box appears, as shown in Figure 1-3.

FIGURE 1-3
Go To dialog box

5. Key **C3** in the *Reference* box.

6. Click **OK**. The highlight moves to **C3**.

7. Move one column to the right by tapping the right arrow one time.

8. Move to cell **A1** by tapping **Ctrl+Home**. Leave the workbook open for the next Step-by-Step.

> **Did You Know?**
>
> You can also go to specific text or numbers in the worksheet by choosing the **Find** command on the **Edit** menu. The Find dialog box opens. In the *Find what* text box, key the data you want to locate in the worksheet and then click **Find Next**. The highlight will move to the next cell that contains the data.

Selecting a Group of Cells

A selected group of cells is called a ***range***. In a range, all cells touch and form a rectangle. The range is identified by the cell in the upper-left corner and the cell in the lower-right corner, separated by a colon. For example, in Figure 1-4, the range C3:E3 is selected.

FIGURE 1-4
Selecting a range

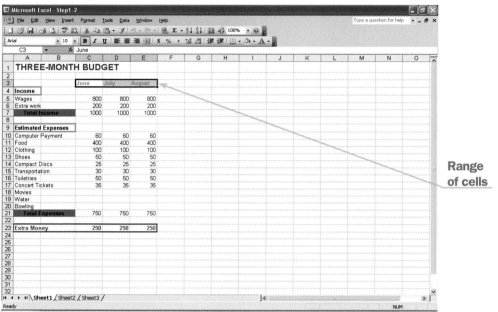

Range of cells

STEP-BY-STEP 1.4

1. Move the highlight to **C3**.

2. Hold down the left mouse button and drag to the right until **E3** is highlighted.

3. Release the mouse button. The range C3:E3 is selected. The column letters C through E and the row number 3 are shaded.

4. Move the highlight to **C5** by tapping the down arrow two times.

5. Hold down the left mouse button and drag down and to the right until **E21** is highlighted.

6. Release the mouse button. The range C5:E21 is selected. Leave the workbook open for the next Step-by-Step.

Entering Data in a Cell

Cells can hold words, numbers, or formulas. Words are used as headings, labels, or notes. Numbers can be values, dates, or times of day. Formulas are equations that result in a value.

STEP-BY-STEP 1.5

1. Move the highlight to **C18** and key **40**. The number appears in the cell and in the formula bar.

2. Tap **Enter**. The highlight moves to C19.

3. Key **20**.

4. Click **Enter** on the formula bar. Notice that the totals in C21 and C23 change as you enter the data.

5. Undo the action by clicking the arrow on the **Undo** button on the Standard toolbar. A menu appears showing what you just did.

6. Choose **Typing '20' in C19** from the menu. The 20 will be removed from C19.

7. Now enter the following data in the cells shown:

Cell	Data
C19	**25**
C20	**15**
D18	**40**
D19	**25**
D20	**15**

8. Leave the workbook open for the next Step-by-Step.

Saving a Worksheet

The first time you save a workbook, the Save As dialog box appears. This is where you give the file a name. After a file has been saved, you may save the latest changes by clicking the Save button on the Standard toolbar.

Hot Tip

If you need help while working with any of Excel's features, use the Office Assistant. The Assistant is an animated character that offers tips, solutions, instructions, and examples to help you work in Excel. It appears on the screen with tips on how to work with data and workbook files. If you have a specific question, you can use the Office Assistant to search for help. To show the Office Assistant if it is not on the screen, open the **Help** menu and choose **Show the Office Assistant**. Key your question and click **Search**. The Assistant displays a list of help topics.

Did You Know?

You can save a file in a new folder by clicking the **Create New Folder** button in the Save As dialog box. In the New Folder dialog box, key a name for the new folder and click **OK**.

S TEP-BY-STEP 1.6

1. Open the **File** menu and choose **Save As**. The Save As dialog box appears.

2. Click the down arrow at the right of the *Save in* box.

3. Choose the location where you want to save the file.

4. In the *File name* box, key **Budget**, followed by your initials.

5. Click **Save**. Leave the workbook open for the next Step-by-Step.

Printing a Worksheet

The Print Preview command on the File menu opens a window that shows you what your worksheet will look like when printed. The Print Preview window looks similar to that shown in Figure 1-5. You can print your worksheet on paper by clicking the Print button on the Standard toolbar. Or, you can use options in the Print dialog box, which is shown in Figure 1-6. Settings in the Print dialog box might differ, depending on the type of printer in use.

FIGURE 1-5
Print Preview window

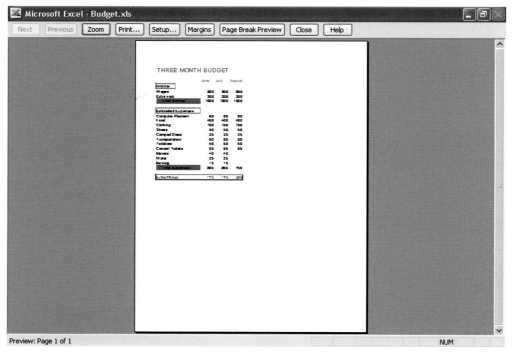

FIGURE 1-6
Print dialog box

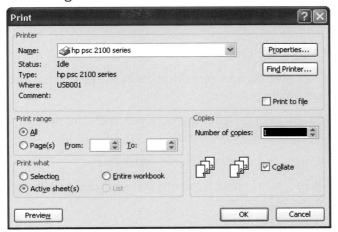

STEP-BY-STEP 1.7

1. Open the **File** menu and choose **Print Preview** to see your worksheet.

2. In the Print Preview window, click **Close**.

3. Open the **File** menu and choose **Print**. Click **OK** to print the worksheet.

4. Open the **File** menu and choose **Close**. If a message box opens asking if you want to save changes (see Figure 1-7), click **Yes**. The workbook closes.

FIGURE 1-7
Saving changes

SUMMARY

In this lesson, you learned:

■ Spreadsheets are used to solve problems involving numbers.

■ A worksheet is a set of columns and rows that meet to form cells. Each cell is identified by a column letter and a row number.

■ You can move to different cells by clicking on a cell with the mouse pointer, using the keyboard, or by using the Go To command.

■ You can enter both words and numbers in the worksheet.

■ You can save changes in a worksheet by using the Save command on the File menu or the Save button on the Standard toolbar.

■ You can switch to the Print Preview window to see how a worksheet will look when it is printed.

■ You can print a worksheet on paper (hard copy).

VOCABULARY *Review*

Define the following terms:

Active cell	Highlight	Spreadsheet
Cell	Name box	Workbook
Columns	Range	Worksheet
Formula bar	Rows	

REVIEW *Questions*

TRUE/FALSE

Circle T if the statement is true or F if the statement is false.

T   F   1. Excel is word-processing software.

T   F   2. A spreadsheet on the computer is called a worksheet.

T   F   3. Columns are labeled with a number at the top of the worksheet.

T   F   4. After you save a workbook file with a name, you can save further changes by clicking the Save button on the Standard toolbar.

T   F   5. The active cell contains the highlight.

WRITTEN QUESTIONS

Write a brief answer to the following questions.

1. What term describes a group of cells?

2. How are rows identified in a worksheet?

3. What term describes the meeting point of a row and column?

4. What keys should you tap to move the highlight to the first cell of the worksheet?

5. What is the difference between a workbook and a worksheet?

PROJECTS

PROJECT 1-1

In the blank space, write the letter of the keystroke from Column 2 that matches the highlight movement in Column 1.

Column 1	Column 2
___1. Right one column	A. Ctrl+Home
___2. Left one column	B. Page Up
___3. Up one row	C. Right arrow
___4. Down one row	D. Home
___5. To the first cell of a row	E. Down arrow
___6. To cell A1	F. Left arrow
___7. To the last cell containing data	G. Ctrl+End
___8. Up one window	H. Up arrow
___9. Down one window	I. Page Down

PROJECT 1-2

In this project, you enter information on how to move around in a worksheet. You can then use this worksheet as a guide.

1.   Open the file **Project1-2** from the data files.

2.   Save the file as **Moving,** followed by your initials.

3.   Enter the following items in the *Tap* column.
    Left arrow
    Right arrow
    Up arrow
    Down arrow
    Home
    Ctrl+Home
    Ctrl+End
    Page Up
    Page Down

4.   Save, preview, print, and close the file.

PROJECT 1-3

For a school science project, you agree to collect and list the type of trash items found within two blocks of the school. To help keep a record, you have prepared a worksheet to list the trash items. Complete the worksheet by doing the following steps:

1. Open the file **Project1-3** from the data files.

2. Save the file as **Litter**, followed by your initials.

3. Enter the following items of trash collected for Week 4. The totals for each category will change as you enter the data.

Plastic Bags	15
Drink Cans	5
Fast Food Containers	20
Newspaper Pages	3
Other Paper Items	10
Water Bottles	17

4. In addition to the items above, you picked up an athletic shoe. Enter a new category in cell **A11** called **Clothing**. Then enter the number **1** in cell **E11**.

5. Save, preview, print, and close the file.

PROJECT 1-4

As a project, the Science Club decided to purchase trees to plant on the school campus. You volunteer to keep track of the trees and the expenses by creating a worksheet.

1. Open the file **Project1-4** from the data files.

2. Save the file as **Tree Project**, followed by your initials.

3. Enter the following data in the correct cells:

Row	Item	Number	Cost per Item
5	Pine	25	$10.00
6	Post Oak	15	$10.00
7	Desert Willow	10	$15.00
8	Red Oak	10	$20.00
9	Maple	5	$25.00
10	Root Starter Solution	5	$5.50
11	Shovels	2	$22.00

4. Save, preview, print, and close the file.

WEB*Project*

PROJECT 1-5

In this lesson, you learned to use the Excel spreadsheet software. Search the Web for the names of other spreadsheet software.

TEAMWORK*Project*

PROJECT 1-6

The purpose of a spreadsheet is to solve problems that involve numbers. In a group, plan the design of a spreadsheet. You should include a main title, column headings, and the following information for each group member: first and last name, grade level, advisory room number, and age. Then, each member should return to his or her computer and enter the data. When finished, compare your spreadsheet with the other members and save the file as **Classmates**.

CRITICAL*Thinking*

ACTIVITY 1-1

The purpose of a spreadsheet is to solve problems that involve numbers. List a way that a spreadsheet might be used by each of the following:

1. Student organization

2. Athletic event

3. Personal collection of items

4. Teacher

ACTIVITY 1-2

You accidentally deleted an entire column in your worksheet. You don't know how to get it back. Use the **Microsoft Excel Help** command on the **Help** menu to learn how to recover the column. Write a brief explanation of the steps you would take to do this. (*Hint*: The answer appears under a topic that relates to "columns.")

WORKSHEET APPEARANCE

Changing Column Width

Worksheets are useful only when they are easy to read and understand. It is important for data in a worksheet to be accurate. It is also important that it looks good.

Sometimes the data you key will not fit in the column. When data you enter is wider than the column, one of the following will happen:

■ A series of number signs (######) appears in the cell.

■ The data that does not fit in the cell is not displayed.

■ The data extends into the next cell if that cell is empty.

■ The data is changed to a different numerical form.

S TEP-BY-STEP 2.1

You will be using a worksheet created to keep track of a group of volunteers. As new information is received, you will update the data.

1. Open **Step2-1** from the data files.

2. Save the workbook as **Volunteers**, followed by your initials.

3. Select cell **B10**.

4. Place the mouse pointer on the right edge of the column B heading. The pointer turns into a double-headed arrow.

5. Drag the arrow to the right until the ScreenTip reads *Width: 15.00*, as shown in Figure 2-1. Release the mouse button. The data now fits within column B.

FIGURE 2-1
ScreenTip shows column width

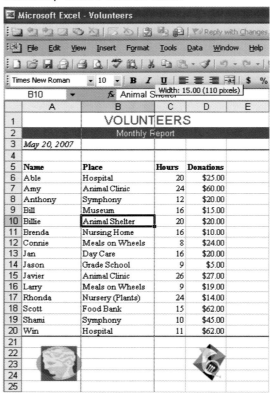

6. Select column **C** by clicking on any cell in the column.

7. Open the **Format** menu, choose **Column**, and then choose **Width** on the submenu. The Column Width dialog box appears, as shown in Figure 2-2.

FIGURE 2-2
Column Width dialog box

STEP-BY-STEP 2.1 Continued

8. Key **6** in the *Column width* box.

9. Click **OK**. The width of column C is changed to 6.

10. Place the mouse pointer on the right edge of the column A heading. Drag the double-headed arrow to the right until the ScreenTip reads *Width: 12.00*

11. Click the **Save** button on the Standard toolbar and leave the worksheet open for the next Step-by-Step.

> **Hot Tip**
>
> You can change the width of several columns at a time by selecting the columns and then dragging the right edge of one of the column headings.

Changing Cell Data

As you work with a worksheet, you might change your mind about data or make a mistake. If so, you can change, replace, or clear cell data.

STEP-BY-STEP 2.2

1. Move the highlight to **A8**. Key **Anthony** to replace the data in the cell and tap **Enter**.

2. Select **B9**, tap the **Delete** key, and then tap **Enter** to remove the cell data.

3. Select **B9** again, key **Museum**, and tap **Enter**.

4. Select **B17** and tap the **F2** key to edit the cell. Tap the spacebar, key **(Plants)**, and tap **Enter**.

5. Move to **C4**, open the **Edit** menu, choose **Clear**, and choose **Contents**.

6. Click the **Save** button and leave the worksheet open for the next Step-by-Step.

Changing Cell Appearance

You can change the appearance of a cell's contents to make it easier to read. You can alter the appearance of cell contents by changing the font, size, style, color, number format, and borders.

> **Hot Tip**
>
> You can access the Format Cells dialog box by *right*-clicking an active cell or range and choosing **Format Cells** on the shortcut menu.

Fonts and Font Sizes

Fonts are designs of type. The *font size* is determined by measuring the height of characters in units called points. The font and font size you choose may affect the readability of the worksheet. The number, types, and sizes of fonts available depend largely on what fonts are installed on your computer. You can choose different fonts for different parts of a worksheet.

Font Style

Bolding, italicizing, or underlining can add emphasis to the contents of a cell. These features are referred to as *font styles*.

S TEP-BY-STEP 2.3

1. Select **A1**.

2. Click the down arrow on the **Font** box on the Formatting toolbar and choose **Arial**.

3. Click the arrow on the **Font Size** button on the Formatting toolbar and choose **14**.

4. Select **A5:D5**.

5. Open the **Format** menu and choose **Cells**. The Format Cells dialog box appears.

6. Click the **Font** tab, as shown in Figure 2-3.

FIGURE 2-3
Font tab in the Format Cells dialog box

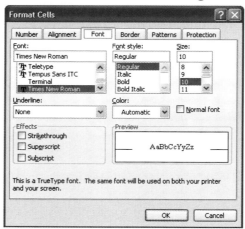

7. In the *Font* list box, scroll and click **Arial**.

8. In the *Font style* list box, click **Bold**.

9. Click **OK**.

10. Click the **Save** button and leave the worksheet open for the next Step-by-Step.

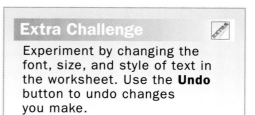

Extra Challenge

Experiment by changing the font, size, and style of text in the worksheet. Use the **Undo** button to undo changes you make.

Color

Changing the color of cells or the data in cells is another way to add emphasis. A palette of colors is available. Use the Fill Color button and palette to select cell color, as shown in Figure 2-4, and the Font Color button and palette to select text color, as shown in Figure 2-5.

FIGURE 2-4
Fill Color palette

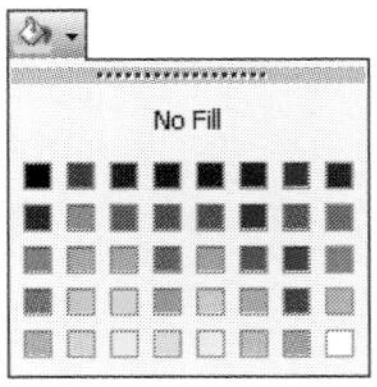

FIGURE 2-5
Font Color palette

S TEP-BY-STEP 2.4

1. Select **A1**.

2. Click the arrow on the **Font Color** button. A menu of colors appears.

3. Click the **Teal** square in the second row of the color palette. (As you point to each square, a ScreenTip displays the name of the color.) The title changes to teal text.

4. Select **A2**.

5. Click the arrow on the **Fill Color** button. A menu of colors appears.

6. Click the **Teal** square in the second row. The cell background is changed to teal.

7. Click the arrow on the **Font Color** button and select **White**.

8. Save your work and leave the worksheet open for the next Step-by-Step.

Borders

You can add emphasis to a cell by placing a *border* around its edges. You can place the border around the entire cell or only on certain sides of the cell. You can add a border by using the Format menu or by using the Borders button menu, as shown in Figure 2-6.

FIGURE 2-6
Borders button menu

STEP-BY-STEP 2.5

1. Select **A4:E20**.

2. Open the **Format** menu and choose **Cells**. The Format Cells dialog box appears.

3. Click the **Border** tab, as shown in Figure 2-7.

FIGURE 2-7
Border tab in the Format Cells dialog box

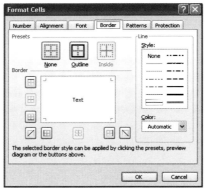

4. In the *Style* box, click the thick, solid line (sixth choice in the second column).

5. Click the arrow on the *Color* box and select the color **Teal**.

6. In the *Border* section, click the top line (first) button and the bottom line (third) button.

7. Click **OK**. When the highlight is moved, a teal line appears above row 4 and below row 20.

8. Save your work and leave the worksheet open for the next Step-by-Step.

Cell Formats

Cell format affects the way data is shown in a cell. The default format is called *General*, which displays data—both words and numbers—exactly as it is entered in a cell. However, you can use several other formats, which are described in Table 2-1.

TABLE 2-1
Cell formats

FORMAT NAME	EXAMPLE	DISPLAY DESCRIPTION
General	1000	The default format; displays either text or numerical data as keyed
Number	1000.00	Displays numerical data with a fixed number of places to the right of the decimal point
Currency	$1,000.00	Displays numerical data preceded by a dollar sign
Accounting	$1,000.00 $ 9.00	Displays numerical data in a **currency** format that lines up the dollar sign and the decimal point vertically within a column
Date	6/8/07	Displays text and numerical data as dates
Time	7:38 PM	Displays text and numerical data as times
Percentage	35.2%	Displays numerical data followed by a percent sign
Fraction	35 7/8	Displays numerical data as fractional values
Scientific	1.00E+03	Displays numerical data in exponential notation
Text	45-875-33	Displays numerical data that will not be used for calculation, such as serial numbers containing hyphens
Special	79410	Displays numerical data that requires a specific format, such as ZIP codes or phone numbers
Custom	000.00.0	Displays formats designed by the user, including formats with commas or leading zeros

STEP-BY-STEP 2.6

1. Select **D6:D20**.

2. Open the **Format** menu and choose **Cells**. The Format Cells dialog box appears.

3. Click the **Number** tab, and click **Currency** in the *Category* list box, as shown in Figure 2-8.

FIGURE 2-8
Number tab in the Format Cells dialog box

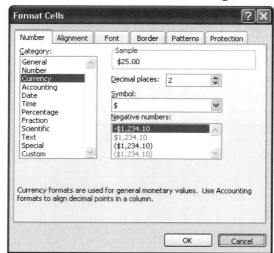

4. Click **OK**.

5. Highlight **A3**.

6. Key today's date in the form *5/20/07* and tap **Enter**.

7. Highlight **A3**.

8. Open the **Format** menu, choose **Cells**, and click the **Number** tab.

9. Click **Date** in the *Category* list box.

10. In the *Type* box, select the form **March 14, 2001**.

11. Click **OK**. If necessary, adjust the width of column A so the full date is visible.

STEP-BY-STEP 2.6 Continued

12. Select **A3**.

13. Click the **Italic** button on the Formatting toolbar. If necessary, adjust the width of Column A. Your screen should look similar to Figure 2-9.

FIGURE 2-9
Changing the appearance of a worksheet

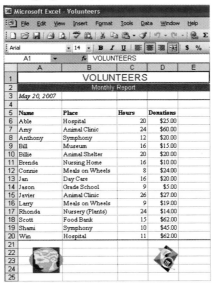

14. Save your work and leave the worksheet open for the next Step-by-Step.

> ### Did You Know?
>
> You can remove the formats you apply to a cell or range of cells by selecting the cell or range, choosing **Clear** on the **Edit** menu, and then clicking **Formats** on the submenu. This removes the formatting *only*.

Copying Data

When entering data in a worksheet, you might want to reuse the same words or numbers in another part of the worksheet. Rather than key the same data over again, you can *copy* the data and *paste* it in another location, as shown in Figure 2-10.

Hot Tip

Data copied to a cell replaces data already in that cell. Check your destination cells for existing data before copying.

FIGURE 2-10
Copying data to another part of the worksheet

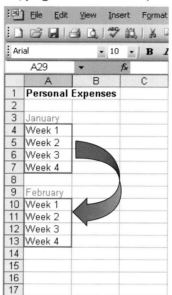

STEP-BY-STEP 2.7

1. Select **B19**.

2. Open the **Edit** menu and click **Copy**.

3. Select cell **B8**.

4. Open the **Edit** menu and click **Paste**.

5. Save, print, and close the file.

SUMMARY

In this lesson, you learned:

- A series of number signs (#####) appears in a cell if the data is wider than the column.

- Worksheet columns can be widened to display data that is too long to fit in the cell.

- Cell data can be changed, replaced, or cleared if you change your mind or make a mistake.

- The appearance of cell data can be changed to make the worksheet easier to read. Font, font size, and font style (bolding, italicizing, and underlining) can be changed.

- Color and borders can be added to a worksheet.

- The appearance of cell data can be changed to a variety of numerical formats.

VOCABULARY *Review*

Define the following terms:

Border	Currency	Font styles
Cell format	Font	Paste
Copy	Font size	

REVIEW *Questions*

TRUE/FALSE

Circle T if the statement is true or F if the statement is false.

T F 1. Column widths can be changed.

T F 2. Once you have entered data in a cell, it cannot be changed.

T F 3. Accounting is the name of a cell format.

T F 4. The currency cell format adds a dollar sign ($) before a number.

T F 5. Only numbers can be copied and pasted in a worksheet.

WRITTEN QUESTIONS

Write a brief answer to the following questions.

1. If cell data is too wide to fit in the column, what symbols appear in the cell?

2. What are three ways to add emphasis to a cell?

3. Which menu contains the Copy and Paste commands?

4. What is the difference between the Fill Color and Font Color buttons?

5. List four of the cell formats discussed in this lesson.

PROJECTS

 PROJECT 2-1

Your neighbor has a dog named Pepper that he cannot keep. You agree to take Pepper, so you prepare a worksheet to determine the expenses.

1. Open **Project2-1** from the data files.

2. Save the file as **Pet Supplies,** followed by your initials.

3. Change the width of column **A** to **12**.

4. Select **A1:A2** and change the font size to **14** and the font color to **Red**.

5. Select **A4:B4** and make it bold.

6. You made a mistake when keying the data in **A14**, so change it to **Food**.

7. Select **B5:B15** and format it for **Currency**.

8. Select **A3:B16**. Add the double-line border to the top and bottom of the range. Change the border color to red.

9. Save, print, and close the file.

 PROJECT 2-2

You agree to help a school coach who is in charge of athletic activities. The coach has been given $1,210 to purchase sports equipment for the school. You create a worksheet to keep track of the equipment costs.

1. Open **Project2-2** from the data files.

2. Save the file as **Sports Equipment**, followed by your initials.

3. Key the following data:

Item	Sport	Quantity	Cost
Basketballs	Basketball	5	28
Hoops	Basketball	3	40
Backboards	Basketball	2	115
Softballs	Softball	20	5
Bats	Softball	7	30
Masks	Softball	3	35
Volleyballs	Volleyball	7	25
Nets	Volleyball	1	125

4. Change the width of column **A** to **12**, column **B** to **10**, column **C** to **8**, and column **D** to **7**.

5. Change the font size of **A1** to **16** and the color to **Plum**.

6. Bold the column headings.

7. Select **D5:D12** and format it for currency.

8. Select **E5:E13** and format it for currency. Adjust the column width, if necessary.

9. Delete the contents of cell **F3**.

10. Select **A1:E1** and apply a fill color of **Pale Blue**.

11. Select **A3:E3**, open the **Format** menu, select **Cells**, and click the **Border** tab.

12. In the *Style* box, select the wide line border (sixth option in the second column). From the *Color* box, select **Plum**. In the *Presets* section, click the **Outline** button.

13. Save, print, and close the file.

PROJECT 2-3

You have collected water samples from various water fountains in the local school. You tested each sample for salt content. You prepare a worksheet to show the results.

1. Open **Project2-3** from the data files.

2. Save the file as **Salt Experiment**, followed by your initials.

3. Widen columns so that all the data shows.

4. Change the main title in cell **A1** to a different font and size **20**.

5. Select **B5:B15** and format it for currency.

6. Select **C5:C15** and format it for percentage. Widen the column if needed.

7. Change the font color of cells in column C to red if the percentage is above 5.50%.

8. In column A, fill the Location cells with light yellow if the percentage is above 8.5%.

9. Select **A3** and key **10:05** as the time.

10. Format **A3** so that the time displays as *10:05 AM*.

11. Select **A4:C4**, open the **Format** menu, select **Cells**, and click the **Border** tab.

12. In the *Style* box, select the wide line border (sixth option in the second column). From the *Color* box, select **Dark Blue**. In the *Presets* section, click the **Outline** button.

13. Save, print, and close the file

WEB*Project*

PROJECT 2-4

To learn more about Excel, go to the Web site *www.msoffice.com*. Click on the topic **Excel** and explore the information.

TEAMWORK*Project*

PROJECT 2-5

In groups, discuss when it is appropriate to add or change each of the following when working with a worksheet:

1. Font color

2. Fill color

3. Border

4. Cell formatting

5. Font size

6. Column width

CRITICAL*Thinking*

ACTIVITY 2-1

To be useful, worksheets must be easy to read. Name ways to do the following:

1. Emphasize certain parts of the worksheet.

2. Make text easier to read.

3. Add interest.

ACTIVITY 2-2

You have learned about formatting a worksheet but you would like to know more. Use the Microsoft Excel Help command on the Help menu to learn more about formatting. (*Hint*: Search for topics that relate to "formatting." The information appears under a topic that relates to formatting worksheets and data.)

WORKSHEET FORMULAS

What Are Formulas?

Numbers entered in cells can be used to calculate values in other cells. The equations that calculate values in a cell are known as *formulas*. Excel recognizes the contents of a cell as a formula when an equal sign (=) is the first character in the cell. For example, if the formula =8+6 is entered in cell B3, the value of 14 is displayed in B3. The formula bar displays the formula =8+6, as shown in Figure 3-1.

FIGURE 3-1
Formula appears in the formula bar and the result displays in the cell

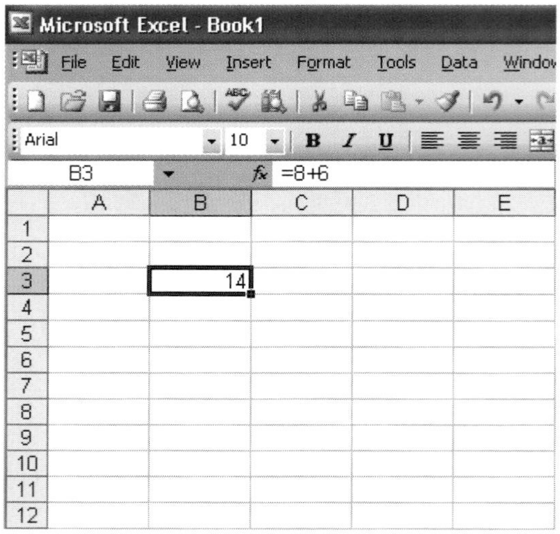

	A	B	C	D	E
1					
2					
3		14			
4					
5					
6					
7					
8					
9					
10					
11					
12					

Formula Formats

A formula has two parts: operands and operators. An *operand* is a number or cell used in formulas. An *operator* tells Excel what to do with the operands. For example, in the formula =B3+5, *B3* and *5* are operands. The plus sign (+) is an operator. It tells Excel to add the value in cell B3 to the number 5. The operators used in formulas are shown in Table 3-1. After you have keyed the formula, enter it by tapping the Enter key.

TABLE 3-1
Formula operators

OPERATOR	OPERATION	EXAMPLE	MEANING
+	Addition	B5+C5	Adds the values in B5 and C5.
-	Subtraction	C8-232	Subtracts 232 from the value in C8.
*	Multiplication	D4*D5	Multiplies the value in D4 by the value in D5.
/	Division	E6/4	Divides the value in E6 by 4.
^	Exponentiation	B3^3	Raises the value in B3 to the third power.

STEP-BY-STEP 3.1

1. Open **Step3-1** from the data files.

2. Save the file as **Computing**, followed by your initials.

3. Highlight **C3**.

STEP-BY-STEP 3.1 Continued

4. Key **=A3+B3** and tap **Enter**. The formula result 181 appears in the cell.

5. In **C4**, key **=A4-B4** and tap **Enter**.

6. In **C5**, key **=A5*B5** and tap **Enter**.

7. In **C6**, key **=A6/B6** and tap **Enter**.

8. Check your results by comparing them to Figure 3-2.

9. Save the worksheet and leave it open for the next Step-by-Step.

FIGURE 3-2
Entering formulas

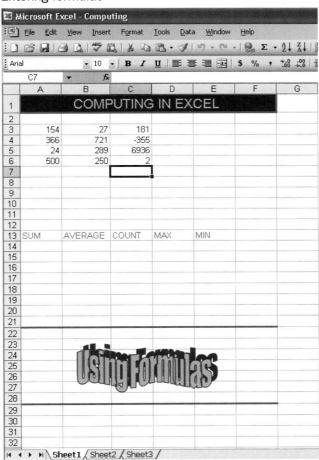

Order of Operations

The sequence used to calculate the value of a formula is called the *order of operations*. Formulas are evaluated in the following order:

1. Items in parentheses are evaluated first.

2. Operators are evaluated in order, as shown in Table 3-2.

3. Equations are evaluated from left to right if two or more operators have the same order of evaluation. For example, in the formula =20-15-2, the number 15 would be subtracted from 20; then, 2 would be subtracted from the difference (5).

TABLE 3-2
Order of operations

ORDER OF OPERATION	OPERATOR	SYMBOL
First	Exponentiation	^
Second	Positive or negative	+ or -
Third	Multiplication or division	* or /
Fourth	Addition or subtraction	+ or -

STEP-BY-STEP 3.2

1. In **D3**, enter **=(A3+B3)*20** and tap **Enter**. The values in A3 and B3 will be added, and then the result will be multiplied by 20. The resulting value is 3620.

2. In **E3**, enter **=A3+B3*20**, the same formula as in D3 but without the parentheses, and then tap **Enter**. The resulting value is 694. This value differs from the value in D3 because Excel multiplied the value in B3 by 20 before adding the value in A3. In D3, the values in A3 and B3 were added together and the sum multiplied by 20. You can see the importance of the parentheses in the order of operations by creating an identical formula without the parentheses.

3. Save the file and leave it open for the next Step-by-Step.

Relative and Absolute Cell References

A *cell reference* identifies a worksheet cell by the column letter and row number. You can use two types of cell references to create formulas: relative and absolute. A *relative cell reference* adjusts to its new location when copied or moved. For example, in Figure 3-3, the formula =A3+A4 is copied from A5 to B5. The formula changes to =B3+B4. When the formula is copied or moved, the cell references change, but the operators remain the same.

FIGURE 3-3
Copying a formula with relative cell references

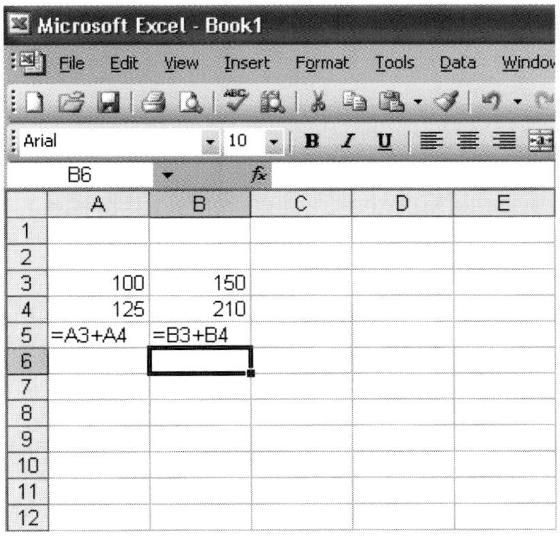

Absolute cell references do not change when moved or copied to a new cell. To create an absolute reference, you insert a dollar sign ($) before the column letter and/or the row number of the cell reference you want to stay the same. For example, in Figure 3-4, the formula =$A$3+$A$4 is copied from A5 to B7 and the formula remains the same in the new location.

FIGURE 3-4
Copying a formula with absolute cell references

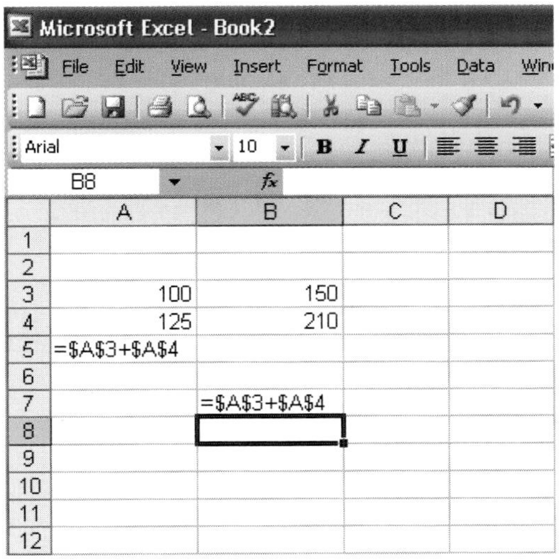

S TEP-BY-STEP 3.3

1. Place the highlight in **D3**. The formula =(A3+B3)*20 (shown in the formula bar) contains only relative cell references.

2. Copy the formula in D3 to D4 by highlighting **D3**. Open the **Edit** menu and select **Copy**. Highlight **D4**. Open the **Edit** menu and select **Paste**. The value in D4 is 21740 and the formula in the formula bar is =(A4+B4)*20. The operators in the formula remain the same, but the relative cell references changed to reflect a change in the location of the formula.

3. Click **D5**, enter **=$A$3*($B$3-200)**, and tap **Enter**. The value in D5 is -26642. The formula contains absolute cell references, which are indicated by the dollar signs that precede row and column references.

4. Copy the formula in **D5** to **D6**. The value in D6 is -26642, the same as in D5.

5. Move the highlight to **D5** and look at the formula in the formula bar. Now move the highlight to **D6** and look at the formula. Because the formula in D5 contains absolute cell references, the formula is exactly the same as the formula in D6.

6. Click **E4**, enter **=$A$4+B4**, and tap **Enter**. This formula contains both a relative and absolute cell reference. The value in E4 is 1087.

7. Copy the formula in **E4** to **E5**. Notice the relative reference B4 changes to B5, but the absolute reference to A4 stays the same. The value in E5 is 655.

8. Copy the formula in **E5** to **F5**. Again, notice the relative reference changes from B5 to C5. The absolute reference to A4 stays the same. The value in F5 is 7302.

9. Save the file and leave it open for the next Step-by-Step.

Using the AutoSum Feature

Worksheet users frequently need to add (sum) long columns or rows of numbers. The AutoSum button on the Standard toolbar makes this operation simple. The AutoSum button is identified by the Greek letter *sigma* (Σ).

STEP-BY-STEP 3.4

1. Highlight **D12**.

2. Click the **AutoSum** button on the Standard toolbar. The range D3:D11 is outlined. Excel has correctly selected the range of cells you would like to sum. The formula =SUM(D3:D11) appears in the formula bar.

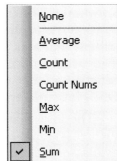

3. Tap **Enter**. D12 displays -27924, the sum of the numbers in column D.

4. Save the file and leave it open for the next Step-by-Step.

> **Extra Challenge**
>
> Auto calculation can be used to check the formula results. D12 contains a function formula that determines the sum of D3:D11. To check the results of the formula, right-click the status bar and click **Sum**. Then select **D3:D11**. The sum in the status bar should equal the value in D12.

| None |
| Average |
| Count |
| Count Nums |
| Max |
| Min |
| ✓ Sum |

Function Formulas

Function formulas are special formulas that do not use operators to calculate a result. Excel has more than 300 function formulas. Commonly used functions are listed in Table 3-3.

TABLE 3-3
Statistical functions

FUNCTION	OPERATION
SUM(number1,number2...)	Displays the sum of the range identified in the argument. For example, =SUM(A4:A9) displays the sum of the numbers contained in the range A4:A9.
AVERAGE(number1,number2...)	Displays the average of the range identified in the argument. For example, =AVERAGE(E4:E9) displays the average of the numbers contained in the range E4:E9.
COUNT(value1,value2...)	Displays the number of cells with numerical values in the argument range. For example, =COUNT(D6:D21) displays 16 if all the cells in the range are filled.
MAX(number1,number2..)	Displays the largest number contained in the range identified in the argument.
MIN(number1,number2..)	Displays the smallest number contained in the range identified in the argument.

Parts of Function Formulas

A function formula contains three parts: the equal sign, a function name, and an argument. The equal sign identifies the data entered as a formula. The function name identifies the operation to be performed. The *argument* is a value, cell, range, or text that acts as an operand in a function formula. The argument is enclosed in parentheses after the function name; for example =SUM(D5:D10), where D5:D10 is the argument.

The Insert Function dialog box, which is shown in Figure 3-5, makes it easy to browse through all of the available functions. The dialog box also provides a brief explanation of any function you choose.

Equal sign
Function name
=SUM(D5:D10)
Argument

Hot Tip

The Insert Function dialog box contains a text box entitled *Search for a function*. Enter a brief description of what you want to do and click Go. Excel will suggest the functions best suited for the task you want to perform.

FIGURE 3-5
Insert Function dialog box

Search function when you need assistance

Function formula name

Brief explanation of function

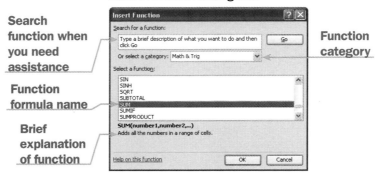

Function category

In the Function Arguments dialog box, which is shown in Figure 3-6, you can select a cell or range to appear in the argument. Click the Collapse Dialog button to go directly to the worksheet to select a cell or range. Then, click the Expand Dialog button to restore the Function Arguments dialog box.

FIGURE 3-6
Function Arguments dialog box

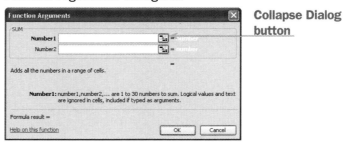

Collapse Dialog button

S TEP-BY-STEP 3.5

1. In **A14,** enter **=SUM(A3:A6)**, and tap **Enter**. The sum of cells A3 through A6, 1044, is displayed in A14.

2. Select **B14**.

3. Open the **Insert** menu and choose **Function**. Click the arrow on the *Or select a category* box and select **All**, as shown in Figure 3-7.

FIGURE 3-7
Selecting a category in the Insert Function dialog box

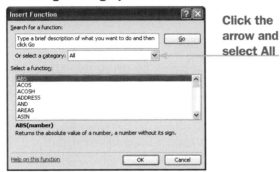

4. In the *Select a function* box, select **AVERAGE** and click **OK**. The Function Arguments dialog box appears.

5. Change the data in the *Number1* box to **B3:B6**. Click **OK**. The result 321.75 appears in cell B14.

6. Select **C14**.

7. Click the **Insert Function** button on the Formula bar.

8. In the *Select a function* box, scroll to and select the **COUNT** function, and click **OK**.

9. Key **C3:C6** in the *Value1* box. Click **OK**. The value 4 appears in C14 to represent the number of cells being counted.

10. Select **D14**.

11. Click the **Insert Function** button. Scroll down and select **MAX** in the *Select a function* box, and click **OK**.

12. Edit the *Number1* box to read **D3:D6**. Click **OK**. The largest (maximum) number in the group of cells is displayed.

13. Select **E14**.

14. Click the **Insert Function** button. Scroll down and select **MIN** in the *Select a function* box, and click **OK**.

15. Edit the *Number1* box to read **E3:E6**. Click **OK**. The smallest (minimum) number in the group of cells is displayed.

16. Save, preview, print, and close the file.

SUMMARY

In this lesson, you learned:

- Formulas entered in a cell begin with an equal sign.

- Formulas perform calculations on values referenced in other cells of the worksheet.

- Worksheet formulas follow the order of operations.

- Relative cell references adjust to a different location when copied or moved.

- Absolute cell references describe the same cell location in the worksheet regardless of where they are copied or moved.

- Formulas can be copied from one cell to another.

- You can sum a group of cells quickly by using the AutoSum button on the Standard toolbar.

- Function formulas are special formulas that do not require operators.

- Excel has more than 300 function formulas.

- Some of the more commonly used function formulas are SUM, AVERAGE, COUNT, MAX, and MIN.

VOCABULARY *Review*

Define the following terms:

Absolute cell reference	Formulas	Operator
Argument	Function formula	Order of operations
Cell reference	Operand	Relative cell reference

REVIEW *Questions*

TRUE/FALSE

Circle T if the statement is true or F if the statement is false.

T   F   1. The order of operations refers to the process of saving a worksheet.

T   F   2. In an absolute cell reference, the $ is inserted before the column letter or row number.

T   F   3. Operations within parentheses are performed before operations outside parentheses in a formula.

T   F   4. The SUM function is used to find the average of a range of cells.

T   F   5. To get a quick total of a range of cells, use the AutoSum button.

WRITTEN QUESTIONS

Write a brief answer to the following questions.

1. Write an example of a formula using the AVERAGE function.

2. What type of cell reference adjusts to its new location when it is copied or moved?

3. Write an example of an absolute cell reference.

4. Explain the steps necessary to display the Insert Function dialog box.

5. What character is keyed first so that Excel recognizes the contents of a cell as a formula?

PROJECTS

PROJECT 3-1

In the space provided, write the worksheet formula that will perform the operation listed.

_____ 1. Use a function formula to add the values of cells A5, A6, A7, and A8.

_____ 2. Multiply the value in cell B7 by 2.

_____ 3. Divide the value in cell C7 by the value in cell D4.

_____ 4. Subtract the value in cell F2 from the value in cell F10.

_____ 5. Divide the value in cell A10 by 3 and then add the value in cell A7.

_____ 6. Use a function formula to find the average of the values in cells G3:G20.

_____ 7. Use a function formula to find how many cells contain numbers within the range B5:B50.

_____ 8. Add the value in cell C6 to the value in cell D6 so that when copied to another cell(s), the value in cell C6 doesn't change.

_____ 9. Use a function formula to find the largest value in the range F6:F9.

_____10. Use a function formula to find the smallest value in the range J1:J8.

 PROJECT 3-2

1. Open **Project3-2** from the data files.

2. Save the file as **Math**, followed by your initials.

3. Enter formulas in the specified cells that perform the operations listed below. After you enter each formula, write the resulting value in the space provided.

Resulting Value		Cell	Operation
_____	a.	C3	Add the values in A3 and B3.
_____	b.	C4	Subtract the value in B4 from the value in A4.
_____	c.	C5	Multiply the value in A5 by the value in B5.
_____	d.	C6	Divide the value in A6 by the value in B6.
_____	e.	B7	Sum the values in the range B3:B6 using a function formula.
_____	f.	D3	Add the values in A3 and A4, and then multiply the sum by 3.
_____	g.	D4	Add the values in A3 and A4 using absolute cell references, and then multiply the sum by B3.
_____	h.	D5	Copy the formula in D4 to D5.
_____	i.	D6	Subtract the value in B6 from the value in A6, and then divide by 2.
_____	j.	D7	Divide the value in A6 by 2, and then subtract the value in B6.

4. Save, print, and close the file.

 PROJECT 3-3

You are a student aide to the coach of the Math team for your school. The Math team, known as the Stars, competes once a month in area contests. To keep track of their scores and related data, you have decided to use a worksheet.

1. Open **Project3-3** from the data files.

2. Save the file as **Stars**, followed by your initials.

3. Enter a formula in **B16** that sums the values in **B6:B14**.

4. Copy the formula in **B16** to **C16:E16**.

5. Enter a formula in **B17** that finds the average of the values in **B6:B14**.

6. Copy the formula in **B17** to **C17:E17**.

7. Enter a formula in **B18** that finds the highest score (MAX) of the values in **B6:B14**.

8. Copy the formula in **B18** to **C18:E18**.

9. Enter a formula in **B19** that finds the lowest score (MIN) of the values in **B6:B14**.

10. Copy the formula in **B19** to **C19:E19**.

11. Enter a formula in **B20** that finds how many team members there are (COUNT) in cells **B6:B14**.

12. Save, print, and close the file.

PROJECT 3-4

You will use a worksheet to record the portions of meat and cheese sold in a sandwich shop during a month.

1. Open **Project3-4** from the data files.

2. Save the file as **Sandwich Servings**, followed by your initials.

3. Enter a formula in **E5** to calculate the total ounces of baloney sold. (*Hint*: Use absolute cell references for C14 and C15.)

4. Copy the formula in **E5** to **E6:E8**.

5. Enter a formula in **E9** to calculate the total ounces of cheddar cheese sold. (*Hint*: Use absolute cell references for C16 and C17.)

6. Copy the formula in **E9** to **E10**.

7. Use the **AutoSum** button to determine the total ounces of meat and cheese in **E11**.

8. Enter a formula in **F5** to determine the percentage of total ounces of baloney that was sold. (*Hint*: Use an absolute cell reference for E11 and divide it by E5.)

9. Copy the formula in **F5** to **F6:F11**.

10. Save, print, and close the file.

WEB*Project*

PROJECT 3-5

Common function formulas were used in this lesson. Excel has more than 300 function formulas. Search the Internet to find a list of the other functions.

TEAMWORK *Project*

PROJECT 3-6

In a group, discuss the following function formulas. Give examples of how each function formula might be used to make a decision.

1. =AVERAGE(range)

2. =COUNT(range)

3. =MAX(range)

4. =MIN(range)

CRITICAL *Thinking*

ACTIVITY 3-1

As a student in geography, you have been asked to do a report on U.S. state populations. You will compare the state populations of the 1990 Census with the state populations of the 2000 Census.

1. Open **Activity3-1** from the data files.

2. Save the file as **State Populations**, followed by your initials.

3. Determine the difference in population between the 2000 Census and the 1990 Census for each state.

4. Find the percentage of population change from 1990 to 2000 for each state.

5. Enter function formulas in C58:C61 that determine the following:
   A. the largest state population for 2000
   B. the smallest state population for 2000
   C. the number of states in the United States
   D. the total population of the United States for 2000

6. In **A58** key the name of the state with the largest population.

7. In **A59** key the name of the state with the smallest population.

8. Save, print, and close the file.

ACTIVITY 3-2

You have worked with worksheet formulas in this lesson. You would like to know more about formulas and how they work in Excel. Use the Microsoft Excel Help command on the Help menu to find more information.

MAKING THE WORKSHEET USEFUL

Searching for and Replacing Data

The Find command enables you to locate specific words or numbers in a worksheet. You can then use the Replace command to change data you have found.

Finding Data

The *Find* command locates data in a worksheet. It is particularly useful when the worksheet is large. The Find command locates a specified string of letters, numbers, or both. For example, searching for *emp* will find the words *employee* and *temporary*. In addition, searching for *85* will find *85*, *850*, and *385*.

Replacing Data

The *Replace* command is an extension of the Find command. Replacing data substitutes new data for the data found. The Replace tab in the Find and Replace dialog box looks like that shown in Figure 4-1. You can perform more specific searches by clicking the Options button within the Find and Replace dialog box. Table 4-1 specifies what actions you can specify in the Find and Replace dialog box.

FIGURE 4-1
Find and Replace dialog box

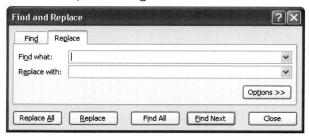

TABLE 4-1
Find and Replace options

SEARCH OPTION	SPECIFIES
Find what	the data you are looking for
Replace with	the data that will be inserted in the cell
Format	the format of the data you are looking for
Within	whether you will search the worksheet or the entire workbook
Search	whether the search will look across rows or down columns
Look in	whether the search will examine cell contents or formulas
Match case	whether the search must match the data's capitalization
Match entire cell contents	whether the search must match all contents of the cell

STEP-BY-STEP 4.1

1. Start Excel, if necessary, and open **Step4-1** from the data files. (Errors will be corrected in later steps.)

2. Save the file as **Cat and Dog Names**, followed by your initials.

3. Move the highlight to **A1**.

4. Open the **Edit** menu and choose **Find**.

5. Key **HOLLY** in the *Find what* box.

STEP-BY-STEP 4.1 Continued

6. Click the **Find Next** button. The highlight will move to **B12**.

7. Click the **Replace** tab in the Find and Replace dialog box.

8. Key **BEN** in the *Replace with* box.

9. Click **Replace**. The word *HOLLY* is replaced by *BEN* in B12.

10. Click the **Close** button to close the dialog box.

11. Save the workbook and leave it open for the next Step-by-Step.

Using the Fill Command

F*illing* copies data into adjacent cell(s). The Fill command on the Edit menu has several options on its submenu, including Down, Right, Up, and Left. Choose Down to copy data to the cell(s) directly below the original cell. Fill Up copies data into the cell(s) directly above the original cell. When you fill to the right or to the left, the data is copied to the cell(s) to the right or left of the original cell. All options make multiple copies if more than one destination cell is selected. Filling can be used only when the destination cells are adjacent to the original cell.

> **Hot Tip**
>
> Sometimes you might want to fill in a series of numbers or dates. For example, you might want a column to contain months such as January, February, March, and so on. To fill cells with a series of data, begin by entering data in at least two cells. Then select the starting cells and drag the fill handle (the square handle on the lower right edge of the selected cell) over the range of cells you want to fill.

STEP-BY-STEP 4.2

1. Select **A4**.

2. Open the **Edit** menu, choose **Fill**, and then choose **Down** on the submenu. The data in A3 is copied to A4.

3. Select **B5**.

4. Open the **Edit** menu, choose **Fill**, and then choose **Right** on the submenu. The data in A5 is copied to B5.

5. Select **A5**.

6. Open the **Edit** menu, choose **Fill**, and then choose **Down** on the submenu. The data in A4 replaces the data in A5.

7. Save the file and leave it open for the next Step-by-Step.

Freezing Titles

Often a worksheet can become so large that it is difficult to view the entire worksheet on the screen. As you scroll to other parts of the worksheet, titles at the top or side of the worksheet might disappear from the screen, making it difficult to identify the contents of particular columns or rows. For example, the worksheet title *Popular Cat and Dog Names* in previous Step-by-Steps might have scrolled off the screen when you were working in the lower part of the worksheet.

Freezing keeps row or column titles on the screen no matter where you scroll in the worksheet. As shown in Figure 4-2, rows 1 and 2 are frozen as indicated by the solid line below row 2.

FIGURE 4-2
Freezing titles

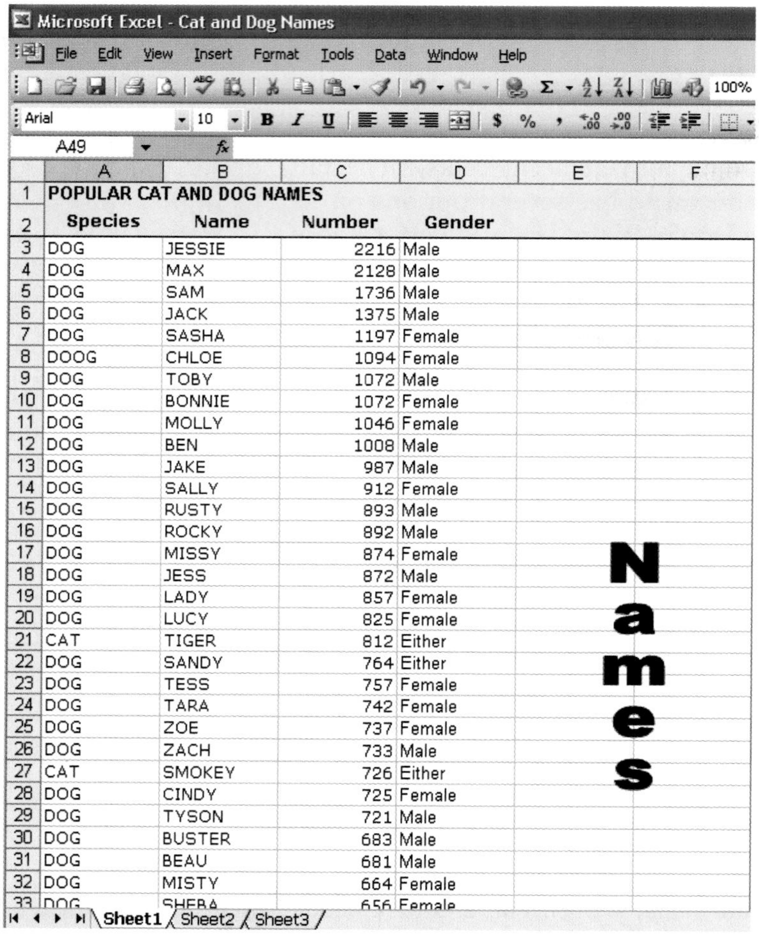

	A	B	C	D	E	F
1	POPULAR CAT AND DOG NAMES					
2	Species	Name	Number	Gender		
3	DOG	JESSIE	2216	Male		
4	DOG	MAX	2128	Male		
5	DOG	SAM	1736	Male		
6	DOG	JACK	1375	Male		
7	DOG	SASHA	1197	Female		
8	DOOG	CHLOE	1094	Female		
9	DOG	TOBY	1072	Male		
10	DOG	BONNIE	1072	Female		
11	DOG	MOLLY	1046	Female		
12	DOG	BEN	1008	Male		
13	DOG	JAKE	987	Male		
14	DOG	SALLY	912	Female		
15	DOG	RUSTY	893	Male		
16	DOG	ROCKY	892	Male		
17	DOG	MISSY	874	Female		
18	DOG	JESS	872	Male		
19	DOG	LADY	857	Female		
20	DOG	LUCY	825	Female		
21	CAT	TIGER	812	Either		
22	DOG	SANDY	764	Either		
23	DOG	TESS	757	Female		
24	DOG	TARA	742	Female		
25	DOG	ZOE	737	Female		
26	DOG	ZACH	733	Male		
27	CAT	SMOKEY	726	Either		
28	DOG	CINDY	725	Female		
29	DOG	TYSON	721	Male		
30	DOG	BUSTER	683	Male		
31	DOG	BEAU	681	Male		
32	DOG	MISTY	664	Female		
33	DOG	SHEBA	656	Female		

STEP-BY-STEP 4.3

1. Select **A3**.

2. Open the **Window** menu and choose **Freeze Panes**. The title and column headings in rows 1 and 2 are now frozen. A darkened gridline appears between rows 2 and 3.

3. Scroll to the lower part of the worksheet so that cell **A34** is under cell A2. You will notice that the column headings remain at the top of the screen no matter where you move.

4. Open the **Window** menu and choose **Unfreeze Panes**. The title and column headings are no longer frozen.

5. Select **B3**.

6. Open the **Window** menu and choose **Freeze Panes**. The title and column headings in rows 1 and 2, and column A are now frozen. A darkened gridline appears between rows 2 and 3, and between columns A and B.

7. Scroll to the right side of the worksheet so that cell **O3** is next to cell A3. You will notice that column A remains on the left of the screen no matter where you move.

8. Open the **Window** menu and choose **Unfreeze Panes**. The title, column headings, and column A are no longer frozen.

9. Save the file and leave it open for the next Step-by-Step.

Checking Spelling in a Worksheet

Excel has a dictionary tool called *spelling* that checks the spelling of words in a worksheet. Excel uses the same dictionary that is available in Microsoft Word. When the spelling checker finds a word that is not in the dictionary, it displays a dialog box similar to the one shown in Figure 4-3.

FIGURE 4-3
Checking the spelling

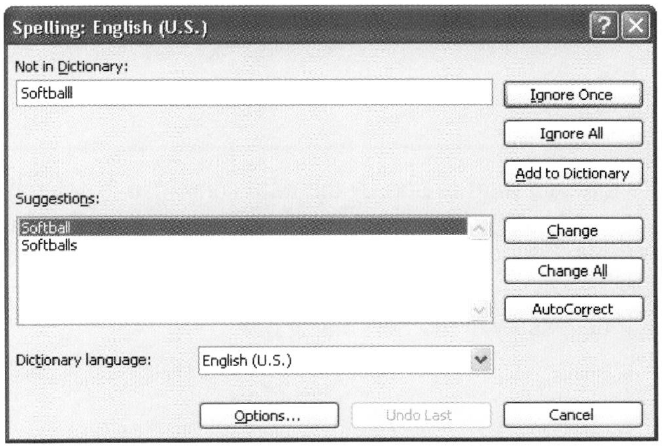

STEP-BY-STEP 4.4

1. Select **A1**.

2. Click the **Spelling** button on the Formatting toolbar. The Spelling dialog box appears. The Spelling tool has incorrectly identified *SASHA* as a misspelled word and has offered several suggestions for change. Click **Ignore Once**.

3. The Spelling tool has correctly identified *doog* as a misspelled word and has offered several suggestions.

4. Click **DOG** in the *Suggestions* box, if necessary. Then, click **Change**. The Spelling tool corrects the spelling.

5. Next, the Spelling tool identifies *TESS* as a misspelled word. However, Tess is the correct spelling. (The term is identified as "Not in Dictionary" because it is not a commonly used English word.)

6. Click **Ignore all**. A message box indicating that the spelling check is complete appears, as shown in Figure 4-4. Click **OK**.

FIGURE 4-4
Message box indicates spelling check is complete

7. Save the file and leave it open for the next Step-by-Step.

Sorting Data

Sorting organizes data in an order that is more meaningful. In an ascending sort, data with letters is sorted in alphabetic order (A to Z) and data with numbers is sorted from lowest to highest. You can also sort in descending order in which data with letters is sorted from Z to A and data with numbers is sorted from highest to lowest.

If you have column headings for data, you most likely will not want those to be sorted along with the data contained in the columns.

STEP-BY-STEP 4.5

1. Click **A3** to indicate that you want to sort by the data contained in column A.

2. Open the **Data** menu and choose **Sort**. The Sort dialog box appears, similar to Figure 4-5. Select **Species** in the *Sort by* box. To prevent Excel from including the headings in the sort, select the **Header row** option if necessary in the Sort dialog box.

STEP-BY-STEP 4.5 Continued

FIGURE 4-5
Sort dialog box

3. Click **Ascending**, if necessary.

4. Click **OK**. The data is sorted from A to Z according to the Species. Your screen should appear similar to Figure 4-6.

FIGURE 4-6
Sorting data in a worksheet

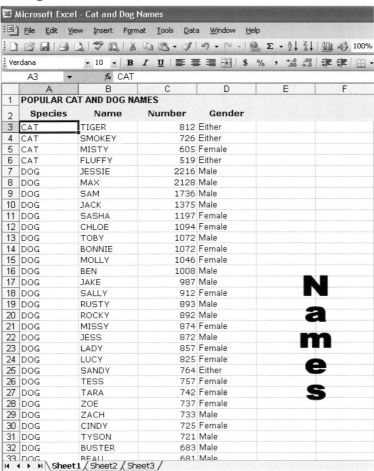

STEP-BY-STEP 4.5 Continued

5. Click **C3** to make the *Number* column the new sort column.

6. Click the **Sort Ascending** button on the Standard toolbar. The data is sorted numerically from smallest to largest.

7. Save the file and leave it open for the next Step-by-Step.

Adding a Picture to a Worksheet

You might want to change the appearance of a worksheet by adding a picture. For example, some companies like to include their logos on their worksheets. In addition, pictures are sometimes added to illustrate data contained in a worksheet, as shown in Figure 4-7.

FIGURE 4-7
Pictures improve worksheet appearance

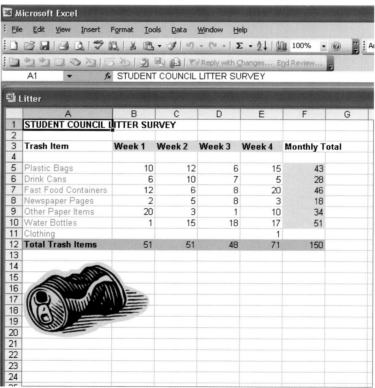

Inserting a Picture in a Worksheet

Clip art is a graphic that is already drawn and available for use. You can insert a picture or clip art from Office Online or from a file that contains a picture. Office Online is a collection of art that can be accessed via the Internet.

Editing a Picture

Once a picture has been inserted in a worksheet, you can move it or edit it to fit your needs. Many of the edit functions are contained on the Picture toolbar, as shown in Figure 4-8, which you can display by right-clicking any toolbar and selecting Picture on the toolbar submenu. Table 4-2 explains methods for editing pictures.

FIGURE 4-8
Picture toolbar

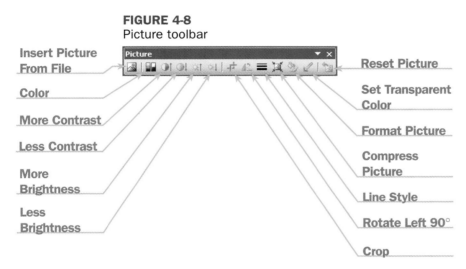

Insert Picture From File

Color

More Contrast

Less Contrast

More Brightness

Less Brightness

Reset Picture

Set Transparent Color

Format Picture

Compress Picture

Line Style

Rotate Left 90°

Crop

TABLE 4-2
Editing pictures

ACTION	SELECT THE PICTURE AND THEN:
Move the picture	Drag it to the desired position.
Restore the picture to the original format	Click the Reset Picture button on the Picture toolbar.
Resize the picture	Drag the sizing handles on the sides of the picture.
Crop the picture (trim the edges)	Click the Crop button on the Picture toolbar and then drag the sizing handles.
Change the brightness of the picture	Click the More Brightness or Less Brightness buttons on the Picture toolbar.
Change the contrast of the picture	Click the More Contrast or Less Contrast buttons on the Picture toolbar.
Make a color in the picture transparent	Click the Set Transparent Color button on the Picture toolbar, and then click a color in the picture.

STEP-BY-STEP 4.6

1. Click **E8**.

2. Open the **Insert** menu, choose **Picture**, and then select **From File** on the submenu. The Insert Picture dialog box appears.

3. Navigate to the data files for this lesson, and select **Dog**.

4. Click the **Insert** button. Your screen should appear similar to Figure 4-9.

FIGURE 4-9
Inserting a picture

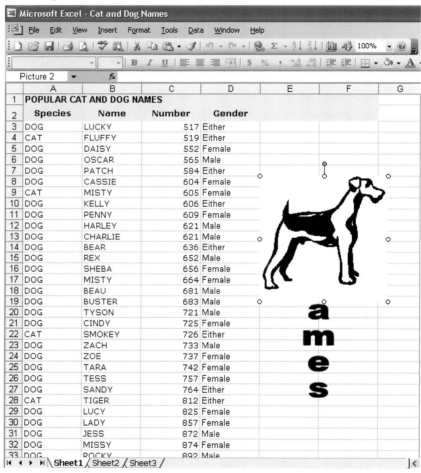

STEP-BY-STEP 4.6 Continued

5. Drag the lower-right sizing handle toward the middle of the picture so the bottom of the picture is even with the top of row 14. This makes the picture smaller.

6. Click on the center of the picture and drag it so the top of the picture is even with the top of row 41 and even with the left edge of column E. This positions the picture.

7. Click **F3**.

8. Open the **Insert** menu, choose **Picture**, and then select **From File** on the submenu. The Insert Picture dialog box appears.

9. Choose **Cat** from the data files and click **Insert**.

10. Drag the lower-right sizing handle toward the middle of the picture so the bottom of the picture is even with the top of row 13. This makes the picture smaller.

11. If the Picture toolbar is not already displayed, right-click on a toolbar and then click **Picture**.

12. Click the **Crop** button on the Picture toolbar, which adds crop handles around the picture edges.

13. Close the **Picture** toolbar.

14. Drag the lower-right handle toward the middle of the picture so the bottom of the picture is even with the top of row 9.

15. Drag the upper-left handle toward the middle of the picture so the top of the picture is even with the top of row 5.

16. Click in the middle of the cat picture and drag to position it so the top edge is even with the top of row 3 and the left edge is even with the left edge of column E.

17. Save, preview, print, and close the file.

SUMMARY

In this lesson, you learned:

■ You can search for specific data in a worksheet. You can also replace data you have searched for with other specific data.

■ The data in a worksheet can be copied to another location by using the Fill command on the Edit menu. This command saves time by eliminating the need to rekey specific data.

■ When a worksheet becomes large, the column or row titles will disappear from the screen as you scroll to other parts of the worksheet. You can keep the titles on the screen at all times by freezing them.

■ You can check the spelling of words in a worksheet by using the Spelling command on the Tools menu.

■ Data in a worksheet may be sorted in alphabetic or numeric order.

■ Pictures may be inserted in a worksheet to make its appearance more attractive.

VOCABULARY *Review*

Define the following terms:		
Clip art	Freezing	Spelling
Filling	Replace	Sorting
Find		

REVIEW *Questions*

TRUE/FALSE

Circle T if the statement is true or F if the statement is false.

T F 1. The Freeze Panes command freezes rows above and columns to the right of the highlight.

T F 2. The Find command can only be used with words, not numbers.

T F 3. Data can be sorted by using the Edit menu.

T F 4. The spell check tool checks for misspelled words by comparing your data to a dictionary.

T F 5. The Fill commands are available only if you are copying data to cells that are adjacent to the original cell.

WRITTEN QUESTIONS

Write a brief answer to the following questions.

1. Which menu contains the Fill command?

2. What dialog box will help you search for data and replace it with new data?

3. What command keeps the titles of a worksheet on the screen no matter where the highlight is moved?

4. Describe the two ways that data can be sorted alphabetically.

5. Which menu contains the Sort command?

PROJECTS

PROJECT 4-1

You have volunteered to help with a survey from the school cafeteria. Random students were asked to taste various frozen treats during their lunch period. Each student responded to a survey. You will use a spreadsheet to find the results for the cafeteria manager.

1. Open the file **Project4-1** from the data files.

2. Save the file as **Kool Treats**, followed by your initials.

3. Replace all occurrences of **None** with **Low**.

4. Replace all occurrences of **Good** with **Excellent**.

5. Sort the **Rating** column in descending order.

6. Check the worksheet spelling and change any misspellings.

7. Save, preview, print, and close the file.

PROJECT 4-2

The school cafeteria manager was very complimentary of the worksheet you prepared in Project 4-1. Since it will be displayed in the school cafeteria for other students to see, you have decided to make it even better. You decide to show the order of flavors rather than the ratings.

1. Open the file **Project4-2** from the data files.

2. Save it as **Kool Treats Display**, followed by your initials.

3. You discover a mistake and can correct it by filling down from cell **A16** to **A17**.

4. Sort the data in ascending order according to the flavor.

5. Freeze the title and column headings so that you can scroll down to check for space to position a picture, and yet still see the headings.

6. Unfreeze the panes.

7. Add an appropriate picture to make the worksheet appealing. (You can find clip art by opening the **Insert** menu, selecting **Picture**, and then Clip Art. In the Clip Art task pane, search for appropriate art.)

8. Save, preview, print, and close the file.

PROJECT 4-3

Your teacher has asked you to help organize a list of students for a new course that is being taught on Fridays. You decide to use a spreadsheet to accomplish this.

1. Open the file **Project4-3** from the data files.

2. Save it as **Friday Class**, followed by your initials.

3. Complete the grade column by using the **Fill Down** command to copy the data from C3 to C4 through C8, from C9 to C10 through C14, and from C15 to C16 and C17.

4. Find all occurrences of the number **2** in column **D** and replace with **4**.

5. Complete column **E** by using the **Fill Right** command to copy data from D3 to E3, D4 to E4, and so forth until you complete all cells through **E17**.

6. Sort by last name in ascending order.

7. Add color, bold font style, and a picture to make the worksheet more readable and appealing.

8. Save, preview, print, and close the file.

PROJECT 4-4

You enjoy attending movies at the local theater. You notice that next year there will be a class at school called Movie Interpretation and have decided that you might be interested in enrolling. The class will cover the top grossing movies for all time. You decide to use a spreadsheet to learn about the top 50.

1. Open the file **Project4-4** from the data files.

2. Save it as **Top Movies**, followed by your initials.

3. Freeze the column headings in rows 1 through 5.

4. Scroll to the bottom of the worksheet to see the entire list of movies.

5. Unfreeze rows 1 through 5.

6. Change all spellings of the word **Pottor** to **Potter**.

7. Sort the **Rank** column in ascending order.

8. Add small pictures along the side of the worksheet to add color and interest.

9. Save, preview, print, and close the file.

WEB*Project*

PROJECT 4-5

Microsoft Office maintains a large collection of clip art that can be inserted in a worksheet. To see what is available, go to *www.msoffice.com* and look at the various categories of clip art.

PROJECT 4-6

In this lesson, you learned how to check the spelling of words in a worksheet. There are several online dictionaries that contain words that may not be included in the dictionary used by Excel. Search the Web for online legal dictionaries, medical dictionaries, and dictionaries that use foreign words.

TEAMWORK*Project*

PROJECT 4-7

Excel will sort numerical and alphabetic data in both ascending and descending order. In groups, discuss when you might want to sort the following:

- Alphabetic data in ascending order

- Alphabetic data in descending order

- Numeric data in ascending order

- Numeric data in descending order

CRITICAL *Thinking*

ACTIVITY 4-1

As a science project, you have chosen to observe daily temperatures. You will record the nighttime low and daytime high temperature for each day for a one-month period. You will use the local weather station as your source of information. Set up a worksheet that can be used to record this data. Include the following in your worksheet:

- Month
- Day
- Date
- Nighttime low
- Daytime high

Make your worksheet easy to read by using bold and italic font styles, pictures, and color. Save the file as **Temperatures**. When you have completed the worksheet, print and close the file.

ACTIVITY 4-2

You would like to design your own calendar for the next month. Using a worksheet, you will record the dates, note special events, and add pictures and color. An example to get you started is shown in Figure 4-10.

FIGURE 4-10
Sample calendar

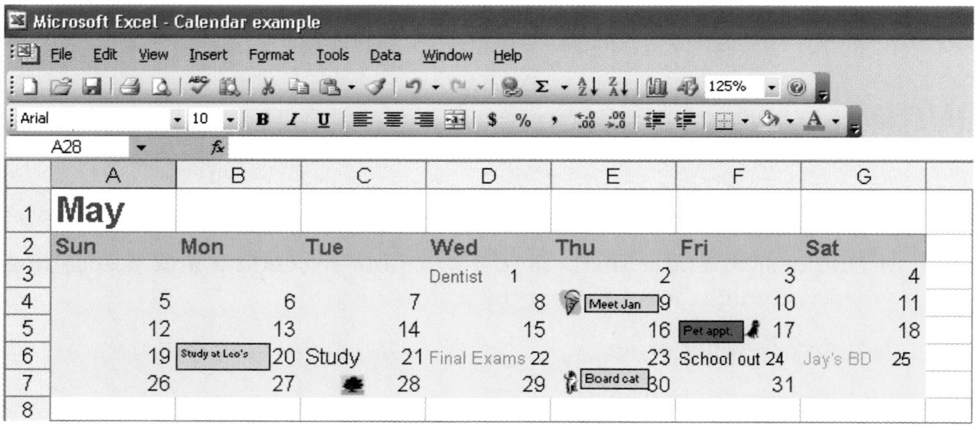

WORKSHEET CHARTS

What Is a Chart?

A *chart* is a graphical representation of data contained in a worksheet. Charts make the data of a worksheet easier to understand. For example, the worksheet in Figure 5-1 shows the enrollment of four grade levels for three years. You might be able to detect the changes in the enrollment by carefully examining the worksheet. However, the increases in the enrollment of each grade are easier to see when the data is illustrated in a chart, such as the one shown in Figure 5-2.

FIGURE 5-1
Worksheet data

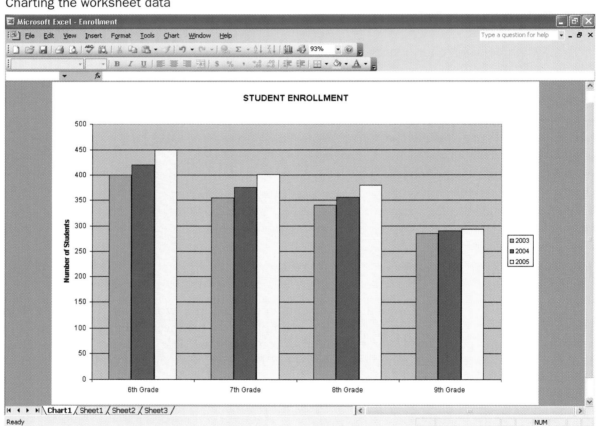

FIGURE 5-2
Charting the worksheet data

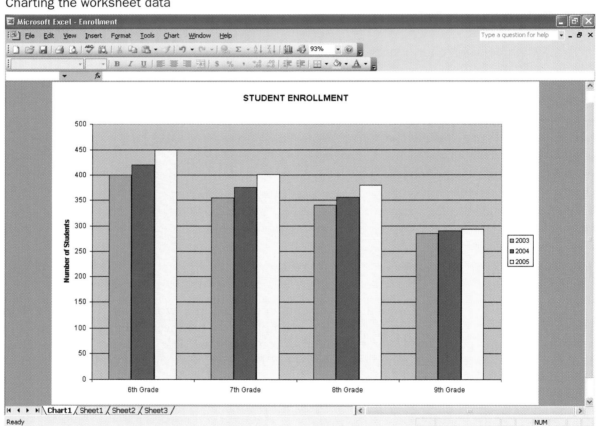

Types of Charts

In this lesson, you create three of the most commonly used worksheet charts: column chart, pie chart, and line chart. These charts, and several other types of charts, are illustrated in Figure 5-3.

FIGURE 5-3
Charts available in Excel

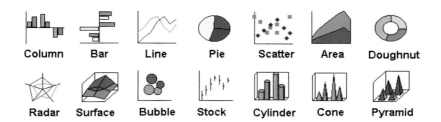

Column   Bar   Line   Pie   Scatter   Area   Doughnut

Radar   Surface   Bubble   Stock   Cylinder   Cone   Pyramid

Column Chart

A *column chart* uses bars of varying heights to illustrate values in a worksheet. It is useful for showing relationships among categories of data. For example, the column chart in Figure 5-2 has one vertical column to show the enrollment of a grade for each of three years. It shows how the enrollment of one grade compares to enrollments of other grades.

Did You Know?

Businesses often use column, bar, and line charts to illustrate growth over several periods. For example, the changes in yearly production or income over a 10-year period can be shown easily in a column chart.

Pie Chart

A *pie chart* shows the relationship of a part to a whole. Each part is shown as a "slice" of the pie. For example, a school office could create a pie chart of the enrollment of grades in a year, as shown in Figure 5-4. Each slice represents the portion of enrollment given for each grade.

Did You Know?

Businesses often use pie charts to indicate the magnitude of an expense in comparison to other expenses. Pie charts are also used to illustrate the company's market share in comparison to its competitors.

FIGURE 5-4
Each "slice" of a pie chart represents part of a larger group

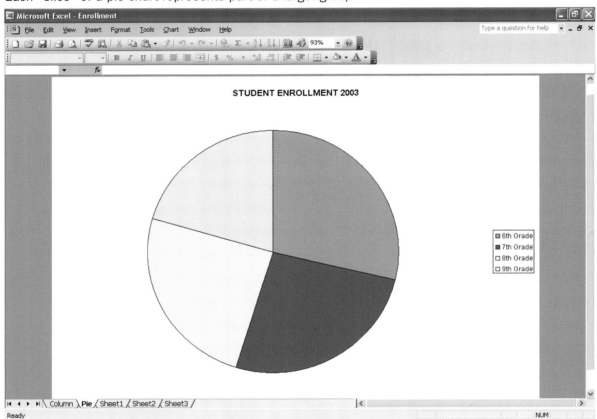

Line Chart

A *line chart* is similar to the column chart, except the columns are replaced by points connected by a line. The line chart is ideal for illustrating trends over time.

Creating a Chart from Worksheet Data

You can create and display charts in two ways: by placing the chart on a chart sheet or by embedding the chart in the worksheet. A *chart sheet* is a separate sheet in the workbook on which you can create and store a chart. You can name the chart sheet to identify its contents and access it by clicking its tab. Use a chart sheet when it is inconvenient to have the chart and data on the same screen or when you plan to create more than one chart from the same data.

An *embedded chart* is created within the worksheet. The primary advantage of an embedded chart is that it can be viewed at the same time as the data from which it is created. When you print the worksheet, the chart is printed on the same page.

The easiest way to create a chart is with the *Chart Wizard*, which is an on-screen guide that helps you prepare a chart. The Chart Wizard presents four steps for preparing a chart:

Step 1, Select the Chart Type. Lets you select from the various types of charts (see Figure 5-3).

Step 2, Chart Source Data. Lets you verify the data from which the chart will be created.

Step 3, Chart Options. Lets you specify various chart options, as described in Table 5-1.

TABLE 5-1
Characteristics related to chart options

CHART OPTION TAB	OPTION FUNCTION
Titles	Headings that identify the contents of the chart or the axes in the chart; most charts have a chart title and titles for each axis.
Axes	Lines that establish a relationship between data in a chart; most charts have a horizontal or X-axis and a vertical or Y-axis.
Gridlines	Lines through a chart that relate the data in a chart to the axes.
Legend	List that identifies patterns or symbols used in a chart.
Data Labels	Text or numbers that identify the values depicted by the chart objects directly on the chart.
Data Table	Data series values displayed in a grid below the chart.

Step 4, Chart Location. Lets you specify where the chart is to be placed.

S TEP-BY-STEP 5.1

1. Open **Step5-1** from the data files, and save it as **Computer Costs**, followed by your initials. Column A contains computer brands and column B contains the computer prices.

2. Select the range **A3:B7**. This is the data to be charted.

3. Open the **Insert** menu and choose **Chart**. The Step 1 of 4 Chart Wizard dialog box opens, as shown in Figure 5-5.

FIGURE 5-5
Step 1 of the Chart Wizard

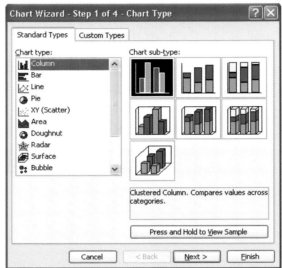

4. Click **Column** in the *Chart type* list, if it is not already selected.

5. From the *Chart sub-type* options, click the first chart sub-type box if it is not already selected. The description identifies the selected chart as *Clustered Column. Compares values across categories*.

6. Preview the chart you are about to create by clicking and holding the **Press and Hold to View Sample** button.

7. Click **Next**. The Step 2 of 4 Chart Wizard dialog box appears, as shown in Figure 5-6. In this dialog box, Excel has created a sample chart.

STEP-BY-STEP 5.1 Continued

FIGURE 5-6
Step 2 of the Chart Wizard

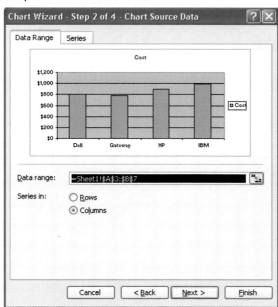

8. Click **Next**. The Step 3 of 4 dialog box appears, as shown in Figure 5-7. The tabs at the top of the dialog box indicate chart options that you can change.

FIGURE 5-7
Step 3 of the Chart Wizard

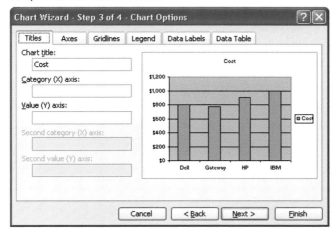

9. Click the **Titles** tab if it is not already selected.

STEP-BY-STEP 5.1 Continued

10. In the *Chart title* text box, key **COMPUTER COSTS**; in the *Category (X) axis* text box, key **Brand Names**; and in the *Value (Y) axis* text box, key **Cost**. As you enter the titles, they appear in the sample chart area on the right side of the dialog box. When you finish, the dialog box should appear similar to Figure 5-8.

FIGURE 5-8
Enter chart titles on the Titles tab

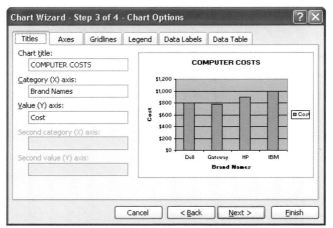

11. Click the **Legend** tab.

12. Click the **Show legend** text box to remove the check mark. This chart uses only one series of data and does not need a legend to distinguish among data.

13. Click **Next**. The Step 4 of 4 Chart Wizard dialog box appears, as shown in Figure 5-9.

FIGURE 5-9
Chart location

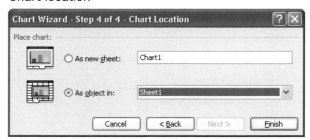

14. Click **As new sheet**.

15. Key **Column** in the text box. The dialog box should look similar to Figure 5-10.

STEP-BY-STEP 5.1 Continued

FIGURE 5-10
Step 4 of the Chart Wizard

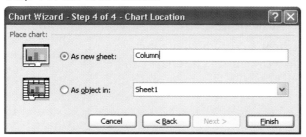

16. Click **Finish**. The chart appears on a chart sheet with a sheet tab named *Column*. The chart should appear similar to Figure 5-11.

FIGURE 5-11
Finished chart sheet

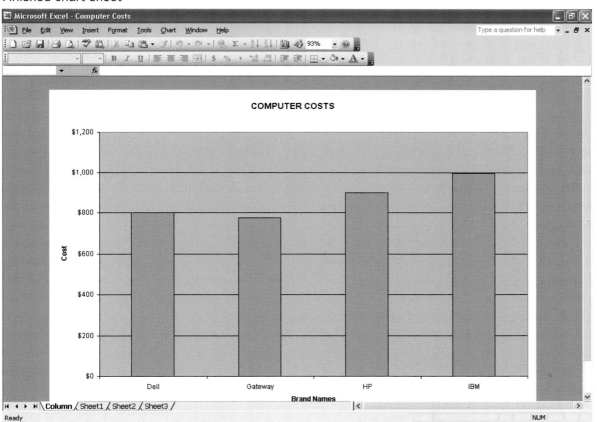

17. Save the workbook and leave it open for the next Step-by-Step.

Switching Between Chart Sheets and Worksheets

A chart sheet is closely related to the worksheet data from which it is created. If you change the data in a worksheet, these changes are automatically made in the chart created from the worksheet.

To return to the worksheet from which a chart was created, click the tab of the worksheet. The chart can be accessed once again by clicking the sheet tab with the chart name on it.

Zoom Command

You can use the *Zoom* command to enlarge a chart sheet or worksheet to see it in greater detail, or reduce it to see more on your screen. You can use the preset zoom settings or enter your own between 10% and 400% of the actual size. When you choose the Fit Selection option, the sheet is automatically sized to fit the screen. You can choose the Zoom command on the View menu or use the Zoom button on the Standard toolbar.

> **Hot Tip**
>
> Excel might display the Chart toolbar, which contains buttons that are useful in editing a chart. As you work more with charts you might want to use these buttons. To access the Chart toolbar, right-click in any existing toolbar and choose **Chart** from the shortcut menu. If you do not want the Chart toolbar displayed, you can close it.

STEP-BY-STEP 5.2

1. Click the **Sheet1** tab. The worksheet appears.

2. Edit the contents of **A6** to be **Compaq**.

3. Click the **Column** sheet tab. The chart sheet appears. The label for the third column has changed.

4. To see the labels more closely, click the arrow on the **Zoom** button. Click **100%**. Scroll to view all areas of the chart.

5. To reduce the sheet to fit the screen, open the **View** menu and choose **Zoom**. The Zoom dialog box appears.

6. Click **Fit selection** and then click **OK**.

7. Save the file and leave it open for the next Step-by-Step.

Renaming a Chart Sheet

Renaming a chart sheet is particularly useful after you have prepared several charts from the same data on a worksheet. These charts could become difficult to distinguish by their chart sheet number and are easier to recognize with more descriptive names.

> **Hot Tip**
>
> You can delete chart sheets by right-clicking the chart sheet tab, and clicking **Delete** on the shortcut menu.

STEP-BY-STEP 5.3

1. Right-click the **Column** sheet tab.

2. Click **Rename** on the shortcut menu.

3. Key **Cost Chart** on the sheet tab. (You can also change the name of the chart sheet by choosing the **Sheet** command on the **Format** menu and choosing **Rename** on the submenu, or by double-clicking the sheet tab, which highlights the name, and keying the new name.)

4. Click outside the sheet tab.

5. Save the workbook and leave it open for the next Step-by-Step.

Previewing and Printing a Chart

You preview and print a chart the same way you do a worksheet. You can click the Print Preview button to preview the sheet. You click the Print button to send the sheet directly to the printer.

STEP-BY-STEP 5.4

1. Click the **Print Preview** button. The chart appears in the preview window.

2. Click the **Print** button in the Print Preview window.

3. In the Print dialog box, click **OK**.

4. Save and close the file.

> ### Hot Tip
> You can print the chart with or without the worksheet data you used to create the chart. To print the chart only, select the chart by clicking it, and on the **File** menu, choose **Print**. To print the chart and the worksheet data, deselect the chart by clicking outside of it, and then open the **File** menu and choose **Print**.

Creating an Embedded Chart

An embedded chart appears within a worksheet rather than on a separate sheet. An embedded chart is created in the same way as a chart on a sheet with one exception. In the last step of the Chart Wizard (step 4), you click the *As object in* button rather than the *As new sheet* button.

Because embedded charts are displayed directly on the worksheet, there is the possibility that they can interfere with other worksheet data by covering it or by appearing in an area that is inconvenient for printing. You can move an embedded chart by dragging it to a different part of the worksheet. You can also change the size of an embedded chart by dragging the *image handles*, which are small black squares that appear at the corners and sides of an embedded chart.

> ### Computer Concepts
> Embedded charts are useful when you want to print a chart next to the data the chart illustrates. When a chart will be displayed or printed without the data used to create the chart, a separate chart sheet is usually more appropriate.

STEP-BY-STEP 5.5

Computer Corner is a store that sells a variety of computer products. The manager would like to determine which products comprise the largest portion of their sales by illustrating the product sales in a pie chart.

1. Open **Step5-5** from the data files, and save it as **Product Sales**, followed by your initials.

2. Select the range **A4:B8**.

3. Click the **Chart Wizard** button on the Standard toolbar.

4. Click the **Pie** chart type.

5. Click the pie chart in the upper-left corner of the *Chart sub-type* section, if it is not already selected. The description identifies the selected chart as *Pie. Displays the contribution of each value to a total.*

6. Click **Next**. The Step 2 Chart Wizard dialog box appears.

7. Click **Next**. The Step 3 Chart Wizard dialog box appears.

8. Click the **Titles** tab if it is not selected and key **Monthly Sales** in the *Chart title* text box.

9. Click the **Legend** tab and make sure the **Show legend** box is not checked.

10. Click the **Data Labels** tab and click the **Category name** and **Percentage** check boxes.

11. Click **Next**. The Step 4 Chart Wizard dialog box appears.

12. Click **As object in** if it is not already selected, and then click **Finish**.

13. Use the image handles to fit the chart within **C10:F25**. Then click outside of the chart. Your screen should look similar to Figure 5-12.

STEP-BY-STEP 5.5 Continued

FIGURE 5-12
Creating an embedded pie chart

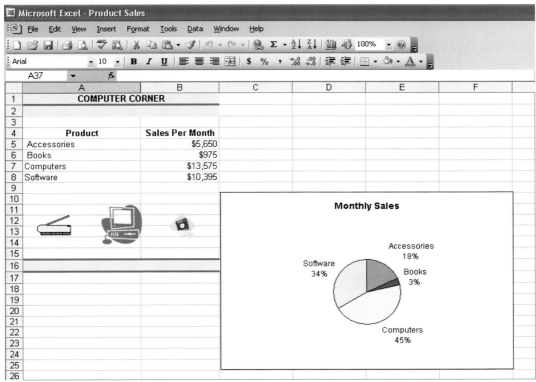

14. Save and print the worksheet and leave the file open for the next Step-by-Step.

Creating Other Types of Charts

In previous Step-by-Steps you created a column chart and a pie chart. Now you learn to create a three-dimensional chart.

Three-Dimensional Charts

Excel enables you to make charts look as though they are three-dimensional. Area, bar, column, cone, cylinder, line, surface, pie, and pyramid charts are available in three-dimensional formats.

STEP-BY-STEP 5.6

1. Save the *Product Sales* workbook as **Product Sales 3D**, followed by your initials.

2. Right-click the white space in the pie chart embedded in the worksheet. A shortcut menu appears.

3. Choose **Chart Type** on the menu. The Chart Type dialog box appears.

4. Click the middle chart in the top row of the *Chart sub-type* section. The chart description *Pie with a 3-D visual effect* appears at the bottom of the dialog box.

5. Click **OK**. You are returned to the worksheet. Click outside the chart to deselect it. Your screen should look similar to Figure 5-13.

FIGURE 5-13
3-D pie chart

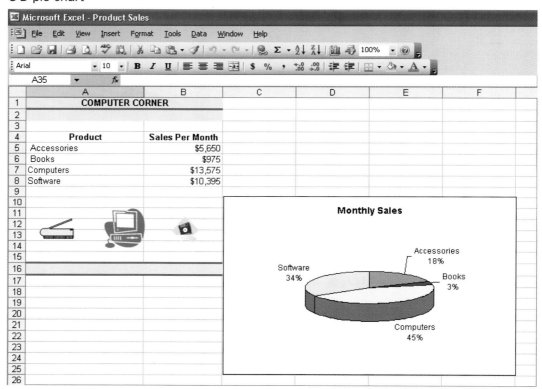

6. Save, print, and then close the file.

Editing a Chart

The Chart Wizard is a quick and easy way to create professional-looking charts. However, you might want to edit the chart to suit your specific needs. For example, you might want to change a title font or the color of a column. Figure 5-14 shows six areas of the chart that can be changed. Clicking once on the part selects it; double-clicking it opens a dialog box in which you can make formatting changes. Each dialog box contains tabs with options for editing specific chart characteristics, as described in Table 5-2. Right-clicking a part displays a shortcut menu with options such as clearing data, inserting data, or changing chart types.

FIGURE 5-14
Six parts of the chart

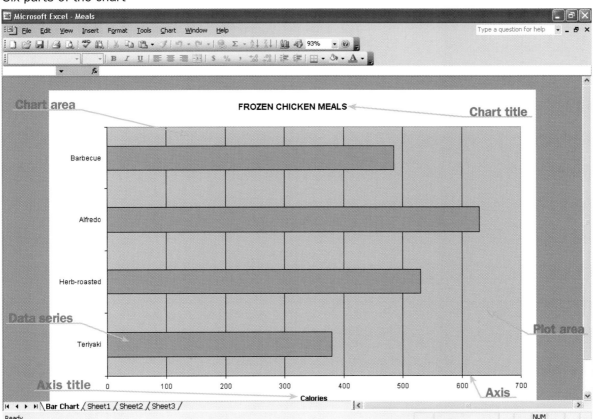

TABLE 5-2
Charts can be edited using Format dialog boxes

FORMAT DIALOG BOX	TABS IN THE DIALOG BOX
Format Chart Title	Patterns—designates the border and color of the chart title. Font—designates the font, font size, and color of characters in the chart title. Alignment—designates the justification and orientation of the chart title.
Format Axis Title	Patterns—designates the border and color of the axis title. Font—designates the font and font size of characters in the axis title. Alignment—designates the justification and orientation of the axis title.
Format Axis	Patterns—designates the border and color of the axis. Scale—designates characteristics of the axis scale. Font—designates the font and font size of characters in the axis. Number—designates the format of numbers in the labels in the axis (for example, currency, text, date). Alignment—designates the orientation of the labels in the axis.
Format Data Series	Patterns—designates the border and color of the data series. Axis—designates whether the data is plotted on a primary or secondary axis. Y Error Bars—designates the treatment of points that extend beyond the scale of the chart. Data Labels—designates the words or values that may appear on the points of a graph. Series Order—designates which data series will appear first in clustered charts. Options—designates the other characteristics unique to the chart type.
Format Plot Area	Patterns—designates the border and color of the plot area.
Format Chart Area	Patterns—designates the border and color of the chart background. Font—designates the font and font size of characters in the chart area.

STEP-BY-STEP 5.7

1. Open **Step5-7** from the data files, and save it as **Meals**, followed by your initials. This is a worksheet containing nutritional facts about frozen chicken meals.

2. Click the **Bar Chart** sheet tab. The sheet contains a chart that indicates the calories of each meal.

3. To add a subtitle, click the chart title **FROZEN CHICKEN MEALS**. A shaded border with handles surrounds the title.

4. Click to the right of the last *S* in the title. An insertion point appears.

5. Tap **Enter**. The insertion point becomes centered under the first line of the title.

6. Key **Nutrition**. The subtitle appears in the chart.

7. To change the font size of the Value Y axis label, double-click **Calories**. The Format Axis Title dialog box appears.

8. Click the **Font** tab. The axis label is currently 10 points.

9. Choose **12** in the *Size* box.

10. Click **OK**. You are returned to the chart sheet. The Value Y axis label is now larger.

11. To change the color of the bars, right-click one of the bars and select **Format Data Series** on the shortcut menu. The Format Data Series dialog box appears.

12. Click the **Patterns** tab if it is not already selected.

13. Click any bright yellow in the *Area* box. A bright yellow color appears in the *Sample* box.

14. Click **OK**. You are returned to the chart sheet. The chart appears with bright yellow bars. Your screen should appear similar to Figure 5-15 on the next page.

STEP-BY-STEP 5.7 Continued

FIGURE 5-15
Editing a chart

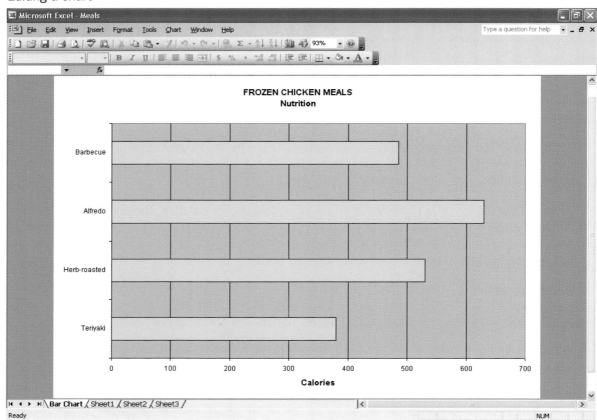

15. Save the workbook and leave it open for the next Step-by-Step.

Changing the Type of Chart

After creating a chart, you can change it to a different type. The Chart Type dialog box is the same dialog box that appears in the Step 1 Chart Wizard dialog box (see Figure 5-5).

> **Computer Concepts**
>
> Not all charts are interchangeable. For example, data that is suitable for a pie chart is often not logical in a scatter chart. However, most line charts are easily converted into column or bar charts.

STEP-BY-STEP 5.8

1. Open the **Chart** menu and choose **Chart Type**.

2. Click **Line** in the *Chart type* box.

3. Click the middle box in the first column of the *Chart sub-type* section if it is not already selected. The description identifies the selected chart as *Line with markers displayed at each data value*.

4. Click **OK**. The new line chart appears.

5. Rename the chart sheet as **Line Chart**. Your line chart should appear as shown in Figure 5-16.

FIGURE 5-16
Changing a column chart to a line chart

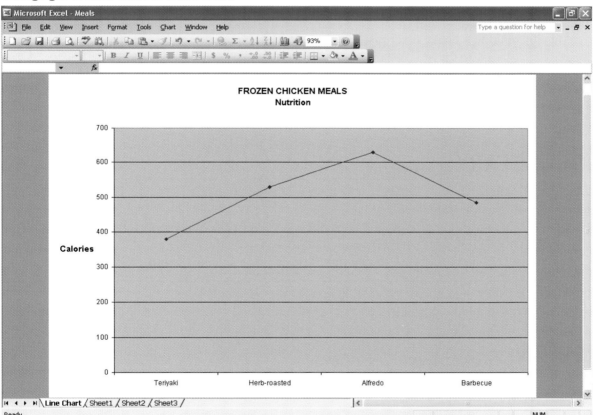

6. Save, print, and close the file.

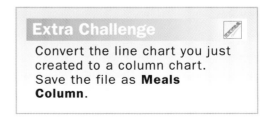

Extra Challenge

Convert the line chart you just created to a column chart. Save the file as **Meals Column**.

SUMMARY

In this lesson, you learned:

- A chart is a graphical representation of worksheet data. You can create several types of worksheet charts. Several types of charts can also be created in a three-dimensional format.

- Charts can be embedded within a worksheet or created on a chart sheet. A chart sheet is a separate worksheet within the workbook. An embedded chart is created on the same worksheet that contains the data being charted.

- The Chart Wizard is a four-step, on-screen guide that helps you prepare a chart from an Excel worksheet. You can use the Chart Wizard to prepare an embedded chart or a chart in a chart sheet.

- A chart created from data on a worksheet is considered part of the same workbook. When you save the workbook, you also save the charts you have created from worksheet data.

- You can rename a chart sheet just as you rename a worksheet.

- You can print a chart from a chart sheet.

- You can edit a chart by selecting the part you want to modify and then accessing the Format dialog box. You can change the type of chart in the Chart Type dialog box.

VOCABULARY *Review*

Define the following terms:

Chart	Column chart	Line chart
Chart sheet	Embedded chart	Pie chart
ChartWizard	Image handles	Zoom

REVIEW *Questions*

TRUE/FALSE

Circle T if the statement is true or F if the statement is false.

T F **1.** Charts make the data of a worksheet easier to understand.

T F **2.** Pie charts are the best way to represent data groups that are part of a whole.

T F **3.** When the worksheet data changes, charts created from that data also change.

T F **4.** A column chart uses bars that run horizontally in the plot are.

T F **5.** A chart sheet is a separate sheet and is not found in the workbook.

FILL IN THE BLANK

Complete the following sentences by writing the correct word or words in the blanks provided.

1. A(n)_____ is a four-step, on-screen guide that aids in preparing a chart from worksheet data.

2. A(n)_____ is a graphical representation of data.

3. The _____ command is used to enlarge a chart sheet or worksheet to see it in greater detail.

4. A(n) _____ chart is created on the same sheet as the data being charted.

5. _____ are small black squares that appear at the corners and sides of an embedded chart.

PROJECTS

PROJECT 5-1

The file Project5-1 contains the names of the National Park System's least visited parks and the attendance for 2002. Create a column chart to illustrate the data for the five least attended parks.

1. Open **Project5-1** from the data files, and save it as **Parks,** followed by your initials.

2. Create a column chart from the data in **A3:B8** in a chart sheet.

3. Title the chart **Least Visited Parks**.

4. Title the Y-axis **Attendance in 2002**. No X-axis title is needed.

5. Do not include a legend in the chart.

6. Name the chart sheet **Column Chart**.

7. Preview the chart.

8. Save, print, and close the file.

PROJECT 5-2

You have been walking each morning to stay in shape. Over the past five weeks you have recorded your walking distance in file Project5-2.

1. Open **Project5-2** from the data files, and save it as **Exercise,** followed by your initials.

2. Create an embedded line chart from the data in **A5:B9**.

3. Insert **Walking Distance** as the chart title.

4. Title the X-axis **Week**. Title the Y-axis **Miles**.

5. Do not include a legend in the chart.

6. Use the chart handles to position the chart in the range **A18:G34** on the worksheet.

7. Right-click the Value Axis labels, and click **Format Axis** on the shortcut menu.

8. In the Format Axis dialog box, click the **Scale** tab.

9. Change the *Maximum value* to **16**, the *Major unit* to **2**, and the *Minor unit* to **0.4**, if necessary. Click **OK**.

10. Save the file. Print the worksheet with the embedded chart, and close the file.

PROJECT 5-3

The file Project5-3 contains the number of calories in a typical fast food meal.

1. Open **Project5-3** from the data files, and save it as **Calories**, followed by your initials.

2. Create a pie chart in a chart sheet from the data in **A4:B7**.

3. Title the chart **Calorie Awareness**.

4. Place a legend on the right side of the chart that identifies each item.

5. Include percentages as data labels next to each slice.

6. Name the chart sheet **Pie Chart**.

7. Edit font sizes so the chart title is **24** points, the slice percentages are **18** points, and the legend is **18** points.

8. Switch to the worksheet. Edit the content of **B4** to be **450**.

9. Switch back to the chart sheet to see that the chart has been updated with the edited data.

10. Save the file. Print the chart and close the file.

PROJECT 5-4

The file Project5-4 contains the number of calories in a typical fast food meal and a similar meal with fewer calories.

1. Open **Project5-4** from the data files, and save it as **Fewer Calories**, followed by your initials.

2. Create a three-dimensional pie chart on a chart sheet from the data in **C4:D7**.

3. Title the pie chart **Eating Better**.

4. Do not include a legend in the chart.

5. The pie chart should include the category names and percentages for each slice.

6. Name the chart sheet **3D Pie Chart**.

7. Change the font size of the chart title to **18** points and bold it.

8. Change the font size of the data labels to **14** points.

9. Preview the chart.

10. Save the file. Print the chart and close the file.

PROJECT 5-5

The file Project5-5 contains the scores for assignments in Social Studies class. Your teacher would like to see the scores for Assignment 1 for the seventh graders charted in a column chart.

1. Open **Project5-5** from the data files, and save it as **Social Studies Class**, followed by your initials.

2. Create an embedded three-dimensional column chart from the data in **B3:C5**. (*Hint*: Click the first chart in the second row of the *Chart sub-type* section.)

3. Title the chart **Assignment 1**.

4. Title the Category (X) axis **7th Grade Students**.

5. Title the Value (Z) axis **Scores**.

6. Do not include gridlines, a legend, or data labels in the chart.

7. Use the image handles to fit the chart within **A20:E36**.

8. Change the font size of the chart title to **20** points.

9. Change the font size of the axis titles to **14** points.

10. Double-click a column to display the Format Data Series dialog box. Click the **Patterns** tab if necessary, and change the color to bright blue.

11. Double-click the plot area and change it to medium green.

12. Double-click the chart area and change it to a lighter shade of green.

13. Double-click the chart walls and floor and change to red.

14. Preview the chart.

15. Save the file. Print the chart and close the file.

WEB*Project*

PROJECT 5-6

Microsoft maintains and frequently updates a newsletter on its Web site. There is a special section on Excel. Go to **www.msoffice.com** and search for information about charts. Write a brief report about your findings.

TEAMWORK *Project*

PROJECT 5-7

Using a daily newspaper and working in groups, search for and make a list of current topics that could easily be displayed in a chart format.

CRITICAL *Thinking*

ACTIVITY 5-1

For each situation, determine what type of worksheet chart you believe would be the most appropriate to represent the data. Justify your answer by describing why you believe the chart is most appropriate.

Situation 1. A movie theater has kept track of daily tickets sold for the first week's showing of a current movie. The movie may be nominated for an Academy Award. The theater manager would like to see how the attendance increased or decreased during the week.

Situation 2. A high school counselor works with students who come from eight middle schools. She has recorded the name of the middle school and the number of students from each one. She would like to illustrate how some of the middle schools supply significantly more students than other middle schools.

Situation 3. You receive an allowance on a monthly basis from your parents. You usually spend your money on things like food, entertainment, school supplies, clothing, and miscellaneous items. In order to prove to your parents that you need an increase in your allowance, you create a chart to illustrate your spending habits.

MICROSOFT EXCEL

COMMAND SUMMARY

FEATURE	MENU COMMAND	TOOLBAR BUTTON	LESSON
Bold Data	Format, Cells, Font	**B**	2
Borders around Cells	Format, Cells, Border		2
Chart, Create a	Insert, Chart		5
Chart, Preview a	File, Print Preview		5
Column Width, Specific	Format, Column, Width		2
Copy by Filling	Edit, Fill		4
Clip Art, Insert	Insert, Picture, Clip Art		4
Data, Copy	Edit, Copy		2
Data, Paste	Edit, Paste		2
Data Ascending, Sort	Data, Sort		4
Data Descending, Sort	Data, Sort		4
Data, Replace	Edit, Replace		4
Fill a Cell with Color	Format, Cells, Patterns		2
Font, Change a	Format, Cells, Font	Arial	2
Font, Color	Format, Cells, Font	A	2
Font Size, Change the	Format, Cells, Font	10	2
Function Formula, Insert a	Insert, Function	f_x	3
Italicize Data	Format, Cell, Font	*I*	2
Picture from a File, Insert	Insert, Picture, From File		4
Spelling Check	Tools, Spelling		4
Sum a Range (AutoSum)	Insert, Function	Σ	3
Titles, Freeze the	Window, Freeze Panes		4
Titles, Unfreeze	Window, Unfreeze Panes		4
Worksheet, Name a	Format, Sheet, Rename		5
Worksheet, Open a	File, Open		1
Worksheet, Preview a	File, Print Preview		1
Worksheet, Print a	File, Print		1
Worksheet, Save a Named	File, Save		1
Worksheet, Save an Unnamed	File, Save As		1
Zoom	View, Zoom	100%	5

REVIEW *Questions*

TRUE/FALSE

Circle T if the statement is true or F if the statement is false.

T F 1. A worksheet is a computerized spreadsheet in Excel.

T F 2. Once data has been entered in a cell, it cannot be changed without deleting it first.

T F 3. Numbers entered in cells can be used to calculate values in other cells.

T F 4. Freezing keeps data from being changed.

T F 5. A chart can be displayed within the worksheet.

MATCHING

Match the description in Column 2 with the term in Column 1.

Column 1	Column 2
___ 1. Active cell	A. An on-screen guide that aids in creating a chart
___ 2. Paste	B. Tells Excel what to do with a number or cell used in formulas
___ 3. Operator	C. Organizes data in an order that is more meaningful
___ 4. Sorting	D. The cell that contains the highlight
___ 5. Chart Wizard	E. To copy text from one cell and place it in another cell

PROJECTS

PROJECT 1

The worksheet in *Project1* is a research project about the history of shoes. (This information was obtained from the Web site *www.centuryinshoes.com*.) Change the appearance of the worksheet to make it easier to read.

1. Open **Project1** from the data files, and save it as **Shoe History**, followed by your initials.

2. Change the size of the text in **A1** to **16** points.

3. Change the width of column **B** to **44**.

4. Change the size of the text in **A2:C2** to **12** points.

5. Change the data in **A9** to **Mid 1500s**.

6. Copy the data in **C3** and paste in **C11**.

7. Select **B3:B12** and add an outline border that is thick and a lime color.

8. Save, print, and close the file.

PROJECT 2

One of your favorite articles of clothing to wear is jeans. Jeans are made from a fabric originally produced in Europe called *jean*. It was named after sailors from Genoa, Italy, who wore clothing made from it. Later it was called denim. The workbook *Project2* is a list of important events in the development of jeans.

1. Open **Project2** from the data files, and save it as **Jeans**, followed by your initials.

2. Change the width of column **A** to **10**, column **B** to **15**, column **C** to **20**, and column **D** to **42**.

3. Change **A4:A14** to number format with no decimals and no comma separator.

4. Sort **A4:D14** by **Era** in ascending order.

5. Select **A1** and change the font to **Bazooka** (if Bazooka is not available, use a font of your choice), the font size to **14**, the font color to blue, and the fill color to gold.

6. Bold the text in **A3:D3**; then change the fill color to light blue, and the font color to white.

7. Fill **A15:D15** with light blue.

8. Select **D17:D21** and add a thick gold border to the bottom.

9. Fill **D17** with gold.

10. Insert the picture **Blue Jeans** from the data files.

11. Size and move the picture so that it fits in the middle of **C17:C21**.

12. Check the spelling and change misspellings as appropriate.

13. Save the file and leave it open for the next project.

PROJECT 3

You decide to add a chart to the *Jeans* file.

1. Create a line chart as an object in Sheet1 using the data in **B4:B14**.

2. In the Step 2 of 4 Chart Wizard dialog box, select the **Series** tab and enter **Sheet1!$A$4:$A$14** in the *Category (X) axis labels* box.

3. Enter the chart title **The Era of Jeans**.

4. Enter **Year** for the X-axis label.

5. Enter **Popularity Scale** for the Y-axis label.

6. Do not include a legend.

7. Move the chart so that it fits in **A23:D38**.

8. Rename **Sheet1** as **Jeans Era**.

9. Change the chart area color to gold.

10. Save, preview, print, and close the file.

PROJECT 4

The file *Project4* is a workbook that contains a list of school holidays for this school year. You will determine how many days are holidays and display them in a chart.

1. Open **Project4** from the data files, and save it as **Holidays**, followed by your initials.

2. Select **B11** and create a formula to find the total of **B3:B10**.

3. Bold the text in **A11**.

4. Select the data in **B7** and fill down to **B8**.

5. Freeze the titles in **A2:B2**. Scroll down to see the pictures at the bottom of the worksheet until they are just below the title area.

6. Delete the picture of the bells.

7. Choose one of the remaining pictures and move it to replace the bells.

8. Delete any pictures that are left. Unfreeze the panes.

9. Create a three-dimensional pie chart in a chart sheet using the data in **A3:B10**.

10. Title the chart **Vacation Days**. Place a legend at the bottom of the chart to identify the slices. Include percentages next to each slice.

11. Name the chart sheet **Pie Chart**.

12. Edit font sizes so the chart title is **22** points, the slice percentages are **15** points, and the legend is **12** points.

13. Select **Sheet1**, and create a column chart in a chart sheet using the data in **A3:B10**.

14. Title the chart **Vacation Days**. No X-axis label is needed. The Y-axis label is **Number of Days**. No legend is needed.

15. Name the chart sheet **Column Chart**.

16. Change the color of the data series to one of your choice.

17. Change the color of the plot area to a complimentary color of your choice.

18. Change the chart title to 20 points.

19. Change the font color of the value axis title to a color of your choice.

20. Preview your completed work.

21. Save the file, print each chart, and close the file.

PROJECT 5

Your family is considering the purchase of a new cell phone. To help them make a good decision, you found an article in a consumers' magazine and copied the information into a worksheet. *Project5* is a comparison of brands.

1. Open **Project5** from the data files, and save it as **Phones,** followed by your initials.

2. Select **A1** and change the text to bold, the size to **18**, and fill the cell with a color of your choice.

3. Select **A3:I3** and change the text to bold and fill it with a different color than the one you selected for A1.

4. Widen all columns to better display data. (*Hint*: All columns except C and G *must* be widened.)

5. Select **C4:C10** and format for currency with no decimal.

6. Select **C12** and use a formula to find the average price of **C4:C10**.

7. Select **C13** and use a formula to find the lowest price of **C4:C10**.

8. Select **C14** and use a formula to find the highest price of **C4:C10**.

9. Select **A12:C15** and add an outline border that is the same color as the fill color in **A3:I3**.

10. Enter a formula in **G4** to multiply the price in **C4** by the tax rate in **C15**. (*Hint*: Make C15 an absolute cell reference.)

11. Copy the formula in **G4** to **G5:G10**.

12. Enter a formula in **H4** to calculate the total price. (*Hint*: The price plus the tax gives you total price.)

13. Copy the formula in **H4** to **H5:H10**.

14. Format **G4:G10** and **H4:H10** for currency with no decimal.

15. Sort the data by the **Price** column from lowest to highest.

16. Clear all data in **I3:I10**.

17. To make the worksheet more appealing, add the same fill color used in A3:H3 to **A17:H17**.

18. Select **A12:C15** and change the text to bold.

19. Save, print, and close the file.

PORTFOLIO *Checklist*

Include the following files from this unit in your student portfolio:

Lesson 1

___ Budget

___ Moving

___ Litter

___ Tree Project

___ Classmates

Lesson 2

___ Volunteers

___ Pet Supplies

___ Sports Equipment

___ Salt Experiment

Lesson 3

___ Computing

___ Math

___ Stars

___ Sandwich Servings

___ State Populations

Lesson 4

___ Cat and Dog Names

___ Kool Treats

___ Kool Treats Display

___ Friday Class

___ Top Movies

___ Temperatures

Lesson 5

___ Computer Costs

___ Product Sales

___ Product Sales 3D

___ Meals

___ Parks

___ Exercise

___ Calories

___ Fewer Calories

___ Social Studies Class

Unit Review

___ Shoe History

___ Jeans

___ Holidays

___ Phones

MICROSOFT ACCESS

Unit 5

 Estimated Time for Unit: 6 hours

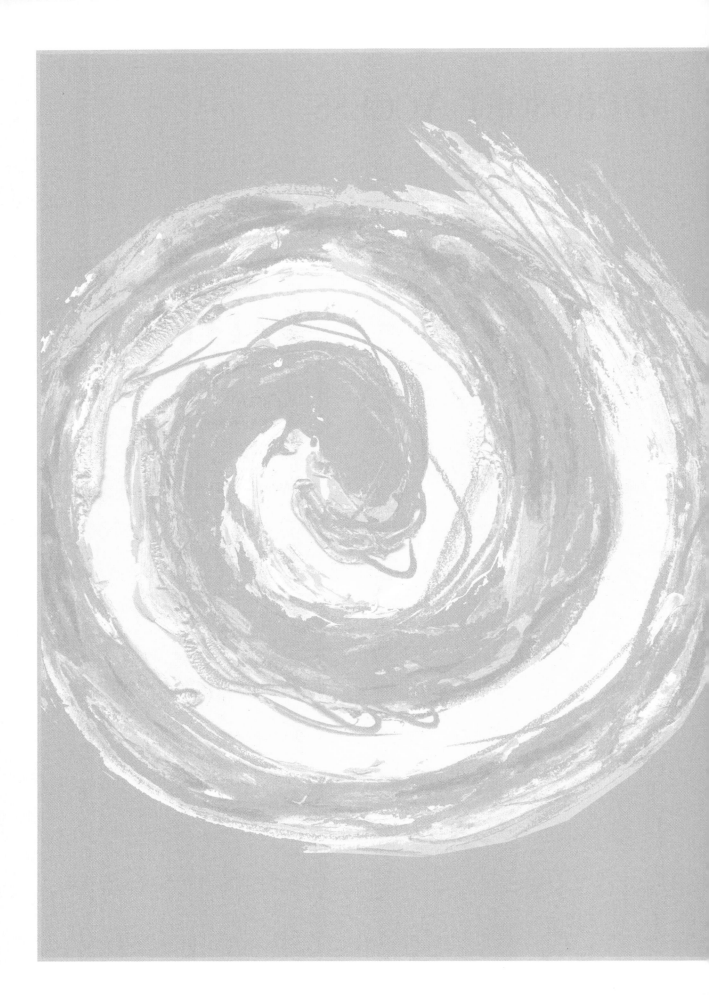

ACCESS BASICS

What Is Access?

Access is the database application of the Microsoft Office 2003 suite of programs. A *database* helps you to store large amounts of information. A database is like a filing cabinet that contains folders of documents. Compared to a paper filing system, a database has the following advantages:

1. Records can be retrieved quickly. You can find the information you need by tapping keys rather than searching through folders in a filing cabinet.

2. Records can be used easily. You can sort records quickly in various ways, find a specific record, or select a group of records.

3. Records can be stored using very little space. You can store large amounts of data in a database. Filing cabinets of paper in folders require large amounts of space.

S TEP-BY-STEP 1.1

1. With Windows running, click **Start** on the taskbar.

2. Point to **All Programs** (in Windows 2000, point to **Programs**), and then **Microsoft Office**. Click **Microsoft Office Access 2003**.

3. Access opens and the Access startup screen appears, as shown in Figure 1-1. Leave this screen open for the next Step-by-Step.

FIGURE 1-1
Access startup screen

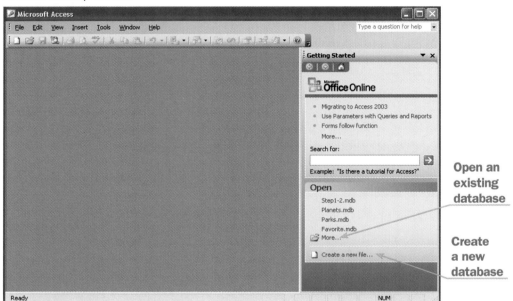

Opening a Database

When you open a database, the Database window appears, as shown in Figure 1-2. The Objects bar, on the left side of the window, lists the types of database objects. In the middle of the window, three ways for creating a table and one existing table named *State Information* are listed. You will learn more about database objects later in this lesson.

FIGURE 1-2
Database window

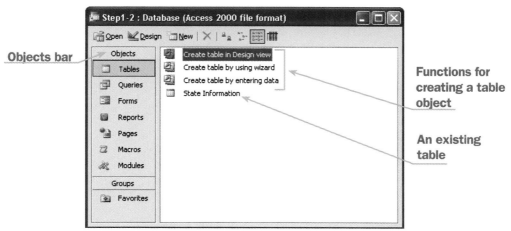

Objects bar

Functions for creating a table object

An existing table

STEP-BY-STEP 1.2

1. Click the **More . . .** option in the Open section of the Getting Started task pane. The Open dialog box displays. If the **More . . .** option is not displayed, choose **Open . . .** instead.

2. Open the file **Step1-2** from the data files. The Database window appears, as previously shown in Figure 1-2. Leave the database open for the next Step-by-Step. (Note: If a security warning appears asking if you want to block unsafe expressions, click **Yes**. A message will display asking you to restart Access. Click **OK**, and then close and restart Access. Reopen **Step1-2** from the data files. Another security warning displays asking if you want to open this file or cancel. Click **Open**. Ask your instructor for instructions on how to keep this message from displaying.)

The Access Screen

Like other Microsoft Office 2003 programs, the Access screen has a title bar, menu bar, and toolbar. At the bottom of the screen is the status bar. If necessary, click the down arrow in the Objects bar to view the other objects. Figure 1-3 shows the Access screen with the *Step1-2* database open.

FIGURE 1-3
Access screen

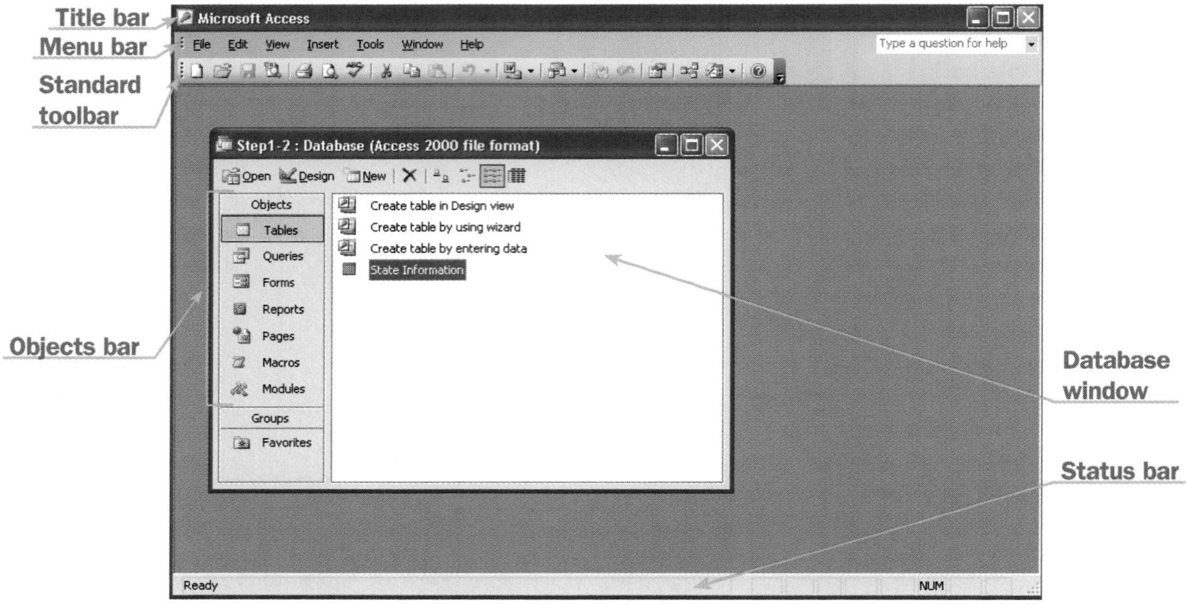

Title bar
Menu bar
Standard toolbar
Objects bar
Database window
Status bar

As you use Access, different windows and dialog boxes will appear on the screen. Unlike Word and Excel, Access does not have a standard view. In Access the screen changes based on how you use the database.

Database Objects

When a database is saved, the file that is saved contains a group of objects. These objects work together to store data, retrieve data, display data, and print reports. The Objects bar in the Database window displays a button for each type of object. If necessary, click the down arrow on the bar to view the additional objects.

Table 1-1 briefly explains the purpose of each type of object.

TABLE 1-1
Database objects

OBJECT	DESCRIPTION
Table	Tables store data in a format similar to that of a worksheet. All database information is stored in tables.
Query	Queries search for and retrieve data from tables based on specific information. A query is a question you ask the database.
Form	Forms allow you to display data in a special format. You might, for example, create a form that matches a paper form.
Report	Reports also display data in a special format. Reports, however, are used for printing data. You can even do Math in a report.
Page	Data access pages let you design database objects so that they can be put on the Web.
Macro	Macros let you perform more than one activity with a single command.
Module	Modules are like macros but use a programming language to create more difficult database jobs.

S TEP-BY-STEP 1.3

1. Make sure **Tables** is selected on the Objects bar. Highlight the **State Information** table in the database objects window, and click the **Open** button. The table appears, as shown in Figure 1-4.

FIGURE 1-4
Database table

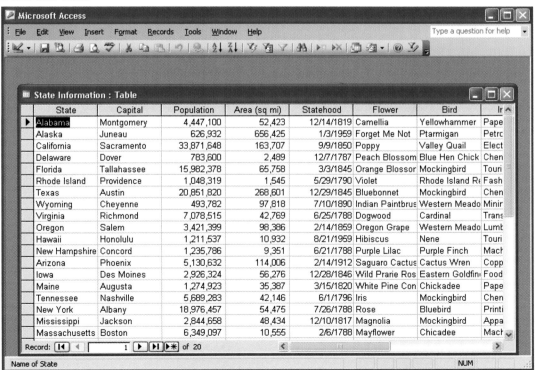

STEP-BY-STEP 1.3 Continued

2. Open the **File** menu and choose **Close** to close the table. The database objects window is visible again.

3. Click **Queries** on the Objects bar. There is one query object named *Mockingbird*. This query locates the states with the mockingbird as the state bird.

4. Click **Forms** on the Objects bar. There is one form object named *State Information Form*.

5. Open the **File** menu and choose **Close** to close the database. Leave Access open for the next Step-by-Step.

Database Terms

Four terms are necessary to know when working with databases. These terms relate to the way data is organized in a table. A *record* is a complete set of data. In the *State Information* table, each State is stored as a record. In a table, a record appears as a row, as shown in Figure 1-5.

Each record is made up of *fields*. For example, the capital of each state is placed in a special field that is created to accept state capitals. In a table, fields appear as columns. In order to identify the fields, each field has a *field name*. The data entered into a field is called an *entry*. In the *State Information* database, for example, the first record has Alabama as an entry in the State field.

FIGURE 1-5
Records and fields

State	Capital	Population	Area (sq mi)	Statehood	Flower	Bird	Ir
Alabama	Montgomery	4,447,100	52,423	12/14/1819	Camellia	Yellowhammer	Pape
Alaska	Juneau	626,932	656,425	1/3/1959	Forget Me Not	Ptarmigan	Petro
California	Sacramento	33,871,648	163,707	9/9/1850	Poppy	Valley Quail	Elect
Delaware	Dover	783,600	2,489	12/7/1787	Peach Blossom	Blue Hen Chick	Chen
Florida	Tallahassee	15,982,378	65,758	3/3/1845	Orange Blossor	Mockingbird	Touri
Rhode Island	Providence	1,048,319	1,545	5/29/1790	Violet	Rhode Island Re	Fash
Texas	Austin	20,851,820	268,601	12/29/1845	Bluebonnet	Mockingbird	Chen
Wyoming	Cheyenne	493,782	97,818	7/10/1890	Indian Paintbrus	Western Meado	Minir
Virginia	Richmond	7,078,515	42,769	6/25/1788	Dogwood	Cardinal	Trans
Oregon	Salem	3,421,399	98,386	2/14/1859	Oregon Grape	Western Meado	Lumb
Hawaii	Honolulu	1,211,537	10,932	8/21/1959	Hibiscus	Nene	Touri
New Hampshire	Concord	1,235,786	9,351	6/21/1788	Purple Lilac	Purple Finch	Mach
Arizona	Phoenix	5,130,632	114,006	2/14/1912	Saguaro Cactus	Cactus Wren	Copp
Iowa	Des Moines	2,926,324	56,276	12/28/1846	Wild Prarie Ros	Eastern Goldfin	Food
Maine	Augusta	1,274,923	35,387	3/15/1820	White Pine Con	Chickadee	Pape
Tennessee	Nashville	5,689,283	42,146	6/1/1796	Iris	Mockingbird	Chen
New York	Albany	18,976,457	54,475	7/26/1788	Rose	Bluebird	Printi
Mississippi	Jackson	2,844,658	48,434	12/10/1817	Magnolia	Mockingbird	Appa
Massachusetts	Boston	6,349,097	10,555	2/6/1788	Mayflower	Chicadee	Mach

Creating a Database

The first step in creating a database is to create the file that will hold the database objects. To do this, you open the File menu and choose New. The Access startup screen appears, as shown in Figure 1-6.

FIGURE 1-6
Access startup screen

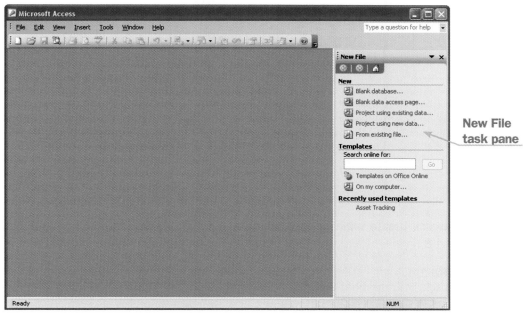

*S*TEP-BY-STEP 1.4

1. Open the **File** menu and choose **New**. The Access startup screen appears, as shown in Figure 1-6.

2. In the New File task pane on the right side of the screen, choose **Blank database** and the File New Database dialog box appears.

STEP-BY-STEP 1.4 Continued

3. In the *File name* box, key **Dogs** followed by your initials, and then click **Create**. Your Database window should look like that shown in Figure 1-7.

FIGURE 1-7
Database window

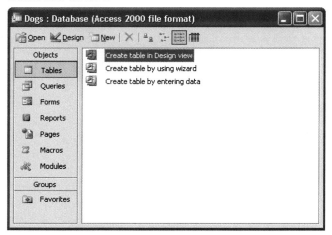

4. Double-click **Create table by entering data**. A new table appears in Datasheet view, as shown in Figure 1-8.

FIGURE 1-8
New table in Datasheet view

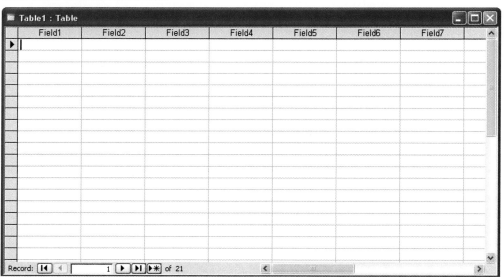

5. Open the **File** menu and choose **Close** to go back to the Database window. Leave the window open for the next Step-by-Step.

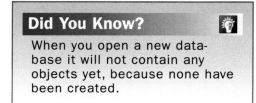

Did You Know?

When you open a new database it will not contain any objects yet, because none have been created.

Creating Tables

Creating a table is the next step after creating a database. The most common way is to create the table in *Design view*. This is the view where you will design new tables and change the design of existing tables.

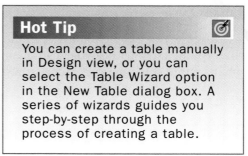

Hot Tip

You can create a table manually in Design view, or you can select the Table Wizard option in the New Table dialog box. A series of wizards guides you step-by-step through the process of creating a table.

STEP-BY-STEP 1.5

1. Click **Tables** on the Objects bar, if necessary, and then click **New**. The New Table dialog box appears, as shown in Figure 1-9.

FIGURE 1-9
New Table dialog box

2. Choose the **Design View** option and click **OK**. The Design view window opens. Leave the window on the screen for the next Step-by-Step.

Designing a Table

Now you are ready to design your table. You create the table's fields in the Design view window. As you can see in the window on your screen, each field in a table is divided into three sections: Field Name, Data Type, and Description. You will insert data in each of these three sections to create a table.

Field Names

First you have to decide what data you need to store. For example, suppose you want to create a database of your family members' birthdays. Some fields to include would be each person's name, address, and birthdate. An example of a record would be: Halie Jones (name), 3410 Vicksburg Ave., Dallas, TX 75224 (address), and 10/28/89 (birth date). You will key the names of these fields in the Field Name column. It is best to create meaningful field names that describe the data.

Data Type

After keying the field name, tap the Tab key to move to the Data Type column. Then determine the type of data to be stored in each field. Choose an appropriate data type that tells Access what kind of information can be stored in the field. Table 1-2 briefly describes the basic data types.

TABLE 1-2
Data types

DATA TYPE	DESCRIPTION
Text	The Text data type allows letters and numbers. A text field can hold up to 255 characters. Data such as names and addresses is stored in fields of this type.
Memo	The Memo data type also allows letters and numbers. A memo field is different because it can hold thousands of characters.
Number	The Number data type holds numeric data.
Date/Time	The Date/Time data type holds dates and times.
Currency	The Currency data type is formatted for dollar amounts.
AutoNumber	The AutoNumber data type is increased by Access for each new record added.
Yes/No	A Yes/No field can hold the values Yes/No, True/False, or On/Off.
OLE Object	The OLE Object data type is used for some of the more advanced features. It allows you to store graphics, sound, and even objects such as spreadsheets in a field.
Hyperlink	The Hyperlink data type is used to store a hyperlink.
Lookup Wizard	The Lookup Wizard creates a field that allows you to choose a value from another table or from a list.

Description

The last step in designing a table is to key a description for each field. The description explains the data in the field.

Hot Tip

Choosing the correct data type is important. For example, you might think a telephone number or ZIP code should be stored in a field with a Number data type. However, you should only use Number data types when you plan to do Math with the data. You won't be adding or subtracting ZIP codes. Numbers that will not be used in Math are best stored as Text.

STEP-BY-STEP 1.6

To help your family in choosing a dog, you will create a database listing dog breeds and some basic physical features.

1. Key **Breed** in the first row of the Field Name column.

2. Tap the **Tab** (or **Enter**) key. The data type will default to Text, which is appropriate for the name of the breed.

3. Tap **Tab** to move to the Description column.

4. Key **Name of breed** and tap **Enter** to move to the next row.

5. Key the other fields and descriptions shown in Figure 1-10. All of the fields are Text data type.

FIGURE 1-10
Defining fields in a table

Field Name	Data Type	Description
Breed	Text	Name of breed
Group	Text	Name of group
Height	Text	Average height
Weight	Text	Average weight

6. Click in the **Data Type** box for the Group field. A down arrow will appear.

7. Click the arrow and choose **Lookup Wizard** from the drop-down menu that appears. The Lookup Wizard screen displays.

8. Choose **I will type in the values that I want** and click **Next**. A second Lookup Wizard screen displays.

9. Leave the *Number of columns* at 1 and key the Lookup values as shown in Figure 1-11, using the Tab key to move down through the list. Click **Finish** when finished.

FIGURE 1-11
Lookup Wizard screen

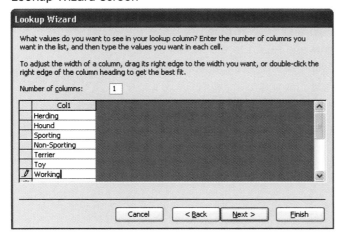

STEP-BY-STEP 1.6 Continued

10. In the first blank row, key **Grooming** in the Field Name column and tap **Tab**.

11. Click the arrow in the **Data Type** field and choose **Yes/No** from the drop-down menu that appears.

12. Tap **Tab**.

13. Key **Is grooming necessary?** in the Description column. Tap **Tab**. Leave the Design view window on the screen for the next Step-by-Step.

Naming and Saving a Table

After designing a table, you must give it a name and save the design. You should choose a name that describes the data to be stored in the table.

STEP-BY-STEP 1.7

1. Open the **File** menu and choose **Save**. The Save As dialog box appears, as shown in Figure 1-12.

FIGURE 1-12
Save As dialog box

2. Key **Breed Information** in the *Table Name* box and click **OK**.

3. A message box appears asking if you want to create a primary key. Click **No**.

4. Open the **File** menu and choose **Close** to close the Design view window and return to the Database window. Note that your *Breed Information* table now appears as an object, as shown in Figure 1-13. Leave the Database window open for the next Step-by-Step.

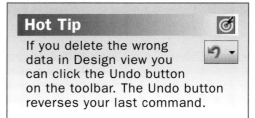

Hot Tip

If you delete the wrong data in Design view you can click the Undo button on the toolbar. The Undo button reverses your last command.

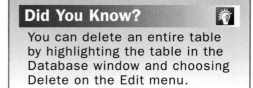

Did You Know?

You can delete an entire table by highlighting the table in the Database window and choosing Delete on the Edit menu.

STEP-BY-STEP 1.7 Continued

FIGURE 1-13
Database window showing *Breed Information* table as an object

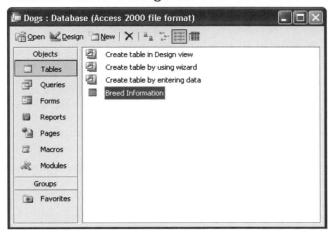

Changing Tables

To change the design of a table, you must be in Design view. In Design view, you can make changes to the names of fields, data formats, and descriptions. You can add fields to the end of the list, or you can insert a new row for a field between existing fields.

STEP-BY-STEP 1.8

1. Highlight the **Breed Information** table in the Database window if it's not selected already.

2. Click the **Design** button. The table appears in Design view.

3. Place the insertion point in the **Grooming** field name.

4. Click the **Insert Rows** button on the toolbar. A blank row is inserted above the Grooming field.

5. In the blank row, key **Color** as the Field Name, choose **Text** as the Data Type, and key **Available colors** as the Description.

6. Place the insertion point in the **Grooming** field name.

7. Click the **Delete Rows** button on the toolbar. The Grooming field is deleted.

8. Click the **Undo** button on the toolbar. The Grooming field reappears.

9. Click the **Save** button on the toolbar to save the design changes. Remain in this screen for the next Step-by-Step.

Navigating and Entering Records in Datasheet View

Once a table is created and designed, you can enter records directly into the table using *Datasheet view*. In Datasheet view, the table appears in a form similar to a spreadsheet, as you saw earlier in the lesson. As with a spreadsheet, the intersection of a row and a column is called a cell.

Entering data in Access is the same as in Excel. Tap Enter or Tab to move to the next field as you enter the data. If you don't key the correct data type, an error message appears.

After entering records in a table in Datasheet view, you do not need to save the changes. Access saves them for you automatically. Remember to always save changes to the table design in Design view.

You can use the mouse to move the insertion point to a cell in the table. You can also use the keys in Table 1-3 to navigate through a table.

> **Did You Know?**
>
> You can switch to the Datasheet or Design view using options on the View menu.

TABLE 1-3
Navigating in Datasheet view

KEY	DESCRIPTION
Enter, Tab, or right arrow	Moves to the following field.
Left arrow or Shift+Tab	Moves to the previous field.
End	Moves to the last field in the current record.
Home	Moves to the first field in the current record.
Up arrow	Moves up one record and stays in the same field.
Down arrow	Moves down one record and stays in the same field.
Page Up	Moves up one screen.
Page Down	Moves down one screen.

S TEP-BY-STEP 1.9

1. Click the **View** button on the toolbar to switch to Datasheet view. The *Breed Information* table looks like that shown in Figure 1-14. (Notice how the View button changes to a different icon. Clicking it will switch you back to Design view.)

FIGURE 1-14
Datasheet view

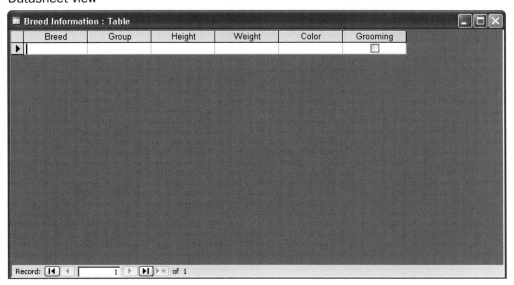

2. Key **Afghan** in the Breed field. Tap **Tab**.

3. Click the down arrow in the Group field and choose **Hound** from the lookup list. Tap **Tab**.

4. Key **27** in the Height field. Tap **Tab**.

5. Key **55** in the Weight field. Tap **Tab**.

6. Key **All colors** in the Color field. Tap **Tab**.

7. The Grooming field has a blank check box in it. Click the check box or tap the spacebar to place a check in the box. Tap **Tab**. Leave the database table open for the next Step-by-Step.

Hot Tip

To preview a database table, open the **File** menu and choose **Print Preview** or click the **Print Preview** button on the toolbar. If necessary, click the magnifying glass with a plus (+) sign to enlarge the table.

Printing a Table

You can print a database table in Datasheet view. Open the File menu and choose the Print command to display the Print dialog box. As shown in Figure 1-15, you can choose to print all the records, only those selected, or to print specific pages.

FIGURE 1-15
Print dialog box

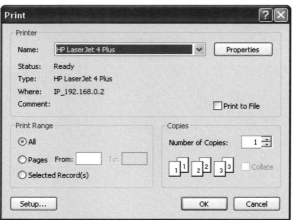

STEP-BY-STEP 1.10

1. Open the **File** menu and choose **Print**. The Print dialog box appears, as shown in Figure 1-15.

2. Click **Setup**. The Page Setup dialog box appears, as shown in Figure 1-16.

FIGURE 1-16
Page Setup dialog box

STEP-BY-STEP 1.10 Continued

3. For the margins, key **.5** in the Left box and **.5** in the Right box.

4. Click **OK**.

5. In the Print dialog box, click **Properties**. The Properties dialog box appears.

6. Click on the Layout tab, if necessary. (If the Layout tab is not displayed, click the Tab that displays the Orientation options.)

7. In the Orientation options, click **Landscape**.

8. Click **OK**.

9. In the Print dialog box, click **All** from the Print Range options, if it isn't already selected. Click **OK.**

10. Close the table. The record has been saved in the table automatically.

> **Hot Tip**
>
> You can also click the Print button on the toolbar to print the database table. However, the Print dialog box will not appear for updates to the page setup.

Exiting Access

As in other Microsoft Office 2003 programs, you exit Access by opening the File menu and choosing Exit. Exiting Access takes you back to the Windows desktop. Remember to remove any floppy disks, and properly shut down Windows before turning off the computer.

STEP-BY-STEP 1.11

1. Open the **File** menu and choose **Close**. The database closes.

2. Open the **File** menu and choose **Exit**. The Windows desktop appears (assuming no other programs are open and maximized).

SUMMARY

In this lesson, you learned:

■ Access is the database application of the Microsoft Office 2003 suite of programs. A database helps you to store large amounts of information. A database is like a filing cabinet that contains folders of documents.

■ You can open an existing database from the File menu or from the Getting Started task pane displayed on the right side of the screen. The Access screen has a title bar, menu bar, and toolbar. Access, however, does not have a standard document view.

■ When a database is saved, the file that is saved contains a group of objects. These objects work together to store data, retrieve data, display data, and print reports. The object types are tables, queries, forms, reports, macros, and modules.

■ A record is a complete set of data. Each record is made up of fields. Each field is identified by a field name. The actual data entered into a field is called an entry.

■ Creating a database creates a file that will hold database objects. To store data, a table must first be created. In Design view, you can create fields and assign data types and descriptions to the fields. Once a table has been created and designed, you can enter records in Datasheet view.

■ As in other Microsoft Office 2003 applications, you exit Access by choosing the Exit command from the File menu.

VOCABULARY *Review*

Define the following terms:

Database	Entry	Field name
Datasheet view	Field	Record
Design view		

REVIEW *Questions*

TRUE/FALSE

Circle T if the statement is true or F if the statement is false.

T   F   1. Using a database is more efficient than a paper filing system.

T   F   2. Opening a database automatically displays the data in the table.

T   F   3. Access has a standard document view that remains on the screen as long as a database is open.

T   F   4. A database file is a group of database objects.

T   F   5. Fields are identified by field names.

WRITTEN QUESTIONS

Write a brief answer to the following questions.

1. Which window appears after you open a database?

2. List three types of database objects.

3. Which database object allows you to search for and retrieve data?

4. What is the term for the data entered in a field?

5. Which view is used to design tables?

PROJECTS

PROJECT 1-1

You decide to make some updates to the database listing dog breeds.

1. Start Access.

2. Open the **Project1-1** database from the data files. (If a security warning appears stating that the file may not be safe, click **Open** to open the file.)

3. Open the **Breed Information** table in Design view.

4. Change the data type for the Height and Weight fields to **Number**.

5. At the end of the table, add a new field named **Lifespan** with the **Number** data type, and **Average lifespan** as the description.

6. Save the changes and switch to Datasheet view.

7. Key **12** in the blank Lifespan field.

8. Print the table in landscape orientation.

9. Close the table and database.

PROJECT 1-2

Add the information that you have collected from the Web to the *Breed Information* table.

1. Open the **Project1-2** database from the data files.

2. Open the **Breed Information** table in Datasheet view.

3. Insert the records shown in Figure 1-17. In the Group field, click the down arrow and choose a value from the lookup list.

FIGURE 1-17

Breed	Group	Height	Weight	Color	Grooming	Lifespan
Basset	Hound	13	45	Black, white, tan	☐	13
Beagle	Hound	13	35	Black, white, tan	☐	13
Boxer	Working	22	45	Fawn, brindle	☐	12
Brittany Spaniel	Sporting	17	33	White, brown	☐	12
Bulldog	Non-Sporting	12	30	Red brindle	☐	7
Chihuahua	Toy	6	3	All colors	☐	13
Cocker Spaniel	Sporting	14	24	All colors	☑	14
Dachsund	Non-Sporting	10	15	All colors	☐	12
Dalmatian	Non-Sporting	22	49	White, black	☐	13
English Setter	Sporting	25	59	White, black	☑	11
Golden Retriever	Sporting	24	65	Golden	☐	12
Great Dane	Working	36	120	Brindle	☐	8
Irish Setter	Sporting	32	70	Chestnut	☑	12
Poodle	Non-Sporting	15	25	All colors	☑	15
Schnauzer	Terrier	18	33	Black	☑	13
Scottish Terrier	Terrier	10	19	Black	☑	12

4. Print the table in landscape orientation.

5. Close the table and database.

 PROJECT 1-3

Your assignment in English class is to create a list of Pulitzer Prize winners for poetry.

1. Create a new database named **Pulitzer**.

2. With the Pulitzer database open, create a new table named **Poetry** using the field names, data types, and descriptions shown in Figure 1-18.

FIGURE 1-18

Field Name	Data Type	Description
Name	Text	Name of Pulitzer prize winner
Poem	Text	Title of poem
Year	Number	Year of prize

3. Save the table as **Poetry**. No primary key is necessary.

4. Switch to Datasheet view and enter the records shown in Figure 1-19.

FIGURE 1-19

Name	Poem	Year
Carl Sandburg	Corn Huskers	1919
Robert Frost	New Hampshire	1924
Leonora Speyer	Fiddler's Farewell	1927
George Dillon	The Flowering Stone	1932
Archibald MacLeish	Conquistador	1933
Robert Frost	A Further Range	1937

5. Print the table.

6. Open the **Poetry** table in Design view.

7. Change the data type for the Year field to **Text**.

8. Save the change.

9. Switch to Datasheet view and add the records as shown in Figure 1-20.

FIGURE 1-20

Name	Poem	Year
Marya Zaturenska	Cold Morning Sky	1938
Vincent Benet	Western Star	1944
W.H. Auden	The Age of Anxiety	1948
Marianne Moore	Collected Poems	1952

10. Print the table.

11. Close the table and database.

PROJECT 1-4

For the past year, you have worked at the City Zoo as a volunteer for a few hours each week. You will create a list of animals that have been recently added to the zoo. This information will be used in the zoo's monthly newsletter.

1. Create a new database named **Zoo Animals**.

2. With the Zoo Animals database open, create a new table named **Recent Additions** using the field names, data types, and descriptions shown in Figure 1-21.

    FIGURE 1-21

Field Name	Data Type	Description
Name	Text	Name of animal
Continent	Text	Name of continent
Classification	Text	Classification of animal
Zoo Location	Text	Location of animal in zoo
Cage or Habitat	Number	Number of cage or habitat
Arrival Date	Date/Time	Arrival date of animal

3. Use the Lookup Wizard and add lookup values for the Continent field. Key the lookup values from Figure 1-22.

    FIGURE 1-22

Col1
Africa
Asia
Australia
Europe
North America
South America

4. Use the Lookup Wizard and add lookup values for the Classification field. Key the lookup values from Figure 1-23.

    FIGURE 1-23

Col1
Bird
Fish
Mammal
Reptile

5. Save the table as **Recent Additions** and close it. No primary key is necessary.

6. Open the table in Datasheet view and enter the record shown in Figure 1-24. In the Continent and Classification fields, click the down arrow and choose a value from the lookup list.

    FIGURE 1-24

Name	Continent	Classification	Zoo Location	Cage or Habitat	Arrival Date
Canary	Africa	Bird	C	6	2/27/2006
				0	

7. Print the table.

8. Close the table and database.

PROJECT 1-5

1. Open the **Project1-5** database from the data files.

2. Open the **Recent Additions** table in Design view.

3. Change the data type for the Cage or Habitat field to **Text**.

4. Save the changes and switch to Datasheet view.

5. Insert the records shown in Figure 1-25. In the Continent and Classification fields, click the down arrow and choose a value from the lookup list.

FIGURE 1-25

Name	Continent	Classification	Zoo Location	Cage or Habitat	Arrival Date
Ostrich	Africa	Bird	E	6	3/15/2006
Baboon	Africa	Mammal	E	2	3/15/2006
Kangaroo	Australia	Mammal	E	10	3/18/2006
Rattlesnake	North Americ	Reptile	S	20	3/27/2006
Bald Eagle	North Americ	Bird	W	2	3/31/2006
Llama	South Ameri	Mammal	E	8	4/2/2006
Gorilla	Africa	Mammal	E	4	4/12/2006
Indian Elephant	Asia	Mammal	N	4	4/25/2006
Piranha	South Ameri	Fish	S	30	5/1/2006

6. Print the table in landscape orientation.

7. Close the table and database.

WEB*Project*

PROJECT 1-6

Use the Web to search for a site that lists dog breeds. A possible Web site to access is *www.akc.org/breeds/recbreeds/group.cfm*. Open the **Project1-6** database from the data files. Choose one of the breeds not already listed in the *Breed Information* table. (This is the same table that you created in Project 1-2.) Search the Web site for information on the breed such as the group, height, weight, color, lifespan, and grooming requirements. Insert the information as a new record in the *Breed Information* table. When finished, print the table in landscape orientation.

TEAMWORK*Project*

PROJECT 1-7

The purpose of a database is to organize data so it can be retrieved quickly, used easily, and stored efficiently. In a group, list six types of data used either at home or school that would be ideal for storing in a database. Discuss and list the reasons why the data is ideal.

CRITICAL *Thinking*

ACTIVITY 1-1

Select a type of collection or a personal interest and create a database to organize it. Name the database **MyCollection**.

Create and design a table for your data using the Table Wizard. Carefully consider the fields your database will need.

To start the Table Wizard, double-click *Create table by using wizard* in the Database window and follow the screens to create your table. In the first screen, choose the Personal category and one of the Sample tables. In the Sample Fields column, select the fields for your new table. When finished with the first screen, click the **Next** button. In the second screen, enter the name of your table and choose *No, I'll set the primary key*. When finished with the second screen, click **Finish**. The table will appear in Datasheet view. Enter at least two records in the table. Change the margins if necessary and print the table. Close the table and exit Access.

ACTIVITY 1-2

When creating a database with many of the same types of fields, it is helpful to know how to copy the definition of a field. Use the Help feature and search for the steps to copy a field's definition within a table. Write down these basic steps.

LESSON 2

MANIPULATING DATA

OBJECTIVES

In this lesson, you will:

- Edit a record and undo a change.
- Select records and fields.
- Delete a record.
- Cut, copy, and paste data.
- Change the layout of a datasheet.

Estimated Time: 1.5 hours

Editing Records

To make editing records easier, Access provides navigation buttons on your screen. The navigation buttons are used to move around the datasheet. These buttons may not be necessary when working with databases as small as those you used in the previous lesson. The navigation buttons are useful when databases get larger. Figure 2-1 shows the locations of the navigation buttons.

FIGURE 2-1
Navigation buttons

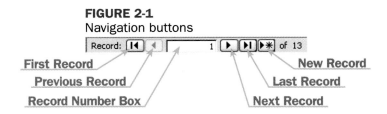

The First Record button is used to move quickly to the top of the table. The Last Record button is used to move to the bottom of the table. There are also buttons used to move to the next or previous record. To move to a specific record number, click the Record Number box and key the number of the record into the field. Tap the Tab key to move to the specified record. To add a new record, click the New Record button.

An arrow to the left of the record indicates the current record. The computer keeps track of the current record using a *record pointer*. When you move among records in Datasheet view, you are actually moving the record pointer.

If you use the Tab key to move to a cell, Access highlights the contents of the cell. As in a spreadsheet, you can replace the contents of the cell by keying data while the existing data is highlighted. If you click a cell with the mouse, the insertion point appears in the cell, allowing you to edit the contents.

Hot Tip

There are three ways to undo changes to a cell. If you make a mistake keying data in a cell, you can open the Edit menu and choose Undo typing or click the Undo typing button on the toolbar. This reverses your last action. If you have already entered the data in a cell and moved to the next cell (or any cell), open the Edit menu and choose Undo Current Field/Record or click the Undo Current Field/Record button on the toolbar. You can also tap the Esc key to restore the contents of the entire record.

STEP-BY-STEP 2.1

You and your family are planning a vacation to one of the National Parks. You created a list of the National Parks along with the possible outdoor activities.

1. Start Microsoft Access and open **Step2-1** from the data files.

2. Open the **National Parks** table in Datasheet view.

3. Click the **Last Record** button at the bottom of the table to move the record pointer to the last record.

4. Click the **First Record** button to move the record pointer to the first record.

5. Click the **Next Record** button to move the record pointer to the next record.

6. In the second record, the Hiking field is not checked when hiking is allowed in the Badlands National Park. Tap the **Tab** key until the check box in the Hiking field is highlighted.

7. Click in the check box or tap the spacebar to place a check in the box. Tap the **Tab** key.

8. Move the mouse pointer to the State field in the third record. Click to place the pointer at the beginning of the field (where the pointer becomes a thick plus sign). The entire field will be highlighted.

9. Key **Oklahoma** and tap the **Tab** key.

STEP-BY-STEP 2.1 Continued

10. Tap the **Esc** key. The word *Oklahoma* changes back to *Texas*.

11. The entry in the Year Established field of the third record is highlighted. Tap the **Delete** key. The entry is deleted.

12. Click the **Undo typing** button on the toolbar. The Year Established field entry reappears. Leave the table on the screen for the next Step-by-Step.

Selecting Records and Fields

You can quickly select records and fields by clicking the record or field selectors. *Field selectors* are at the top of a table and contain the field name. Figure 2-2 shows the State field selected. *Record selectors* are located to the left of a record's first field. Clicking in the upper-left corner of the datasheet selects all records in the database.

FIGURE 2-2
Record and field selectors

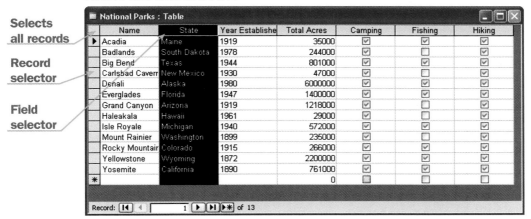

You can select more than one field by clicking the field selector in one field, holding down the Shift key, and clicking the field selector in another field. The two fields, and all the fields in between, will be selected. You can use the same method to select more than one record. You can also select more than one field or record by clicking and dragging across the field or record selectors.

S TEP-BY-STEP 2.2

1. Click the **State** field selector to select the entire column.

2. Click the **Year Established** field selector to select the entire column.

3. Select the **State** field again.

STEP-BY-STEP 2.2 Continued

4. Hold down the **Shift** key and click the **Total Acres** field selector. The State, Year Established, and Total Acres fields are selected, as shown in Figure 2-3.

FIGURE 2-3
Selecting multiple columns

Name	State	Year Established	Total Acres	Camping	Fishing	Hiking
Acadia	Maine	1919	35000	☑	☑	☑
Badlands	South Dakota	1978	244000	☑	☐	☑
Big Bend	Texas	1944	801000	☑	☑	☑
Carlsbad Cavern	New Mexico	1930	47000	☑	☐	☑
Denali	Alaska	1980	6000000	☑	☑	☑
Everglades	Florida	1947	1400000	☑	☑	☑
Grand Canyon	Arizona	1919	1218000	☑	☐	☑
Haleakala	Hawaii	1961	29000	☑	☐	☑
Isle Royale	Michigan	1940	572000	☑	☑	☑
Mount Rainier	Washington	1899	235000	☑	☐	☑
Rocky Mountain	Colorado	1915	266000	☑	☑	☑
Yellowstone	Wyoming	1872	2200000	☑	☑	☑
Yosemite	California	1890	761000	☑	☑	☑
*			0	☐	☐	☐

Record: ◄◄ ◄ 1 ► ►► ►* of 13

5. Click the record selector of the **Yellowstone** record. The entire record is selected.

6. Select the **Everglades** record. Leave the table on the screen for the next Step-by-Step.

> **Hot Tip** 🎯
>
> To delete an entire record, select the record and open the **Edit** menu and choose **Delete Record** or tap the **Delete** key. You can also click the **Delete Record** button on the toolbar.

Deleting Records

When deleting a record a message box appears, as shown in Figure 2-4, warning you that you are about to delete a record. Click Yes to permanently delete the record or No to not delete the record. Once you've deleted a record using the Delete Record command, you cannot use the Undo command or Esc key to restore it.

FIGURE 2-4
Message warning that you are about to delete a record

> **Did You Know?** 💡
>
> You can delete more than one record by holding down the Shift key, clicking the record selector in each field, and then selecting Delete Record.

You cannot delete fields in Datasheet view the same way you delete records. As you learned in Lesson 1, you can delete fields in Design view only.

S TEP-BY-STEP 2.3

1. Click the **Previous Record** button to move to the Denali record.

2. Click the **Delete Record** button on the toolbar. A message appears, as shown in Figure 2-4, warning you that you are about to delete the record.

3. Click **Yes**. The record is deleted. Leave the table on the screen for the next Step-by-Step.

Cutting, Copying, and Pasting Data

The Cut, Copy, and Paste commands in Access work the same way as in other Office programs. You can use the commands to copy and move data within a table or between tables.

When you select a record and choose the Cut command, you will get the same message as when you use the Delete command. The difference is that with the Cut command, you can restore the record to the end of the table by using the Paste Append command.

> **Hot Tip**
>
> To cut or copy an entire record, select the record and choose **Cut** or **Copy** on the **Edit** menu or click the **Cut** or **Copy** buttons on the toolbar.

S TEP-BY-STEP 2.4

1. Select the **Acadia** record.

2. Click the **Copy** button on the toolbar.

3. Click the **New Record** button. The new record appears at the bottom of the database. Click the **Paste** button on the toolbar to insert the information copied from record 1.

4. In the new record 13, change the name to **Zion** and the state to **Utah**.

5. In the Total Acres field, delete the existing text and key **147000**.

6. Select the **Haleakala** record.

7. Click the **Cut** button on the toolbar. The message saying that you are about to delete a record appears.

8. Click **Yes**.

> **Did You Know?**
>
> You can move and copy an entire object. In the Database window, select the object (table, query, form, or report), open the **Edit** menu and choose **Cut** or **Copy**. Open the database in which you want to paste the object, open the **Edit** menu and choose **Paste**.

STEP-BY-STEP 2.4 Continued

9. Select the empty record at the end of the table.

10. Open the **Edit** menu and choose **Paste Append**. The Haleakala record appears, as shown in Figure 2-5. Leave the table on the screen for the next Step-by-Step.

FIGURE 2-5
Using the Cut and Paste buttons to add a record

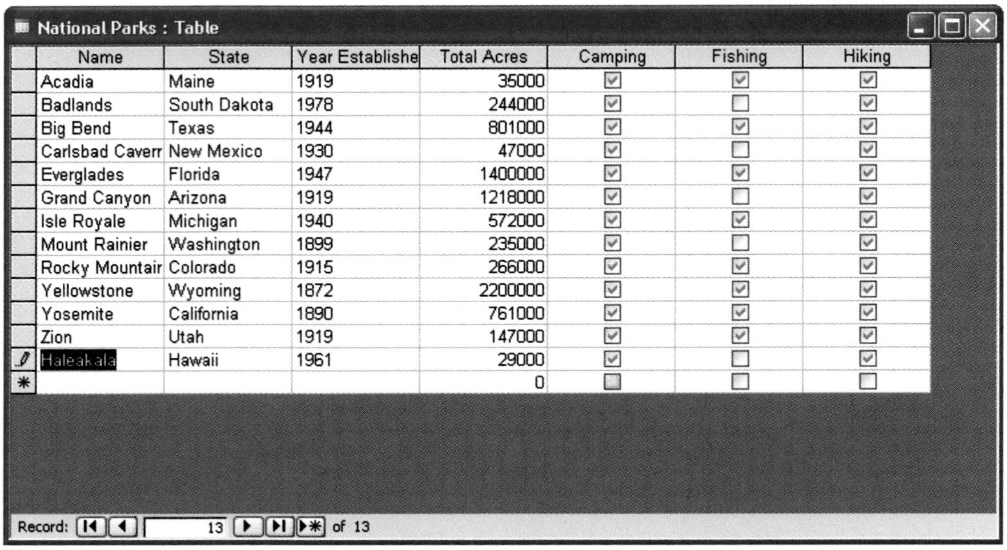

	Name	State	Year Establishe	Total Acres	Camping	Fishing	Hiking
	Acadia	Maine	1919	35000	☑	☑	☑
	Badlands	South Dakota	1978	244000	☑	☐	☑
	Big Bend	Texas	1944	801000	☑	☑	☑
	Carlsbad Caverr	New Mexico	1930	47000	☑	☐	☑
	Everglades	Florida	1947	1400000	☑	☑	☑
	Grand Canyon	Arizona	1919	1218000	☑	☐	☑
	Isle Royale	Michigan	1940	572000	☑	☑	☑
	Mount Rainier	Washington	1899	235000	☑	☐	☑
	Rocky Mountain	Colorado	1915	266000	☑	☑	☑
	Yellowstone	Wyoming	1872	2200000	☑	☑	☑
	Yosemite	California	1890	761000	☑	☑	☑
	Zion	Utah	1919	147000	☑	☑	☑
⫽	Haleakala	Hawaii	1961	29000	☑	☐	☑
*				0	☐	☐	☐

Record: |◄| |◄| 13 |►| |►I| |►*| of 13

Changing Datasheet Layout

You can make many changes to the datasheet layout, including changing row height and column width, rearranging columns, and freezing columns.

Changing Row Height

You can adjust the row height in a datasheet, but the adjustment affects all the rows. To change the height, position the pointer on the lower border of a row selector, and it will turn into a double arrow, as shown in Figure 2-6. Using the double arrow, click and drag the row border up or down to adjust the row height. You can also specify an exact row height, as shown in Figure 2-7.

FIGURE 2-6
Adjusting the row height

Name
Acadia
Badlands
Big Bend

FIGURE 2-7
Row Height dialog box

S TEP-BY-STEP 2.5

1. Position the mouse pointer on the lower border of the record selector for **Acadia**. You will know you have the pointer correctly positioned when it changes to a double arrow, as shown in Figure 2-6.

2. Click and drag the row border down slightly to increase the height of the row. When you release the mouse button, all rows are affected by the change.

3. Select the **Badlands** record.

4. Open the **Format** menu and choose **Row Height**. The Row Height dialog box, shown in Figure 2-7, appears.

5. Key **25** in the Row Height box and click **OK**. The row height changes to a height that allows the data to be read more easily. Leave the table on the screen for the next Step-by-Step.

Changing Column Width

The column widths provided by default are usually too wide or too narrow for the data. Adjusting column width is similar to adjusting row height. To adjust the column width, place the mouse pointer in the field selector on the border of the column. The pointer changes to a double arrow. Click and drag to the width you want. Unlike rows, which must all have the same height, each field can have a different width.

Hot Tip

Instead of choosing **Row Height** on the **Format** menu, you can right-click the record selector. Select **Row Height** on the shortcut menu that appears.

When you choose Column Width on the Format menu, the Column Width dialog box appears, as shown in Figure 2-8. You can key a specific width or click the Best Fit button. The Best Fit option automatically selects the best width for the data in the column.

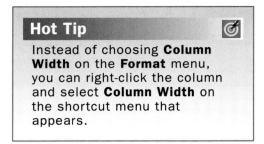

Hot Tip

Instead of choosing **Column Width** on the **Format** menu, you can right-click the column and select **Column Width** on the shortcut menu that appears.

FIGURE 2-8
Column Width dialog box

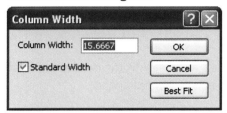

STEP-BY-STEP 2.6

1. Position the pointer on the right border of the **Year Established** field selector.

2. Click and drag to make the column wide enough so all the field name fits in the column.

3. Select the **Total Acres** field.

4. Open the **Format** menu and choose **Column Width**. The Column Width dialog box appears, as shown in Figure 2-8.

5. Click **Best Fit**. The column narrows.

6. Select the **Camping** field.

7. Open the **Format** menu and choose **Column Width**. The Column Width dialog box appears.

8. Key **10** into the Column Width box and click **OK**.

9. Change the width of the **Fishing** and **Hiking** fields to **10**.

10. Print the table in landscape orientation. Leave the table on the screen for the next Step-by-Step.

Rearranging Columns

Access allows you to rearrange fields by dragging them to a new location. First, select the field you want to move. Then, click and hold down the mouse button on the field selector and drag the field to the new location. A vertical bar follows your mouse pointer to show you where the field will be inserted. Release the mouse button to insert the field in its new location.

S TEP-BY-STEP 2.7

1. Select the **Total Acres** field.

2. Click and drag the **Total Acres** field to the left until the vertical bar appears between the State and Year Established fields. Release the mouse button. The Total Acres column appears between the State and Year Established columns, as shown in Figure 2-9. Leave the table on your screen for the next Step-by-Step.

FIGURE 2-9
Rearranging fields

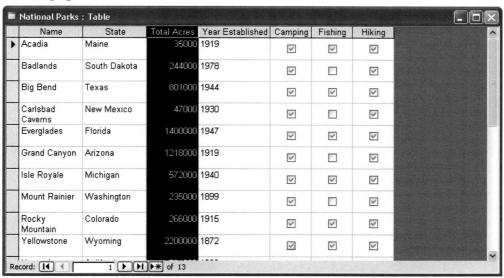

Changing Field Properties

When you created fields for a table in Lesson 1, you added only the field name, data type, and description. Now you will learn how to change the *field properties* to add more detail to the data type.

In Design view, you can view and change the field properties in a table. Figure 2-10 shows the field properties available for a Text data type. The field properties are somewhat different for each data type. Table 2-1 lists the most common field properties.

FIGURE 2-10
Field properties in Design view

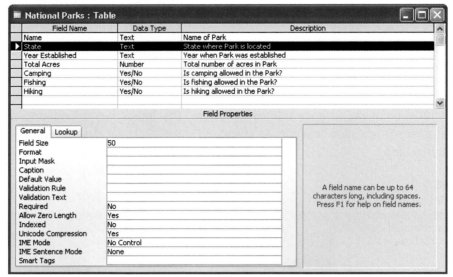

TABLE 2-1
Field properties

OBJECT	DESCRIPTION
Field Size	Field Size is the number of characters allowed in the field. A field can contain up to 255 characters. The default size is 50.
Format	The Format field property allows you to select how you want to display numbers, dates, times, and text. For example, the default format for dates is 10/28/2006. You can change the format to 28-Oct-06 or Tuesday, October 28, 2006.
Caption	The Caption field property is used instead of field names in a table. For example, if the field name is Address, you could enter Home Address in the caption field property.
Default Value	Another useful field property is Default Value. Use this field property when you have a field that usually contains the same value. For example, if most of the people in a database of names and addresses live in California, you can enter CA as the Default Value of the State field. The State field will automatically contain CA, unless you change it to another state.
Required	The Required field property determines if you must enter a value in the field. For example, in a student database, you might choose that each field requires a telephone number. If you try to enter a record without including a telephone number, Access will alert you that you must enter one.
Decimal Places	Number and Currency fields have a field property called Decimal Places. You can choose a number of decimal places here instead of the automatic setting.

S TEP-BY-STEP 2.8

1. Open the **National Parks** table in Design view.

2. Select the **Name** field.

3. Under the *Field Properties* section beside Field Size, double-click **50** to highlight it. Key **40**.

4. In the *Caption* box, key **Park Name**.

5. Click in the **Required** field property box. A down arrow will appear at the right end of the box.

6. Click the down arrow and choose **Yes** from the menu.

7. Select the **State** field.

8. Change the Field Size to **40** and the Required field property to **Yes**.

9. Select the **Total Acres** field.

10. Click in the **Format** field property box. A down arrow appears.

11. Click the down arrow. A menu of numeric formats appears.

12. Choose **Standard**.

13. Click in the **Decimal Places** property box. A down arrow appears.

14. Click the down arrow and choose **0**.

15. Save the table design. A message may appear stating that some data may be lost because you changed the setting for a field size to a shorter size. Click **Yes** to continue. Another message may appear asking if you want the existing data tested with the new rules. Click **Yes**.

16. Switch to Datasheet view to see the format changes to the Total Acres field. The Name field now contains the caption you entered. The other changes are not visible.

17. Print the table in portrait orientation.

18. Save and close the table and then close the database by clicking the **Close** button in the Database window.

SUMMARY

In this lesson, you learned:

■ The navigation buttons are used to move around the datasheet. They allow you to move to the first record, the last record, the previous record, or the next record. You can also use a navigation button to add a new record.

■ There are three ways to undo changes to cells. If you make mistakes while keying data in a cell, you can click the Undo typing button. If you have already entered data and moved to the next cell, tap the Esc key. To reverse all the changes to the previous record, open the Edit menu and choose Undo Saved Record.

■ To delete a record, use the Delete Record command. Entire records and fields can be selected by clicking the record and field selectors. Cut, Copy, and Paste are available in Datasheet view to move and copy data. The Paste Append command pastes a record at the end of the database.

■ You can make many changes to a datasheet. You can change the row height and column width. You can also rearrange columns.

■ Field properties allow you to add more detail to the data type of a field. Some of the more common field properties are Field Size, Format, Caption, Default Value, Format, Required, and Decimal Places.

VOCABULARY*Review*

Define the following terms:		
Field properties	Record pointer	Record selectors
Field selectors		

REVIEW*Questions*

TRUE/FALSE

Circle T if the statement is true or F if the statement is false.

T   F   1. If you click a cell with the mouse, the insertion point appears in the cell.

T   F   2. Holding down the Alt key allows you to select more than one field.

T   F   3. In Access, you can use the Cut, Copy, and Paste commands.

T   F   4. Changing the height of one row changes the height of all datasheet rows.

T   F   5. You can delete records and fields in Datasheet view.

WRITTEN QUESTIONS

Write a brief answer to the following questions.

1. What is the record pointer?

2. How do you delete a record in Datasheet view?

3. What does the Paste Append command do?

4. Which key can you tap to undo changes to a cell if you have already entered data and moved to the next cell?

5. In what view do you change field properties?

PROJECTS

PROJECT 2-1

Last semester a new club called the Future Business Leaders Club was formed. Any student from the entire school district is invited to join. As President of the club, you have created a database to keep the information about each member.

1. Open the **Project2-1** database from the data files.

2. Open the **Members** table in Datasheet view.

3. Go to **record 7** and change the address to **628 Elmwood Drive**.

4. Go to **record 14** and change the interest to **Books**.

5. Go to **record 13** and change the first name to **Alex**.

6. Go to **record 3** and change the dues paid to **30**.

7. Undo your last change.

8. Delete record 5.

9. Change the width of the Address field to **22** and the Zip Code field to **11**.

10. Change all other field widths using Best Fit.

11. Change the row height to **15**.

12. Change the left and right margins to **.5** inches and print the table in landscape orientation.

13. Close the table. Click **Yes** if prompted to save changes to the layout of the table. Close the database.

PROJECT 2-2

You decide to update the database since a member has paid his dues and a new member has joined.

1. Open the **Project2-2** database.

2. Open the **Members** table in Datasheet view.

3. Copy record **2** and paste it at the bottom of the table.

4. In the pasted record, change the First Name to **Michelle**, the Interest to **Jewelry**, the Dues Owed to **15**, the Dues Paid to **0**, and the Date Joined to **1/12/2007**.

5. Move the **Date Joined** field to between the Zip Code and Interest fields.

6. Change the dues paid for Matt Matthews to **15**.

7. Change the left and right margins to **.5 inches** and print the table in landscape orientation.

8. Close the table. Click **Yes** if prompted to save changes to the layout of the table. Close the database.

PROJECT 2-3

To make the Members information easier to read, you decide to update some of the field properties. Also, two new members have joined the club.

1. Open the **Project2-3** database.

2. Open the **Members** table in Design view.

3. Format the **Dues Owed** and **Dues Paid** fields for **Currency**.

4. Select **Medium Date** from the Format field properties for the **Date Joined** field.

5. Make the **Zip Code** field **Required**.

6. Save the table design. A message may appear asking if you want to continue. Click **Yes**. Another message may appear asking if you want the existing data tested with the new rules. Click **Yes**.

7. Switch to Datasheet view and insert the following records at the end of the table.

Jackson   Sarah   Maxwell   4540 Crestview Drive   Denver   CO   80255   12-Jan-07 Clothing $15.00 $15.00

Williams   Tyler   Northridge   2252 Elkhurst Street   Denver   CO   80274   12-Jan-07 Cars $15.00 $0.00

8. Change the left and right margins to **.5 inches** and print the table in landscape orientation.

9. Close the table. Click **Yes** if prompted to save changes to the layout of the table. Close the database.

WEB *Project*

PROJECT 2-4

Use the Web to search for a site that lists the National Parks. Open the **Project2-4** database from the data files. Choose two parks not already listed in the *National Parks* table. (This is the same table that you created in Lesson 2.) Use the Web to search for the same information on the two parks that appear in the table. Add two new records (one for each National Park) using the New Record button. When finished, save and print the table.

TEAMWORK *Project*

PROJECT 2-5

In a group, create a database of CDs you own and would be willing to share with others.

1. List on a separate piece of paper at least six fields that will describe the CDs. For example, you could list the title, artist or group name, owner name, or person currently using the CD.

2. Determine the data types and field properties for each field.

3. Create the new database and name it **CD Club**, followed by three letters to identify it.

4. Design the table using descriptive field names. When finished, name the table **CD List**.

5. Each person in the group should add the information on two of his or her CDs to the table.

6. When finished, adjust the columns to see all of the data. Save and print the table in landscape orientation.

CRITICAL *Thinking*

ACTIVITY 2-1

Open the MyCollection database you created for the Critical Thinking Activity in Lesson 1. Add two new records using the New Record button. Select a field and make a change to the data. Delete an entire record. Copy one record and paste it into the table as a new record. If necessary, increase the column width and row height to see all the data. Rearrange the columns. Print and close the table.

FINDING AND SORTING DATA

OBJECTIVES

In this lesson, you will:

- Find data in a database.
- Create and use a query.
- Create and use a filter.
- Sort a database.

Estimated Time: 1.5 hours

Using Find

The Find command is the easiest way to quickly locate data in a database. The Find command allows you to search the database for specific information. There are several options to choose from when using the Find command. These options appear in the Find and Replace dialog box, shown in Figure 3-1.

FIGURE 3-1
Find and Replace dialog box

You can access the Find and Replace dialog box by opening the Edit menu and choosing Find or by clicking the Find button on the toolbar. The Find command is available when a datasheet is displayed.

Hot Tip

Use the Find command when searching for one record at a time. Use the Filter tool when searching for more than one record. You will learn about filters later in this lesson.

STEP-BY-STEP 3.1

1. Open **Step3-1** from the data files. This database includes a table of information on the United States.

2. Open the **State Information** table in Datasheet view.

3. Place the insertion point in the **Flower** field of the first record.

4. Click the **Find** button. The Find and Replace dialog box appears.

5. Key **Magnolia** into the *Find What* box.

6. Be sure the **Flower** field appears in the *Look In* box.

7. Click the down arrow to the right of the *Match* box and choose **Any Part of Field** from the list.

8. Be sure **All** appears in the *Search* box. The *Match Case* and *Search Fields As Formatted* options should not be selected.

9. Click the **Find Next** button. The record for Mississippi is selected, as shown in Figure 3-2.

> **Did You Know?**
>
> When using the Find command, you can click Find Next to display the next record that matches the specific information. When the entire database has been searched, a message appears telling you that the search item was not found.

FIGURE 3-2
Finding data

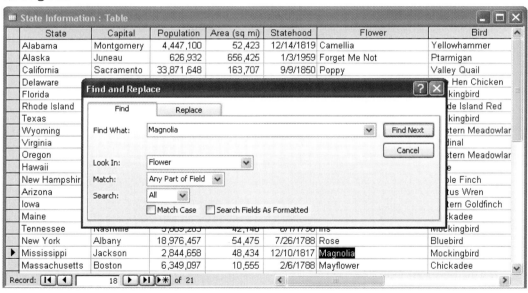

STEP-BY-STEP 3.1 Continued

10. Click **Find Next** again. The record for Louisiana is selected.

11. Click **Find Next** again. A message appears telling you that the search item was not found. There are two states with the Magnolia as the state flower. Click **OK**.

12. Click **Cancel** to close the Find and Replace dialog box.

13. Close the table and leave the database open for the next Step-by-Step.

Using Queries

The Find command is an easy way to find data. Sometimes you will need to find data based on more specific information. For example, you may need to search for states with a population greater than 20 million. You cannot do that with the Find command. A *query* will let you search for data based on more specific information. A query is a question that you ask the database.

Creating a Query in Design View

The first step in creating a query is to open the database and click Queries on the Objects bar. Then click the New button to create a new query. The New Query dialog box appears, as shown in Figure 3-3. You can choose to create a query in Design View or to use one of the Query Wizards.

FIGURE 3-3
New Query dialog box

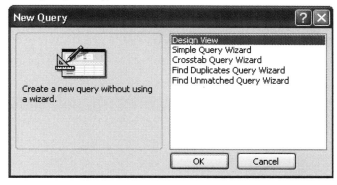

S TEP-BY-STEP 3.2

1. Click **Queries** on the Objects bar.

2. Click the **New** button. The New Query dialog box appears, as shown in Figure 3-3.

3. Choose **Design View**, if it is not already selected, and click **OK**. The Show Table dialog box appears from which you select a table to query, as shown in Figure 3-4.

FIGURE 3-4
Show Table dialog box

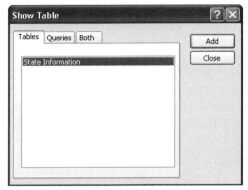

4. Select the **State Information** table in the Show Table dialog box and click **Add**. The fields of the *State Information* table appear in the query window. Click **Close** to close the Show Table dialog box. Leave the query window on the screen for the next Step-by-Step.

The query window is divided into two parts. The top part of the window shows the available tables and fields (the *State Information* table and its fields are shown in Figure 3-5).

FIGURE 3-5
Query window

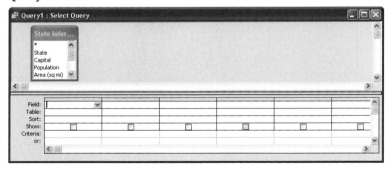

The bottom part of the window contains a grid that allows you to specify the information needed to create a query. To create a query, you must supply three pieces of information: the fields you want to search, what you are searching for (called the *search criteria*), and what fields you want to display with the results. The Field row is where you select a field to be part of the query. Click the down arrow to display the available fields. To include more than one field in a query, click in the next column of the Field row and choose another field.

The Sort row allows you to sort the results of the query. Click the Show check box if you want the field to be displayed in the query results. Normally, this will be checked. Sometimes you may want to search by a field that does not need to appear in the query results.

For the fields you want to search, enter the search information in the Criteria row. For example, if you want to find only records that contain the word *Cardinal* in the Bird field, you would key *Cardinal* into the Criteria row of the Bird field.

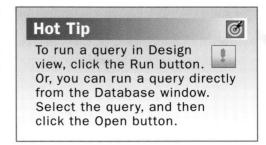

Hot Tip

To run a query in Design view, click the Run button. Or, you can run a query directly from the Database window. Select the query, and then click the Open button.

STEP-BY-STEP 3.3

1. In the query grid, click the down arrow in the **Field** row of the first column and choose **State**, as shown in Figure 3-6.

   FIGURE 3-6
   Selecting fields to query

   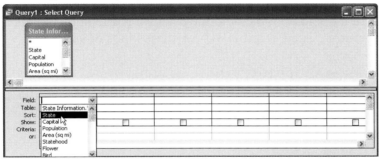

2. Click in the **Sort** row of the **State** column, click the down arrow, and choose **Ascending** from the menu. This tells Access to sort the selected records by the State name in ascending order.

3. Click the in the **Field** row of the second column, click the down arrow, and choose **Bird** from the menu.

4. In the **Criteria** row of the **Bird** column, key **Mockingbird**. This tells Access to display any records with the mockingbird as the state bird.

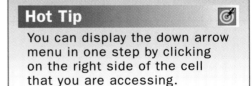

Hot Tip

You can display the down arrow menu in one step by clicking on the right side of the cell that you are accessing.

5. Open the **File** menu and choose **Save**. You are prompted for a name for the query.

6. Key in **Mockingbird** and click **OK**.

7. Open the **File** menu and choose **Close**.

STEP-BY-STEP 3.3 Continued

8. To run the query, highlight **Mockingbird** in the Database window and click **Open**. The results of the query appear, as shown in Figure 3-7.

FIGURE 3-7
Results of the Mockingbird query

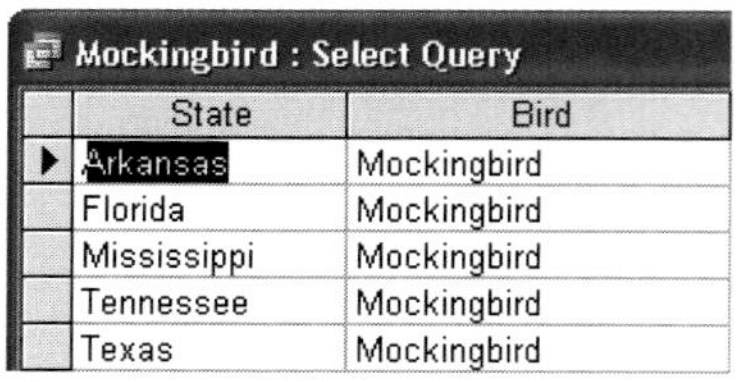

State	Bird
Arkansas	Mockingbird
Florida	Mockingbird
Mississippi	Mockingbird
Tennessee	Mockingbird
Texas	Mockingbird

Mockingbird : Select Query

9. Open the **File** menu and choose **Print** to print the table with the query applied. Click **OK**.

10. Open the **File** menu and choose **Close** to close the results of the query. Leave the database open for the next Step-by-Step.

You can create a more detailed query by using operators. For example, you might want to find all the students in a database table who have a 3.50 grade point average or higher. You can use the relational operators listed in Table 3-1 for these kinds of searches.

TABLE 3-1
Relational operators

OPERATOR	DESCRIPTION
>	Greater than
<	Less than
=	Equal to
>=	Greater than or equal to
<=	Less than or equal to
<>	Not equal

STEP-BY-STEP 3.4

1. Click **Queries** on the Objects bar.

2. Click the **New** button. Choose **Design View** and click **OK**.

3. Select the **State Information** table in the Show Table dialog box and click **Add**. Close the Show Table dialog box.

4. In the query grid, click the down arrow in the **Field** row of the first column and choose **State**.

> **Hot Tip**
>
> To modify a query, open it in Design view. You can change the fields to be searched, the search criteria, and the fields to be displayed in the query results.

STEP-BY-STEP 3.4 Continued

5. Click the in the **Field** row of the second column, click the down arrow, and choose **Population** from the menu.

6. Click in the **Sort** row of the **Population** column, click the down arrow, and choose **Descending** from the menu. This tells Access to sort the selected records by population in descending order.

7. In the **Criteria** row of the **Population** column, key **>18000000**. This tells Access to display any records with a population greater than 18 million.

8. Open the **File** menu and choose **Save**. You are prompted for a name for the query.

9. Key **Large Populations** and click **OK**.

10. Open the **File** menu and choose **Close**.

11. To run the query, highlight **Large Populations** in the Database window and click **Open**. The results of the query appear, as shown in Figure 3-8.

FIGURE 3-8
Results of the Large Populations query

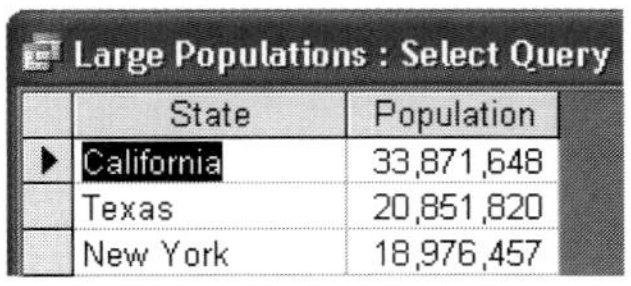

Large Populations : Select Query	
State	Population
California	33,871,648
Texas	20,851,820
New York	18,976,457

12. Open the **File** menu and choose **Print** to print the table with the query applied. Click **OK**.

13. Open the **File** menu and choose **Close** to close the results of the query. Leave the database open for the next Step-by-Step.

Using the Simple Query Wizard

You can also create a query using the Simple Query Wizard. The Simple Query Wizard will ask you questions and then create a query based upon your answers. When creating a query using the wizard, you do not have as many options to choose from as when you create a query in Design view. For instance, you can choose the fields to display, however you cannot sort, group, or specify search criteria.

STEP-BY-STEP 3.5

1. Click **Queries** on the Objects bar.

2. Click the **New** button. The New Query dialog box appears.

STEP-BY-STEP 3.5 Continued

3. Choose **Simple Query Wizard** and click **OK**. The Simple Query Wizard dialog box appears, as shown in Figure 3-9.

FIGURE 3-9
Simple Query Wizard dialog box

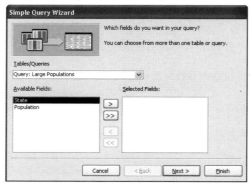

4. Click the down arrow in the **Tables/Queries** box and choose **Table: State Information**. The fields from the State Information table will appear in the Available Fields list.

5. In the Available Fields list, choose **State** and click **>**. The field name will appear in the Selected Fields list.

6. Do the same for the **Capital**, **Population**, **Area**, and **Industry** fields.

7. Click **Next**. The Simple Query Wizard dialog box changes to ask if you would like a detail or summary query. Choose **Detail** if not already selected.

8. Click **Next**. The Simple Query Wizard dialog box changes to ask you for a title, as shown in Figure 3-10.

FIGURE 3-10
Keying a title for the query

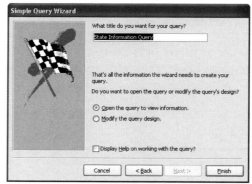

9. If not already there, key **State Information Query**. Be sure the option to open the query to view the information is selected.

10. Click **Finish**. The results of the query appear.

STEP-BY-STEP 3.5 Continued

11. Open the **File** menu and choose **Print** to print the results of the query. Click **OK**.

12. Open the **File** menu and choose **Close** to close the results of the query. Leave the database open for the next Step-by-Step.

Using Filters

Queries are very powerful and flexible tools. A query is a very powerful and flexible way to search for information. In many cases, however, less power is enough. A *filter* displays selected records in a database more easily than a query. Think of a filter as a simpler form of a query. A filter "filters out" the records that do not match the specified criteria. When you use a filter, all of the fields are displayed, and the filter cannot be saved for use again later. Table 3-2 briefly describes the four types of filters.

TABLE 3-2
Four types of filters

FILTER	DESCRIPTION
Filter by Form	Select records by keying the criteria into a form.
Filter by Selection	Highlight data in a cell, or part of the data in a cell, as the criteria (fastest and easiest option).
Filter Excluding Selection	Excludes the data that is highlighted in a cell.
Advanced Filter/Sort	Works like a query; use to create a more difficult search.

STEP-BY-STEP 3.6

1. In the Database window, click **Tables** on the Objects bar.

2. Open the **State Information** table in Datasheet view.

3. Open the **Records** menu and choose **Filter**, and then select **Advanced Filter/Sort** on the submenu. The Filter window appears, as shown in Figure 3-11.

FIGURE 3-11
Design view for an advanced filter

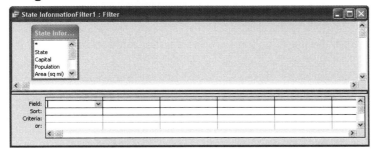

STEP-BY-STEP 3.6 Continued

4. Click the down arrow in the **Field** row of the first column. Scroll down and choose **Industry** from the menu.

5. Key **Tourism** into the **Criteria** field of the first column.

6. Click the **Apply Filter** button on the toolbar. The filter is applied, and only the states with tourism as the major industry are displayed, as shown in Figure 3-12.

FIGURE 3-12
A filter displaying the states with tourism as the major industry

State	Capital	Population	Area (sq mi)	Statehood	Flower	Bird
Florida	Tallahassee	15,982,378	65,758	3/3/1845	Orange Blossom	Mockingbird
Hawaii	Honolulu	1,211,537	10,932	8/21/1959	Hibiscus	Nene

7. Print the table with the filter applied. (*Note:* Be sure to change the left and right margins to .5 inches and select landscape orientation.)

8. Click the **Remove Filter** button, or open the **Records** menu and choose **Remove Filter/Sort**, to remove the filter and display all records.

9. Open the **Records** menu and choose **Filter**, and then select **Filter by Form** on the submenu. A form appears, as shown in Figure 3-13.

FIGURE 3-13
Filter by Form

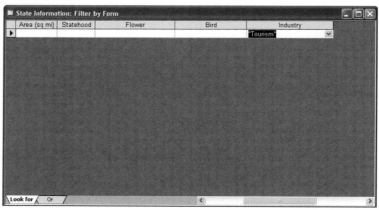

10. Click the down arrow in the **Industry** field. (Tourism was the criteria in the previous filter.)

11. Choose **Paper** from the list of options. (*Note:* You may need to scroll down the list of options.)

STEP-BY-STEP 3.6 Continued

12. Click the **Apply Filter** button on the toolbar. The filter is applied, and only the states with paper as the major industry are displayed, as shown in Figure 3-14.

FIGURE 3-14
A filter displaying the states with paper as the major industry

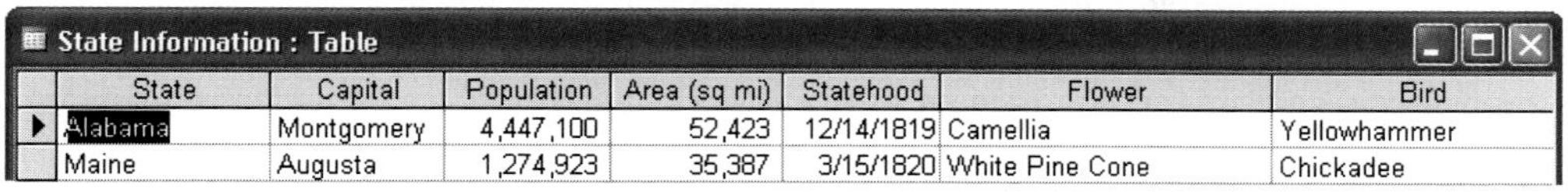
State Information : Table

State	Capital	Population	Area (sq mi)	Statehood	Flower	Bird
Alabama	Montgomery	4,447,100	52,423	12/14/1819	Camellia	Yellowhammer
Maine	Augusta	1,274,923	35,387	3/15/1820	White Pine Cone	Chickadee

13. Print the table with the filter applied. (Be sure to change the left and right margins to .5 inches and select landscape orientation.)

14. Click the **Remove Filter** button, or open the **Records** menu and choose **Remove Filter/Sort**.

15. To create a Filter by Selection, highlight **Chickadee** in the **Bird** field for **Maine**.

16. Open the **Records** menu and choose **Filter**, and then select **Filter by Selection** on the submenu. The filter is applied, and only the states with the chickadee as the state bird are displayed, as shown in Figure 3-15.

FIGURE 3-15
A filter displaying the states with the chickadee as the state bird

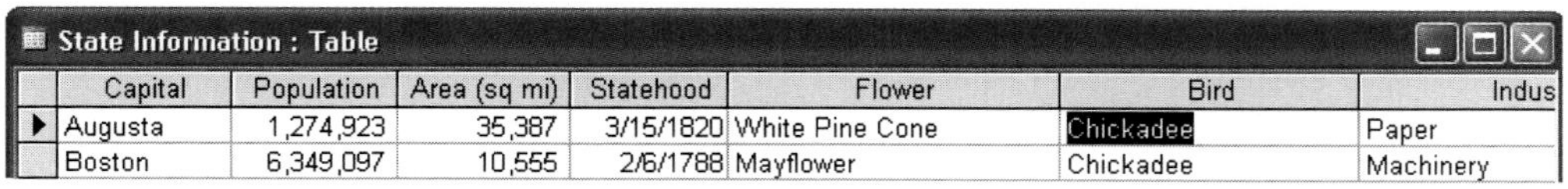
State Information : Table

Capital	Population	Area (sq mi)	Statehood	Flower	Bird	Indus
Augusta	1,274,923	35,387	3/15/1820	White Pine Cone	Chickadee	Paper
Boston	6,349,097	10,555	2/6/1788	Mayflower	Chickadee	Machinery

17. Print the table with the filter applied. (Be sure to change the left and right margins to .5 inches and select landscape orientation.)

18. Click the **Remove Filter** button, or open the **Records** menu and choose **Remove Filter/Sort**. Close the table. Click **Yes** to save changes to the design of the table. Leave the database open for the next Step-by-Step.

Sorting

Sorting is an important part of working with a database. Often you will need records to appear in a specific order. An ***ascending sort*** arranges records from A to Z or smallest to largest. A ***descending sort*** arranges records from Z to A or largest to smallest. Access provides buttons on the toolbar to quickly sort the records of a table.

STEP-BY-STEP 3.7

1. Open the **State Information** table in Datasheet view. Suppose you want to sort the records from the state with the smallest area of land to the largest. Place the insertion point in the first record of the **Area (sq mi)** field.

2. Click the **Sort Ascending** button. The records appear in order by area.

3. Suppose you want to sort the records from largest population to the smallest population. Place the insertion point in the first record of the **Population** field.

4. Click the **Sort Descending** button. The states are sorted from the largest population to the smallest.

5. Print the table. (Be sure to change the left and right margins to .5 inches and select landscape orientation.)

6. Close the table. If asked to save the design of the table, click **Yes**. Close the database.

SUMMARY

In this lesson, you learned:

- The Find command is the easiest way to locate data in the database. The Find command searches the database for specified information.

- A query will let you search for data based on more specific information. A query is a question that you ask the database.

- A filter displays selected records in a database more easily than a query. A filter "filters out" the records that do not match the specified criteria. When you use a filter, all of the fields are displayed, and the filter cannot be saved for use again later.

- Sorting is an important part of working with a database since often you will need records to appear in a specific order.

VOCABULARY *Review*

Define the following terms:		
Ascending sort	Filter	Search criteria
Descending sort	Query	

REVIEW *Questions*

TRUE/FALSE

Circle T if the statement is true or F if the statement is false.

T F 1. The Find command can search for data in all fields.

T F 2. The Find Next button in the Find dialog box finds the next record that matches the criteria you've specified.

T F 3. A query automatically displays all fields in the table.

T F 4. Filters cannot be saved for later use.

T F 5. An ascending sort arranges records from Z to A.

WRITTEN QUESTIONS

Write a brief answer to the following questions.

1. What is the easiest way to quickly locate data in a database?

2. What are the three pieces of information you must supply when creating a query?

3. What menu is used to access the command that creates a filter?

4. What button is used to sort records from largest to smallest?

5. Which type of filter selects records by keying the criteria into a form?

PROJECTS

PROJECT 3-1

Your teacher is on the planning committee for the National Teachers Conference to be held in your city this summer. She has asked you to help her create a database of information on the best restaurants in the city. This information will be included in the packet given to each teacher at the conference.

1. Open the **Project3-1** database file from the data files.

2. Open the **Restaurants** table in Datasheet view.

3. Use the **Find** command to locate the first restaurant that serves Chinese food.

4. Use the **Find** command to locate any other restaurants that serve Chinese food.

5. Close the table.

6. Create a query that displays the restaurants with meal prices that are low. Have the query display the **Restaurant Name, Type of Food, Location, Lunch,** and **Dinner** fields. Sort the **Restaurant Name** field in ascending order. Save the query as **Lower Priced Restaurants**.

7. Run the query and print the results. Close the query. Leave the database open for the next project.

PROJECT 3-2

Your teacher asks you to sort the information so it is easier to find a restaurant by the type of food. Also, you create a list of restaurants in the downtown area since this is where the conference will be held.

1. Open the **Restaurants** table in the **Project3-1** database in Datasheet view.

2. Sort the table so that the restaurants are displayed by type of food in ascending order.

3. Print the results of the sort.

4. Create a filter to display only the restaurants located in the downtown (DT) area. You do not have to sort the records.

5. Print the results of the filter.

6. Remove the filter to show all the records in the table. Close the table. If asked to save the design of the table, click **Yes**. Close the database.

PROJECT 3-3

Your family has decided that a large dog would be the best choice for them. You create a query to search for information about large dogs.

1. Open the **Project3-3** database from the data files.

2. Open the **Breed Information** table in Datasheet view.

3. Use the **Find** command to locate the first dog in the Working group.

4. Use the **Find** command to locate any other dogs in the Working group.

5. Close the table.

6. Create a query, using the **Breed Information** table that displays the dogs that weigh more than 35 pounds. Have the query display the **Breed, Weight, Color, Grooming**, and **Lifespan** fields. Sort the **Weight** field in descending order. Save the query as **Large Dogs**.

7. Run the query and print the results. Close the query. Leave the database open for the next project.

PROJECT 3-4

Your father likes to hunt. He has asked the family to consider getting a dog from the Sporting group.

1. Open the **Breed Information** table in the **Project3-3** database in Datasheet view.

2. Sort the table so that the dogs are displayed by the shortest to longest lifespan.

3. Print the results of the sort.

4. Create a filter to display only the dogs in the Sporting group. You do not have to sort the records.

5. Print the results of the filter.

6. Remove the filter to show all the records in the table. Close the table. If asked to save the design of the table, click **Yes**. Close the database.

WEB*Project*

PROJECT 3-5

Use the Web to search for a site that lists information on the United States. A possible Web site to access is www.50states.com. Open the **Project3-5** database from the data files. Choose five states not already listed in the *State Information* table. (This is the same table that you used previously in this lesson.) Search the Web site for the following information on each state: capital, population, area, year admitted to statehood, state flower, state bird, and major industry. Add the five new records to the table (one for each state).

When finished, sort the table by the Statehood field in ascending order. Which state was the first to be admitted to statehood? Write down your answer. Sort the table by the Statehood field in descending order. Which state was the last to be admitted to statehood? Write down your answer. When finished, print the table (change the margins to .5 inches and select landscape orientation).

TEAMWORK *Project*

PROJECT 3-6

In a group, create a database of favorite restaurants in your city.

1. List on a separate piece of paper the fields in the database.

2. Determine the data types and field properties for each field.

3. Create the new database and name it **Favorites**, followed by three letters to identify it.

4. Design the table using descriptive field names. When finished, name the table **Restaurants**.

5. Each person in the group should add the information on four of their favorite restaurants to the table.

6. Decide on what types of sorts, filters, and queries to create for the table.

7. Create and apply at least one filter, one sort, and one query to the table. Print the table after applying each.

CRITICAL *Thinking*

ACTIVITY 3-1

You and your dad have decided to see at least one baseball game at each of the Major League baseball stadiums. Together you will visit the stadiums at different times throughout your lives. You have already collected information on the top ten baseball stadiums to visit. Open the **Activity3-1** database from the data files. Open the **Baseball Stadiums** table. Sort the table to find the oldest stadium. Write down your answer. Sort the table to find the stadium with the largest capacity. Write down your answer. Print the table.

FORMS AND REPORTS

Creating Forms

Datasheet view is useful for many of the ways you work with a database table. Often, however, you may want an easier way to enter and view records. A *form* is a database object used to enter or display data in a database. For example, the form shown in Figure 4-1 places all of the fields from the Members table into an easy-to-use layout.

FIGURE 4-1
Forms can make entering and viewing data easier

The Form Wizard makes the process of creating a form easy. It asks you questions about the fields, layout, and format and then creates a form based on your answers. You can also use the AutoForm feature. It automatically creates a form to display all the fields and records of a database table.

Using the Form Wizard

To create a form, click Forms on the Objects bar. Click the New button and the New Form dialog box appears, as shown in Figure 4-2. The New Form dialog box gives you several options for creating a form. In the next Step-by-Step, you will use the Form Wizard option. The New Form dialog box also asks you to specify the table or query to use for the form. In complex databases, you may have to choose from several tables or queries.

> **Hot Tip**
>
> You can also create a form using the Form Wizard by double-clicking **Create form by using wizard** in the Database window.

FIGURE 4-2
New Form dialog box

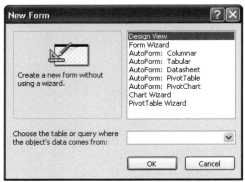

S TEP-BY-STEP 4.1

You are the newly elected Secretary of the Future Business Leaders Club. To make it easier when adding a new member to the database, you decide to create a form.

1. Open the **Step4-1** database from the data files.

2. Click **Forms** on the Objects bar.

3. Click **New**. The New Form dialog box appears, as shown in Figure 4-2.

> **Did You Know?**
>
> Forms can be created in Design view by placing fields on a blank form. Creating a form in Design view gives you more flexibility.

4. Choose the **Form Wizard** option and the **Members** table from the drop-down list.

5. Click **OK**. The Form Wizard dialog box appears, as shown in Figure 4-3. Leave the Form Wizard dialog box on the screen for the next Step-by-Step.

STEP-BY-STEP 4.1 Continued

FIGURE 4-3
Form Wizard dialog box

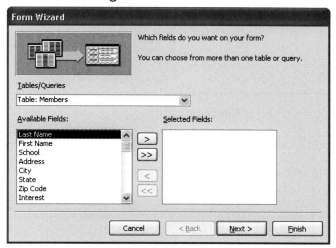

Choosing Fields for the Form

The next step is to choose the fields you want to appear on the form. To add a field to the form, click the field name in the *Available Fields* list and click the > button. To add all of the fields at once, click the >> button.

S TEP-BY-STEP 4.2

1. Click **>>**. All of the field names appear in the *Selected Fields* list.

2. Click the **Next** button. The Form Wizard dialog box changes to ask you to select a layout for the form, as shown in Figure 4-4.

FIGURE 4-4
Selecting a layout for a form

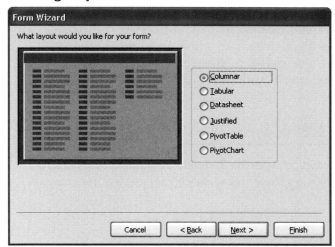

3. Leave the dialog box open for the next Step-by-Step.

Choosing a Layout for the Form

You have a choice of six different layouts for the form: Columnar, Tabular, Datasheet, Justified, PivotTable, and PivotChart. The Columnar layout is the most common type. The form in Figure 4-1 is an example of a Columnar layout. As data is entered, the insertion point moves down the fields.

STEP-BY-STEP 4.3

1. If not already selected, click the **Columnar** option.

2. Click **Next**. This dialog box asks you to choose a style, as shown in Figure 4-5.

FIGURE 4-5
Choosing a style for a form

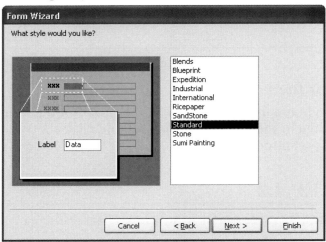

3. Leave the dialog box open for the next Step-by-Step.

Choosing a Style and Name for the Form

Choose a style to make your form look different. There are several styles from which to choose. After you choose a style, you are asked to name the form. You should select a name that best describes the form.

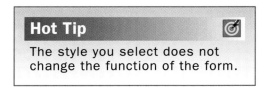

Hot Tip

The style you select does not change the function of the form.

STEP-BY-STEP 4.4

1. If not already selected, choose the **Standard** style from the list. The preview box shows you what this form style looks like. It should look similar to the preview box shown in Figure 4-5.

2. Click the other styles to see what they look like.

3. Choose the **SandStone** style and click **Next**. The final Form Wizard dialog box appears, as shown in Figure 4-6.

STEP-BY-STEP 4.4 Continued

FIGURE 4-6
Naming the form

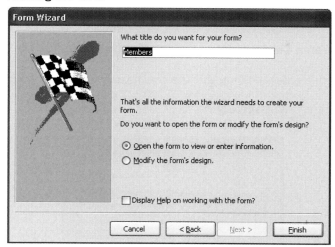

4. Key **Membership Form** into the title box.

5. Click the **Open the form to view or enter information** button if it's not chosen already.

6. Click **Finish**. Access creates the form, which should look like the form shown in Figure 4-7.

FIGURE 4-7
Membership form

Membership Form	
Last Name	Berry
First Name	Jared
School	Pine Springs
Address	5902 Sierra Street
City	Denver
State	CO
Zip Code	80231
Interest	Sporting goods
Dues Owed	$25.00
Dues Paid	$25.00
Date Joined	15-Sep-06

Record: 1 of 17

7. Open the **File** menu and choose **Close** to close the form. Leave the database open for the next Step-by-Step.

Using the AutoForm Feature

The AutoForm feature automatically creates a form that displays all the fields and records of the database table. This is the fastest way to create a simple form because no detailed questions are asked about the fields, layout, or format.

S TEP-BY-STEP 4.5

1. If not already selected, click **Forms** on the Objects bar.

2. Click **New**. The New Form dialog box appears.

3. Choose the **AutoForm: Columnar** option and the **Members** table from the drop-down list.

4. Click **OK**. AutoForm creates the form with the columnar layout, as shown in Figure 4-8.

FIGURE 4-8
Form created with the AutoForm feature

5. Open the **File** menu and choose **Close**. A message will appear asking if you want to save changes to the form.

6. Click **Yes**. The Save As dialog box appears.

7. Key **Members AutoForm** into the *Form Name* box.

8. Click **OK**. Leave the database open for the next Step-by-Step.

Using Forms

Using a form is the same as using Datasheet view. The same keys move the insertion point among the fields. You see the same navigation buttons at the bottom of the form, as shown in Figure 4-9. As with Datasheet view, you can move to a specific record by clicking in the Record Number box and entering the number of the record you want to see.

FIGURE 4-9
Navigation controls at the bottom of the form

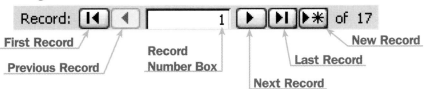

Table 4-1 lists the ways to move around when a form is displayed, including keyboard shortcuts.

TABLE 4-1
Navigating a form

TO MOVE TO THE...	BUTTON	KEYBOARD SHORTCUT
First record	First Record button	Ctrl+Home
Last record	Last Record button	Ctrl+End
Next record	Next Record button	Page Down
Previous record	Previous Record button	Page Up

To add a new record, click the Next Record button until the blank record at the end of the database appears, or click the New Record button. Key the new record. To change an existing record, display the record and make changes in the fields of the form.

After entering or editing records in a form, you do not need to save the changes. Access saves them for you automatically.

You can print forms the same way you print tables. To print all the records in the form, open the File menu and choose Print. In the Print dialog box, choose All from the Print Range options. To print only one record, display the record on the screen. Open the File menu and choose Print. Click the Selected Record(s) option from the Print Range options.

> **Hot Tip**
>
> You can preview a form the same way you preview a table in Datasheet view. To preview a form, open the **File** menu and choose **Print Preview** or click the **Print Preview** button on the toolbar. If necessary, click the magnifying glass with a plus (+) sign to make the form larger.

S TEP-BY-STEP 4.6

1. Open the **Membership Form**.

2. Click the **New Record** button. A blank record appears in the form.

3. Enter the following information in the form:

Last Name: **Patel**

First Name: **Paul**

School: **Pine Springs**

Address: **4546 Arapahoe Drive**

City: **Denver**

State: **CO**

STEP-BY-STEP 4.6 Continued

Zip Code: **80231**

Interest: **Computers**

Dues Owed: **$15.00**

Dues Paid: **$0.00**

Date Joined: **11-Feb-07**

4. Click in the record number box. Delete the 18, key **4**, and tap **Enter**.

5. Change the Interest field to **Sporting Goods**.

6. Go to record **14** and change the Address field to **6302 Rosebud Lane**.

7. Display record **18**, and then open the **File** menu and choose **Print**. The Print dialog box appears.

8. Click the **Selected Record(s)** option in the *Print Range* section, and click **OK**. (The printed form may cut off the data in some of the fields.)

9. Open the **File** menu and choose **Close** to close the form. Leave the database open for the next Step-by-Step.

Creating Reports

Databases can become large as records are added. Printing the database from Datasheet view may not always be the most desirable way to put the data on paper. A *report* is a database object used to organize, summarize, and print all or some of the data in a database. Figure 4-10 shows an example of a database report.

Printing a database from Datasheet view is a kind of a report. Printing from Datasheet view, however, is much less flexible than creating a report and printing it.

Using the Report Wizard

The Report Wizard makes the process of creating a report easy. It asks you questions about the fields, layout, and format and then creates a report based on your answers. You can also use the AutoReport feature. It automatically creates a report to display all the fields and records of a database table.

Hot Tip

You can also create a report using the Report Wizard by double-clicking **Create report by using wizard** in the Database window.

FIGURE 4-10
Database report

School	Last Name	First Name	Dues Owed	Dues Paid
Maxwell				
	Fleming	Jamie	$15.00	$15.00
	Jackson	Sarah	$15.00	$15.00
	Knight	Cameron	$25.00	$25.00
	Padilla	Jose	$25.00	$25.00
Summary for 'School' = Maxwell (4 detail records)				
Sum			$80.00	$80.00
Northridge				
	Chang	Michelle	$15.00	$0.00
	Chang	Laura	$25.00	$25.00
	Foley	John	$15.00	$0.00
	Foley	David	$25.00	$25.00
	Mitchell	Maggie	$25.00	$0.00
	Williams	Tyler	$15.00	$0.00
Summary for 'School' = Northridge (6 detail records)				
Sum			$120.00	$50.00
Pikes Peak				
	Fisher	Chris	$25.00	$10.00
	Gordon	Tara	$25.00	$15.00
	Matthews	Matt	$15.00	$15.00
	Simon	Heather	$15.00	$15.00
Summary for 'School' = Pikes Peak (4 detail records)				
Sum			$80.00	$55.00
Pine Springs				
	Berry	Jared	$25.00	$25.00
	Johnston	Ashley	$25.00	$25.00
	Patel	Paul	$15.00	$0.00
	Ross	Alex	$25.00	$10.00
Summary for 'School' = Pine Springs (4 detail records)				
Sum			$90.00	$60.00
Grand Total			$370.00	$245.00

Membership Dues Report

To create a report, click Reports on the Objects bar, and click the New button. The New Report dialog box appears, as shown in Figure 4-11. The New Report dialog box gives you several options for creating a report. In the next Step-by-Step, you will use the Report Wizard option. The New Report dialog box also asks you to specify the table or query to use for the report. Choose a table if you want to include the entire table in the report. Choose a query to include only certain data in the report.

FIGURE 4-11
New Report dialog box

STEP-BY-STEP 4.7

For the next meeting of the Future Business Leaders Club, you create a report listing the members and the membership dues.

1. Click **Reports** on the Objects bar.

2. Click **New**. The New Report dialog box appears, as shown in Figure 4-11.

3. Choose the **Report Wizard** option and the **Members** table from the drop-down list.

4. Click **OK**. The Report Wizard dialog box appears, as shown in Figure 4-12. Leave the Report Wizard dialog box on the screen for the next Step-by-Step.

FIGURE 4-12
Report Wizard dialog box

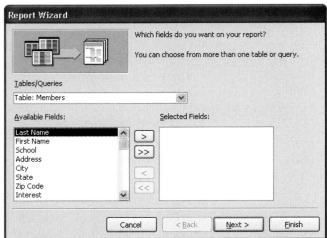

Choosing Fields for the Report

Select fields for the report in the Report Wizard dialog box shown in Figure 4-12. You can select fields the same way you did when creating a form using the Form Wizard.

STEP-BY-STEP 4.8

1. Highlight **Last Name** in the *Available Fields* list. Click **>**. The Last Name field is now listed in the *Selected Fields* box.

2. Do the same for the **First Name**, **School**, **Dues Owed**, and **Dues Paid** fields. Your screen should appear similar to Figure 4-13.

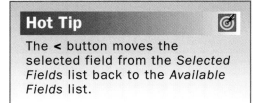

Hot Tip

The **<** button moves the selected field from the *Selected Fields* list back to the *Available Fields* list.

STEP-BY-STEP 4.8 Continued

FIGURE 4-13
Choosing fields

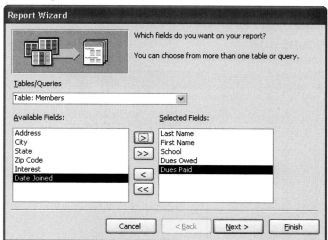

3. Click **Next**. The Report Wizard now gives you the option to group the report. Leave the Report Wizard dialog box on the screen for the next Step-by-Step.

Grouping and Sorting the Report

Grouping a report allows you to break it into parts based on the data in a field. In the report you are creating now, you will group the report by school. To group a report, choose the field(s) you want grouped from the Report Wizard dialog box shown in Figure 4-14.

FIGURE 4-14
Grouping a report by fields

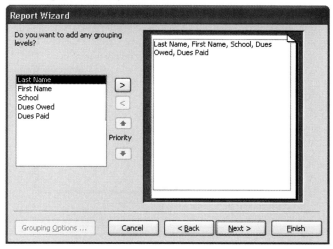

Sorting the report works together with grouping. You can sort a report by one or more fields. The dialog box shown in Figure 4-15 allows you to choose the fields for sorting the report. *Sorting* orders the records in a group based on the selected field(s). For example, you could group a student's report by grade and then sort it by last name. The report would list the students in alphabetic order by grade.

FIGURE 4-15
Sorting a report

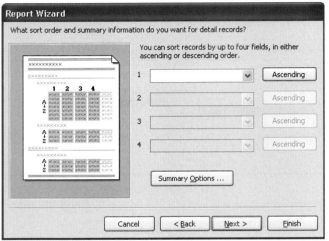

S TEP-BY-STEP 4.9

1. Highlight **School** and click **>**. Your screen should appear similar to Figure 4-16.

FIGURE 4-16
Report grouped by school

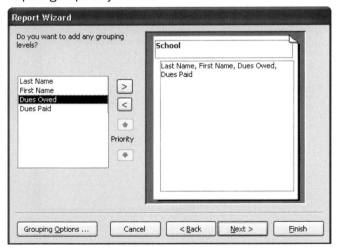

2. Click **Next**. The Report Wizard asks you which fields you want to sort by, as shown in Figure 4-15.

3. Choose **Last Name** as the first sort field by clicking the down arrow next to the number 1 box. For this report, you will sort by one field only. Leave the Report Wizard dialog box displayed for the next Step-by-Step.

Summary Options

One of the most useful features of reports is the ability to create summaries within them. Each group of records in a report can be followed by totals, averages, or other summary information. The Summary Options dialog box allows you to specify summaries for fields in the report.

S TEP-BY-STEP 4.10

1. Click the **Summary Options** button. The Summary Options dialog box appears.

2. Click the **Sum** check box for both the **Dues Owed** and **Dues Paid** fields. The report will total the Dues Owed and Dues Paid fields. Your screen should appear similar to Figure 4-17.

FIGURE 4-17
Summary Options dialog box

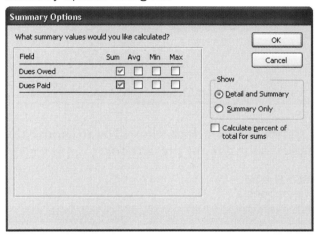

3. Click **OK** to close the Summary Options dialog box.

4. Click **Next**. The Report Wizard asks you to choose a layout and page orientation. Leave the Report Wizard dialog box on the screen for the next Step-by-Step.

Layout, Orientation, and Style

Next, you'll choose the layout and orientation for your report, as shown in Figure 4-18. The layout options let you choose how you want data to appear on the page. When you choose a layout, a sample is shown in the preview box on the left side of the dialog box. You can also choose from Landscape or Portrait orientation.

FIGURE 4-18
Layout options

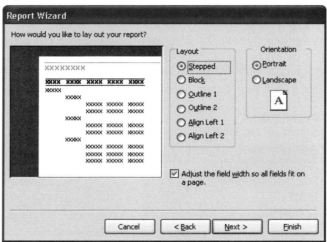

The next dialog box, shown in Figure 4-19, allows you to choose a style for the report. When you choose a style, a sample is shown in the preview box.

FIGURE 4-19
Style options

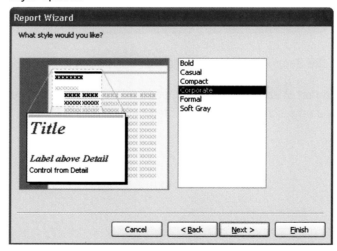

STEP-BY-STEP 4.11

1. Choose the **Outline 2** layout. The sample layout is shown in the preview box. Click the other options to look at the other layouts. When you have seen all of the available options, choose **Stepped** as the layout.

2. Choose **Portrait** as the page orientation, if it is not already selected. Make sure the **Adjust the field width so all fields fit on a page** box is checked. Your screen should appear the same as Figure 4-18.

3. Click **Next**. The Report Wizard asks you to select a style, as shown in Figure 4-19.

4. Choose the **Casual** style. The sample style is shown in the preview box. Click on the other options to look at the other styles. When you have seen all of the available options, choose **Corporate** as the style.

5. Click **Next**. The final Report Wizard dialog box appears. Leave the Report Wizard on the screen for the next Step-by-Step.

Naming the Report

The final step is naming the report, as shown in Figure 4-20. Use a name that best describes the data in the report. A report name can be up to 64 characters including letters, numbers, spaces, and some special characters. For example, if a report from a database of students prints the students by grade in last name order, you might name the report *Students by Grade*.

Computer Concepts

The style of a report tells the reader of the report something about the data. For example, it is best to display some types of reports in a formal style and others in a casual style.

FIGURE 4-20
Naming the report

After creating a report, you do not need to save it. Access saves it for you automatically with the title you entered into the Report Wizard. You will, however, need to save any modifications made later to the design of the report.

STEP-BY-STEP 4.12

1. Key **Membership Dues Report** as the title of the report.

2. Make sure the option to preview the report is selected and click **Finish**. The report appears in a window, as shown in Figure 4-21.

FIGURE 4-21
Previewing a report

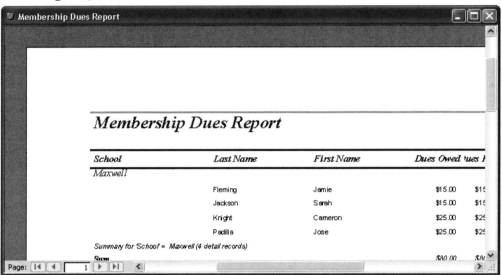

3. Scroll through the report to see the various categories.

4. Click the **Print** button to print the report.

5. Open the **File** menu and choose **Close**. The report will be saved automatically. Close the database.

SUMMARY

In this lesson, you learned:

■ The Form Wizard makes the process of creating a form easy. It asks you questions about the fields, layout, and format and then creates a form based on your answers. You can also use the AutoForm feature. It automatically creates a form to display all the fields and records of a database table.

■ Using a form is the same as using Datasheet view. The same keys move the insertion point among the fields.

- A report is a database object used to organize, summarize, and print all or some of the data in a database. The Report Wizard makes the process of creating a report easy. It asks you questions about the fields, layout, and format and then creates a report based on your answers.

- Grouping a report allows you to break it into parts based on the data in a field. Sorting the report works together with grouping. Sorting orders the records in a group based on the selected field(s).

VOCABULARY *Review*

Define the following terms:

Form	Report	Sorting
Grouping		

REVIEW *Questions*

TRUE/FALSE

Circle T if the statement is true or F if the statement is false.

T   F   1. The style you select for a form has an effect on the function of the form.

T   F   2. Database reports are prepared by creating a report object.

T   F   3. The Report Wizard always includes all fields in a report.

T   F   4. Like file names, report names can contain only eight characters.

T   F   5. The AutoForm feature is the quickest way to create a simple form because no detailed questions are asked about the fields, layout, and format.

WRITTEN QUESTIONS

Write a brief answer to the following questions.

1. What are the six different layouts for a form?

2. How do you move to a specific record using a form?

3. How does grouping affect a report?

4. What view is similar to a Tabular layout for a database?

5. What should you choose in the New Report dialog box to include only certain data in your report?

PROJECTS

 PROJECT 4-1

For the past year, you have worked at the City Zoo as a volunteer for a few hours each week. A large amount of money was donated one year ago to the zoo. This money was used to improve the zoo and add some more animals. The new animals have been arriving since February. To make it easier to add the information on the new animals, you decide to create a form.

1. Open the **Project4-1** database from the data files. Create a new form with the Form Wizard using the **New Animals** table.

2. Add the **Name, Continent, Classification, Zoo Location, Cage or Habitat**, and **Arrival Date** fields.

3. Use the **Columnar layout** and the **Standard** style.

4. Title the form **New Animal Form** and open the form.

5. Add a new record with the following information:

   Name: **Lion**

   Continent: **Africa**

   Classification: **Mammal**

   Zoo Location: **N**

   Cage or Habitat: **10**

   Arrival Date: **5/12/2006**

6. Go to record **2** (Ostrich), and change the Zoo Location to **W**.

7. Print Record **2**. (Be sure the *Selected Record(s)* option is selected in the Print dialog box.)

8. Close the form and leave the database open for the next project.

PROJECT 4-2

The zoo veterinarians check on the new animals every day to be sure that they are adjusting to their new habitats. To make their jobs easier, the veterinarians have asked for a report listing the new animals by their location in the zoo.

1. Use the Report Wizard to create a report. Use the **New Animals** table and choose the **Name, Zoo Location, Cage or Habitat,** and **Arrival Date.**

2. Group the report by **Zoo Location** and sort it by **Cage or Habitat.**

3. Choose the **Block** layout, **Portrait** orientation, and **Compact** style.

4. Title the report **New Animals by Zoo Location.** Select the option to preview the report.

5. Print the report.

6. Close the report and the database.

PROJECT 4-3

The database of restaurants created for the National Teachers Conference needs updating. To make it easier to update, you decide to create a form.

1. Open the **Project4-3** database from the data files.

2. Create a new form for the **Restaurants** table using the **AutoForm: Columnar** option.

3. After the form is created, scroll through the records until you find the information on **Rosa's Cafe.** Change the Location to **SW.**

4. Print the information on **Rosa's Cafe.**

5. Save the form as **Restaurant Form.**

6. Close the form and leave the database open for the next project.

PROJECT 4-4

Your teacher asks you to create a report listing the restaurants by the type of food. This information goes into a packet that each teacher will receive at the conference.

1. Use the Report Wizard to create a report using all the fields in the **Restaurants** table. Group the report by **Type of Food** and sort it by **Restaurant Name**.

2. Choose the **Stepped** layout, **Portrait** orientation, and **Corporate** style.

3. Title the report **Restaurants by Type of Food**. Select the option to preview the report.

4. Print the report.

5. Close the report and the database.

WEB*Project*

PROJECT 4-5

Create a database of information on water parks throughout the United States. Name the database **Water Parks**. Use the Web to search for the location (state and city) of each park and the price of an adult ticket. Create the table with the **Name, State, City,** and **Ticket Price** fields. Name the table **Park Information**. Add one record for each park to the table. You should add at least five records (water parks) to the table. When finished, create a report listing the water parks in alphabetical order. Name the report **Water Parks**. Preview and print the report.

TEAMWORK*Project*

PROJECT 4-6

In Project 3-6 of Lesson 3, as a group you created a database of favorite restaurants called **Favorites**. In this same group, use the Favorites database and create three reports named **Type of Food, Location,** and **Meal Prices**. Group each report according to the name of the report. Preview and print each report.

CRITICAL*Thinking*

ACTIVITY 4-1

Open the **MyCollection** database you created for the Critical Thinking Activity 1-1 in Lesson 1. (This database was updated in Critical Thinking Activity 2-1 in Lesson 2.) Use the Form Wizard to create a Justified form that includes the fields of your database table. Choose an attractive style for the form. Title the form **Address Form**. Add a record to the table using the new form. Print the record and close the form. Close the database.

MICROSOFT ACCESS

COMMAND SUMMARY

FEATURE	MENU COMMAND	TOOLBAR BUTTON	LESSON
Close	File, Close	☒	1
Close a Table	File, Close	☒	1
Column Width	Format, Column Width		2
Copy Record	Edit, Copy	🗐	2
Cut Record	Edit, Cut	✂	2
Database (create)	File, New	🗋	1
Delete Record	Edit, Delete Record	▶✕	2
Delete Row	Edit, Delete Rows	➡	1
Design View	Highlight name of Object, Design	↙	1
Exit Access	File, Exit		1
Field Properties	Highlight name of Table, Design	↙	2
File, Create	File, New	🗋	1
Filter, Records, Apply	Filter, Apply Filter/Sort	▽	3
Filter, Create	Records, Filter		3
Filter, Records, Remove	Filter, Remove Filter/Sort	▽	3
Find Data	Edit, Find	🔍	3
First Record		⏮	2
Form, Create	Forms, New		4
Insert Row	Insert, Rows	▤	1
Last Record		⏭	2
New Record		▶✱	2
Next Record		▶	2
Open Existing Database	File, Open	📂	1
Paste Record	Edit, Paste	📋	2
Previous Record		◀	2
Print	File, Print	🖨	1
Query, Create	Queries, New		3

FEATURE	MENU COMMAND	TOOLBAR BUTTON	LESSON
Report, Create	Reports, New		4
Row Height	Format, Row Height		2
Save	File, Save	💾	1
Sort Ascending	Records, Sort, Sort Ascending	⬇	3
Sort Descending	Records, Sort, Sort Descending	⬇	3
Start Access	Start, All Programs, Microsoft Office, Microsoft Office Access 2003		1
Table, Create	Tables, New		1
Table, Modify	Highlight name of Table, Design	◪	1
Undo Changes in Cell	Edit, Undo Typing	↩	2
Undo Changes in Previous Cell	Edit, Undo Current Field/ Record or Esc key		2
View, Datasheet		▦ ▾	1
View, Design		◪ ▾	1

REVIEW *Questions*

TRUE/FALSE

Circle T if the statement is true or F if the statement is false.

T F 1. A record appears as a column in Datasheet view.

T F 2. The navigation buttons are used to move around the datasheet.

T F 3. Queries allow the most complex searches.

T F 4. A field can contain up to 356 characters.

T F 5. You can click the Undo button to restore a record after you have deleted it using the Delete Record command.

WRITTEN QUESTIONS

Write a brief answer to the following questions.

1. What data type is used to store dollar amounts?

2. What option makes Access choose the width of a column?

3. What button displays the results of a filter?

4. Which layout is the most common type for a form?

5. Which database object is created to organize, summarize, and print all or some of the data in a database?

PROJECTS

PROJECT 1

For a Science project, you have created a database of information on the planets. By sorting the database, you can easily find the data that you need to include in your project.

1. Open the **Project1** database from the data files.

2. Open the **Planets** table in Datasheet view.

3. Sort the table to answer each of the following questions. Write down your answers.
    A. Sort the table by **Distance** in ascending order. Which planet is closest to the sun?
    B. Sort the table by **Distance** in descending order. Which planet is farthest from the sun?
    C. Sort the table by **Revolution** in descending order. Which planet takes longest to revolve around the sun?
    D. Sort the database by **Rotation** in ascending order. Which planet takes the shortest time to rotate on its axis?
    E. Sort the database by **Diameter** in descending order. Which planet is the largest?
    F. Sort the database by **Moons** in descending order. Which planet has the most moons?

4. Move the **Moons** column between the **Planet** and **Distance** fields.

5. Change the column width for all of the fields to **Best Fit**.

6. Print the table.

7. Close the table. Click **Yes** if prompted to save changes to the table.

8. Close the database.

PROJECT 2

You decide to create a database of your friends containing the information that you use frequently.

1. Create a new database named **Friends** followed by your initials.

2. With the *Friends* database open, create a new table named **Friend Information**. Add the following fields to the table:

Field Name	Data Type	Description
Last Name	Text	Last name of friend
First Name	Text	First name of friend
Phone Number	Text	Friend's phone number
E-mail Address	Text	Friend's e-mail address
Birthday	Date/Time	Friend's birthday

3. When finished, save the table as **Friend Information**. No primary key is necessary.

4. Switch to Datasheet view and enter the information on five of your friends. Key the Birthday field in the format XX/XX/XXXX. If you do not know some of the information, leave the field blank.

5. Open the **Friend Information** table in Design view.

6. Change the format for the Birthday field to **Medium Date**.

7. Save the change.

8. Switch to Datasheet view and change the column width for all of the fields to **Best Fit**.

9. Print the table.

10. Close the table. Click **Yes** if prompted to save changes to the table.

11. Close the database.

PROJECT 3

This week at the city zoo, third grade classes from each grade school will be taking field trips. Some of the third grade teachers have requested information on the location of certain animals at the zoo.

1. Open the **Project3** database from the data files.

2. Open the **New Animals** table, and use the Find command to locate the animals classified as **Reptile**.

3. Create a filter to display only the animals located in the southern (**S**) area of the zoo. You do not have to sort the records.

4. Print the results of the filter.

5. Remove the filter to show all the records in the table. Close the table. If asked to save the design of the table, click **Yes**.

6. Create a query that displays the animals that are from **Africa**. Have the query display the **Name, Continent,** and **Classification** fields. Sort the **Name** field in ascending order. Save the query as **Animals from Africa**.

7. Run the query and print the results. Close the query and the database.

PROJECT 4

You have created a database with information on dog breeds. To make it easier to add the information on a new dog, you decide to create a form.

1. Open the **Project4** database from the data files. Create a new form with the Form Wizard using the **Breed Information** table.

2. Add the **Breed, Group, Height, Weight, Color, Grooming,** and **Lifespan** fields.

3. Use the **Columnar layout** and the **Standard** style.

4. Title the form **New Dog Form** and open the form.

5. Add a new record and add the following information in the form:
   Breed: **Border Collie**
   Group: **Herding**
   Height: **20**
   Weight: **40**
   Color: **All colors**
   Grooming: **No**
   Lifespan: **13**

6. Go to the **Golden Retriever** record. Print the record. (Be sure the *Selected Record(s)* option is selected in the Print dialog box.)

7. Close the form and leave the database open for the next project.

PROJECT 5

Your family wants to decide on the new dog after dinner this evening. You create a report listing the information on the various dog breeds.

1. Use the Report Wizard to create a report using all the fields in the **Breed Information** table. Group the report by **Group** and sort it by **Weight**.

2. Choose the **Stepped** layout, **Portrait** orientation, and **Bold** style.

3. Title the report **Dog Breeds by Group**. Select the option to preview the report.

4. Print the report.

5. Close the report and the database.

PORTFOLIO *Checklist*

Include the following files from this unit in your student portfolio:

Lesson 1
____ Dogs (Breed Information)
____ Project1-1 (Breed Information)
____ Project1-2 (Breed Information)
____ Pulitzer (Poetry)
____ Zoo Animals (Recent Additions)
____ Project1-5 (Recent Additions)
____ Project1-6 (Recent Additions)
____ MyCollection

Lesson 2
____ Step2-1 (National Parks)
____ Project2-1 (Members)
____ Project2-2 (Members)
____ Project2-3 (Members)
____ Project2-4 (National Parks)
____ CDClub (CDList)
____ MyCollection

Lesson 3
____ Step3-1 (State Information)
____ Project3-1 (Restaurants)
____ Project3-3 (Breed Information)
____ Project3-5 (State Information)
____ Favorites (Restaurants)
____ Activity3-1 (Baseball Stadiums)

Lesson 4
____ Step4-1 (Members)
____ Project4-1 (New Animals)
____ Project4-3 (Restaurants)
____ Water Parks (Park Information)
____ Favorites (Restaurants)
____ MyCollection

Unit Review
____ Project1 (Planets)
____ Friends (Friend Information)
____ Project3 (New Animals)
____ Project4 (Breed Information)

MICROSOFT PUBLISHER

Unit 6

Lesson 1 — 1.5 hrs.
Publisher Basics

Lesson 2 — 2.5 hrs.
Enhancing Publisher Documents

Estimated Time for Unit: 4 hours

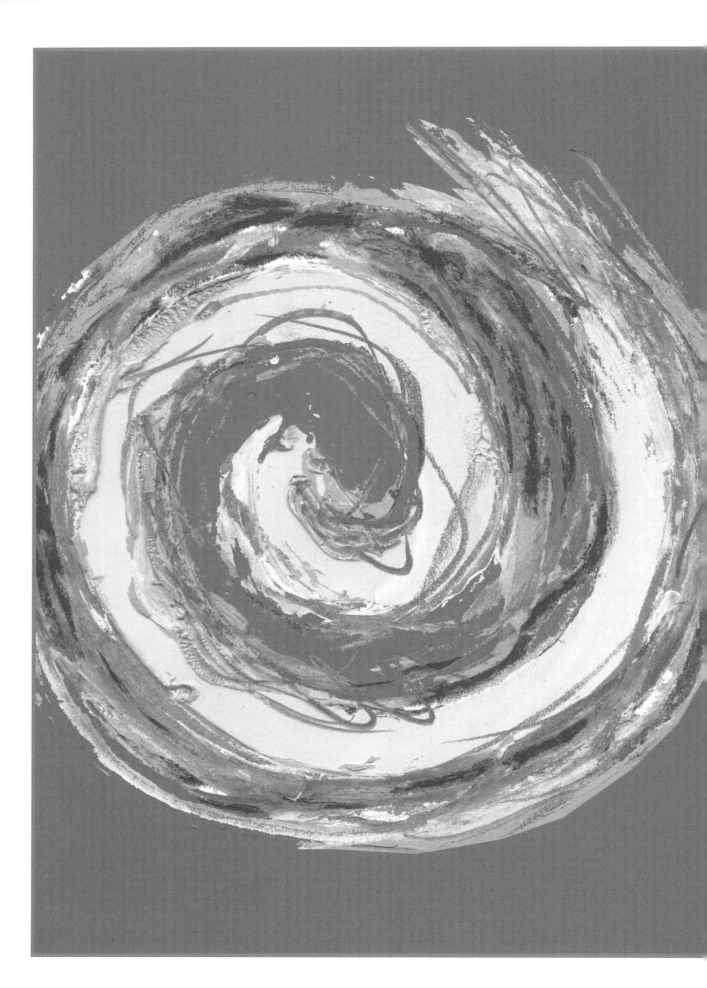

PUBLISHER BASICS

What Is Publisher?

Publisher is the desktop publishing application in the Microsoft Office 2003 suite of programs. *Desktop publishing* is used to design many different publications. Some of these documents could include business cards, flyers, and greeting cards. Publisher contains hundreds of predesigned templates you can use to create professional-looking projects. All you have to do is add your own style and text.

STEP-BY-STEP 1.1

1. With Windows running, click **Start** on the task bar.

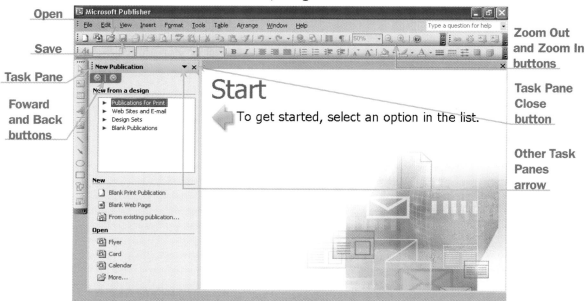

2. Point to **All Programs** (in Windows 2000, point to **Programs**) and then **Microsoft Office**. Click **Microsoft Office Publisher 2003**.

3. Publisher opens and the Publisher startup screen appears, as shown in Figure 1-1. Leave the screen open for the next Step-by-Step.

FIGURE 1-1
Microsoft Office Publisher 2003 opening screen

Start a Project

When you first start Publisher, no publication is open. You must select from one of the options in the New Publication task pane. This task pane on the left side of the screen helps you start, create, and edit your Publisher project. If you choose to create a new publication, the program opens a new publication, which is temporarily titled Publication1. Each time you open a new publication to create another project, the default name will change by one number. If you close and then reopen Publisher, the default naming starts over again.

Task Panes

As you work in Publisher, different task panes appear. You can view other task panes by using the Other Task Panes arrow on the task pane title bar. The navigation arrows (Back and Forward) make it easy to view task panes that have been used before. The Close button on the upper right side of the task pane hides the task pane. Look at Figure 1-1 and find the Other Task Panes arrow, the Back and Forward arrows, and the Close button.

The task pane you will use first is the New Publication task pane. In this task pane, the *New from a design* section creates new publications using a publication wizard or a design set. The *New* section starts a blank publication. The *Open* section opens an existing publication. See Figure 1-2.

FIGURE 1-2
Microsoft Publisher screen

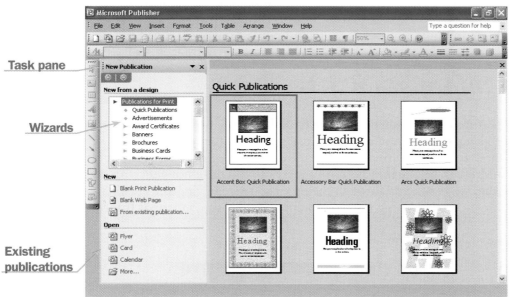

New from a Design

Wizards use built-in templates that are the framework for various types of publications. Publisher comes with more than 25 wizards.

When *Publications for Print* is selected in the task pane, the available wizards are listed below it. When you select a wizard from the list, designs for that type of publication are shown in the pane on the right.

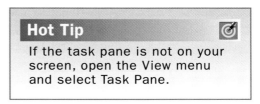

Hot Tip

If the task pane is not on your screen, open the View menu and select Task Pane.

In Figure 1-2, there are diamonds or arrows next to the wizards listed in the task pane. When a wizard with an arrow next to it is chosen, a list of subcategories appears. These subcategories represent more detailed publications. Wizards with diamonds do not have additional subcategories.

When you select *Design Sets* in the *New from a design* section of the task pane, the window to the right shows groups of available publications. These show the types of designs you can use. A *design set* is a group of documents (letterheads, business cards, envelopes, and so forth) that use the same design or theme. There are also design sets that offer certain layouts for special events, holidays, and fund-raising.

New

The *New* section of the task pane has several options to start a new publication, including *Blank Print Publication*. A **blank publication** is one you use to make a document from scratch using whatever format, colors, and designs you like. You can also choose to create a new Web page or a new publication based on an existing one.

Open

This section of the task pane lists recently saved publications. To open an existing publication that is not listed, choose *More*. (If the *More* option is not displayed, choose *Open* instead.) The Open Publication dialog box appears so you can open a previously saved file.

Personal Information Sets

A helpful feature of Publisher is the personal information sets. You can use a **personal information set** to keep information about your businesses, other organizations, or your home and family. Then, when you are creating a publication, Publisher automatically inserts information such as names, addresses, phone numbers, and logos. If you have not yet created a personal information set, Publisher will walk you through the process. You can view the Personal Information dialog box (see Figure 1-3) by opening the Edit menu and choosing Personal Information.

FIGURE 1-3
Personal Information dialog box

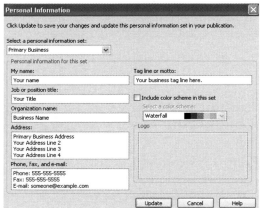

STEP-BY-STEP 1.2

1. Select **Publications for Print** in the *New from a design* section. This is in the New Publications task pane displayed on the left. The screen appears, as shown in Figure 1-2.

2. Click **Business Cards** in the list of wizards. Many designs will appear on the right (see Figure 1-4).

STEP-BY-STEP 1.2 Continued

FIGURE 1-4
Business Card wizards

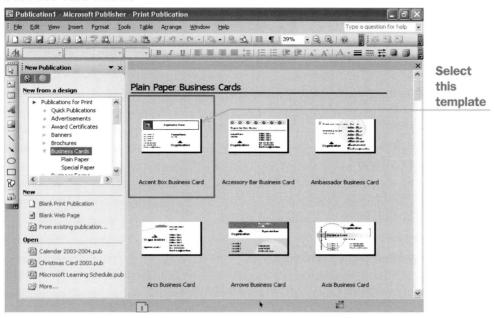

3. Click the **Accent Box Business Card** template, as shown in Figure 1-4. The Business Card Options task pane appears on the left side of the screen (see Figure 1-5) and the Accent Box Business Card template appears on the right.

FIGURE 1-5
Business Card Options task pane

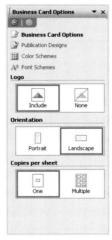

4. If you have not created a personal information set, the Personal Information dialog box will open (see Figure 1-3). If it does not open automatically, click the **Edit** menu and choose **Personal Information** to display the Personal Information dialog box. (Delete the existing information in each of the text boxes as you complete Steps 5–11.)

STEP-BY-STEP 1.2 Continued

5. In the *Select a personal information set* box, select **Primary Business**, if necessary.

6. In the *My name* box, key **Sam Goldman**.

7. In the *Job or position title* box, key **Associate**.

8. In the *Organization name* box, key **Galaxy Entertainment**.

9. In the *Address* box, key the following:

1504 Pine Tree Road
Graham, TX 76450

10. In the *Phone, fax, and e-mail* box, key the following:

Phone: 940-555-9213
Fax: 940-555-9211
E-mail: sgoldman@galaxyent.com

11. In the *Tag line or motto* box, key **Come see the stars!**

12. Click the **Update** button to save your changes. Your card will look similar to the one in Figure 1-6. The logo may be different, but will be edited later in this lesson. Leave your card open for the next Step-by-Step.

FIGURE 1-6
Business card with updated personal information

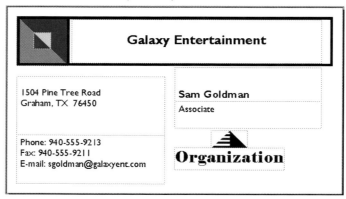

Save a Publication

The first time you save a publication, the Save As dialog box appears in which you can name the publication. Once a publication has been saved, the Save command updates the latest version.

STEP-BY-STEP 1.3

1. From the File menu, choose **Save As**. The Save As dialog box appears.

2. Key **Card**, followed by your initials, in the *File name* text box. (If necessary, navigate to the folder where you have been instructed to save your work.)

3. Click **Save** and leave the card open for the next Step-by-Step.

Add a Logo

You can make changes to your card by clicking on the item in the window. For example, if you want to change the title of Associate, click on the item. A blinking insertion point appears so that you can key a new title.

To create a new logo for the card, click on the existing logo. A Logo Wizard icon appears. When you click the icon, the task pane on the left displays designs and options you can use to customize a logo. You can apply a different design, create a logo with Publisher, or insert an existing picture file as a logo. You can also remove the graphic from the logo or add lines of text.

STEP-BY-STEP 1.4

1. Click the logo portion of your business card to select it. See Figure 1-7. (Your logo may look different.) The Logo Wizard icon appears so you can edit your logo.

FIGURE 1-7
Editing the logo

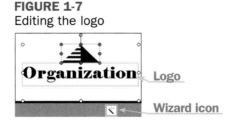

STEP-BY-STEP 1.4 Continued

2. Click the Logo Wizard icon. The Logo Designs task pane appears. See Figure 1-8.

FIGURE 1-8
Logo Options and Logo Designs task pane

3. The *Apply a design* section of the task pane lists the different designs available. Click the **Open Oval** design. The logo design changes.

4. Select the word **Organization** (or other company name) in the logo part of your business card. Key **Galaxy Entertainment**. Click outside the text box to close it. Leave the file open for the next Step-by-Step.

Print a Publication

You print your publication by opening the File menu and choosing Print. The Print dialog box appears. Use the Print dialog box to print all or part of a publication or to change the way your publication looks on the printed page.

Close a Publication

Unlike other Microsoft Office 2003 programs, the Publisher program does not have a Close Window button in the upper-right corner. The Close button in the upper-right corner closes the entire Publisher program. To close your publication project but not the entire Publisher program, open the File menu and choose Close.

S TEP-BY-STEP 1.5

1. Save the file by clicking the **Save** button on the toolbar. A message appears asking if you want to save the new logo to the Primary Business personal information set. Click **Yes**. Your business card will look similar to the one in Figure 1-9.

FIGURE 1-9
Modified business card

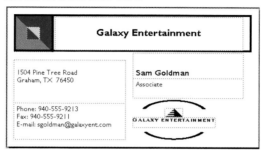

2. In the Business Card Options task pane, under *Copies per sheet,* choose **Multiple**.

3. Open the **File** menu and choose **Print**. In the Print dialog box, click **OK** to print your business card.

4. Click the **Save** button to save the business card.

5. Open the **File** menu and choose **Close**.

> **Hot Tip**
>
> If the Business Card Options task pane is not displayed, click the Other Task Panes arrow at the top of the task pane. Choose Business Card Options from the menu.

Design Sets

The Design Sets option allows you to design an entire series of documents that include the same design, information, and logo. This way you can keep the same format in all the documents you make.

S TEP-BY-STEP 1.6

1. In the *New from a design* section of the New Publication task pane, click **Design Sets**. The Accent Box templates display on the right side of the screen by default since the Accent Box design set is the first in the list. Click on **Master Sets**. The Master Sets submenu appears. Click on the different submenu titles to see the different designs Publisher has for you to use, and then click on **Accent Box** again.

STEP-BY-STEP 1.6 Continued

2. Scroll down through the Accent Box templates, and click **Accent Box Special Offer Flyer**. The Flyer Options task pane appears. See Figure 1-10.

FIGURE 1-10
Flyer Options task pane

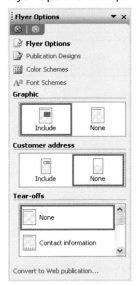

3. In the Tear-offs section, click **Coupon**. Your flyer is updated to include a coupon.

4. Open the **Edit** menu and choose **Personal Information**. Verify that the data entered in Step-by-Step 1.2 is still correct. (Notice that the logo was updated to reflect the changes you made earlier.) Click **Update** if necessary (or **Cancel** if no changes were made).

5. Save the file as **Flyer**, followed by your initials. Leave the publication open for the next Step-by-Step.

Edit a Publication from a Design Set

You can make changes to the flyer using the same methods you applied on your business card. To better view the text you are changing, magnify or reduce your view using the Zoom In and Zoom Out buttons on the Standard toolbar. To change the font type or font size of the text in your flyer, use the Font box or Font Size box on the Formatting toolbar. Click on the font or font size you want and any highlighted text changes to the new choice.

STEP-BY-STEP 1.7

1. Click the *Promotion Title* portion of the flyer. The entire title is automatically selected. This allows you to edit the title.

2. Key **2 for 1 Special**.

STEP-BY-STEP 1.7 Continued

3. In the *Date of Sale* box, click to select **00/00/00** and key next Saturday's date. You may need to click on the **Zoom In** button on the toolbar once or twice to enlarge your editing area.

4. In the *Time of Sale* box, click to select **00:00** and key **10:00 a.m. – 11:00 p.m**.

5. Click in the box that asks you to describe your location (the text will be selected automatically). Key **Located next to Graham National Bank**.

6. Click to select the *Free Offer* attention getter and then click the wizard icon. The Attention Getter Designs task pane appears. See Figure 1-11.

FIGURE 1-11
Attention Getter Designs task pane

7. In the task pane, scroll and click the **Shadowed Starburst** design. Notice that the logo design changes.

8. Click on the **Free Offer** logo and key **1 Day Only!**

9. Click on the picture in your flyer to select it. Click on the picture again so the selection handles change color and have *X*s in them. The Picture toolbar appears. (It may be floating or docked with the other toolbars.)

10. Open the **Insert** menu from the Menu toolbar. Choose **Picture** and choose **Clip Art** on the submenu. The Clip Art task pane appears.

11. In the *Search for* text box, key **Stars** and click the **Go** button.

12. In the results that are displayed, click a star-related picture to insert it in the flyer.

STEP-BY-STEP 1.7 Continued

13. Click in the box to the right of the clip art that contains the phone number, and key **940-555-9213**.

14. Click in the tag line (motto) box. Select the text **Come see the stars!**

15. Click the down arrow on the Font Size button (on the Formatting toolbar) and select **20** to change the font size of the tag line.

16. Click in the text box under the picture to select all the text. Key the following:
Galaxy Entertainment is happy to offer an out-of-this-world special. For one day only, rent any game, video, or DVD and get a second one free.

17. Tap **Enter** until the text is centered horizontally.

18. Click in the box that contains the bulleted text *List items here*, to select the list. Key the following text:
Latest games
Newest videos and DVDs
Best arcade in town
Great snacks

19. Click the *Name of Item or Service* text box on the coupon. Key **Popcorn and Candy**.

20. Click the *00% OFF* text box. Key **15% OFF**.

21. Click in the box (on the coupon) that asks you to describe your location, and key **Located next to Graham National Bank.** (You may need to click the **Zoom In** button again to enlarge your edit area.)

22. Click in the box (on the coupon) that contains the phone number. Key **940-555-9213**.

23. Click in the box that contains the coupon's expiration date (*00/00/00*). Key the date for the Saturday following the next one. (The coupon will expire one week after the 2 for 1 special date.)

24. Click on the picture in the coupon section of the flyer. Click on the picture again so the selection handles change color and have *Xs* in them. The Picture toolbar appears.

25. The Clip Art task pane should open. If not, open the **Insert** menu on the Menu toolbar. Choose **Picture** and choose **Clip Art** on the submenu.

STEP-BY-STEP 1.7 Continued

26. In the *Search for* text box, key **Popcorn**. Click a popcorn-related picture to insert into the flyer. Your flyer will look similar to Figure 1-12.

FIGURE 1-12
Completed flyer with Attention Getter and Coupon

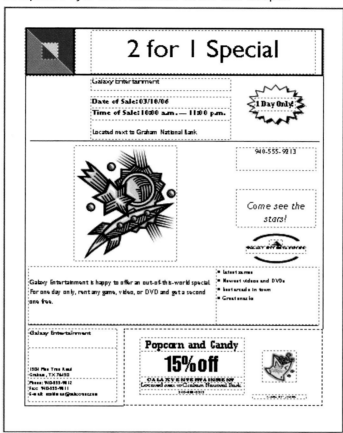

27. Save, print, and close the flyer.

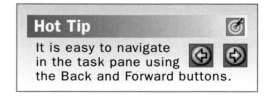

Hot Tip

It is easy to navigate in the task pane using the Back and Forward buttons.

Other Types of Publications

Publisher allows you to create many other types of publications using the processes you have already learned in this lesson.

STEP-BY-STEP 1.8

1. In the New Publication task pane, choose **Design Sets**.

2. By default, the Accent Box design set is selected (within the Master Sets). Click **Accent Box Calendar**. The Calendar Options task pane appears. See Figure 1-13.

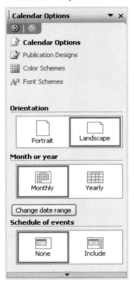

FIGURE 1-13
Calendar Options task pane

3. In the *Orientation* section of the task pane, click **Portrait**. The calendar changes to portrait orientation.

4. In the *Month or year* section of the task pane, select **Yearly**.

5. Your calendar will look similar to Figure 1-14.

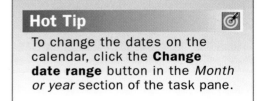

Hot Tip

To change the dates on the calendar, click the **Change date range** button in the *Month or year* section of the task pane.

STEP-BY-STEP 1.8 Continued

FIGURE 1-14
Completed calendar

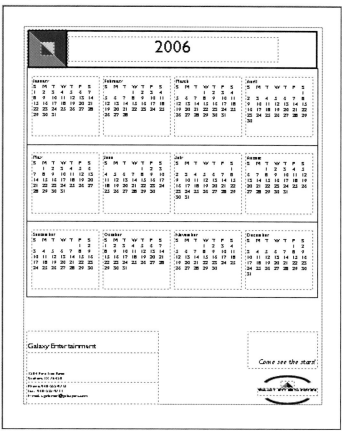

6. Save the file as **Calendar**, followed by your initials.

7. Print your calendar and close the file.

SUMMARY

In this lesson, you learned:

- Microsoft Publisher is a program that produces professional-looking documents in almost any format. Publisher makes this process easy by using wizards and design sets.

- You can create publications with publication wizards. Wizards use predesigned templates that supply the framework for different types of publications.

- By using design sets, you can make a series of documents that have the same design, information, and logo. This helps you keep a consistent look throughout the documents you produce.

- Publisher helps you easily add logos and clip art or make changes to your publication once it has been created.

- Updating the Personal Information dialog box lets you personalize any publication with your own information.

VOCABULARY*Review*

Define the following terms:

Blank publication	Desktop publishing	Publisher
Design set	Personal information set	Wizard

REVIEW*Questions*

TRUE/FALSE

Circle T if the statement is true or F if the statement is false.

T   F   1. To start a new publication, choose the *Open a publication* option.

T   F   2. By choosing *Blank Print Publication*, you can create a new publication based on an existing one.

T   F   3. You can use design sets to create a series of documents with the same design.

T   F   4. Logo options include removing the graphic and adding lines of text.

T   F   5. You cannot use the Personal Information dialog box to customize your publication with business information.

WRITTEN QUESTIONS

Write a brief answer to each of the following questions.

1. List the three options that are listed in the *New* section of the task pane.

2. When does the Logo Wizard icon appear?

3. Which option in the task pane allows you to create a series of documents (letterheads, business cards, and envelopes) with the same design?

4. What option would you select in the task pane to retrieve any files you have saved?

5. What does it mean when a wizard category has an arrow next to it?

PROJECTS

PROJECT 1-1

Create a business card for your personal use.

1. Start Publisher, if necessary.

2. In the *Open* section of the New Publication task pane, click **More**, if necessary, and locate **Project1-1** in the data files. If the **More** option is not displayed, choose **Open** instead.

3. Save the file as **Card1**, followed by your initials.

4. Edit the personal information to include your name, address, phone number, and e-mail address. Add your school's name in the *Organization name* text box. Leave the *Tag line or motto* text box blank. Click **Update**.

5. Use the Logo Wizard button to change the logo design.

6. In the logo text box, key the year you will graduate. (*Hint:* Key **Class of 2010.**)

7. Click the *Other Task Panes* arrow and select **Business Card Options**. In the Business Card Options task pane, select **Multiple** under *Copies per sheet*, if necessary, and then print the business cards.

8. Save the file. Click **Yes** if asked whether to save the new logo to the Primary Business personal information set. Close the document.

PROJECT 1-2

Create a flyer for a fund-raiser at your school or other organization.

1. Start Publisher, if necessary.

2. In the *New from a design* section, click **Publications for Print** and click **Flyers**.

3. From the *Flyers* section, choose **Fundraiser** and select a design.

4. Save the file as **Flyer1**, followed by your initials.

5. Edit the personal information to add your school's (or other organization's) address, phone number, and e-mail address. Click **Update**.

6. In each of the text boxes, key information about a fund-raiser that takes place in two weeks. Be sure to include times, dates, and places.

7. Save and print the flyer. Close the document.

PROJECT 1-3

Create a letterhead for your school or organization.

1. Start Publisher, if necessary.

2. From the *New from a design* section, click **Publications for Print** and click **Letterhead**.

3. Choose a letterhead design and delete the logo that is automatically inserted.

4. Save the file as **Letterhead**, followed by your initials.

5. Print the letterhead. Close the document.

PROJECT 1-4

Create a postcard for a club or organization to which you belong.

1. Start Publisher, if necessary.

2. From the *New from a design* section, click **Publications for Print** and click **Postcards**.

3. Select the **Accessory Bar Informational Postcard**.

4. Save the file as **Postcard**, followed by your initials.

5. Key the name of a club or organization in the **Product/Service Information** text box.

6. Key information about an upcoming meeting in the center text box. Be sure to include the time, date, and place for the meeting.

7. Delete the logo.

8. Save and print the postcard. Close the document.

WEB*Project*

PROJECT 1-5

Create a presidential campaign flyer.

1. Using the World Wide Web, find interesting facts about a historical American hero or heroine.

2. Open Publisher and design a campaign flyer that announces your hero's/heroine's decision to run for President. Be sure to list interesting facts about your candidate.

3. Preview the document.

4. Save the document as **President** followed by your initials.

5. Print and close the document.

TEAMWORK*Project*

PROJECT 1-6

In small groups, work together to design a menu for a new restaurant.

1. Open Publisher, if necessary.

2. In the *New from a design* section, click **Publications for Print**.

3. From the submenu, click **Menus**.

4. Choose any menu template from the *Daily Special* section and create a menu.

5. Save the document as **Menu** with the initials of the group.

6. Print copies of the menu for each member of the group and close the document.

7. Share your menu with the other groups.

CRITICAL*Thinking*

ACTIVITY 1-1

You are asked to change the color scheme and the font scheme of the **Flyer** file you created in this lesson. Use the Help system to find information on color schemes and font schemes and how to change them in a publication. Write a paragraph that defines font and color schemes and explains the procedure for changing them. Save the paragraph as **Critical Thinking Activity 1-1**, followed by your initials. Modify your publication by changing the color scheme and font scheme of the **Flyer** document. Save the file as **Flyer Scheme**, followed by your initials.

ENHANCING PUBLISHER DOCUMENTS

Enhance Your Publisher Documents

As we saw in Lesson 1, the personal information sets, design sets, and wizards in Microsoft Publisher are easy to use. In this lesson, you will learn about some useful tools for enhancing your publications. By using Design Gallery objects, it is easy to add text, calendars, coupons, and reply forms to your Publisher projects. By adding color and pictures to your project, you can make attractive and professional-looking publications. With these tools, you can design professional publications for your school, business, and even for yourself.

STEP-BY-STEP 2.1

1. Start Microsoft Office Publisher 2003, if necessary, and select **Publications for Print** from the New Publication task pane displayed on the left.

2. From the *Publications for Print* submenu, choose **Brochures**. Click **Price List** from the submenu. The Price List Brochures templates appear on the right. See Figure 2-1.

FIGURE 2-1
Price List Brochures templates

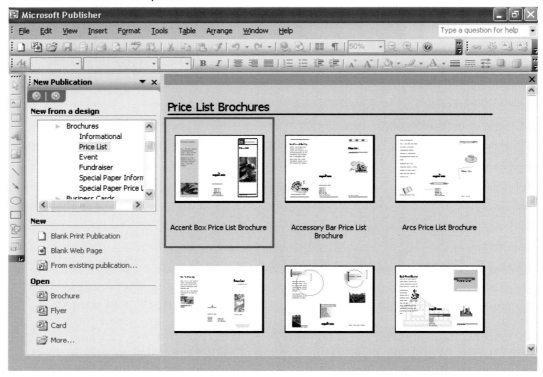

3. Click the **Blends Price List Brochure** template. (You may need to scroll to locate this template.)

4. If you have not created a personal information set, a Personal Information dialog box appears. Click **OK** to display the Personal Information dialog box. If a message does not appear, open the **Edit** menu. Choose **Personal Information** to display the Personal Information dialog box. Delete any information in the boxes.

STEP-BY-STEP 2.1 Continued

5. In the *Select a personal information set* box, select **Primary Business**, if necessary, and key the following:

My name:	**Sarah Jacobs**
Job or position title:	**Summer Camp Counselor**
Organization name:	**St. Charles Athletic Club**
Address:	**2109 Clarkson Valley Road**
	St. Charles, IL 60174

Phone, fax, and e-mail:

Phone: 208-555-9694

Fax: 208-555-9699

E-mail: sjacobs@scac.com

Tag line or motto:	**Fitness Made Fun!**

(*Hint:* If there is a logo in the Personal Information dialog box, it remains until you delete it in the next Step-by-Step exercise.)

6. Click the **Update** button to close the Personal Information dialog box.

7. Save the file as **Brochure**, followed by your initials. Leave the publication open for the next Step-by-Step.

Enter Text

When developing projects, you will need to add your own information. When using Publisher templates, you can add text directly into text boxes or panel headings. A *panel heading* is the area provided for the title or heading of a project or section of a project. You can also add text by copying information stored in other Microsoft programs into a publication. This time-saving technique will be discussed later in this lesson.

Microsoft Publisher gives you the flexibility to resize and reposition text boxes. If a text box is difficult to read, you can select the area and zoom in for better viewing and editing.

To assist you in navigating and managing your text, the *page navigator* is located in the lower-left side of the window. It allows you to move quickly from one page to another, which is very useful when your publication contains multiple pages of text.

STEP-BY-STEP 2.2

1. The *Brochure* file should be open from the previous Step-by-Step. Close the Brochure Options task pane.

2. Display page **1** if necessary (by using the page navigator), and click the Zoom In (+) button to zoom to **75%**.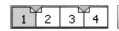

3. Right-click the logo in the second panel of the brochure. From the submenu, select **Delete Object**.

4. Right-click the picture in the first panel of the brochure. From the submenu, select **Delete Object**.

5. Change the text (in the first panel) that reads *BACK PANEL HEADING* to read **OUR MISSON** by clicking on the text and keying the replacement text. Center the text vertically by highlighting it and clicking the **Center** button on the Standard toolbar. Center the text horizontally by placing the cursor in front of the text and tapping **Enter**.

6. Click in the text box below *OUR MISSION* to select all the text. Key the following:
   It is our mission to provide a fun and friendly atmosphere to meet your fitness needs. We promise a clean, safe environment in which you can strengthen your body and your mind. Join us at the St. Charles Athletic Club…where we make fitness fun!

7. Select the text you just entered and click the **Bold** button on the Standard toolbar. Change the font size to **12**.

8. In the third panel, select all the text in the *Price List* text box. Key **SPORTS CAMP**. Bold and center it.

9. In the telephone number text box, change the text to read **208-555-9694**.

10. In the same panel, right-click on the picture and from the submenu, select **Delete Object**. Your brochure should look like Figure 2-2.

STEP-BY-STEP 2.2 Continued

FIGURE 2-2
Page 1 view of the St. Charles Athletic Club Price List brochure

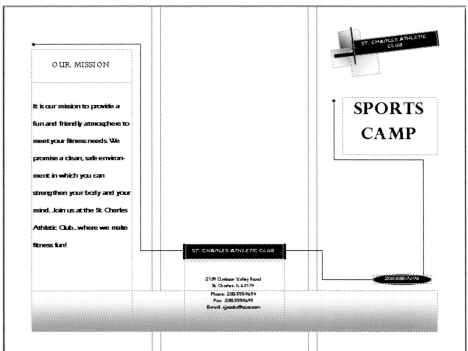

11. Click **2** in the page navigation area to switch to the page 2 view.

12. Click the text that reads *Main Inside Heading* to highlight it. Replace it with **St. Charles Athletic Club**.

13. Click in the text box below the main inside heading to select the text. Click the **Font Size** down arrow and choose **16** point. Then key:

Basketball, soccer, and tennis will be offered to children ages 9-12 in an all-day sports camp. An all-day camp for children ages 5-8 will teach swimming, field games, and tennis. Check our price list to select individual classes.

Our camp is designed to improve skills in a variety of sports. Along with skill improvement, we will focus on sportsmanship and fun!

14. In the second panel, click in the text box that reads *Price List*, and center the text.

15. Zoom in to **100%**. Highlight the first row of text that reads *List your product or service here* and replace it with **All-Day Camp (Kids 9-12)**.

16. Click to highlight the text that reads *Include description if necessary* and key **Lobby, 8:30 a.m. – 3:30 p.m.**

STEP-BY-STEP 2.2 Continued

17. Replace *$00.00* with **$110.00**.

18. Continue to enter the text as shown in Table 2-1.

TABLE 2-1
Text to key in Brochure publication

Basketball (Kids 9-12)	Center Court, 8:30 a.m. - 10:30 a.m.	$50.00
Soccer (Kids 9-12)	Field 1, 10:30 a.m. - 12:30 p.m.	$50.00
Tennis (Kids 9-12)	Court 10, 12:30 p.m. - 2:30 p.m.	$50.00
All-Day Camp (Kids 5-8)	Lobby, 8:30 a.m. - 3:30 p.m.	$110.00
Swimming (Kids 5-8)	Pool, 8:30 a.m. - 10:30 a.m.	$50.00
Field Games (Kids 5-8)	Field 2, 10:30 a.m. - 12:30 p.m.	$50.00
Tennis (Kids 5-8)	Court 7, 12:30 p.m. - 2:30 p.m.	$50.00

19. At this point, your publication should look like Figure 2-3. Save the file and leave the publication open for the next Step-by-Step.

FIGURE 2-3
Page 2 view of the Sports Camp Price List brochure

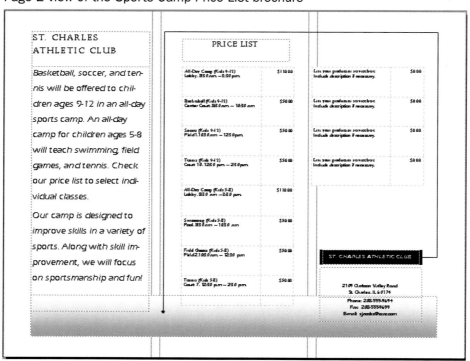

Add Design Gallery Objects and Add Color

Within Microsoft Publisher, you can create original coupons, logos, and borders. You can also choose predesigned objects from the Design Gallery. *Design Gallery objects* are ready-made objects that you can quickly insert into your project. Some Design Gallery objects are calendars, advertisements, and reply forms. By clicking the Design Gallery Object button on the Objects toolbar (typically docked on the left side of the screen), you can see many choices. Your own designs can also be stored in the Design Gallery.

> **Hot Tip**
>
> Creating your own business cards and brochures allows you to be creative and show your customers your personal design style.

STEP-BY-STEP 2.3

1. The *Brochure* file should be open from the previous Step-by-Step. Switch to the page **1** view. From the Objects toolbar, click the **Design Gallery Object** button. The Design Gallery dialog box appears. See Figure 2-4.

FIGURE 2-4
Design Gallery dialog box

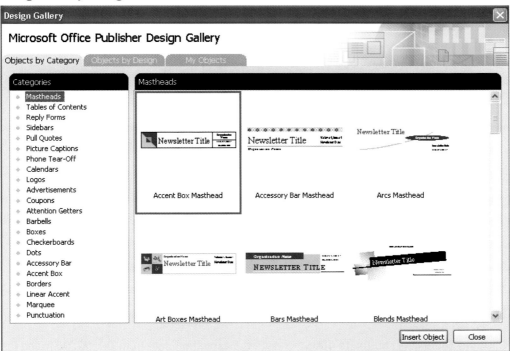

STEP-BY-STEP 2.3 Continued

2. In the *Categories* list click **Coupons**. Click the **Top Oval Coupon**. Click the **Insert Object** button located at the lower-right side of the dialog box.

3. The Top Oval coupon appears on the brochure. Left-click and move the coupon until it is centered and near the top of the second panel. See Figure 2-5.

> **Hot Tip**
>
> Publisher has design sets that offer specific layouts for special events, holidays, and fundraisers.

FIGURE 2-5
Top Oval Coupon centered

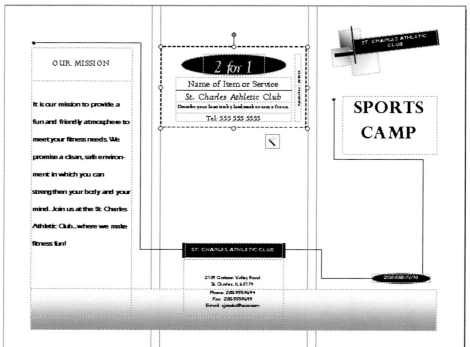

4. Select and replace the text that reads *2 for 1* with **10% Discount**.

5. Select and replace the text that reads *Name of Item or Service* with **For additional siblings**.

6. Select and replace the text that reads *Describe your location by landmark or area of town* with **Summer Sports Camp Special.**

7. Select and replace the text that reads *Tel: 555 555 5555* with **208-555-9694**.

8. Click the Zoom In (+) button to **400%**. Change the expiration date from *00/00/00* to the last Monday in July. Resize your editing area to **75%**.

9. Switch to the page **2** view. Right-click the table frame in the third panel and select **Delete Object**. Click the **Design Gallery Object** button on the Objects toolbar. In the *Categories* section of the Design Gallery dialog box, click **Reply Forms**. Scroll down and click **Sign-Up Form (Narrow)**. Click the **Insert Object** button.

STEP-BY-STEP 2.3 Continued

10. The sign-up form appears on the brochure. Drag and drop to center the form near the top of the third panel.

11. Select and replace the text that reads *Sign-Up Form Title* with **Sign-Up Form**.

12. Select the first occurrence of *Type the event name here* and delete the text. (You may need to click on the Zoom In (+) button on the toolbar to enlarge your editing area.) Right-click on the box and choose **Format Text Box** on the menu. The Format Text Box dialog box appears. Select the **Colors and Lines** tab if necessary. Click the down arrow in the *Color* box of the *Fill* section. Choose a blue color in the box. Slide the *Transparency* slider to **80%**, and click **OK**.

13. Repeat Step 12 for all of the boxes that contain *Type the event name here*.

14. Delete all of the *00:00* under the Time column.

15. Delete all of the *$00.00* under the Price column. Your brochure should appear similar to Figure 2-6.

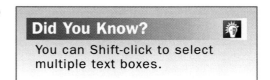

Did You Know?

You can Shift-click to select multiple text boxes.

FIGURE 2-6
Brochure with edited sign-up form

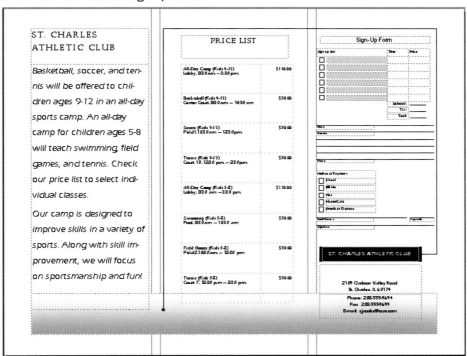

16. Save the file and leave the publication open for the next Step-by-Step.

Insert Pictures

One of the best ways to personalize a flyer or brochure is to add artwork and photographs. This is easily done by using the Clip Art feature that is built into Microsoft Publisher. To save time and to make them user friendly, you can save the clip art pictures or your own pictures that you use the most in the Design Gallery. Once an object is placed into a publication, it can be resized, rotated, or flipped to fit your needs.

STEP-BY-STEP 2.4

1. The *Brochure* file should be open from the previous Step-by-Step. Click 1 in the page navigation area to switch to page 1 view. Zoom to **75%**.

2. From the **Insert** menu, choose **Picture**. Choose **Clip Art** from the submenu.

3. In the *Search for* text box of the *Clip Art* task pane, key **soccer** and then click **Go.**

4. Select the picture of the soccer ball shown in Figure 2-7. If that picture is not available, choose a similar one.

5. Close the Clip Art task pane and close the picture toolbar. Then, size and position the picture as shown in Figure 2-7.

> **Hot Tip**
>
> To move an object, select it and drag it to the desired position.

FIGURE 2-7
Brochure with soccer ball picture positioned correctly

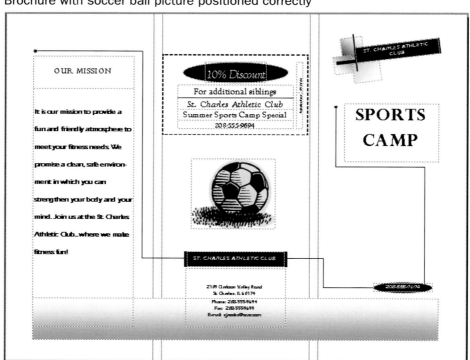

STEP-BY-STEP 2.4 Continued

6. Make sure the clip art is still selected. Open the **Insert** menu and choose **Add Selection to Design Gallery**. The Add Object dialog box appears. See Figure 2-8.

FIGURE 2-8
Add Object dialog box

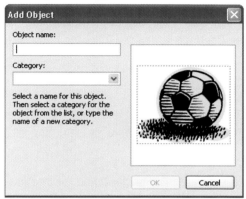

7. Name the picture (object) **Soccer**, followed by your initials. Name the category **Sports**. Then click **OK**.

8. Click the **Design Gallery Object** button to open the Design Gallery dialog box. Select the **My Objects** tab. Click the **Sports** category if necessary and the Soccer clip art appears.

9. Click **Close** to close the Design Gallery dialog box.

10. Save, print, and close the brochure. Leave Publisher open for the next Step-by-Step.

Create a Newsletter

Many schools, businesses, and professional organizations produce personalized, multipaged newsletters throughout the year. Once you choose a newsletter template, the columns, color schemes, and font schemes can be changed to meet your needs.

STEP-BY-STEP 2.5

1. Publisher should be open from the previous Step-by-Step. Choose **Publications for Print**, if necessary. Scroll down and click **Newsletters** in the list of wizards. Several template designs appear on the right.

2. Scroll and click the **Blends Newsletter** template. The Newsletter Options task pane appears on the left side of the screen. The Blends template appears on the right. Close the Newsletter Options task pane.

STEP-BY-STEP 2.5 Continued

3. Make sure that you are on page **1** and Zoom to **100%**.

4. Select and replace the text that reads *Newsletter Title* with **The Club Connection.**

5. Select and replace the text that reads *Newsletter Date* with today's date.

6. In the text boxes below *Inside this issue*, delete the first *Inside Story.* Key **Construction Update** and key **1** as the page number. Continue keying the following in the rest of the boxes:

Board Elections	**1**
Calendar	**2**
Tennis News	**3**

Delete the rest of the text in the table frame by selecting all the text. Right-click and choose **Delete Text**.

7. Select and replace the text that reads *Special points of interest* with **Quick Updates:**. Select and replace the text behind the first bullet with **The Saturday "Hoop Dreams" basketball team captured the league crown. They will compete in the Heartland double-elimination tournament next month.**

8. Tap **Enter.** Behind the second bullet key **If you need a new locker in the upstairs locker room, please contact Julie Wright.**

9. Select the picture and caption in the middle of the page and delete them.

10. Using the page navigator, switch to the page **2/3** view. Select and replace the text in the top text frame (the panel heading) of page 2 with **The Club Connection** if necessary. (This should appear automatically.)

11. Select and delete all of the text boxes (titles, text, and frames), pictures, and caption boxes on page **2**. Only the panel headings with "Page 2" and "The Club Connection" remain.

STEP-BY-STEP 2.5 Continued

12. On the Objects toolbar, click the **Design Gallery Object** button. On the Design Objects task pane, click **Calendars**. Scroll and click **Blends Calendar** and then click the **Insert Object** button. Position and resize the calendar as shown in Figure 2-9.

FIGURE 2-9
Calendar positioned correctly

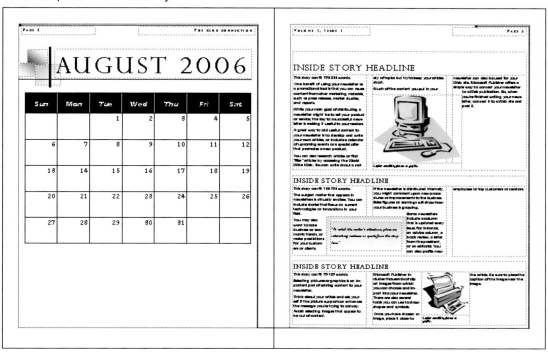

STEP-BY-STEP 2.5 Continued

13. On page **3**, select and delete the text frames for the first two titles and stories. Delete the picture and caption box as well as the text box in the center of the page as shown in Figure 2-10.

Hot Tip ⊚

Using a calendar created with a publication program can be a helpful tool for time management.

FIGURE 2-10
Page with frames deleted

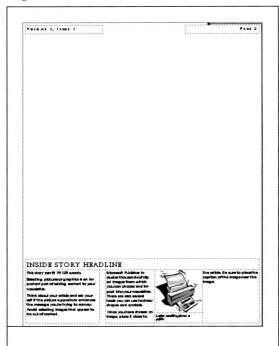

14. From the Objects toolbar, click the **Design Gallery Object** button. On the Design Gallery Objects task pane, click **Coupons**. Click the **Tilted Box Coupon** and click the **Insert Object** button. Center the coupon in the middle of the page above the text and picture that remain at the bottom of the page.

15. Click the **Design Gallery Object** button again. Click **Pull Quotes** and select the **Blends Pull Quote**. Click the **Insert Object** button. Position and resize the quote box as shown in Figure 2-11.

STEP-BY-STEP 2.5 Continued

FIGURE 2-11
Coupon and pull quote positioned correctly

16. Highlight the text in the pull quote and replace it with the following:

"Those who do not find time for exercise will have to find time for illness." Earl of Derby

Change the font size to **22**. If necessary, **center** the pull quote in the text box.

17. On the coupon, select and replace *Name of Item or Service* with **Tennis Balls**.

18. Select and replace the text that reads *Describe your location by landmark or area of town* with **Sign up for the Tennis League and receive free tennis balls.**

19. Replace *Tel: 555 555 5555* with **208-555-9694**.

20. Zoom in to **400%**. Change the expiration date from *00/00/00* to a date one month from today. Resize your editing area to **75%**.

STEP-BY-STEP 2.5 Continued

21. Delete the picture and caption box under the coupon.

22. Switch to the page **4** view. Right-click and delete the logo. Select the text in the Attention Getter (text in the oval) and replace it with **We're on the Web at www.scac.com.**

23. Select and replace the text in the picture caption with **We now have DSL connections in our Media Lounge**.

24. In the upper-left corner, delete the e-mail address.

25. Save the file as **Newsletter** followed by your initials. Leave the publication open for the next Step-by-Step.

> **Hot Tip**
>
> If you delete an object by accident, use the Undo command or Ctrl+Z to restore the deleted object.

Insert Text from a Word Document

When developing projects in Publisher, you can save time by inserting preexisting text from Word documents. This technique can save time when producing projects.

STEP-BY-STEP 2.6

1. The *Newsletter* file should be open from the previous Step-by-Step. Switch to the page **1** view. In the top panel heading, highlight the text that reads *LEAD STORY HEADLINE* and key **CONSTRUCTION UPDATE**.

2. Minimize Publisher. Locate and open **Step2-6a.doc** from the data files.

3. From the **Edit** menu, choose **Select All**. Word highlights all of the text in the document. Right-click in the highlighted text and choose **Copy** from the menu. Close the document and switch to Publisher.

> **Hot Tip**
>
> Some programs have a Select All command to select all parts of a drawing or text.

4. Select the text in the frames below *CONSTRUCTION UPDATE*. Right-click and select **Paste** from the menu. Select all the pasted text and change the font size to **11**.

5. In the next text frame, highlight the text that reads *SECONDARY STORY HEADLINE* and key **BOARD ELECTIONS**.

6. Switch to Word. Locate and open **Step2-6b.doc** from the data files.

7. From the **Edit** menu, choose **Select All**. Word highlights all of the text in the document. Right-click in the highlighted text and choose **Copy** from the menu. Close the document and switch to Publisher.

8. Select the text in the frames below *BOARD ELECTIONS*. Right-click and select **Paste** from the menu. Select all the pasted text and, if necessary, change the font size to **9**.

STEP-BY-STEP 2.6 Continued

9. Switch to the page **2/3** view.

10. Switch to Word. Locate and open **Step2-6c.doc** from the data files.

11. From the **Edit** menu, choose **Select All**. Right-click in the highlighted text and choose **Copy** from the menu. Close the document and switch to Publisher.

12. Paste the table into the newsletter and move it so it is located below the calendar on page **2**. Change the font size within the table to **11**.

13. Move to page **3**, and replace the text that reads *INSIDE STORY HEADLINE* with **TENNIS NEWS**.

14. Switch to Word. Locate and open **Step2-6d.doc** from the data files.

15. From the **Edit** menu, choose **Select All**. Right-click in the highlighted text and choose **Copy** from the menu. Close the document and switch to Publisher.

16. Select the text in the frames below *TENNIS NEWS.* Right-click and select **Paste** from the menu. Select the pasted text and change the font size to **11**. Your pages should appear similar to Figure 2-12.

FIGURE 2-12
Completed newsletter, pages 2 and 3

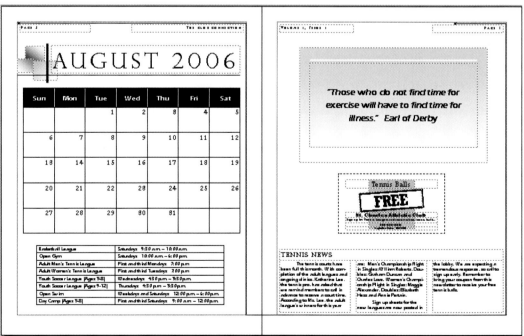

17. Save, print, and close the newsletter.

SUMMARY

In this lesson, you learned:

■ Microsoft Publisher has built-in designs in the Design Gallery that can enhance your publications.

■ When you design publications, you can enter your own text or insert text from a Word document (or other document). Once the text is entered, you can change the font, style, size, and position of the text.

■ Adding pictures and color to brochures and newsletters will personalize your project and can make it look more professional.

VOCABULARY *Review*

Define the following terms:

Design Gallery objects	Page navigator	Panel heading

REVIEW *Questions*

TRUE/FALSE

Circle T if the statement is true or F if the statement is false.

T F 1. The Design Gallery objects can only be used in the flyers and brochures templates.

T F 2. You can view text in a publication easily by using the Zoom In feature.

T F 3. Once a clip art has been selected, you can resize it to fit your publication.

T F 4. A panel heading is the area provided for the title or heading of a project.

T F 5. Once text has been entered in the panel heading text box, it cannot be resized.

WRITTEN QUESTIONS

Write a brief answer to the following questions.

1. Where will you find the brochure options in Publisher?

2. What is the quickest way to view a different page in a working Publisher document?

3. List the steps for adding color to a text box.

4. What are Design Gallery objects?

5. How do you add a new picture to the Design Gallery?

PROJECTS

PROJECT 2-1

1. In the *Open* section of the New Publication task pane, select the **Newsletter** publication. Use the page navigator to view page **4**.

2. Select and delete the text in the upper-right corner. From the **Objects** toolbar, click the **Design Gallery Object** button. In the **Design Gallery** dialog box, click **Sidebars**. Click the **Blends Sidebar** and click the **Insert Object** button. Resize the sidebar in the column, leaving room at the bottom for the next project.

3. Select and replace *Special points of interest:* with **Kitchen Connections**.

4. Select and replace *Briefly highlight your point of interest here* with **Weekly Specials Offered This Month**.

5. List the foods you would like served at the grill. Change the font size to fit the sidebar.

6. Save as **Newsletter1** followed by your initials. Leave the publication open for the next Project.

PROJECT 2-2

1. The *Newsletter1* publication should be open from the previous Project. The page navigator indicates you are on page **4**. Zoom to **75%**.

2. From the **Insert** menu, choose **Picture**. Choose **Clip Art** from the submenu.

3. In the *Search for* text box, key **Food** and then click **Go**.

4. Select a picture. Close the Clip Art task pane and close the picture toolbar. Then, size and position the picture to fit the Kitchen Connections sidebar.

5. Save, print, and close the newsletter.

WEB*Project*

PROJECT 2-3

1. Using the World Wide Web, find information about recovering from sore muscle pain. Using Microsoft Office Word 2003, key a paragraph about the information you found. Save the document as **Muscle Pain** followed by your initials. Close this document.

2. In the *Open* section of the *New Publication* task pane, select the **Newsletter1** publication.

3. Use the page navigator to view page **4**. Select and replace the text that reads *BACK PAGE STORY HEADLINE* with **DEALING WITH MUSCLE PAIN.**

4. Minimize Publisher. Locate and open the **Muscle Pain** document.

5. From the **Edit** menu, choose **Select All**. Right-click in the highlighted text and choose **Copy** from the menu. Close the document and close Word.

6. Maximize Publisher. Select the text in the frames below *DEALING WITH MUSCLE PAIN* and paste the copied text. Select the pasted text and change the font size to fit the area.

7. Move the computer picture and the caption to the third panel. Resize if needed.

8. Save the newsletter as **Completed Newsletter**, followed by your initials. Print and close the file.

TEAMWORK *Project*

PROJECT 2-4

With a friend, think of a hobby or activity that you both enjoy. Then, using Microsoft Office Publisher 2003, create an informational flyer that introduces others to your hobby. Use the available wizards and graphics in Publisher to produce the flyer. Save the project as **Informational Flyer**, followed by the initials of the group.

CRITICAL *Thinking*

ACTIVITY 2-1

You are asked to design a newsletter that involves tables and charts. In order to make the table look more professional, you want to add an object. Use the Help system to find information on adding objects to tables in Publisher. Write a paragraph that explains the procedure for adding objects to a table, and save the file as **Adding Objects to a Table** followed by your initials.

MICROSOFT PUBLISHER

COMMAND SUMMARY

FEATURE	MENU COMMAND	TOOLBAR BUTTON	LESSON
Add Design Gallery objects		🖻	2
Center text and objects		≣	2
Enlarge documents	View, Zoom	🔍	1
Navigate back		◄	1
Navigate forward		►	1
Open existing files	File, Open	📂	1
Open wizard		🖊	1
Print file	File, Print	🖨	1
Save file	File, Save	💾	1
Show other task panes		▼	1
Start Publisher	Start, All Programs, Microsoft Office, Microsoft Office Publisher 2003	🏁 start	1
View different pages		1 2 3 4	2

REVIEW *Questions*

TRUE/FALSE

Circle T if the statement is true or F if the statement is false.

T F   1.   To add a picture to a Publisher project, click the + key on the View menu.

T F   2.   In Publisher, you should use the *Design Sets* option to create a layout for special events, such as holidays.

T F   3.   Using the *From existing publication* option allows you to create a series of documents that include the same design, information, and logo.

T F   4.   The page navigator allows you to move quickly from one page to another.

T F   5.   You will need to retype Word documents into Microsoft Office publications.

WRITTEN QUESTIONS

Write a brief answer to each of the following questions.

1. List at least three documents that you can create with Microsoft Office Publisher.

2. What type of information can be updated in Publisher's Personal Information dialog box?

3. Describe how to insert a picture into a Publisher document.

4. List some articles that could be put in a school newsletter.

5. Describe how to insert text from a Word Document into a Publisher project.

PROJECTS

PROJECT 1-1

Use Microsoft Publisher to create an award certificate for a special teacher at your school.

1. Start Microsoft Publisher and from *Publications for Print*, select any of the Award Certificates, **Plain Paper** templates.

2. Save the publication as **Certificate** followed by your initials.

3. Key the name of a teacher who sponsors one of the school's clubs in the *Name of Recipient* text box.

4. In the text area below the words *in recognition of valuable contributions to*, key the name of the club sponsored by this teacher.

5. In the logo text box, key the name of your school.

6. Review and change or delete anything that does not relate to your project (for example pictures, logos, e-mail addresses, and so forth).

7. Save, print, and close the publication.

PROJECT 1-2

Use Microsoft Publisher to design a thank-you note for sponsors of the Band Fund-raiser.

1. Start Microsoft Publisher if necessary, and from *Publications for Print*, select **Greeting Cards**.

2. Choose any **Thank you** template and save the publication as **Thanks** followed by your initials.

3. Click **Select a suggested verse** located at the bottom of the task pane. The Suggested Verse dialog box appears.

4. In the Suggested Verse dialog box, click **It's great to know you can count on some people**. Notice that the first part of the message is applied to the front, and an accompanying second message appears in the inside of your card. Click **OK**.

5. Click to the page **2/3** view using the page navigator at the bottom of the screen.

6. On page 2, delete the words *Thank You* in the first text box and in the text box below, delete the defaulted text and key the following:

   Thank you so much for your help with the Band Fund-raiser. Because of the tremendous response this year, we will be able to travel to the state competition.

7. Bold and center the text.

8. Change the font size to **12**.

9. Delete the logo on page **2**.

10. Click to page **4** view using the page navigator.

11. In the *Organization Name* text box, key the name of your school.

12. In the *Address* text box, key the address of your school.

13. Delete the *Phone/Fax/E-mail* text box.

14. In the logo text box, key the name of your school, if necessary.

15. Review and change or delete anything that does not relate to your project (for example pictures, logos, e-mail addresses, and so forth).

16. Save, print, and close the publication.

PROJECT 1-3

Use Microsoft Publisher to create an advertisement about a soccer camp to be placed in the local paper.

1. Start Microsoft Publisher if necessary, and from *Publications for Print*, select **Advertisements**.

2. Select the **Equal Emphasis Advertisement**.

3. Save the project as **Soccer Advertisement**, followed by your initials.

4. Right-click on the picture of the clock and, from the drop-down menu, select **Change Picture**. Click **Clip Art** and key **soccer** in the *Search for* textbox. Click **Go**. Select a picture.

5. Minimize Publisher. Locate and open **Project3.doc** from the data file. Copy the text from the Word document into the text box next to the soccer picture. If necessary, change the text font size to fit the text box.

6. Highlight the text in the *Advertisement Heading* and key **SOCCER CAMP**.

7. In the text box for the hours and date, key **Saturday, June 10th from 9 a.m. to 12 Noon**.

8. In the location text box, key **Field 3 at the St. Charles Athletic Club**.

9. In the *Organization Name* text box, key **St. Charles Athletic Club,** if necessary.

10. Bold and center all text boxes.

11. Delete the picture of the computer disks.

12. In the logo text box, key **St. Charles Athletic Club,** if necessary.

13. Click the logo wizard and select a different logo design.

14. Move the logo so it is centered in the area available.

15. Review and change or delete anything that does not relate to your project (for example pictures, logos, e-mail addresses, and so forth).

16. Save, print, and close the advertisement.

PROJECT 1-4

Use Microsoft Publisher to create a postcard to remind families about the Saturday morning soccer camp.

1. Start Microsoft Publisher, if necessary, and from *Publications for Print,* select **Postcards**.

2. Select **Reminder** from the menu and choose any *Reminder Postcards* template.

3. Save your card as **Soccer Postcard**, followed by your initials.

4. Replace the picture with one relating to soccer.

5. Replace the text of the postcard with the following message:

    Don't forget about Soccer camp! We will meet this Saturday on Field 3. Camp begins at 9:00 a.m.

6. Add any additional information that will be helpful including the date, times, and location of the camp.

7. Center all the postcard text boxes both vertically and horizontally.

8. Use the Design Gallery Object button to insert the Attention Getter design of your choice above the logo. Inside the Attention Getter, key **Don't Forget!**

9. Use the page navigator to view the back of the postcard.

10. Use the **Back** button to return to the Postcard Options task pane. Under *Copies per sheet*, select **One**, if necessary.

11. Review and change or delete anything that does not relate to your project (for example pictures, logos, e-mail addresses, and so forth).

12. Save, print, and close the publication.

PORTFOLIO *Checklist*

Include the following files from this unit in your student portfolio:

Lesson 1

_____ Card

_____ Flyer

_____ Calendar

_____ Card1

_____ Flyer1

_____ Letterhead

_____ Postcard

_____ President

_____ Menu

_____ Flyer Scheme

Lesson 2

_____ Brochure

_____ Newsletter

_____ Newsletter1

_____ Completed Newsletter

_____ Informational Flyer

_____ Adding Objects to a Chart

_____ Muscle Pain

Unit Review

_____ Certificate

_____ Thanks

_____ Soccer Advertisement

_____ Soccer Postcard

CAPSTONE SIMULATION

NEW YEAR'S EVE DINNER DANCE

Estimated Time: 8 hrs.

Background

The Evergreen Youth Club has 31 members who work in the community on many different projects. They help keep the city park clean, raise money for local charities, and improve their own leadership skills.

This New Year's Eve, the club is hosting a dinner dance at Evergreen Community Center. The club members will plan the event, make arrangements for entertainment and food, decorate the community center, and sell tickets and sponsorships. The club has organized dinners and activities in the past, but this is the first year for the New Year's Eve Dinner Dance. The theme is Hawaiian; so, everyone will be asked to dress Hawaiian.

The purpose of the event is to offer a place for youth to have fun on New Year's Eve without alcohol. Tickets will be $15 each and will include dinner, dancing, snacks, and New Year's party favors. Money raised from the event will fund the club's trip to Denver next summer. During the three-day trip, the club will visit Fun World, attend a youth leadership conference, and be the governor's guests for the day at the state capitol.

You have been elected chair of the event. Your responsibilities are to make sure committees do their jobs, to answer questions, and to take care of last-minute arrangements or problems that arise. Scott Sims is the club's adult advisor. He will check with you periodically about the progress of the planning.

NOVEMBER 6

The club will meet tomorrow night to plan for the New Year's Eve Dinner Dance. You decide to create a PowerPoint presentation with the information that you already know about the event. Open Microsoft PowerPoint and create a presentation (5–6 slides) with this information. You can include information from the background paragraphs above. Also, include a list of the committees (see Figure 1-1) and ask the members to sign up for one. Include clip art to make the presentation look interesting. Save the presentation as **Dinner Dance Presentation**. Print the slides as handouts (six slides per page). Close the presentation.

NOVEMBER 7

Committee meeting held. The New Year's Eve Dinner Dance was discussed.

NOVEMBER 13

Last week at the club's meeting, you passed around a committee sign-up sheet. You asked everyone to volunteer to work on a committee or to be a committee chair. Using the committee sign-up sheet, you create a committee list to give to committee chairs.

1. Open Microsoft Word.

2. Create a Committee List from the committee sign-up sheet shown in Figure 1-1.

FIGURE 1-1

Evergreen Youth Club
New Year's Eve Dinner Dance
Committee Sign-up Sheet

Ticket Sales Committee
Sell at least 85 tickets. Report ticket sales to Event Chair by December 29. Turn in money to Finance Chair.
Chair: *Austin Aldridge*
1. *Britney Haddock*
2. **Landon Lewis**
3. *Josh Acker*

Decorations Committee
Plan decorations with a Hawaiian theme. Submit expenses to Finance Committee. Decorate Community Center before the event and clean up decorations after the event.
Chair: *Ashley Wyatt*
1. *Te Yung*
2. *Matt Gunter*
3. *Emily Katz*

Program Committee
Plan the program for the evening by December 1. Get band (or disc jockey) and party favors—such as party hats, confetti, and nonalcoholic champagne. Submit expenses to Finance Committee.
Chair: *Zack Sartor*
1. **Danielle Rogers**
2. *Tyler Miller*
3. *Ashley Stone*

Food Committee
Plan the dinner menu and snacks by December 10. Get bids from three caterers. Book caterer once decision is made. Submit expenses to Finance Committee.
Chair: *Michelle Poole*
1. **Caitlyn Cortez**
2. *Madison Mixco*
3. *Jamal Johnson*

Finance Committee
Accept receipts for reimbursement and pay bills. By January 15, submit an end report to Event Chair that shows income and expenses.
Chair: **Taylor Glass**
1. *Jordan Eagle*
2. *Katie Clements*

Sponsorship Committee
By December 10, locate at least five corporations, businesses, or individuals to sponsor the event with $200 sponsorships. Buy thank-you gifts for sponsors. Submit expenses to Finance Committee.
Chair: **Cody Carrizales**
1. *LaChell Jackson*
2. *Samantha Bledsoe*
3. *Jose Rodriguez*

3. Save the file as **Committee List,** followed by your initials.

4. Change all margins to .75 inches.

5. If necessary, adjust the font size to make sure all data fits on one page.

6. Save, print, and close.

NOVEMBER 16

Zack Sartor, chair of the Program Committee, called you to ask about the phone numbers and addresses of the people on his committee. You decide it would be helpful if all committee chairs had this information about their committee members. Use the sign-up sheet and the club's roster to create a database that includes the names, addresses, and phone numbers of all committee members. You can give each committee chair his or her committee list at the meeting on November 20. (Do not enter records for members who are not on a committee.)

1. Open Microsoft Access.

2. Create a new database and name it **Committee Members,** followed by your initials.

3. With the Committee Members database open, create a new table named **Member Information.** Use the field names and data types listed below. Add your own field descriptions.

FIELD NAME	DATA TYPE
First Name	Text
Last Name	Text
Address	Text
City	Text
State	Text
Zip Code	Text
Phone Number	Text
Committee	Text

4. Switch to datasheet view and enter the records from the roster in Figure 1-2. (Do not enter records for members who are not on a committee.) When finished, adjust all column widths to best fit.

5. Create a filter named **Food** to show only members on the Food Committee.

6. Apply the filter and print the list in landscape orientation.

7. Create filters for the other five committees (Ticket Sales, Sponsorship, Finance, Decorations, and Program). Apply each filter and print the list in landscape orientation.

8. Close the table and database. Save the changes to the layout of the table.

FIGURE 1-2

Evergreen Youth Club Membership Roster

Josh Acker *Ticket sales*
79 Treetop Boulevard
Evergreen, CO 80498-9710
303-555-7700

Austin Aldridge *Ticket sales*
9345 Snow Hill
Evergreen, CO 80498-9340
303-555-8779

Samantha Bledsoe *Sponsorship*
4551 Rocky Road
Evergreen, CO 80499-4511
303-555-6632

Cody Carrizales *Sponsorship*
9212 Bear Road
Evergreen, CO 80498-9121
303-555-4739

Kyle Chen
3445 West Willow
Evergreen, CO 80498-3334
303-555-9911

Katie Clements *Finance*
8776 Hunter's Way
Evergreen, CO 80499-8771
303-555-0412

Caitlyn Cortez *Food*
456 Bear Road
Evergreen, CO 80498-4600
303-555-8246

Kristi Duncan
8998 Hunter's Way
Evergreen, CO 80498-9988
303-555-1290

Jordan Eagle *Finance*
78 Beaver Road
Evergreen, CO 80499-7811
303-555-6034

Taylor Glass *Finance*
4423 Pine Alley
Evergreen, CO 80499-4332
303-555-7702

Matt Gunter *Decorations*
5360 Shadow Lane
Evergreen, CO 80498-6030
303-555-7351

Britney Haddock *Ticket sales*
1265 Green Street
Evergreen, CO 80498-1221
303-555-4001

LaChell Jackson *Sponsorship*
7832 Hunter's Way
Evergreen, CO 80498-7382
303-555-6092

Jamal Johnson *Food*
902 East Lake
Evergreen, CO 80498-9002
303-555-6080

Emily Katz *Decorations*
4077 Sky View
Evergreen, CO 80499-4117
303-555-5910

Landon Lewis *Ticket sales*
598 Pine Valley
Evergreen, CO 80499-5800
303-555-4025

Tyler Miller *Program*
9090 Wren Avenue
Evergreen, CO 80499-9191
303-555-1209

Madison Mires *Food*
1009 Elk Crossing
Evergreen, CO 80499-1019
303-555-6978

Michelle Poole *Food*
876 Leaf Avenue
Evergreen, CO 80499-8176
303-555-4826

Jose Rodriguez *Sponsorship*
799 Beaver Road
Evergreen, CO 80499-7990
303-555-7677

Danielle Rogers *Program*
2331 Sunset Street
Evergreen, CO 80498-2113
303-555-5732

Zack Sartor *Program*
8001 Lake View
Evergreen, CO 80499-8010
303-555-1188

Renee Sokora
4590 Elk Crossing
Evergreen, CO 80498-4951
303-555-8004

Ashley Stone *Program*
4561 Yucca Avenue
Evergreen, CO 80498-4615
303-555-5294

Evan Strange
6857 Berry Hill
Evergreen, CO 80498-6580
303-555-9843

Melissa Tait
3311 Doe Road
Evergreen, CO 80499-3300
303-555-7998

Tyrone Thomas
3489 Redwood
Evergreen, CO 80499-4839
303-555-2119

Robbie Vickers
5776 Brookview
Evergreen, CO 80499-7777
303-555-3223

Natt Whitaker
807 Pine Alley
Evergreen, CO 80499-8171
303-555-6060

Ashley Wyatt *Decorations*
5055 Eagle Landing
Evergreen, CO 80499-5150
303-555-8712

Te Yung *Decorations*
709 Maple Avenue
Evergreen, CO 80498-7099
303-555-8824

NOVEMBER 17

December is an important month for telling the local youth about the dinner dance. Open Microsoft Publisher and create a flyer describing the dinner dance. You can use information from the background paragraphs on the first page of this simulation. Be creative to make the flyer look interesting. Save the flyer as **Dinner Dance Flyer**. Print and close the flyer.

NOVEMBER 18

You need a budget based on the club's previous dinners and estimates of costs for this year's dinner and dance. Create the following budget to give to all the committee chairs at the next committee meeting.

1. Open Microsoft Excel.

2. Key the data as shown in Figure 1-3 in a new worksheet.

FIGURE 1-3

	A	B	C	D
1	NEW YEAR'S EVE DINNER DANCE			
2	Budget			
3			Estimated	Estimated
4	Committee	Item	Income	Expenses
5	Ticket			
6		85 Tickets X $15	$1,275	
7				
8	Sponsorship			
9		5 Sponsors X $200	$1,000	
10				
11	Food			
12		Meals		$680
13		Snacks		$75
14		Paper Goods		$25
15				
16	Program			
17		Music		$500
18		Party Favors		$170
19				
20	Decorations			
21		Decorations		$150
22				
23	Sponsorship			
24		Gifts for Sponsors		$100
25				
26	Event Chair			
27		Postage		$15
28		Printing/Copying		$50
29				
30	Totals			
31				
32	Estimated			
33	Profit			
34				

3. Increase the width of column A to **12** and column B to **18**.

4. Format columns C and D for **Currency** with **0** decimals.

5. Use a function in cell **C30** to get the total income budgeted.

6. Use a function in cell **D30** to get the total expenses budgeted.

7. Create a formula in cell **D33** to subtract the budgeted expenses from budgeted income to get estimated profit.

8. Boldface cells **C30, D30,** and **D33.**

9. Save the file as **Budget,** followed by your initials.

10. Print and close.

NOVEMBER 19

Many topics need to be discussed at the committee meeting tomorrow. Create an agenda so that everyone will be aware of the topics and you won't forget anything.

1. Open Microsoft Word.

2. Create a new document and key the handwritten data up to the Roman numeral one (I), as shown in Figure 1-4. Bold AGENDA and space between the lines as indicated in the figure (DS = double space, TS = triple space).

FIGURE 1-4

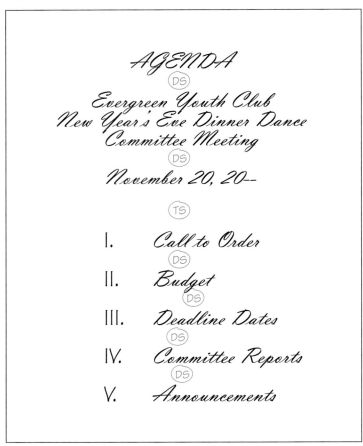

3. Save the file as **Agenda,** followed by your initials.

4. Change the top margin to **2.75** inches and the left and right margins to **1.75** inches.

5. Set a right tab at **2** inches and a left tab at **2.25** inches.

6. Key the remaining data using the tabs you set.

7. Save, print, and close.

NOVEMBER 20

Committee meeting held. Topics discussed according to the agenda.

NOVEMBER 21

At the committee meeting, it was decided that you should write a memo to all Evergreen Youth Club members. Encourage them to help committees and to buy tickets.

1. Open Microsoft Word.

2. Create a new document and key **MEMORANDUM** centered and boldfaced.

3. Triple-space and then set a right tab at **1.25** inches and a left tab at **1.5** inches.

4. Key the rest of the memo as shown in Figure 1-5.

FIGURE 1-5

MEMORANDUM

        To: All members of the Evergreen Youth Club

   From: *Student's Name*

   Date: November 21, 20--

 Subject: New Year's Eve Dinner Dance

Plans for the New Year's Eve Dinner Dance are under way. Thanks to all of you who signed up and are working on committees. If your committee hasn't met, it will meet soon. Not only is this a chance for you to have fun, it is also a fund-raiser for our club. Any profits we make will go toward our trip to Denver next summer. Please help all you can.

Remember that each member must purchase a ticket to participate in the dinner and dance on New Year's Eve. This year the theme is Hawaiian, so wear your grass skirts and Hawaiian shirts. Ashley Wyatt and her committee will be decorating the community center with coconut trees, sand, and other related items. The dinner menu also will follow the Hawaiian theme, so get ready for some fresh pineapple!

Disc jockey Jammin' Jay Jay Jones will be playing dance music. He'll also be taking requests. At midnight, everyone will be given confetti to throw, noise makers to use, and nonalcoholic champagne to drink. We'll have dance contests and games. Bring all your friends!

New Year's Eve Dinner Dance
December 31
7:00 p.m.
Evergreen Community Center
$15 per person

For tickets, call Austin Aldridge at 303-555-8779.

5. Save the file as **Member Memo**, followed by your initials.

6. Change the top margin to **1.5** inches and the left and right margins to **1.5** inches.

7. Save, print, and close.

To send a memo to every member, you need to add the members who aren't on a committee to the database.

8. Open the **Committee Members** database and the **Member Information** table.

9. Add to the table the records of those who are not on a committee. See Figure 1-2.

10. Sort the table by Last Name in ascending order.

11. Print the table in landscape orientation. Close the table and database.

NOVEMBER 29

Austin Aldridge just reported that his committee has already sold 25 tickets. Create a worksheet to record ticket sales.

1. Open Microsoft Excel.

2. Key the data in a new worksheet, as shown in Figure 1-6. Adjust column widths as needed.

FIGURE 1-6

	A	B	C
1	NEW YEAR'S EVE DINNER DANCE		
2	Ticket Sales		
3			
4	Committee		
5	Member	Tickets Sold	
6			
7	Austin Aldridge	9	
8	Britney Haddock	6	
9	Landon Lewis	7	
10	Josh Acker	3	
11			
12	Total	25	
13			

3. Save the file as **Tickets**, followed by your initials.

4. Use a function in cell B12 to get the total number of tickets sold.

5. Save, print, and close.

DECEMBER 10

The club's advisor, Scott Sims, wants a list of all the sponsors for the dinner and dance. He would also like to know which member on the Sponsorship Committee sold each sponsorship. You call Cody Carrizales, chair of the Sponsorship Committee, to get this information. Create a database of the sponsors.

1. Open Microsoft Access.

2. Create a new database and name it **Sponsors**, followed by your initials.

3. With the *Sponsors* database open, create a new table named **Sponsor Information**. Use the field names and data types listed below. Add your own field descriptions.

FIELD NAME	DATA TYPE
Sponsor	Text
Contact	Text
Address	Text
City	Text
State	Text
Zip Code	Text
Phone Number	Text
Amount	Currency
Member	Text

4. Switch to Datasheet view and enter the records from Figure 1-7. When finished, adjust all column widths to best fit.

FIGURE 1-7

Sponsor	Contact	Address	City	State	Zip Code	Phone Number	Amount	Member
Evergreen Outfitters	Skip Vance	6072 Bear Crossing	Evergreen	CO	80498-1021	303-555-1030	$200.00	Jose Rodriguez
Cool T-Shirts	Jamie Hunt	9823 82nd Street	Evergreen	CO	80498-7811	303-555-9006	$200.00	LaChell Jackson
Extreme Pizza	Dave Rivera	301 Pine Valley	Evergreen	CO	80499-5992	303-555-3030	$200.00	Cody Carrizales
KTET Radio	Brad Johnson	4910 Digital Lane	Evergreen	CO	80499-6070	303-555-9990	$200.00	Cody Carrizales
Peoples Bank	Joy Daniel	101 Main Street	Evergreen	CO	80499-8000	303-555-8512	$200.00	Samantha Bledsoe

5. Print the table in landscape orientation. Close the table and database.

DECEMBER 17

Austin Aldridge called to give you an update on ticket sales. Update your spreadsheet.

1. Open Microsoft Excel.

2. Open the **Tickets** file that you created previously.

3. Save the file as **Tickets 2,** followed by your initials.

4. Update the worksheet with the following information: Austin has sold a total of 23 tickets, Britney has sold 17 total, Landon has sold 13 total, and Josh has sold 15 total.

5. Key **Goal** in cell **A14.**

6. Key **# To Go** in cell **A16.**

7. Key **85** in cell **B14.**

8. Create a formula in cell **B16** to find how many more tickets need to sell before reaching the goal.

9. Save, print, and close.

DECEMBER 28

Scott Sims suggested that you send a letter to each of the sponsors thanking them for supporting the event.

1. Open Microsoft Word.

2. Create a new document and key the information as shown in Figure 1-8.

FIGURE 1-8

```
                         Evergreen Youth Club
                            1200 Main Street
                        Evergreen, CO  80498-1201
                             303-555-0075


December 28, 20--

Sponsor
Attention:  Contact's name
Address
City, State  ZIP

Ladies and Gentlemen:

Thank you for sponsoring our New Year's Eve Dinner Dance.  Your thoughtfulness and
generosity will help keep the youth of Evergreen safe and alcohol-free on New Year's Eve.

As we have told you, our club continues to give back to the community in many ways.  We work
one day each month in the Evergreen Park to keep it clean and free of trash.  We have also
helped the city plant flowers there for the past two years.  In addition, the Evergreen Youth Club
raises money for local charities by having car washes, garage sales, and bake sales.

We have other fund-raisers to pay for club trips.  The money earned from the New Year's Eve
Dinner Dance will fund a trip to Denver next summer.  During the three-day trip, the club will
visit Fun World, attend a youth leadership conference, and be the governor's guests for the day at
the state capitol.

Your sponsorship of this event shows that you are interested in today's youths, who will be the
leaders of tomorrow.  Thank you for your gift.

Sincerely,



Student's Name
Event Chair
```

3. Save the document as **Thanks,** followed by your initials.

4. Change all the margins to 1 inch.

5. Save, print, and close.

DECEMBER 29

The Ticket Sales Committee has made its final report to you. Update the spreadsheet.

1. Open Microsoft Excel.

2. Open the **Tickets 2** file that you previously created.

3. Save the file as **Tickets 3,** followed by your initials.

4. Update the worksheet with the following total sales: Austin sold 30 tickets, Britney sold 21, Landon sold 22, and Josh sold 19.

5. Key **# Above Goal** in cell **A16.**

6. Edit the formula in cell **B16** to subtract **B14** from **B12** to get a positive number.

7. Save, print, and close.

DECEMBER 31

The New Year's Eve Dinner Dance started at 7 p.m. After dinner, everyone hung out, played games, and danced until midnight. At midnight, everyone celebrated the New Year. The party ended at 12:15 a.m., and everyone had a good time.

JANUARY 8

You and Taylor Glass, the Finance Committee Chair, reviewed the income and expenses. Now you need to create a Financial Report to submit to the Evergreen Youth Club advisor, Scott Sims.

1. Open Microsoft Excel.

2. Open the **Budget** file that you previously created.

3. Save the file as **Budget Report**, followed by your initials.

4. Change the subtitle in cell **A2** to **Financial Report, January 8, 20--**.

5. Insert a new column to the right of column C.

6. Key the new data as shown in Figure 1-9 in the new column D you have created, in column F, and in A35.

FIGURE 1-9

	A	B	C	D	E	F
1						
2						
3				Actual		Actual
4				Income		Expenses
5						
6				1380		
7						
8						
9				1000		
10						
11						
12						732
13						71.78
14						25.4
15						
16						
17						395
18						168.49
19						
20						
21						147.59
22						
23						
24						103.75
25						
26						
27						10.44
28						43.88
29						
30						
31						
32						
33						
34						
35	Actual Profit					

7. Copy the formula in cell **C30** to cells **D30** and **F30**.

8. Create a formula in cell **F35** to subtract **F30** from **D30**. Boldface the data in cell **F35**.

9. Format columns D and F for **Currency** with **2** decimals.

10. Insert two blank rows after row 31.

11. Key **Difference** boldfaced in cell **A32**.

12. Create a formula in cell **D32** to subtract **D30** from **C30**.

13. Create a formula in cell **F32** to subtract **F30** from **E30**.

14. Change the font size of the entire spreadsheet to **10** (if it is 10 already, make it 8) and the left and right margins to 1 inch.

15. Save, print, and close.

16. Open Microsoft Word and the **Member Memo** file that you previously created. Save the file as **SS Budget Memo**.

17. Replace the current data in the file with the new data, as shown in Figure 1-10.

FIGURE 1-10

MEMORANDUM

To:	Scott Sims
From:	*Student's Name*
Date:	January 8, 20--
Subject:	New Year's Eve Dinner Dance Financial Report

Attached is the financial report for the New Year's Eve event. I think that it was a great success. I look forward to meeting with you on January 15 to discuss suggestions for next year's event.

---

18. Save, print, and close. Attach the *Budget Report* to the *SS Budget Memo*.

Congratulations! You were a great Event Chair and the club appreciates you!

APPENDIX A

WINDOWS BASICS

OBJECTIVES

In this appendix, you will:

- Put your desktop in order.
- Open programs using the Start button.
- Shut down your computer.
- Move, resize, open, and close a window.
- Use scroll bars.
- Use menus.
- Use Windows Help.

This appendix explains Windows 2000 and Windows XP software. It holds the information you need to move around your desktop and manage the resources you work with every day. It also talks about the Windows Help system.

Starting Windows

If Windows is already set up, it should start automatically. If your computer is on a network, you may need some help from your teacher.

STEP-BY-STEP A.1

1. Turn on the computer.

2. After a few moments, Windows 2000 or Windows XP appears.

Navigating in Windows

The Mouse

A *mouse* is a tool that rolls on a flat plane and has one or more buttons. The mouse allows you to control the graphics and text on the screen. The *pointer*, which appears as an arrow on the screen, shows where the mouse is located. The four most common mouse operations are point, click, double-click, and drag.

OPERATION	DESCRIPTION
Point	Moving the mouse pointer to a specific item on the screen.
Click	Pressing the mouse button and quickly releasing it while pointing to an item on the screen. (The term *click* comes from the noise you hear when you press and release the button.)
Double-click	Clicking the mouse button twice quickly while keeping the mouse still.
Drag	Pointing to an object on the screen, pressing and holding the left mouse button, and moving the pointer while the button is pressed. Letting go of the button ends the drag operation.

The Desktop

When Windows starts up, the desktop displays on the screen. The *desktop* is the space where you access and work with programs and files. Figure A-1 shows a typical desktop screen. Your screen may vary slightly from that shown in the figure. For example, your screen may display icons that were installed with Windows or shortcut icons you've created. You can adapt and arrange your desktop by creating files, folders, and shortcuts.

FIGURE A-1
Typical desktop screen

The main features of the desktop screen are labeled and numbered on the figure and discussed below:

1. The Start button brings up menus that give you a variety of options. You can start a program, open a document, find help, or shut down the computer.

2. The Quick Launch toolbar has icons that show the desktop or quickly starts programs.

3. The taskbar tells you the names of all open programs.

4. My Computer allows you to see what files and folders are located on your computer.

5. Internet Explorer is a Web browser that allows you to connect to the Internet.

6. My Network Places shows all the folders and printers that are on hand for you.

7. The Recycle Bin is a place to get rid of files or folders that are no longer needed.

8. Other icons stand for programs waiting to be opened.

9. Windows makes it easy to connect to the Internet. Just click the Launch Internet Explorer Browser button on the Quick Launch toolbar. The Quick Launch toolbar is located to the right of the start menu. It allows you to quickly access programs.

With Windows you can include Web content into your work by using the Active Desktop. Active Desktop is an interface that lets you put "active items" from the Internet on your desktop. You can use *channels* to adapt the information from the Internet to your computer. By showing the Channel bar on your desktop, you can add, subscribe to, or view channels.

S TEP-BY-STEP A.2

1. Click the **Launch Internet Explorer Browser** button on the Quick Launch toolbar.

2. Click the **Show Desktop** button on the Quick Launch toolbar. It displays the Windows desktop.

Desktop

3. Click the **Internet Explorer** button on the taskbar. You return to the browser window.

4. Choose **Close** on the **File** menu to close Internet Explorer.

5. Point to the **Start** button.

6. Click the left mouse button. A menu of choices emerges above the Start button, as shown in Figure A-2.

FIGURE A-2
Start menu in Windows XP

7. If you are using *Windows 2000*, point to **Settings**. Then click **Control Panel** on the submenu. If you are using *Windows XP*, click **Control Panel**. A new window appears. The title bar at the top tells you that Control Panel is the name of the open window. If needed, click the button in the Task pane that says **Switch to Classic View**. Leave this window open for the next Task.

Using Windows

Many of the windows you will work with have similar features. You can work more capably by familiarizing yourself with some of the common elements. They are shown in Figure A-3 and explained below.

FIGURE A-3
Window elements

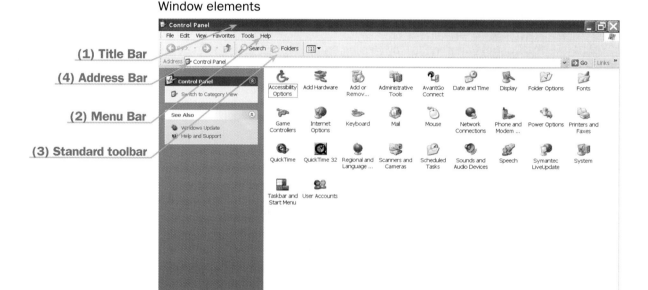

(1) Title Bar
(4) Address Bar
(2) Menu Bar
(3) Standard toolbar

1. A title bar is at the top of every window. It contains the name of the open program, window, document, or folder.

2. The menu bar lists available menus. From this, you can choose a variety of commands. Every option that is available for the current window is accessible through a menu.

3. The standard toolbar, located directly below the menu bar, contains common commands you can use by clicking the correct button.

4. The Address bar tells you which folder's contents are being displayed. You can key a Web address in the Address bar without first opening your browser.

5. At the bottom of the window is the status bar. It gives you directions on how to access menus and summarizes the actions of the commands that you choose. If the status bar does not appear on your screen, open the **View** menu and choose **Status Bar**.

Moving and Resizing Windows

Sometimes you will have several windows open on the screen at the same time. To work more effectively, you may need to move or change the size of a window.

STEP-BY-STEP A.3

1. Switch to the List view by clicking the **View** button and choosing **Icon**.

2. Move the Control Panel window by clicking on the title bar and holding the left mouse button down. Continue to hold the left mouse button down and drag the Control Panel until it appears to be centered on the screen. Release the mouse button.

3. Point anywhere on the border at the bottom of the Control Panel window. The pointer turns into a vertical two-headed arrow.

4. While the pointer is a two-headed arrow, click the left mouse button and drag the bottom border of the window down to enlarge the window.

5. Point to the border on the right side of the Control Panel window. The pointer turns into a horizontal two-headed arrow.

6. While the pointer is a two-headed arrow, click and drag the border of the window to the right to enlarge the window.

STEP-BY-STEP A.3 Continued

7. Point to the lower-right corner of the window border. Place your pointer on the sizing handle. The pointer becomes a two-headed arrow pointing diagonally.

8. Drag the border upward and to the left to resize both sides at the same time until the window is about the same size as the one shown in Figure A-4. Leave the window on the screen for the next Task.

FIGURE A-4
Scroll bars, arrows, and boxes

Scroll Bars

A *scroll bar* appears on the edges of windows any time there is more to be displayed than a window can show at its current size (see Figure A-4). A scroll bar can appear along the bottom edge (horizontal) and/or along the right side (vertical) of a window. A scroll bar appeared in the last step of the preceding exercise because the window was too small to show all the icons at once.

Scroll bars are a convenient way to bring another part of the window's contents into view. On the scroll bar is a sliding box called the *scroll box*. The scroll box shows your place within the window. *Scroll arrows* are at the ends of the scroll bar.

STEP-BY-STEP A.4

1. On the horizontal scroll bar, click the scroll arrow that points to the right. The contents of the window shift to the left.

2. Click and hold the mouse button on the same scroll arrow. The contents of the window scroll quickly across the window. Notice that the scroll box moves to the right end of the scroll bar.

STEP-BY-STEP A.4 Continued

3. You can also scroll by dragging the scroll box. Drag the scroll box on the horizontal scroll bar to the left.

4. Drag the scroll box on the vertical scroll bar to the middle of the scroll bar.

5. The final way to scroll is to click on the scroll bar. Click the horizontal scroll bar to the right of the scroll box. The contents scroll left.

6. Click the horizontal scroll bar to the left of the scroll box. The contents scroll right.

7. Resize the Control Panel until the scroll bar disappears. Leave the window open for the next Task.

Other Window Controls

Three other key window controls, located on the right side of the title bar, are the ***Maximize button***, the ***Minimize button***, and the ***Close button*** (see Figure A-5). When a window is maximized, the Maximize button is replaced by the Restore Down button (see Figure A-6). The ***Restore Down button*** returns the window to the size it was before the Maximize button was clicked.

FIGURE A-5
Maximize, Minimize, and Close buttons

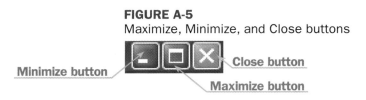

Minimize button

Close button

Maximize button

FIGURE A-6
Restore Down button

STEP-BY-STEP A.5

1. Click the **Maximize** button. The window enlarges to fill the screen.

2. Click the **Restore Down** button.

3. Click the **Minimize** button. The window is reduced to a button on the taskbar.

4. Click the **Control Panel** button on the taskbar to open the window again.

5. Click the **Close** button to close the window.

Menus and Dialog Boxes

You look at the menu to find out what a restaurant has to offer. The same is true of computers. *Menus* in computer programs contain options for performing certain actions.

If you choose a menu option with an arrow beside it, a submenu opens that lists additional options. A menu item followed by an ellipsis (…) shows that a dialog box will appear when chosen. A *dialog box*, like the Turn off computer dialog box shown in Figure A-7, appears when more information is needed before the command can be done. You may have to key information, choose from a list of options, or simply confirm that you want the command to be performed. To back out of a dialog box without performing an action, tap Esc, click the Close button, or choose Cancel (or No).

FIGURE A-7
Turn off computer dialog box

STEP-BY-STEP A.6

1. Click the **Start** button. A menu appears.

2. If you are using *Windows 2000*, click **Shut Down**. The Shut Down Windows dialog box appears. If you are using *Windows XP*, the button on the Start menu and the title on the dialog box is *Turn Off Computer*, as shown in Figure A-7.

3. Click **Cancel** to back out of the dialog box without shutting down.

Menus can be accessed from a menu bar in a Windows application (see Figure A-8). A menu bar appears under the title bar in each Windows program and consists of a row of menu names, such as File and Edit. Each name in the menu bar stands for a separate ***drop-down menu***. Drop-down menus are easy to use because the commands are in front of you on the screen, as shown in Figure A-8. Like a menu in a restaurant, you can view a list of choices and pick the one you want.

FIGURE A-8
Drop-down menu

You can give commands from drop-down menus. Use either the keyboard or the mouse. Each menu and each choice on a menu is set apart by an underlined letter called a ***mnemonic***. To open a menu using the keyboard, tap Alt plus the mnemonic letter shown on the menu name. To display a menu using the mouse, simply place the pointer on the menu name and click the left button.

Drop-down menus have items with right-pointing arrows that open submenus. Ellipses open dialog boxes. Choosing an item without an ellipsis or a right-pointing arrow executes the command. To close a menu without choosing a command, tap Esc or click anywhere outside of the menu.

S TEP-BY-STEP A.7

1. If you are using *Windows 2000*, open the Notepad accessory by clicking **Start**, **Programs**, **Accessories**, and then **Notepad**. If using *Windows XP*, open the Notepad application by clicking **Start**, **All Programs**, **Accessories**, and then **Notepad** (see Figure A-9).

FIGURE A-9
Opening menus in an application

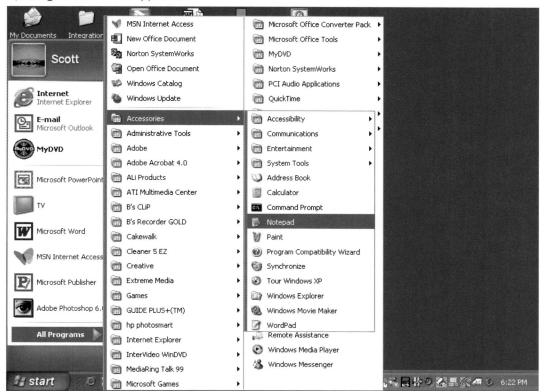

2. Click **Edit** on the menu bar. The Edit menu appears.

3. Click **Time/Date** to display the current time and date.

STEP-BY-STEP A.7 Continued

4. Click **File** on the menu bar. The File menu appears. Point to **Exit**. The Exit option is selected (see Figure A-10).

FIGURE A-10
Exit command on the File menu

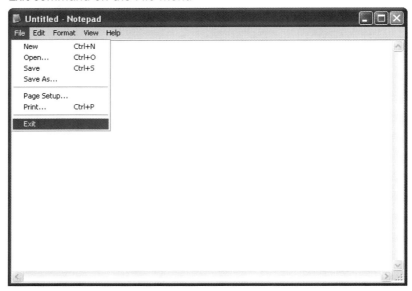

5. Click **Exit**. A save prompt dialog box appears.

6. Click **No**. The Notepad window closes (without saving your document) and you return to the desktop.

Windows Help

This appendix has covered only a few of the many features of Windows. For more information, Windows has a user-friendly Help system. Use Help as a quick reference when you are unsure about a function. You can choose to search the Help system using the Index or Search options. Additional information about a program can be found in that program's Help menu on the menu bar.

Many topics in the Help program are linked. A *link* is represented by colored, underlined text. By clicking a link, the user "jumps" to a linked document that contains more information.

Using the buttons on the toolbar controls the display of information. Both Windows 2000 and Windows XP have Back and Forward buttons. Back and Forward buttons allow you to move between previously displayed Help entries. The Options button offers navigational choices. It also offers options to customize, refresh, and print Help topics.

The Contents tab (or Locate in Contents button in Windows XP) allows you to browse through the topics by category. Click a book icon to see extra Help topics. Click a question mark to display detailed Help information in the right frame of the Help window.

S TEP-BY-STEP A.8

1. If you are using *Windows 2000*, open the Windows Help program by clicking the **Start** button, and then **Help**. If you are using *Windows XP*, click **Start** and then **Help and Support**.

2. If you're using *Windows 2000*, click the **Hide** button on the toolbar to remove the left frame. If you are using *Windows XP*, skip to step 5.

3. Click the **Show** button to display the left frame again.

4. Click the **Contents** tab if it is not already selected.

5. *Windows 2000* users: Click **Introducing Windows 2000 Professional** and then click **How to Use Help**.

   Windows XP users: Click **What's new in Windows XP**.

6. *Windows 2000* users: Click **Find a Help Topic**.

   Windows XP users: Click **What's new topics** in the left pane and then **What's new for Help and Support** in the right pane.

7. Read the Help window and leave it open for the next Task.

When you want to search for help on a particular topic, use the Index tab and key in a word. Windows will search alphabetically through the list of Help topics to find an appropriate match. Double-click a topic to see it explained in the right frame of the Help window. Sometimes a Topics Found dialog box will appear that displays subtopics related to the item. Find a subtopic that you'd like to learn more about and double-click it.

S TEP-BY-STEP A.9

1. *Windows 2000* users: Click the **Index** tab.

   Windows XP users: Click the **Index** button.

2. *Windows 2000* users: Begin keying **printing** until *printing* is highlighted in the list of index entries.

   Windows XP users: Begin keying **help** until *help and support for Windows XP* is highlighted in the list of index entries.

3. *Windows 2000* users: Click **printing Help topics** and then **from a Server** to display information in the right frame.

   Windows XP users: Double-click **copying and printing Help topics**. Then double-click **To print a Help topic or page**.

STEP-BY-STEP A.9 Continued

4. *Windows 2000* users: Read the Help window. Then print the information by following the instructions you read.

   Windows XP users: Read the Help window. Then print the information by clicking the **Print** button on the toolbar.

5. *Windows 2000* users: Click the **Back** button to return to the previous Help screen.

   Windows XP users: Click the **Back arrow** button to return to the previous Help screen.

6. *Windows 2000* users: Click the **Forward** button to advance to the next Help screen.

   Windows XP users: Click the **Forward arrow** button to advance to the next Help screen.

7. Close the Help program by clicking the **Close** button.

The Search function is like the Index function. However, it will perform a more thorough search of the words that you key. By using the Search option, you can show every incident of a certain word throughout the Windows Help system. Double-click on the topic most similar to what you are looking for. The information is displayed in the Help window.

If you need help using the Windows Help program in Windows 2000, choose *Introducing Windows, How to Use Help* from the Contents tab. However, if you are using Windows XP, choose *What's new in Windows XP* from the Home page and then *What's new topics*.

If you are using a Microsoft Office application, you can also get help by using the Office Assistant feature.

Other Features

One of Windows' primary features is its file management abilities. Windows comes with two file management utilities: My Computer and Windows Explorer. The Recycle Bin function also helps you manage files. When open, these utilities display a standard toolbar like the one shown in Figure A-11. Your toolbar may look different from Figure A-11 if it has been customized. To adapt your toolbar, choose Toolbars on the View menu and Customize on the submenu.

FIGURE A-11
Windows XP Standard toolbar

The Back and Forward buttons let you move back and forth between folder contents that have already been seen. The Up button moves you up one level in the ladder of folders. The Undo button allows you to reverse your most recent action. The Delete button removes the selected text. The View button lists options for displaying the contents of the window.

My Computer

There is an icon on your desktop labeled My Computer. Double-clicking this icon opens the My Computer window. It looks similar to the one shown in Figure A-12. The My Computer program is helpful because it allows you to see what is on your computer. Double-click the icon for the drive you want to view. That drive's name appears in the title bar. The window displays all the folders and files on that drive.

FIGURE A-12
Windows XP My Computer window

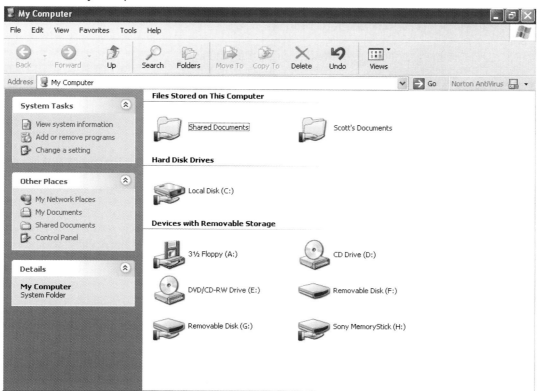

Because computer disks have such a large capacity, it is not unusual for a floppy disk to contain dozens of files or for a hard disk to contain hundreds or thousands of files. A disk can be divided into folders to organize files. A *folder* is a place where files and other folders are stored. They help keep documents organized on a disk. Folders group files that have something in common. You can also have folders within a folder. For example, you could create a folder to group all of the files you are working on in computer class. Within that folder, you could have several other folders that group files for each chapter.

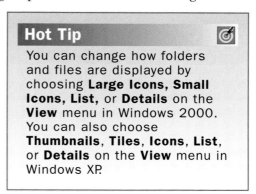

Hot Tip

You can change how folders and files are displayed by choosing **Large Icons, Small Icons, List,** or **Details** on the **View** menu in Windows 2000. You can also choose **Thumbnails, Tiles, Icons, List,** or **Details** on the **View** menu in Windows XP.

STEP-BY-STEP A.10

1. Double-click the **My Computer** icon on your desktop.

2. Double-click the drive where you want to create a new folder.

3. Open the **File** menu, choose **New**, and then choose **Folder** on the submenu. A folder titled *New Folder* appears, as shown in Figure A-13.

4. Name the folder **Time Records**. Tap **Enter**.

5. Open the **File** menu and choose **Close** to close the window.

FIGURE A-13
New folder (Tiles view)

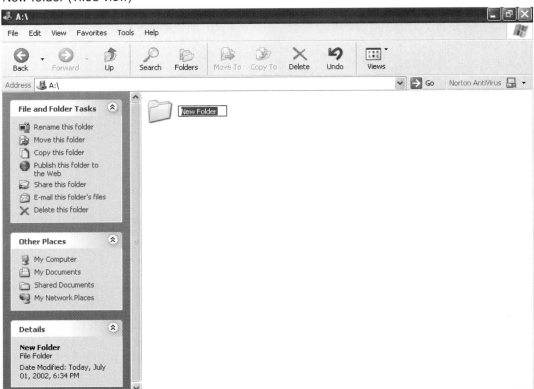

Windows Explorer

Another way to view the folders and files on a disk is to use the Windows Explorer program. The Explorer window is split into two panes. The left pane shows a hierarchical or "tree" view of how the folders are organized on a disk. The right side, or Contents pane, shows the files and folders located in the folder that is currently selected in the tree pane. Explorer is a useful tool for organizing and managing the contents of a disk because you can create folders, rename them, and easily delete, move, and copy files.

STEP-BY-STEP A.11

1. *Windows 2000* users: Open Windows Explorer by clicking **Start**, **Programs**, **Accessories**, and then **Windows Explorer**.

   Windows XP users: Open Windows Explorer by clicking **Start**, **All Programs**, **Accessories**, and then **Windows Explorer**.

2. In the tree pane, click the drive where the *Time Records* folder you just created is located.

3. Select the **Time Records** folder in the Contents pane of the Explorer window.

4. Open the **File** menu and choose **Rename**.

5. Key **Finance**. Tap **Enter**.

6. Leave Windows Explorer open for the next Task.

Recycle Bin

Another icon on the desktop that you learned about earlier is the Recycle Bin. It looks like a wastebasket. It is a place to get rid of files and folders that you no longer need. Items that have been "thrown away" will remain in the Recycle Bin. They can be restored until you empty the Recycle Bin.

STEP-BY-STEP A.12

1. Windows Explorer should still be open from the previous Task.

2. Right-click the **Finance** folder.

3. Choose **Delete** on the shortcut menu. The Confirm Folder Delete dialog box appears.

4. Click **Yes**. The folder is removed.

5. Open the **File** menu and choose **Close** to close Windows Explorer.

SUMMARY

In this appendix, you learned:

■ The desktop organizes your work. Clicking the Start button displays options for opening programs and documents. It can also shut down the computer.

■ You can connect to the Internet using the Internet Explorer browser. You can also use the Active Desktop and channels to incorporate Web content into your work.

■ Windows can be moved, resized, opened, and closed. If the contents of the window cannot be seen, scroll bars allow you to move to the part of the window you want to see. Windows can be maximized to fill the screen or minimized to a button on the taskbar.

■ Menus allow you to choose commands to perform different actions. Menus are accessed from the Start button or from a program's menu bar near the top of the window. When you choose a menu command with an ellipsis (…), a dialog box appears that requires more information before performing the command. Choosing a menu option with an arrow opens a submenu.

■ The Windows Help program provides more information about the many features of Windows. You can access the Help program from the Start button and use the Contents, Index, or Search tabs to get information. You can also get help from the Help menu within Windows programs.

■ Folders group files that have something in common. To organize a disk, it can be divided into folders where files and other folders are stored. Other useful features of Windows include My Computer and Windows Explorer. They also help you organize and manage your files. The Recycle Bin is used for deleting unneeded files or folders.

APPENDIX B

COMPUTER CONCEPTS

What Is a Computer?

A computer is a machine that is used to store, retrieve, and control information (called data) electronically. You enter the data into the computer through a variety of input devices, such as a keyboard, mouse or joystick. The computer processes your input, and then outputs it to a monitor, projector, or printer. Computer software programs run the computer and let you manipulate the data.

Hardware

The parts of the computer that you can physically touch are called hardware. The main parts are the central processing unit (CPU), the monitor, the keyboard, and the mouse. Peripherals are additional components, such as printers and scanners.

Input Devices. You enter information into a computer by keying on a keyboard or by using a mouse. Tablet PCs allow you to input data by writing directly on the computer screen. They use a technology called handwriting recognition to convert your writing to text. A joystick is an input device that moves a pointer, or character, on the screen. A modem is another input device; it receives information via a telephone line. Other input devices include scanners, trackballs, and digital tracking devices. You can use scanners to "read" text or graphics into a computer from a printed page, or to read bar codes (coded labels) to keep track of merchandise in a store or other records. Similar to a mouse, a trackball has a roller ball that you turn to control a pointer on the screen. Digital tracking devices are an alternative to the trackball or mouse. They are situated on the keyboard of a laptop, and allow you to simply press a finger on a small electronic pad to control the pointer on the screen. See Figure B-1.

FIGURE B-1
Keyboard, controller, and mouse

Processing Devices. The central processing unit (CPU) is a silicon chip that processes data and carries out instructions given to the computer. The data bus includes the wiring and pathways by which the CPU communicates with the peripherals and components of the computer.

FIGURE B-2
Motherboard

Storage Devices. The hard drive is a device that reads and writes data to and from a disk. The hard drive is called hard because the disk is rigid, unlike a floppy disk drive. Floppy disk drives read and write data to and from a removable non-rigid disk. The floppy disk is encased in a plastic sleeve to protect its data. The floppy disk's main advantage is portability. You can store data on a floppy disk and transport it for use on another computer. A floppy disk will hold up to 1.4 megabytes (MB) of information. Similar to a floppy disk is a Zip disk. These are portable disks contained in a plastic sleeve, but they will hold 100MB or 250MB of information. A special disk drive called a Zip drive is required to use a Zip disk.

At one time, the largest hard drive was 10MB, or 10,000,000 bytes, of data. A byte stands for a single character of data. At the current time, typical hard drives range from 40 gigabytes (GB) to 120 gigabytes.

Another storage device is the CD, or compact disc, which is a form of optical storage. Compact discs can store 650MB. Information is encoded on the disk by a laser and read by a CD-ROM drive in the computer. These discs have a great advantage over floppies because they can hold vast quantities of information. However, most computers cannot write (or save) information to these discs; CD-ROMs are Read-Only Memory (ROM) devices. Drives are now available that write to CDs. The great advantage of CDs is their ability to hold graphic information—including moving pictures with the highest quality stereo sound.

Similar to a CD, the digital video drive (DVD) can read high-quality cinema-type discs. A DVD is a 5-inch optical disc, and it looks like an audio CD or a compact disc. It is a high-capacity storage device that contains 4.7GB of data. There are two different DVDs that offer even more storage—a 2-layer version with 9.4GB capacity, and double-sided discs with 17GB. These highest-capacity discs are designed to, in time, replace the CD-ROM. A DVD holds 133 minutes of data on each side.

Another storage medium is magnetic tape. This medium is most commonly used for backing up a computer system. This means making a copy of files from a hard drive. Although it is somewhat rare for a hard drive to crash (that is, to have the data or pointers to the data to be partially or totally destroyed), it can and does happen. Therefore, most businesses and some individuals routinely back up files on tape. If you have a small hard drive, you can use floppy disks or CD-ROMs to back up your system.

FIGURE B-3
Hard drive

Output Devices. The monitor on which you view your work is an output device. It provides a visual version of the information stored in or produced by your computer. The monitor for today's system is the SVGA (super video graphics array), which uses a Cathode-ray tube (CRT) similar to a television. It provides a very sharp picture because of the large number of tiny dots, called pixels, that make up the display. It can also present the full spectrum of colors. Most laptop computers use a liquid crystal display (LCD) screen. They do not have as clear a display because it depends on the arrangement of tiny bits of crystal to present an image. However, the latest laptops use new technology that gives quality near or equal to that of a standard monitor.

Printers are another type of output device. They let you produce a paper printout of information. Today, most printers are of the laser type. They use technology similar to a photocopier to produce high-quality print. The laser printer uses heat to fuse a powdery substance called toner to the page. Ink-jet printers use a spray of ink to print. Laser printers give the sharpest image. Ink-jet printers provide nearly as sharp an image, but the wet printouts can smear when they first are printed. Most color printers, however, are ink jet. These printers let you print information in its full array of colors. Laser color printers are available, but are significantly more costly.

Modems are another type of output device that can also serve as an input device. Modems allow computers to communicate with each other by telephone lines. Modems convert information in bytes to sound media. They then convert it back to bytes after receiving data. Modems run at various speeds. Typically, a computer will have a modem that operates at 33.6 Kbps (Kilobytes per second) to 56 Kbps baud (a variable unit of data transmission) per second or better.

Local telephone companies currently offer residential ISDN services that provide connection speeds up to 128 Kbps and digital subscriber line technologies (DSL), which can provide speeds beyond 1.5 Mbps (Megabytes per second). Other alternatives include fast downstream data connections from direct broadcast satellite (DBS), fixed wireless providers, and high-speed cable.

FIGURE B-4
Monitor

Laptops and Docking Stations. A laptop computer is a small folding computer that literally fits in a person's lap. Within the fold-up case is the CPU, data bus, monitor (built into the lid), hard drive (sometimes removable), and 3.5-inch floppy drive. The fold-up case also contains a CD-ROM drive and a trackball or digital tracking device. The advantage of the laptop is that it is moveable. You can work anywhere because you can use power either from an outlet or from the computer's internal, rechargeable batteries. The drawbacks are the smaller keyboard, liquid crystal monitor, smaller capacity, and higher price. Newer laptops, however, offer full-sized keyboards and higher-quality monitors. As technology improves, the storage capacity on smaller devices is making it possible to offer laptops with as much power and storage as a full-sized computer. A docking station is a device into which you slide a closed laptop so that it becomes a desktop computer. Then you can plug in a full-sized monitor, keyboard, mouse, printer, and so on. Such a setup lets you use the laptop like a desktop computer while at your home or office. See Figure B-5.

FIGURE B-5
Laptop and docking station

Personal Digital Assistants (PDA). A Personal Digital Assistant is a pocket-sized electronic organizer that helps you to manage addresses, appointments, expenses, tasks, and memos. This information can be shared with a Windows-based or Macintosh computer through a process called synchronization. By placing your PDA in a cradle that is attached to your computer, you can transfer the data from your PDA into your computer's information manager program. The information is updated on both sides, making your PDA a portable extension of your computer.

FIGURE B-6
Personal Digital Assistant

Functioning

All of the input, processing, storage, and output devices function together to make the manipulation, storage, and distribution of data possible.

Data and Information Management. Data is information entered into and manipulated within a computer. Manipulation includes adding, subtracting, multiplying, and dividing; analysis planning, such as sorting data; and reporting, such as presenting data for others in a chart. Data and information management is what runs the software on the computer hardware.

Memory. There are two kinds of memory in a computer—RAM and ROM. RAM, or Random Access Memory, is a number of silicon chips inside a computer that hold information as long as the computer is turned on. RAM is what keeps the software programs up and running and keeps the visuals on your screen. RAM is where you work with data until you save it to another media, such as a hard or floppy disk. Early computers had simple programs and did little with data, so they had very little RAM—possibly 4 or fewer megabytes. Today's computers run very complicated programs that remain available to the user at the same time as other programs and contain graphics. Both of these tasks take a lot of memory. Today's computers have at least 128 or more megabytes of RAM. ROM, or read-only memory, is the small bit of memory that stays in the computer when it is turned off. It is ROM that lets the computer boot up, or get started. ROM holds the instructions that tell the computer how to begin to load its operating system software programs. Figure B-7 shows random access memory.

FIGURE B-7
Random Access Memory

Speed. The speed of a computer is measured by how fast the drives turn to reach information to be retrieved or to save data. The measurement is in megahertz (MHz). Hard drives on early personal computers worked at 4.77 to 10 megahertz. Today, machines run at 1000 MHz (or 1GHz) or more. Another factor that affects the speed of a computer is how much RAM is available. Since RAM makes up the work area for all programs and holds all the information that you input until you save, the more RAM available, the quicker the machine will be able to operate.

Speed is also measured by how quickly the modem can send and receive information. As mentioned earlier, modem speed is measured in baud. The usual modem runs at 33,600 or 56,000 baud per second or more. The cable modems, DSL lines, ISDN lines, and DSB offer much faster transfers of information.

Communications. Computers have opened up the world of communications, first within offices via LANs (local area networks that link computers within a facility) and, later, via the Internet. Using the Internet, people can communicate across the world instantly with e-mail and attach files that were once sent by mailing a floppy disk. Also, anyone with a modem and an access service can download information from or post information to thousands of bulletin boards. Figure B-8 shows a network diagram.

FIGURE B-8
Diagram of a network

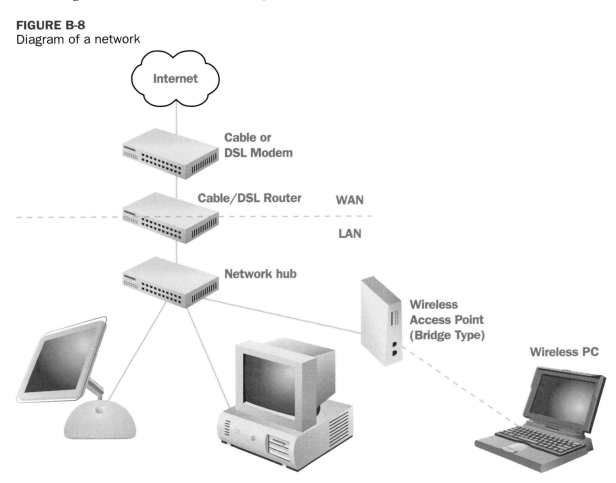

Software

A program is a set of mathematical instructions to the computer. Software is the collection of programs and other data input that tells the computer how to operate its machinery, how to use, store, and output information, and how to accept the input you give it. Software fits into two basic categories: systems software and applications software. A third category, network software, is really a type of application.

Systems Software. Systems software refers to the operating system (OS) of the computer. The OS is a group of programs that is automatically copied in RAM every couple of seconds from the time the computer is turned on until the computer is turned off. Operating systems serve two functions. They control data flow among computer parts, and they provide the platform on which application and network software work. In effect, they allow the "space" for software and translate its commands to the computer. The most popular operating systems in use today are the

Macintosh operating system and a version of Microsoft Windows, such as the Windows program you are currently using.

Macintosh has its own operating system that has evolved over the years since its beginning. Macintosh has used a graphical user interface (GUI) operating system since its introduction in the mid-1970s. The OS is designed so users "click" with a mouse on icons or on text to give commands to the system. Data is available to you in a way that lets you see on-screen what a document will look like when it is printed. Graphics and other kinds of data, such as spreadsheets, can be placed into text documents. However, GUIs take a great deal of RAM to keep all of the graphics and programs operating.

The OS for IBM and IBM-compatible computers (machines made by other companies that operate similarly) originally was DOS (disk operating system). It did not have a graphical interface. The GUI system, Windows™, was developed to make using the IBM/IBM-compatible computer more "friendly." Windows 3.1, however, was a translating system that operated on top of DOS—not on its own.

Windows 3.1 was a GUI system that operated on top of DOS. It allowed you to point and click on graphics and words that then translated to DOS commands for the computer. Graphics and other kinds of data, such as spreadsheets, could be placed into text documents by Object Linking and Embedding (OLE). However, Windows 3.1 did not keep more than one operation going at a time; it merely switched between operations quickly. Using several high-level programs at the same time, however, could cause problems, such as memory failure. Therefore, improvements were necessary and expected.

The improvements came with the release of Windows 95 and then Windows 98. These versions of Windows had their own operating system. Windows 95/98 has DOS built in, but does not operate on top of it—if you go to a DOS prompt from Windows, you will still be operating inside a Windows system, not in traditional DOS. Today's Windows applications are the logical growth of GUI for IBM and IBM-compatible machines. It is a stay-resident, point-and-click system that automatically configures hardware to work together. You should note, however, that with all of its ability comes the need for more RAM or a system running Windows will operate slowly.

Windows 95 and 98 were designed for the consumer. They are easy to use, compatible with most peripheral products, and have features that you would most likely use for personal applications. Windows NT and Windows 2000 were designed for businesses. They include improved features for reliability and security. Windows XP brought these two divergent operating systems back together into one product for all users. It combines the flexibility of Windows 98 with the stability and security of Windows 2000. Newer versions of Windows continue to be released.

Applications Software. When you use a computer program to perform a data manipulation or processing task, you are using applications software. Word processors, databases, spreadsheets, desktop publishers, fax systems, and online access systems are all applications software.

Network Software. Novell™ and Windows NT are two kinds of network software. A traditional network is a group of computers that are hardwired (hooked together with cables) to communicate and operate together. Today, some computer networks use RF (radio frequency) technology to communicate with each other. This is called a wireless network because you do not need to hook the network together with cables. In a typical network, one computer controls the flow of data among the other computers, called nodes, on the network. Network software manages this flow of information. Networks have certain advantages over stand-alone computers. Networks allow communication among the computers; they allow smaller capacity nodes to access the larger capacity of the server. They also allow several computers to share peripherals, such as one printer, and they can make it possible for all computers on the network to have access to the Internet.

History of the Computer

Although various types of calculating machines were developed in the nineteenth century, the history of the modern computer begins about the middle of the last century. The strides made in developing today's personal computer have been truly astounding.

Early Development

The ENIAC, or Electronic Numerical Integrator and Computer, was designed for military use in calculating ballistic trajectories and was the first electronic, digital computer to be developed in the United States. For its day, 1946, it was quite a marvel because it was able to accomplish a task in 20 seconds that took a human three days to do. However, it was an enormous machine that weighed more than 20 tons and contained thousands of vacuum tubes, which often failed. The tasks that it could accomplish were limited, as well.

FIGURE B-9
ENIAC

From this awkward beginning, however, the seeds of an information revolution grew. Major dates in the history of computer development are listed in Table B-1.

TABLE B-1
History of computer development

YEAR	DEVELOPMENT
1948	First electronically stored program
1951	First junction transistor
1953	Replacement of tubes with magnetic cores
1957	First high-level computer language
1961	First integrated circuit
1965	First minicomputer
1971	Invention of the microprocessor (the silicon chip) and floppy disk
1974	First personal computer (made possible by the microprocessor)

These last two inventions launched the fast-paced information revolution in which we now all live and take part.

The Personal Computer

The PC, or personal computer, was mass marketed by Apple beginning in 1977 and then by IBM in 1981. It is this desktop tool with which people are so familiar. Today, they contain much more power and ability than did the original computer that took up an entire room. The PC is a small computer (desktop size or less) that uses a microprocessor to manipulate data. PCs may stand alone, be linked together in a network, or be attached to a large mainframe computer.

FIGURE B-10
Early IBM

Computer Utilities and System Maintenance

Computer operating systems let you run certain utilities and perform system maintenance. When you add hardware or software, you might need to make changes in the way the system operates. Beginning with the Windows 95 version, most configuration changes are done automatically; other operating systems may not. You may also want to customize the way the new software or hardware will interface (coordinate) with your system. Additionally, you can make changes such as the speed at which your mouse clicks, how quickly or slowly keys repeat on the keyboard, and what color or pattern appears on the desktop or in GUI programs.

You need to perform certain maintenance regularly on computers. You should scan all new disks and any incoming information from online sources for viruses (a small program that is loaded onto your computer without your knowledge and runs against your wishes). Some systems do this automatically, but others require you to install software to do it. You should run a program that checks the hard drive to see that there are not bad sectors (areas) and looks for corrupted files. Optimizing or defragmenting the hard disk is another way to keep your computer running at its best. You can also check a floppy disk if it is not working properly. Programs for scanning a large hard drive could take up to half an hour to run. However, checking programs run on a small hard drive or disk might take only a short time. Checking programs often offer the option of "fixing" the bad areas or problems. While this is good, you should be aware that it may result in data loss.

Society and Computers

The Electronic Information Era has probably impacted society as much or more than any other enlightenment era. With the changes of this era have come many new questions and responsibilities. There are issues of ethics, security, safety, and privacy.

Ethics Using Computers

When you access information, you must respect the rights of the creator of that information. Treat electronic information in a copyrighted form the same way as you would a book. The information you transmit must be accurate and fair.

When you use equipment that belongs to your school, you must not:

1. Damage computer hardware nor add or remove equipment without permission.

2. Use an access code or equipment without permission.

3. Read others' electronic mail.

4. Alter data belonging to someone else without permission.

5. Use the computer for play without permission.

6. Access the Internet for non–school-related work during school hours.

7. Add to or take away from software programs without permission.

8. Make unauthorized copies of data or software.

9. Copy software programs to use at home.

10. Copy files or procedures for personal use.

11. Borrow computer hardware for personal use without asking permission.

Security, Safety, and Privacy

The Internet provides us access to improve our economic status and offer life-enhancing features. Businesses throughout the world depend on the Internet every day to get work done. Disruptions in the Internet would create havoc for people around the world.

The terrorist attack on the World Trade Center and the Pentagon made the country more aware of security for the people of the United States and for the country. In response to this attack, President George W. Bush established the Department of Homeland Security. He also created a division called the National Cyber Security Division (NCSD) to protect our interest in the Internet.

The National Cyber Security Division encourages all Internet users to use updated antivirus software and add patches designed to enhance your computer's security. They also ask that you report suspicious activity to law enforcement or a DHS watch office. Electronic communication is the fastest way for terrorists to communicate, so we must all raise our level of security awareness when using computers.

Just as you would not open someone else's mail, you must respect the privacy of e-mail sent to others. When interacting with others online, you must keep private information private. Do not endanger your privacy, safety, or financial security by giving out personal information to someone you do not know. A common scam (trick) is for someone to pretend to work for the online service you are using and ask for your access code or password. Those numbers control your service account. Never give this information out to anyone online. The person can use it and charge money to your account as well as access other personal information about you. Also, do not give out your credit card number, home address, or telephone number online.

Career Opportunities

All of our careers involve the computer. Whether you are a grocery checker using a scanner to read the prices, a busy executive writing a report on a laptop on an airplane, or a programmer creating new software—almost everyone uses computers in their jobs. And, everyone in a business processes information in some way. There are also specific careers available if you want to work primarily with computers.

Schools offer computer programming, repair, and design degrees. The most popular jobs are systems analysts, computer operators, and programmers. Analysts figure out ways to make computers work (or work better) for a particular business or type of business. Computer operators use the programs and devices to conduct business with computers. Programmers write the software for applications or new systems.

There are courses of study in using CAD (computer-aided design) and CAM (computer-aided manufacturing). Computer engineering and architectural design degrees are also available. Scientific research is done on computers, and specialties are available in that area as well. There are positions available to instruct others in computer software use within companies and schools. Technical writers and editors must be available to write manuals on using computers and software. Computer-assisted instruction (CAI) is a system of teaching any given subject on the computer. The learner is provided with resources, such as an encyclopedia on CD-ROM, in addition to the specific learning program with which he or she interacts on the computer. Individuals are needed to create these instruction systems. Designing video games is another exciting and ever-growing field of computer work. And these are just a few of the possible career opportunities in an ever-changing work environment.

FIGURE B-11
Person in a computer-related job

What Does the Future Hold?

The possibilities for computer development and application are endless. Things that were dreams or science fiction only 10 or 20 years ago are a reality today. New technologies are emerging. Some are replacing old ways of doing things. Others are merging with those older methods and devices. We are learning new ways to work and play because of the computer. It is definitely a device that has become part of our lives.

Emerging Technologies

Today, the various technologies and systems are coming together to operate more efficiently. For instance, since their beginnings, Macintosh and Windows-based systems could not exchange information well. Today, you can install compatibility cards in the Power Macintosh and run Windows, DOS, and Mac OS on the same computer and switch between them. Macs (except for early models) can read from and write to MS-DOS and Windows disks. And you can easily network Macintosh computers with other types of computers running other operating systems. In addition, you can buy software for a PC to run the Mac OS and to read Macintosh disks.

Telephone communication is also being combined with computer e-mail so users can set a time to meet online and, with the addition of voice technology, actually speak to each other. This form of communication will certainly evolve into an often-used device.

Another technology is the CUCME (see you, see me) visual system that allows computer users to use a small camera and microphone wired into the computer. When they communicate, the receiver can see and hear them. For the hearing impaired, this form of communication can be more effective than writing alone since sign language and facial expression can be added to the interaction. CUCME is a logical next step from the image transfer files now so commonly used to transfer a static (nonmoving) picture.

A great deal of research and planning has gone into combining television and computers. The combined device has a CPU, television-as-monitor, keyboard, joystick, mouse, modem, and CUCME/quick-cam. This combined medium allows banking, work, entertainment, and communication to happen all through one piece of machinery—and all in the comfort of your home. Another combined technology is printers that function as a copier, fax machine, and scanner.

Trends

There are many trends that drive the computer industry. One trend is for larger and faster hard drives. Forty- and 80-gigabyte hard drives have virtually replaced the 540MB drives, and 200GB drives are becoming common. RAM today is increasing exponentially. The trend is to sell RAM in units of 32 or 64 megabytes to meet the needs of 128, 256, and larger blocks of RAM. All of these size increases are due to the expanding memory requirements of GUIs and new peripherals. Although the capacities are increasing, the actual size of the machines is decreasing. Technology is allowing more powerful components to fit into smaller devices—just as the 3½-inch floppy disk is smaller and holds more data than the obsolete 5¼-inch floppy.

Another trend is the increased use of computers for personal use in homes. This trend is likely to continue as the technologies of the PC and standard home electronics, such as the television, are combined.

Home Offices. More and more frequently, people are working out of their homes. Many companies allow workers to have a computer at home that is linked by modem to the office. Work is done at home and transferred to the office. Communication is by e-mail and telephone. Such an arrangement saves companies workspace and money. Other employees use laptop computers to work both at home and on the road as they travel. These computers, in combination with a modem, allow an employee to work from virtually anywhere.

With downsizing (the reduction of the workforce by companies), many individuals have found themselves unemployed or underemployed (working less or for less money). These people have begun their own businesses out of their homes. With a computer, modem, fax software, printer, and other peripherals, they can contract with many businesses or sell their own products or services. Many make use of the Internet and World Wide Web to advertise their services.

Home Use. As the economy has tightened, many people are trying to make their lives more time- and cost-efficient. The computer is one help in that quest. Maintaining accounting records, managing household accounts and information, and using electronic banking on a computer saves time. Games and other computer interactions also offer a more reasonable way of spending leisure dollars than some outside entertainment. For instance, you may not be able to afford a trip to Paris to see paintings inside the Louvre Museum. However, you might be able to afford a CD-ROM that lets you take a tour on your computer.

This can be quite an educational experience for children and a more restful one for those who might tire on a trip of that size. Young people can benefit from this kind of education as well as using the computer to complete homework, do word processing, and create art and graphics. They can also play games that sharpen their hand-to-eye coordination and thinking skills.

APPENDIX C

CONCEPTS FOR MICROSOFT OFFICE PROGRAMS

Introduction

Microsoft Office is a group of computer programs. Office includes a word-processing program (Word), a spreadsheet program (Excel), a database program (Access), a presentation program (PowerPoint), and a desktop publishing program (Publisher).

The word-processing program (Word) helps you create documents such as letters and reports. The spreadsheet program (Excel) lets you work with numbers to create items such as budgets and loan payments. The database program (Access) helps you create lists of information, such as addresses. The presentation program (PowerPoint) is used to create slides, outlines, speaker's notes, and audience handouts. The desktop publishing program (Publisher) helps you design professional-looking documents.

The programs in Office can be used together. For example, numbers from a spreadsheet can be included in a letter created in the word processor.

Read below for more information on each Office program.

Word

Word is the word-processing program in Microsoft Office. In today's busy world, it is necessary to prepare and send many types of documents. Word processing is the use of a computer and software to produce documents, such as memos and letters (see Figure C-1). You can also create documents that are more complex, such as newsletters with graphics, and documents that can be published as Web pages.

FIGURE C-1
Business letter in Word

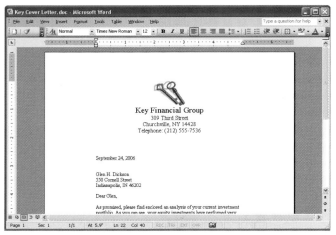

Keying text in Word is easy because it automatically moves, or wraps, text to the next line. After you key your text, you may want to edit it. Use the Spelling and Grammar checker to identify spelling and grammar errors. Correct the errors using the Backspace and Delete keys to delete text and Overtype to type over text. Cut, Copy, and Paste commands allow you to move and copy data. Word also has an Undo command that reverses your last command.

Word has many automated features that help you create and edit documents. AutoCorrect corrects errors as you enter text; AutoFormat As You Type applies built-in formats as you key; AutoComplete suggests the entire word after keying the first few letters; and AutoText inserts frequently used text.

In Word, you can format a document to make it easier to read and more attractive. Formatting includes making decisions about margins, tabs, headings, indents, text alignment, fonts, colors, styles, headers, and footers. Word encourages you to be creative because you can try new formats and change formats in seconds.

You can also enhance documents by adding graphics or pictures to make the page more attractive. Word provides pictures called clip art, as well as shapes, diagrams, and charts. Drawing tools permit you to create your own graphics.

Excel

Excel is the spreadsheet program in Microsoft Office. A *spreadsheet* is a grid of rows and columns containing numbers, text, and formulas. The purpose of a spreadsheet is to solve problems with numbers. Without a computer, you could solve a number problem by creating rows and columns on paper. You would then use a calculator to create solutions. Computer spreadsheets also contain rows and columns (see Figure C-2), but they calculate much faster.

FIGURE C-2
Spreadsheet in Excel

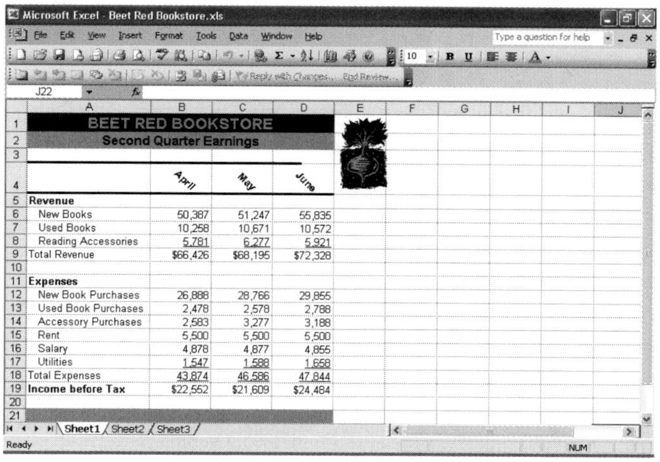

Spreadsheets are used in many ways. For example, a spreadsheet can be used to calculate a grade in a class or to prepare a budget for the next few months. The biggest advantage of spreadsheets is the ability to calculate accurately, quickly, and easily. For example, you might use a spreadsheet to calculate your monthly income and expenses.

Besides calculating rapidly and accurately, spreadsheets are flexible. Making changes to a spreadsheet is usually as easy as pointing and clicking with the mouse. Suppose, for example, you have prepared a budget on a spreadsheet. If you make a change in the spreadsheet, the entire budget will be recalculated. You can imagine the work this change would require if you were calculating the budget with pencil and paper.

Excel uses the term *worksheet* to describe a computerized spreadsheet. Sometimes you may want to use several worksheets that relate to each other. A group of related worksheets is a *workbook*.

Access

Access is the database program in Microsoft Office. A database helps you to store large amounts of information. A database is like a filing cabinet that contains folders of documents. Compared to a paper filing system, a database has the following advantages:

1. Records can be retrieved quickly. You can find the information you need by tapping keys rather than searching through folders in a filing cabinet.

2. Records can be manipulated easily. You can sort records quickly in various ways, find a specific record, or select a group of records.

3. Records can be stored using very little space. You can store large amounts of data in a database. Filing cabinets of paper in folders require large amounts of space.

A database is made up of many small sets of data called *records*. For example, in an Employee database, all the information about an employee is a record (see Figure C-3). Information in a record can include the employee's number, name, social security number, address, birth date, department, and title. In a database, these categories of information are called *fields*. In Access, data is organized into a *table*. Tables store data in a format similar to a spreadsheet. In a table, records appear as rows of data and fields appear as columns.

FIGURE C-3
Employee database in Access

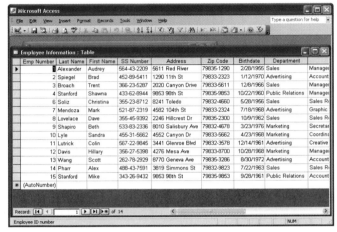

PowerPoint

PowerPoint is the presentation program in Microsoft Office. Presentations can be created using slides, outlines, speaker's notes, and handouts (see Figure C-4). A PowerPoint presentation can include text, clip art, pictures, animations, and hyperlinks. Other Microsoft Office programs can be used with PowerPoint. A Word table can be inserted into a PowerPoint presentation. Excel charts can be inserted into a presentation. A presentation can be saved as a Web page. After you complete a presentation, you can use the rehearsal functions to practice your timing and delivery. PowerPoint presentations are usually viewed using a projector on a screen. You can also use a television monitor or an additional monitor connected to your computer.

FIGURE C-4
Presentation in PowerPoint

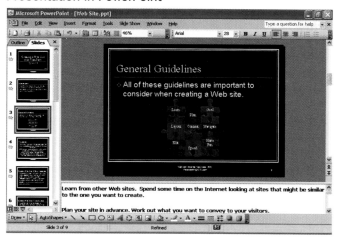

Publisher

Publisher is the desktop publishing program in Microsoft Office. In Publisher, you can create many types of documents, such as business cards, calendars, and stationery (see Figure C-5). Publisher contains hundreds of templates you can use to start a project. Personal information sets can be used to store information about your business, organization, or family. You can add a logo to customize a group of documents by using the By Design Set option. All you have to do is add your own custom touches to create your own professional-looking documents.

FIGURE C-5
Business card in Publisher

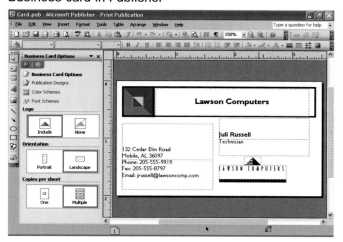

APPENDIX D

KEYBOARDING TOUCH SYSTEM IMPROVEMENT

Introduction

Your Goal – Improve your keyboarding skill using the touch system.

Why Improve Your Keyboarding Skills?

■ To key faster and more accurately every time you use the computer for the rest of your life.

■ To increase your enjoyment while using the computer.

> **Hot Tip**
>
> You will key faster and more accurately when using the touch system instead of looking from the copy and then to the keyboard and tapping keys with one or two fingers—the "hunt and peck" system.

Getting Ready to Build Skills

Get ready by:

1. **a.** Clearing your desk of everything except your book and a pencil or pen.

    b. Positioning your keyboard and book so that you are comfortable and able to move your hands and fingers freely.

    c. Keeping your feet flat on the floor, sitting with your back erect.

2. Taking a two-minute timed writing, page 542, now according to your teacher's directions.

3. Calculating your Words A Minute (WAM) and Errors A Minute (EAM) using the instructions on the timed writing progress chart, page 543. This will be your base score to compare to future timed writings.

4. On the Base Score line (page 543), recording the Date, WAM, and EAM.

5. Repeating the timed writing as many times as you can.

6. Recording each attempt on the Introduction line of the chart.

Skill Builder 1

Your Goal – Use the touch system to key j u y h n m spacebar.

What To Do

1. Place your fingers on the home row as shown in Figure D-1.

FIGURE D-1
Place your fingers on the home row

2. Look at Figure D-2. Notice how later (in step 3) you will tap the letters j u y h n m in a counterclockwise (↺) direction. You will tap the spacebar with your right thumb.

FIGURE D-2
Tap all of these keys with your right index finger—the home finger j

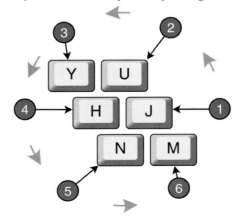

3. Look at your keyboard. Softly say the letters as you tap each key three times (3X), counterclockwise from 1 to 6 with a blank space in between. After tapping each letter in the circle, tap j, called the home key, 3X as shown. Don't worry about errors. Start keying:

jjj uuu jjj yyy jjj hhh jjj nnn jjj mmm

jjj uuu jjj yyy jjj hhh jjj nnn jjj mmm jjj

4. Repeat the same drill as many times as it takes to reach your comfort level.

jjj uuu jjj yyy jjj hhh jjj nnn jjj mmm

jjj uuu jjj yyy jjj hhh jjj nnn jjj mmm jjj

5. Close your eyes and visualize each key under each finger as you repeat the drill in step 4.

6. Look at the following two lines and key:

jjj jjj jjj juj juj juj jyj jyj jyj jhj jhj jhj jnj jnj jnj jmj jmj jmj

jjj jjj jjj juj juj juj jyj jyj jyj jhj jhj jhj jnj jnj jnj jmj jmj jmj

7. Repeat step 4, this time concentrating on a rhythmic, bouncy stroking of the keys.

8. Close your eyes and visualize the keys under your fingers as you key the drill in step 4 from memory.

9. Look at the following two lines and key these groups of letters:

j ju juj j jy jyj j jh jhj j jn jnj j jm jmj j ju juj j jy jyj j jh jhj j jn jnj j jm jmj

jjj ju jhj jn jm ju jm jh jnj jm ju jmj jy ju jh j u ju juj jy jh jnj ju jm jmj jy

10. You may want to repeat Skill Builder 1, striving to improve keying letters that are most difficult for you.

Skill Builder 2

Your Goal - Use the touch system to key f r t g b v.

What To Do

1. Place your fingers on the home row as you did in Skill Builder 1, Figure D-1.

2. Look at Figure D-3. Notice how (later in step 3) you will tap the letters f r t g b v in a clockwise (↻) direction. Tap the spacebar with your right thumb.

FIGURE D-3
Tap all of these keys with your left index finger—the home finger f

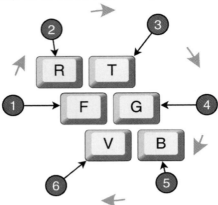

3. Look at your keyboard. Softly say the letters as you tap the keys 3X each, clockwise from 1 to 6, with a blank space in between. After tapping each letter in the circle, tap the home key f 3X as shown. Don't worry about errors. Ignore them.

    fff rrr fff ttt fff ggg fff bbb fff vvv

    fff rrr fff ttt fff ggg fff bbb fff vvv fff

4. Repeat the same drill two more times using a quicker, sharper stroke.

    fff rrr fff ttt fff ggg fff bbb fff vvv

    fff rrr fff ttt fff ggg fff bbb fff vvv fff

5. Close your eyes and visualize each key under each finger as you repeat the drill in step 4.

6. Look at the following two lines and key these groups of letters:

    fff fff fff frf frf frf ftf ftf ftf fgf fgf fgf fbf fbf fbf fvf fvf fvf

    fff fff fff frf frf frf ftf ftf ftf fgf fgf fgf fbf fbf fbf fvf fvf fvf

7. Repeat step 6, this time concentrating on a rhythmic, "bouncy" stroking of the keys.

8. Close your eyes and visualize the keys under your fingers as you key the drill in step 4 from memory.

9. Look at the following two lines and key these groups of letters:

    fr frf ft ftf fg fgf fb fbf fv fvf

    ft fgf fv frf ft fbf fv frf ft fgf

10. You are about to key your first words. Look at the following lines and key these groups of letters:

     jjj juj jug jug jug rrr rur rug rug rug

     ttt tut tug tug tug rrr rur rub rub rub

     ggg gug gum gum gum mmm mum

     mug mug mug hhh huh hum hum hum

11. Complete the Keyboarding Technique Checklist, page 544.

> **Teamwork**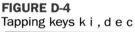
>
> ■ Ask your classmate to call out the letters in random order as you key them with your eyes closed. For example: k i , d e c. Do the same for your classmate.
> ■ Ask your classmate or your teacher to complete the Keyboarding Technique Checklist.

Skill Builder 3

Your Goal – Use the touch system to key k i , d e c.

Keys k i ,

What To Do

1. Place your fingers on the home row, as shown in Figure D-4.

FIGURE D-4
Tapping keys k i , d e c

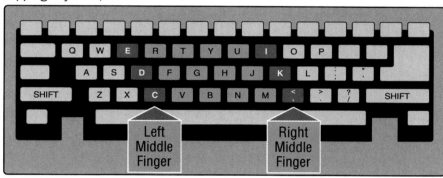

2. Look at your keyboard and locate these keys: k i ,

3. Look at your keyboard as much as you need to. Softly say the letters as you tap each key 3X as shown, with a space between each set of letters.

     kkk iii kkk ,,, kkk iii kkk ,,, kkk iii kkk ,,, kkk iii kkk ,,, kkk iii kkk ,,, kkk

4. Look at the line in step 3 and repeat the drill two more times using a quicker, sharper stroke.

5. Close your eyes and repeat the drill in step 3 as you visualize each key under each finger.

6. Repeat step 5, concentrating on a rhythmic, bouncy stroking of the keys.

Keys d e c

1. Place your fingers on the home row.

2. Look at your keyboard and locate these keys: d e c

3. Look at your keyboard. Softly say the letters as you tap each key 3X as shown, with a space between each set of letters.

   ddd eee ddd ccc ddd eee ddd ccc ddd eee ddd ccc ddd eee ddd ccc ddd

4. Look at the line in step 3 and repeat the drill two more times using a quicker, sharper stroke.

5. Close your eyes and repeat the drill in step 3 as you visualize each key under each finger.

6. Repeat step 5, concentrating on a rhythmic, bouncy stroking of the keys.

7. Look at the following lines and key these groups of letters and words:

   fff fuf fun fun fun ddd ded den den den

   ccc cuc cub cub cub vvv vev vet

   fff fuf fun fun fun ddd ded den den den

   ccc cuc cub cub cub vvv vev vet

8. Complete the Keyboarding Technique Checklist, page 544.

Skill Builder 4

Your Goal – Use the touch system to key l o . s w x and the left Shift key.

Keys l o .

What To Do

1. Place your fingers on the home row as shown in Figure D-5.

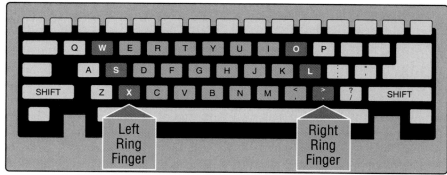

FIGURE D-5
Tapping keys l o . s w x

2. Look at your keyboard and locate the following keys: l o . (period key)

3. Look at your keyboard. Softly say the letters as you tap each key 3X with a space between each set of letters.

   lll ooo lll ... lll ooo lll ... lll ooo lll ... lll ooo lll ... lll ooo lll ... lll ooo lll ... lll

4. Look at the line in step 3 and repeat the drill two more times using a quicker, sharper stroke.

5. Close your eyes and repeat the drill in step 3 as you visualize each key under each finger.

6. Repeat step 5, concentrating on a rhythmic, bouncy stroking of the keys.

Keys s w x

1. Place your fingers on the home row.

2. Look at your keyboard and locate the following keys: s w x

3. Look at your keyboard. Softly say the letters as you tap each key 3X with a space between each set of letters.

   sss www sss xxx sss www sss xxx sss www sss xxx sss www sss xxx sss

4. Look at the line in step 3 and repeat the same drill two more times using a quicker, sharper stroke.

5. Close your eyes and repeat the drill in step 3 as you visualize each key under each finger.

6. Repeat step 5, concentrating on a rhythmic, bouncy stroking of the keys.

Left Shift Key

1. Look at the following two lines and key the line, and then the sentence. Hold down the left Shift key with the little finger of your left hand to make capitals of letters tapped by your right hand.

    jjj JJJ jjj JJJ yyy YYY yyy YYY nnn NNN nnn NNN mmm MMM

    Just look in the book. You can key well.

2. Complete the Keyboarding Technique Checklist, page 544.

Skill Builder 5

Your Goal - Use the touch system to key ; p / a q z and the right Shift key.

Keys ; p /

What To Do

1. Place your fingers on the home row as shown in Figure D-6.

FIGURE D-6
Tapping keys ; p / a q z

2. Look at your keyboard and locate the following keys: ; p /

3. Look at your keyboard. Softly say the following letters as you tap each key 3X with a space in between:

    ;;; ppp ;;; /// ;;; ppp ;;; /// ;;; ppp ;;; ///

    ;;; ppp ;;; /// ;;; ppp ;;; /// ;;; ppp ;;; /// ;;;

4. Look at the lines in step 3 and repeat the drill two more times using a quicker, sharper stroke.

5. Close your eyes and repeat the drill in step 3 as you visualize each key under each finger.

6. Repeat step 5, concentrating on a rhythmic, bouncy stroking of the keys.

Keys a q z

1. Place your fingers on the home row.

2. Look at your keyboard and locate the following keys: a q z

3. Look at your keyboard. Softly say the following letters as you tap each key 3X with a space in between:

   aaa qqq aaa zzz aaa qqq aaa zzz aaa qqq aaa zzz aaa qqq aaa zzz aaa

4. Look at the line in step 3 and repeat the same drill two more times using a quicker, sharper stroke.

5. Close your eyes and repeat the drill in step 3 as you visualize each key under each finger.

6. Repeat step 5, concentrating on a rhythmic, bouncy stroking of the keys.

Right Shift Key

1. Look at the following lines and key them. Hold down the right Shift key with the little finger of your right hand to make capitals of letters tapped by your left hand.

   sss SSS rrr RRR

   Tap the key quickly. Relax when you key.

2. Complete the Keyboarding Technique Checklist, page 544.

Skill Builder 6

Your Goal - Use the touch system to key all letters of the alphabet.

What To Do

1. Close your eyes. Do not look at the keyboard and key all letters of the alphabet as shown:

   aaa bbb ccc ddd eee fff ggg hhh iii jjj

   kkk lll mmm nnn ooo ppp qqq rrr sss

   ttt uuu vvv www xxx yyy zzz

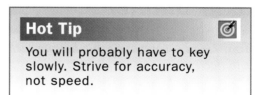

Hot Tip

You will probably have to key slowly. Strive for accuracy, not speed.

2. Repeat step 1, tapping keys with a rhythmic, bouncy touch.

3. Repeat step 1, but faster than you did for step 2.

4. Key the following:

   aa bb cc dd ee ff gg hh ii jj kk ll mm nn oo pp qq rr ss tt uu vv ww xx yy zz

   a b c d e f g h i j k l m n o p q r s t u v w x y z

5. Keep your eyes on the following copy. Do not look at the keyboard and key all letters of the alphabet three times each backwards:

   zzz yyy xxx www vvv uuu ttt sss rrr

   qqq ppp ooo nnn mmm lll kkk jjj iii

   hhh ggg fff eee ddd ccc bbb aaa

6. Repeat step 5, but faster than the last time.

7. Key each letter of the alphabet once backwards:

z y x w v u t s r q p o n m l k j i h g f e d c b a

8. Think about the letters that took you the most amount of time to locate. Go back to the Skill Builder for those letters, and repeat those drills until you are confident about their locations. For example, if you have difficulty with the c key, practice Skill Builder 3 again.

Timed Writing

Prepare to take the timed writing, page 542, according to your teacher's directions.

1. Get ready by:
   a. Clearing your desk of everything except your book and a pencil or pen.
   b. Positioning your keyboard and book so that you are comfortable and able to move your hands and fingers freely.
   c. Keeping your feet flat on the floor, sitting with your back erect.

2. Take a two-minute timed writing, page 542, now according to your teacher's directions.

3. Calculate your Words A Minute (WAM) and Errors A Minute (EAM) scores using the instructions on the timed writing progress chart, page 543.

4. Record the date, WAM, and EAM on the Skill Builder 6 line.

5. Repeat the timed writing as many times as you can and record each attempt.

Skill Builder 7

Your Goal – Improve your keying techniques—which is the secret for improving your speed and accuracy.

What To Do

1. Rate yourself for each item on the Keyboarding Technique Checklist, page 544.

2. Do not time yourself as you concentrate on a single technique you marked with a "0." Key only the first paragraph of the timed writing.

Teamwork

You may want to ask a classmate or your teacher to record your scores.

3. Repeat step 2 as many times as possible for each of the items marked with an "0" that need improvement.

4. Take a two-minute timed writing. Record your WAM and EAM on the timed writing progress chart as 1st Attempt on the Skill Builder 7 line. Compare this score with your base score.

5. Look only at the book and using your best techniques, key the following technique sentence for one minute:

    .   **2**   .   **4**   .   **6**   .   **8**   .   **10**   .   **2**   .   **14**   .   **16**

    Now is the time for all loyal men and women to come to the aid of their country.

6. Record your WAM and EAM on the 7 Technique Sentence line.

7. Repeat steps 5 and 6 as many times as you can and record your scores.

Skill Builder 8

Your Goal – Increase your words a minute.

What To Do

1. Take a two-minute timed writing.

2. Record your WAM and EAM scores as the 1st Attempt on page 543.

3. Key only the first paragraph only one time as fast as you can. Ignore errors.

4. Key only the first and second paragraphs only one time as fast as you can. Ignore errors.

> **Hot Tip**
>
> You can now key letters in the speed line very well and with confidence. Practicing all of the other letters of the alphabet will further increase your skill and confidence in keyboarding.

5. Take a two-minute timed writing again. Ignore errors.

6. Record only your WAM score as the 2nd Attempt on page 543. Compare only this WAM with your 1st Attempt WAM and your base score WAM.

Get Your Best WAM

1. To get your best WAM on easy text for 15 seconds, key the following speed line as fast as you can, as many times as you can. Ignore errors.

    .   **2**   .   **4**   .   **6**   .   **8**   .   **10**

    Now is the time, now is the time, now is the time,

2. Multiply the number of words keyed by four to get your WAM (15 seconds × 4 = 1 minute). For example, if you keyed 12 words for 15 seconds, 12 × 4 = 48 WAM.

3. Record only your WAM in the 8 Speed Line box.

4. Repeat steps 1-3 as many times as you can to get your very best WAM. Ignore errors.

5. Record only your WAM for each attempt.

Skill Builder 9

Your Goal – Decrease errors a minute.

What To Do

1. Take a two-minute timed writing.

2. Record your WAM and EAM as the 1st Attempt on page 543.

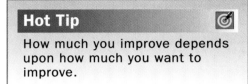

Hot Tip

How much you improve depends upon how much you want to improve.

3. Key only the first paragraph only one time at a controlled rate of speed so you reduce errors. Ignore speed.

4. Key only the first and second paragraphs only one time at a controlled rate of speed so you reduce errors. Ignore speed.

5. Take a two-minute timed writing again. Ignore speed.

6. Record only your EAM score as the 2nd Attempt on page 543. Compare only the EAM with your 1st Attempt EAM and your base score EAM.

Get Your Best EAM

1. To get your best EAM, key the following accuracy sentence (same as the technique sentence) for one minute. Ignore speed.

   Now is the time for all loyal men and women to come to the aid of their country.

2. Record only your EAM score on the Accuracy Sentence 9 line.

3. Repeat step 1 as many times as you can to get your best EAM. Ignore speed.

4. Record only your EAM score for each attempt.

Skill Builder 10

Your Goal – Use the touch system and your best techniques to key faster and more accurately than you have ever keyed before.

What To Do

1. Take a one-minute timed writing.

2. Record your WAM and EAM as the 1st Attempt on the Skill Builder 10 line.

3. Repeat the timed writing for two minutes as many times as necessary to get your best ever WAM with no more than one EAM. Record your scores as 2nd, 3rd, and 4th Attempts.

> **Hot Tip**
>
> You may want to get advice regarding which techniques you need to improve from a class-mate or your teacher.

Assessing Your Improvement

1. Circle your best timed writing for Skill Builders 6-10 on the timed writing progress chart.

2. Record your best score and your base score. Compare the two scores. Did you improve?

	WAM	EAM
Best Score	____	____
Base Score	____	____

3. Use the Keyboarding Technique Checklist on page 544 to identify techniques you still need to improve. You may want to practice these techniques now to increase your WAM or decrease your EAM.

Timed Writing

Every five strokes in a timed writing is a word, including punctuation marks and spaces. Use the scale above each line to tell you how many words you keyed.

```
          .       2    .       4    .       6    .
If you learn how to key well now, it
  8   .       10   .       12   .       14   .       16
is a skill that will help you for the rest
     .       18   .       20   .       22   .       24   .
of your life.  How you sit will help you key
26   .       28   .       30   .       32   .       34   .
with more speed and less errors.  Sit with your
36   .       38   .       40   .       42   .       44
feet flat on the floor and your back erect.
     .       46   .       48   .       50   .       52
To key fast by touch, try to keep your
     .       54   .       56   .       58   .       60
eyes on the copy and not on your hands or
     .       62   .       64   .       66   .       68   .       70
the screen.  Curve your fingers and make sharp,
     .       72   .
quick strokes.
       74   .       76   .       78   .       80   .
Work for speed first. If you make more
     82   .       84   .       86   .       88   .       90
than two errors a minute, you are keying too
     92   .       94   .       96   .       98   .       100
fast. Slow down to get fewer errors. If you
     .       102  .       104  .       106  .       108
get fewer than two errors a minute, go for
   .       110
speed.
```

Timed Writing Progress Chart

Last Name: _____   *First Name:* _____

Instructions

   Calculate your scores as shown in the following sample and footnotes (a) and (b). Repeat timed writings as many times as you can and record your scores for each attempt.

Base Score: *Date* ____ *WAM* ____ *EAM* ____ *Time* ____

Skill Builder	Date	1st Attempt (a) WAM	(b) EAM	2nd Attempt WAM	EAM	3rd Attempt WAM	EAM	4th Attempt WAM	EAM
Sample	9/2	22	3.5	23	2.0	25	1.0	29	2.0
Introduction									
6									
7									
8					-----				
9				-----					
10									
7 Technique Sentence									
8 Speed Line			-----		-----		-----		-----
9 Accuracy Sentence		-----		-----		-----		-----	

(a) Divide words keyed (44) by 2 (minutes) to get WAM (22)

(b) Divide errors (7) by 2 (minutes) to get EAM (3.5)

Keyboarding Technique Checklist

Last Name: _____   *First Name:* _____

Instructions

1. Write the Skill Builder number, the date, and the initials of the evaluator in the proper spaces.

2. Place a check mark (✓) after a technique that is performed satisfactorily. Place a large zero (0) after a technique that needs improvement.

Skill Builder Number:	Sample									
Date:	9/1									
Evaluator:	SL									
Technique										
Attitude										
1. Enthusiastic about learning	✓									
2. Optimistic about improving	✓									
3. Alert but relaxed	✓									
4. Sticks to the task; not distracted	✓									
Getting Ready										
1. Desk uncluttered	✓									
2. Properly positions keyboard and book	✓									
3. Feet flat on the floor	✓									
4. Body erect, but relaxed	0									
Keyboarding										
1. Curves fingers	0									
2. Keeps eyes on the book	✓									
3. Taps the keys lightly; does not "pound" them	0									
4. Makes quick, "bouncy," strokes	0									
5. Smooth rhythm	0									
6. Minimum pauses between strokes	✓									

GLOSSARY

A

Absolute cell reference Worksheet cell reference that does not adjust to the new cell location when copied or moved.

Access The database application of the Office 2003 programs.

Active cell Highlighted worksheet cell ready for data entry.

Active sheet Worksheet that appears on the screen.

Address bar Displays the name of the folder whose contents are being displayed.

Alignment How text is positioned between margins.

And operator Used to find records that meet more than one criteria.

Animate Adding a sound or visual effect.

Animation Text or pictures that have motion.

Argument In Excel, value, cell reference, range, or text that acts as an operand in a function formula.

Ascending sort Sort that arranges records from A to Z or smallest to largest.

AutoContent Wizard Guides you through a series of questions about the type of presentation, output options, presentation style, and presentation options.

Automatic Spelling and Grammar Check Identifies spelling and grammatical errors as you key your text.

Axis Line that identifies the values in a chart; most charts have a horizontal (or X axis) and a vertical (or Y axis).

B

Blank Presentation Feature that lets you create a presentation from scratch, using whatever layout, format, colors, and styles you prefer.

Blank publication In Publisher, used to create a document from scratch using whatever format, colors, and designs are preferred.

Border A line that is placed around text for emphasis or decoration.

Bullet A character or symbol placed before text, usually in a list, to add emphasis.

Broadcast Allows you to deliver a live presentation over the Internet.

C

Cell Intersection of a row and column in a worksheet or table.

Cell format The way data is shown in a cell.

Cell reference Identifies a worksheet cell by the column letter and row number (for example, A1, B2, C4).

Channels Used to adapt the information.

Chart A graphical representation of data.

Chart sheet Area separate from the Excel worksheet in which a chart is created and stored; the chart sheet is identified by a tab near the bottom of the screen.

Chart Wizard Four-step, on-screen guide that aids in preparing a chart from an Excel worksheet.

Clip art Graphics that are already drawn and available for use in documents.

Clipboard A temporary storage place in the computer's memory.

Close Removing a document or window from the screen.

Close button "X" on the right side of the title bar that you click to close a window.

Column chart Chart that uses rectangles of varying heights to illustrate values in a worksheet.

Columns Appear vertically in a worksheet and are identified by letters at the top of the worksheet window.

Copy A copy of the selected text is placed on the clipboard while the original text remains in the document.

Currency A format that displays numerical data preceded by a dollar sign.

Cut Removes selected text from the document and places it on the Clipboard.

D

Data labels Values depicted by the chart objects (such as columns or data points) that are printed directly on the chart.

Data series Group of related information in a column or row of a worksheet that is plotted on a worksheet chart.

Data sheet In PowerPoint, a table that contains sample data and automatically appears when you create a chart.

Database Helps you to store large amounts of information. A database is like a filing cabinet that contains folders of documents. Access is the database application of the Office 2003 programs.

Datasheet view In a database, a form similar to a spreadsheet that allows records to be entered directly into a table.

Default Setting used unless another option is chosen.

Descending sort Sort that arranges records from Z to A or largest to smallest.

Design Gallery objects Ready-made objects that you can quickly insert into your project.

Design set In Publisher, a series of documents (letterheads, business cards, envelopes, etc.) that incorporate the same design.

Design template Are pre-designed graphic styles that you can apply to your slides.

Design view Where you design and modify tables in a database.

Desktop Space where you access and work with programs and files.

Desktop publishing The process of combining text and graphics to create attractive documents. Publisher is the desktop publishing application of the Office 2003 programs.

Diagram A graphical illustration for organizing data.

Dialog box A message box that "asks" for further instructions before a command can be performed.

Drag and Drop A quick method for copying and moving text a short distance.

Drawing tools Tools to use to insert lines and objects that help make a worksheet more informative.

Drop-down menu A list of commands that appears below each menu name on the menu bar.

E

Effects options Allows you to select objects or text to enter the screen in various ways.

Embed Information becomes part of the current file, but is a separate object that can be edited using the application that created it.

Embedded chart Chart created within a worksheet; an embedded chart may be viewed on the same screen as the data from which it is created.

Entry Data entered into a database field.

Excel The spreadsheet application of the Office 2003 programs.

F

Field A category of data that make up records.

Field name Name that identifies a field in a database table.

Field properties Specifications that allow you to customize a database table field beyond choosing a data type.

Field selectors Located at the top of a database table, they contain the field name.

Filling Copies data into the cell(s) adjacent to the original.

Filter Simpler form of a database query that cannot be saved and that displays all fields.

Find   A command which locates in a worksheet.

Folder   A location where files and other folders are stored on a disk.

Font size   Determined by measuring the height of characters in units called points.

Font style   Formatting feature that changes the appearance of text such as bold, italic, and underline.

Fonts   Designs of type.

Form   A database object used to enter or display data.

Format Painter   Used to format an object with the same attributes as another object.

Formatting   Arranging the shape, size, type, and general make-up of a document.

Formatting toolbar   Toolbar that is normally near the top of the screen and which contains buttons for changing formatting.

Formula   Equation that calculates a new value from values currently on a worksheet.

Formula bar   Appears directly below the toolbar in the worksheet; displays a formula when the cell of a worksheet contains a calculated value.

Freezing   Keeps row or column titles on the screen no matter where you scroll in the worksheet.

Full Screen view   A view which removes the toolbars, rulers, and scroll bars from the screen.

Function formula   Special formulas that do not use operators to calculate a result.

G

Graphics   Pictures that help illustrate the meaning of the text or that make the page more attractive.

Grid settings   Sets the spacing between the intersections of the gridlines.

Gridlines   Lines displayed through a worksheet chart that relate the objects (such as columns or data points) in a chart to the axes.

Grouping   In PowerPoint, allows you to work with several objects as though they were one object. In Access, organizing records into parts or groups based on the contents of a field.

Guide settings   A set of crosshairs that help you align an object in the center, left, right, top, or bottom of a slide.

H

Handles   Small boxes that appear around an object when it is selected. You can drag the handles to resize the object.

Handout master   Lets you add items that you want to appear on all your handouts, such as a logo, the date, the time, and page numbers.

Highlight   Entry point of a worksheet; a highlighted cell is indicated by a dark border; to shade text with color to emphasize important text or graphics.

Home page   First page that appears when you start your Web browser.

Hyperlink   Allows you to jump to another location.

I

Icon   Small pictures that represent an item or object.

Image handles   See Handles.

Indent   The space placed between text and a document's margins.

Insertion point   Location on the screen where text will appear when you begin keying.

Integrated software package   Computer program that combines common tools into one package.

Internet   Vast network of computers linked to one another.

Internet Explorer   Office 2003's browser for navigating the Web.

Intranet   A company's private network.

L

Landscape orientation   Documents that are wider than they are long.

Leader   A line of periods or dashes that precedes a tab.

Line chart   Chart that is similar to a column chart except columns are replaced by points connected by a line.

Line spacing   The amount of space between lines of text.

Link   See Hyperlink.

M

Margins Blank spaces around the top, bottom, and sides of a page.

Maximize button Button at the right side of the title bar that you click to enlarge a window to fill the screen.

Media clips A collection of clip art that may be placed on your hard disk when Office is installed.

Menu List of options from which to choose.

Menu bar A bar normally at the top of the screen that lists the names of menus, each of which contains a set of commands.

Minimize button Button at the right side of the title bar that you click to reduce a window to a button on the taskbar.

Mnemonic An underlined letter that is pressed in combination with the ALT key to access items on the menu bar, pull-down menu, and dialog boxes.

Motion path Allows you to use predefined paths for the movement of an object.

Mouse A tool that rolls on a flat plane and allows you to control graphics and text on the screen using one or more buttons.

My Computer Program to help you organize and manage your files.

N

Name box Area on the left side of the worksheet formula bar that identifies the cell reference of the active cell.

Network Neighborhood Displays all of the folders and resources that are available to you through the network connection, if you have one.

Normal view screen Simplified layout of the page so you can quickly key, edit, and format text.

Notes page view Displays your slides on the top portion of the page, with the speaker notes for each slide in the notes pane on the bottom of the page.

Notes master Allows you to include any text or formatting that you want to appear on all your speaker notes.

O

Open Process of loading a file from a disk onto the screen.

Operand Numbers or cell references used in calculations in the formulas of worksheets.

Operator Tells Excel what to do with operands in a formula.

Order of operations In Excel, the sequence used to calculate the value of a formula.

Organization charts Show the hierarchical structure and relationships within an organization.

Outline numbered list A list with two or more levels of bullets or numbering.

Outline tab Displays all of the text in a PowerPoint slide show in outline form.

Overtype mode Allows you to replace existing text with the new text that is keyed.

P

Package for CD Compact all your presentation files into a single, compressed file that fits on a CD.

Page break Separates one page from the next.

Page navigator Allows you to move quickly from one page to another.

Pane An area of a split window that contains separate scroll bars that allow you to move through that part of the document.

Panel heading The area provided for the title or heading of a project or section of a project.

Paste Text is copied from the Clipboard to the location of the insertion point in the document.

Personal information set In Publisher, used to store information about your businesses, other organizations, or your home and family.

Picture toolbar Allows you to adjust the color, contrast, and brightness of your picture. You can also crop, rotate, add a border, compress, or set a transparent color.

Placeholder Reserves a space in the presentation for the type of information you want to insert.

Pointer Appears as an arrow on the screen and indicates the position of the mouse.

Points Unit of measurement for fonts.

Portrait orientation Documents that are longer than they are wide.

PowerPoint The presentation application of the Office 2003 programs.

Presentations Help you show your ideas using slides, outlines, speaker's notes, and audience handouts. A presentation can include text, clip art, graphs, tables, and charts. Presentations can also include multimedia objects such as flash files, animated GIFs, and sound.

Publisher The desktop publishing application of the Office 2003 programs.

Q

Query A search method that allows more specific searches of a database.

Quick Launch toolbar Contains icons you can click to quickly display the desktop or start frequently used programs.

R

Range Selected group of cells on a worksheet identified by the cell in the upper left corner and the cell in the lower right corner, separated by a colon (for example, A3:C5).

Read-only file File that can be viewed but not changed.

Record Complete set of database fields.

Record pointer The pointer that Access uses internally to keep track of the current record.

Record selectors Located to the left of a database table record's first field.

Recycle Bin Place to get rid of files or folders that are no longer needed.

Relative cell reference Worksheet cell reference that adjusts to a new location when copied or moved.

Report A database object used to organize, summarize, and print all or some data.

Replace An extension of the Find command that substitutes new data for the data found.

Restore button Button at the right side of the title bar that you click to resize a maximized window to its previous size.

Rows Appear horizontally in a worksheet and are identified by numbers on the left side of the worksheet window.

S

Save Process of storing a file on disk.

Scale Resizing a graphic so that its proportions are precise.

Scroll arrows Drag to move the window in the corresponding direction one line at a time.

Scroll bar Appears at the bottom and/or right side of a window to allow user to view another part of the window's contents.

Scroll box Box in the scroll bar that indicates your position within the contents of the window.

Search criteria In a query, it's the information for which you are searching.

Selecting Highlighting a block of text.

Selection rectangle The box that appears around a graphic when you select it.

Shading Adding colors or grays to emphasize text.

Sheet tabs Label that identifies a worksheet in a workbook.

Shift-clicking Allows you to select objects that are not close to each other or when the objects you need to select are near other objects you do not want to select.

Show Advanced Timeline This feature displays the time of the animation as a horizontal line graph.

Sizing handles See Handles.

Slide master Controls the formatting for all the slides in the presentation.

Slide pane The workbench for PowerPoint presentations.

Slide Show view Allows you to run your presentation on the computer as if it were a slide projector and preview how it will look.

Slide sorter Displays miniature versions of slides in a presentation and allows you to arrange them.

Slide transitions Determine how one slide is removed from the screen and how the next one appears.

Slides tab Displays slides in a presentation as small pictures or thumbnails.

Snap to Moves an object to the closest gridline on a slide.

Sorting Arranges a list of words or numbers in ascending order (A to Z; smallest to largest) or in descending order (Z to A; largest to smallest).

Spelling and Grammar Checker Used to check the spelling and grammar of a document after you finish keying.

Spreadsheet Grid of rows and columns containing numbers, text, and formulas; the purpose of a spreadsheet is to solve problems that involve numbers. Excel is the spreadsheet application of the Office 2003 programs.

Standard toolbar Toolbar that is normally near the top of the screen and which contains buttons used for common tasks.

Start Button on the taskbar that you click to display menus with a variety of options.

Status bar Bar normally at the bottom of a screen that tells you the status of what is shown on the screen.

Style A predefined set of formatting options that have been named and saved.

T

Table In Access, an arrangement of data in rows and columns, similar to a spreadsheet.

Tabs Mark the place the insertion point will stop when the Tab key is pressed.

Task pane Separate window on the right hand side of the opening screen that contains commonly used commands.

Taskbar Bar normally at the bottom of a screen that displays the Start button and the names of all open programs.

Template A file that contains page and paragraph formatting and text that you can customize to create a new document similar to but slightly different from the original.

Thesaurus A feature for finding a synonym, or a word with a similar meaning, for a word in your document.

Title bar Bar at the top of a window that displays the name of the Office program and the current file.

Toggling Clicking a toolbar button to turn a feature on or off.

Toolbar Bar at the top or bottom of the screen that displays buttons you can click to quickly choose a command.

U

Uniform Resource Locators (URLs) Internet addresses that identify hypertext documents.

V

Vertical alignment How text is positioned between the top and bottom margins of a document.

W

Web browser Software used to display Web pages on your computer monitor.

Web site A collection of related Web pages connected with hyperlinks.

Wizard A program that asks you questions and creates a document, similar to a template, based on the answers. In Publisher, pre-designed templates that provide the framework for various types of publications.

Word The word processing application of the Office 2003 programs.

Word processing The use of a computer and software to produce written documents such as letters, memos, forms, and reports. Word is the word-processing application of the Office 2003 programs.

Word wrap A feature that automatically wraps words around to the next line when they will not fit on the current line.

Workbook Collection of related worksheets in Excel.

Worksheet Computerized spreadsheet in Excel; a grid of rows and columns containing numbers, text, and formulas.

World Wide Web System of computers that share information by means of hypertext links.

Z

Zoom view A view that allows you to magnify and reduce your document on the screen.

INDEX

A

Absolute cell reference, 287

Access, 523, 525–526
  basics of, 345–368
  command summary, 421–422
  create database, 351–361
  create forms and reports, 401–420
  database, 525–526
  exit, 361
  manipulate data, 369–384
  open database, 347–350

Access screen, 348

Access startup screen, 346, 351

Accounting cell format, 273

Action button menu, 229

Active cell, 254

Active Desktop, 492

Add Entrance Effect dialog box, 204

Addition operation, 284

Add Object dialog box, 459

Address Bar, 493–494

Add (sum), 288

Advanced Filter/Sort, 393

Alignment, 125
  change in PowerPoint presentation, 171–172
  decimal, left, right, or center tab stops, 89

of text in Word document, 83–84
  use slide master to change, 163
  vertical, 88–89, 126

All caps, 71

Alphabetical order (A to Z), 302. See also Ascending sort

Animate, 161

Animation, 140, 144, 161

Apple, 517

Applications software, 515

Apply to All Slides, 182

Apply to selected slides, 181

Area chart, 325

Argument, 290

Ascending sort, 302, 395–396

Attention Getter Designs task pane, 439

Auto calculation, 289

AutoContent presentation, 158

AutoContent Wizard, 148, 157–158

AutoContent Wizard dialog box, 157

AutoForm, 405–406

Automatic grammar checking, 52–53

Automatic spell checking, 51, 175

AutoShapes, 197

AutoSum feature, 288–289

AVERAGE(number1,number2...), 289

Axes chart option, 317

Axis, 327–328

Axis title, 327–328

B

Backspace key, 47

Bar chart, 325

Blank presentation, 156–157, 432

Bold, 68, 125

Book icon, 500

Border, 94, 125, 272
  add, to pages in Word, 111–112
  add, to paragraphs in Word, 105–106
  click and drag, 194
  print, around presentation slides, 149

Borders and Shading dialog box
  Borders tab in, 105
  Page Border tab in, 111–112
  Shading tab in, 105

Break dialog box, 87. See also Page break

Broadcasting, 137